Not a Penny in the Post

A Master's Memoirs of the Easton Harriers

J A Harvey

NOT A PENNY IN THE POST

A MASTER'S MEMOIRS OF THE EASTON HARRIERS

J. A. HARVEY

ryelands

First published in Great Britain in 2008

British Library Cataloguing-in-Publication Data
A CIP record for this title is available from the British Library

Profits from the sale of this work
are donated to the Suffolk Punch Trust

ISBN 978 0 9556477 6 5

RYELANDS
An imprint of Halsgrove

Halsgrove House
Ryeland Industrial Estate, Bagley Road,
Wellington, Somerset TA21 9PZ
Tel: 01823 653777
Fax: 01823 216796
email: sales@halsgrove.com
website: www.halsgrove.com

Front cover photograph: Jim Meads

Printed and bound by CPI Antony Rowe Ltd.

CONTENTS

From left to right: Huntsman: Nick Brooks, Betty Kingston-Smith, the Hon. Miss Judith Bull, J.A.H., Geoffrey Ingram-Smith, Sylvia Partridge, Kaye Kingston-Smith, Alan Bridgeford.

LIST OF ILLUSTRATIONS

AUTHOR'S PREFACE

Since the publication of *If St Peter Had Hounds* many people have asked me if I would consider writing an account of the Easton Harriers during my time. I gave this considerable thought and came to the conclusion that I could not separate the doings of the Easton from my own life, since the two were inextricably linked for thirty-five odd years. I started at the very beginning because I thought it of interest to show the slightest encouragement, in this instance a telephone call, can influence the course of one's life.

JAH
Tannington Hall
March 2005

EDITOR'S PREFACE

This book was not quite finished by JAH before his death and there remained some details which had not been finalised. He would also, no doubt, have thanked all the many people who assisted with their memories and their photographs. As I would be bound to find myself in the invidious position of inadvertently omitting some, I will not attempt to name them in his place. They know who they are and he was very grateful. Special and honourable mention must, however, be made to Anne St Quinton who had the unenviable task of converting his extremely rough handwritten notes into a first draft.

Very soon after he started hunting he was encouraged to keep a hunting diary by his great mentor Captain Bernard and it was this habit, carried out to a greater or lesser degree of thoroughness, which made it possible for him to write what amounts to an autobiography in such detail. The diary format has been maintained for the most part and consequently there is a certain amount of repetition but this accurately reflects the annual routine of running a hunt.

Editor

EDITOR'S NOTE

After Tony's death, I was determined to push ahead with publication of this memoir. I would like to thank Bridget Wells-Furby for her able editing of the original and to echo her thanks to all those who have contributed photographs and anecdotes for the completed work. Linda Foulston at Cyber-Press has meticulously designed the book before handing it on to Halsgrove Press for publication. I am very thankful to her.

Those who knew Tony well will recall his extraordinary energy and ability to galvanise others into working with him while enjoying themselves at the same time. Readers will discover the pace of life he set himself and expected others to follow.

Lydia Harvey

GLOSSARY

All on; all hounds present

Babbling; speaking with no scent, an unpardonable sin

Best, to give a hare best; to acknowledge that she has beaten hounds

Blue haze; a thin mist that hovers over the ground, a sure sign of very poor scent

Bone; frost in the ground

Break up (the hare); to devour it completely

Brought to their noses; when the hare has run out of sight and hounds are left with scent only

Bullfinches; a tall, thick hedge, usually just thin enough to enable a horse and rider to push through

Capping on; when the huntsman knows where the hare has run and wants to encourage his hounds in the right direction he rides along the line, takes his hat in his hand and, leaning down, moves the hat in the direction of the line. This gives the same message as doubling the horn (*q.v.*) but is used when hounds are nearby and has the advantage of being quiet and consequently not lifting hounds' heads.

Check; when hounds have temporarily lost the scent

Chop a hare; to kill a hare on its seat without it having run

Clap down; a hunted hare suddenly stops and crouches down

Clean boot; to hunt a human being with no artificial scent

Cope for them; to call for them in a special way

Couples; two collars joined by a short length of chain

Curée; in France most members carry the large, circular, French horn which produces five notes. Different tunes are played to explain what is happening in the forest during the day. At the curée after a kill the tunes are blown simultaneously by all the members and tell the story of the day's hunting.

Does in kindle; pregnant doe hares

Doubling the horn; the same note many times, each time getting louder and faster. Hounds find this very exciting and it is used when the huntsman knows where the hare has gone and wants to put the hounds on the line. *See also* 'capping on'.

Exercise; see Hound exercise

Feathering; hounds are not sure enough of the scent but show their huntsman that they are almost sure

Field Master; the official appointed to control the mounted field

Form; a depression in the ground which is the hare's home

Fresh find; to find the scent of the hunted hare again

Harbourer/harboured; a man who walks about in the late night with one hound on a lead and notes where the deer has decided to spend the day. He will report the age and location of several deer.

Head a hare; to cause a running hare to change direction by being in front of her

Hitting off the line; to find the scent again

Hound exercise; beginning to get hounds fit at the end of the summer by going further with them than walking out (*q.v.*)

Huntsman's change; this involves the horses being held side by side and with a hand on each pommel, the rider swinging across

Jealous; a hound who ignores the hounds hunting the line and goes off across country, speaking to a non-existent line, just to distract the other hounds

Lay hounds on the line; to quickly show hounds the line

Let hounds down; to allow them to become unfit at the end of the season

Leveret; a young hare

Lièvre; French word for hare from which our word leveret comes.

Marking to ground; hounds sniffing at a particular place and speaking to show where the hunted hare is although they cannot go there

Mute, running mute; a hound hunting a scent without speaking

Pate; the head of a hare (for mounting)

Pricking; to see the little toe marks of a hare visible in the ground

Rapport; when the harbourer tells the Master what he has seen

Sally, Old Sally; traditional name for the hare

Scarteen (Ireland pack); unique Irish pack of Kerry Beagles

Scut, save her scut; the tail of a hare

Slot marks; the mark of a deer's feet visible in the ground

Stern; a hound's tail, a curly stern is not desirable

Thrown up; hounds have stopped speaking

Tiger trap; a nearly solid wooden fence built over a ditch which is the same either way.

Travelling Jack; a jack hare who has been 'courting' overnight and is found the next morning a long way from his home territory. He will usually run in a straight line rather than the more normal wide circles.

Trencher-fed; a means of keeping a pack of hounds in past days when each member takes a hound or two to keep over the summer.

Turning hounds; whipping in

Under a blanket; the pack hunting so close together that they could be covered by a blanket

Valeting; cleaning preparing the hunt coat

Walking out; gentle form of exercise carried out each day during the summer

Level crossing, North Green, Kelsale, March 1957 – the incident described on page 3. Captain Bernard, M.H., Ernie Nunn, Kennel Huntsman, John Moyle.

CHAPTER 1

EARLY DAYS TO 1963

I grew up on a farm, Braiseworth Hall in Tannington, and, although many farmers were 'hunting farmers', my family was not one of them. There was no tradition of hunting in my family and the only time hunting affected us was when my father would mention having seen the hounds on his land. These references held no animosity although they were an undoubted nuisance. The carthorses would be unsettled while hounds were in earshot and the younger ones perhaps had to be held for most of the day which was a waste of manpower. There was no tradition of riding horses for pleasure, either, although from an early age I worked with the Suffolk Punch horses on the farm until they were all sold and replaced by Ferguson tractors in the spring of 1954.

This was to change in 1953 when I was sixteen when one day, my father mentioned that our vet, Major Clay, had told him of a cob that was available on a 'meat for manners' basis as the owner, Mrs. Mary Mann, was pregnant. It was a great adventure for me to set off on my bicycle to see the cob as I hardly ever left the farm and did not know the way at all. Armed with careful directions from my father as to where I could find Elm Farm, Dennington, I eventually arrived and immediately liked Monty. Mary insisted that I rode him to see whether I got on with him but this was most embarrassing as I had never been on a saddle and could not rise to the trot having only ever ridden cart horses bare-back. Nevertheless Mary said I could take him and, with his saddle and bridle still on, I set off home with Monty trotting beside my bicycle. As I cycled home with Monty I little realised the significance of what I was doing or that it would introduce me to hunting and the Easton Harriers.

When my father saw how much I was enjoying Monty he said I ought to have some breeches so on the next market day I was taken into Ipswich to be measured for a pair at Edwards in the Buttermarket; there was no such thing as ready made in those days. They cost £8 10s. which seemed to me a terrible

Monty

extravagance as it was more than a farm workers basic wage at that time. I thought it would be interesting to find out the present day price of a pair of made to measure breeches. It took fifteen phone calls before I could find a firm who actually had a breeches maker on the premises. This was Bernard Weatherall in London and they quoted me £881. It is interesting to note that breeches at £8 10s. represented eight and a half days' work for a farm worker in 1953 and £763 represents twenty days at basic pay today.

Nevertheless, one morning at breakfast my father grunted,

'Boy, the hounds meet at Worlingworth Swan. You ought to go.'

I was anxious to go but at the same time apprehensive and frightened of what I might be expected to do. By this time I had acquired a riding cap as well as the breeches but, apart from these, we had to do the best we could. My farm boots were cleaned and polished and I wore these with an old pair of stockings left from when my father had worn plus fours. A sports jacket with shirt and tie made me as presentable as possible. The meet was advertised for 11 o'clock and as I hacked the two miles or so from Braiseworth Hall I became more and more apprehensive. I was so shy that I stopped short of the meet and stood in the gateway of Grange Farm, Worlingworth. I waited very nervously for what seemed like an eternity until they eventually moved off at 12 o'clock. The Easton Harriers had always advertised the time of the meet but moved off at the Master's discretion, a tradition that I later agreed with and maintained throughout my Mastership. I was so scared that I might well have gone home had the wives of some of our farm workers not been at the meet and would have told their husbands that I had chickened out. I stayed well back from the mounted field which numbered about ten and, as I rode, I was thinking how stupid I was to be there as I could barely ride and had certainly never jumped anything.

As these thoughts were going through my mind hounds found their first hare and were away. The cry had me quivering with excitement but not enough to make me jump the first ditch, so I jumped off and led Monty over. This was how I negotiated my first few ditches. This hare was killed on Chandos Farm which was owned by my father and, as the Master had found out who I was in spite of my cringing at the back, he called me up to him to receive the pad. I was too ashamed to get off with all the field looking, so hung tightly to the mane and jumped my first ditch. This momentous first meet was in November 1953 but I did not hunt again until the end of that season when I hacked the ten miles or so to the meet at Kelsale Rising Sun.

During the following summer Mary Mann asked for Monty back but, soon afterwards, my father said he would buy me a hunter and took me to the Cambridge Horse Sales. I was so excited that as we got nearer to Cambridge I started to tremble and shake as though I had the ague. He bought a 4-year-old chestnut mare called Flame for 60 guineas and after getting her home I soon found out that she was not at all as described in the catalogue; the description was one that said almost everything that did not constitute a warranty. I eventually got her going and had my first 'early morning' hunting at Church Farm, Saxtead, after Captain Bernard, the Master, had telephoned my father to ask if I would like to go. My father accepted this almost as a royal command and there was no question that I would not go. Soon after this Colonel Brian Gooch, who lived at Tannington Hall and was Master of the Norwich Staghounds, also telephoned to say that if I brought my hunter down to the Hall his groom, Jim Arris, would clip her out for me. This was a tremendous boost of morale for me to think that a Master of Staghounds should show an interest in me and make this kind offer. I rode her to the Hall and as I entered the stable I could hear strange sounds, which proved to be my first experience of grooms hissing as they worked. When he had finished clipping Jim asked about rugs and of course I had none, so he lent me two old rugs and a surcingle and I rode home with

Colonel Gooch

them rolled up in front of my saddle. The fact that Captain Bernard, Master of the Easton Harriers, had telephoned to invite me to hunt at Church Farm and that Colonel Gooch, Master of Staghounds, had arranged to have my horse clipped, meant a great deal to me and, more importantly, influenced my father. My father wanted me to hunt but at the same time could not bear to think of me losing any time from work. I resolved this problem for him by not actually asking for time off and just going hunting and accepting a mild telling off at tea time. As the conversation at mealtimes was usually about work he would slip in the odd comment like, 'We almost finished the beet at Low Farm. Would have done if we had not been short handed.' I need not have had any conscience about hunting as there was often several hours work to do in the dark after tea. I cannot remember why but lorries often seemed to arrive in the evenings and need unloading after tea, either bags to be carried into the mill or thousands of bricks to be thrown off by hand three at a time, caught in mid air and stacked. Father was doing a lot of building at the time.

In that season (1954–55), which was mostly memorable for the amount of times I fell off, I believe I had around 15 days with the Easton Harriers to add to the two during the previous season. This was enough to leave me with a love of hunting for the rest of my life. During the following summer I had a serious disagreement with my father and, as we were two stubborn souls together, neither would give way and I told my father I would go my own way. Father said that, if I meant what I said, then not to look to him for any help. He immediately telephoned Colonel Gooch to ask him if he knew anyone who would like Flame and she was sold to a lady at Morningthorpe.

Selling this mare left me with no horse to hunt for the last meet of the season, which was at Kelsale Eight Bells. The land at Kelsale was so wet and poorly farmed that no farmer would have started spring cultivations, so it was ideal for the last meet. Another, and perhaps the main reason for it being at Kelsale, was that the Master liked to give one of his famous hunting teas on the last day. He had said to me that he hoped I would come for tea, so Jack Steel and I followed in a car and saw an amazing happening.

Kelsale Parish is a maze of little roads, each one had its level crossing gates opened and shut by a local man, and Captain Bernard knew all their names and would some cheery remark as he passed. On this day he did such a stupid thing that I just could not imagine what he was thinking about. The level crossing gates were shut and he rode with hounds right up to the crossing and stood talking to the crossing keeper. When the train came through, the driver waved and blew his whistle. The combination of the whistle blowing and the train passing right in front of his nose caused the Captain's horse to back away, stamping on some hounds. This set up a chain reaction as hounds fled in all directions; some were stamped on by other horses and their cries of pain further alarmed the others. I was in about the third or fourth car back so saw everything; horses were kicking each other and rearing, with some horses hooves landing on the bonnets of cars. Within a few seconds there was complete pandemonium and it was lucky that no one was seriously hurt. Captain Bernard complained to British Rail, which, I thought, was uncharacteristic and unsporting of him since it was entirely his own fault. He received a letter of apology from British Rail but what he did not know was that the train driver was a cartoonist. This driver came to Framlingham Show where the Master and Ernie Nunn were parading hounds to sketch their likeness and later sent Captain Bernard the cartoon, which hung in his lavatory for many years. I was delighted when one Christmas Eve the doorbell rang and on answering I found Pam Spiller with a copy of the cartoon as a Christmas present for me. I was absolutely delighted and it has hung in the front hall ever since.

The next two years I spent breaking and dealing in horses and the only hunting I had was to improve a horse or show one off; hunting was secondary to earning a living. One deal I shall never forget was the buying of a chestnut mare called Blaze from Buxhall for £45. I rode her home the 25 miles, advertised her, and sold her to a gentleman from Blythburgh for £75

Flame

on the proviso that I hunted her for one day. He had bought her for his daughter but did not want her to try the mare out for the first time, so I hacked her to the meet at Stonham Ten Bells. We had a good straight run on a 'travelling jack' and I was so thrilled by how well she went that I asked the man to promise to give me first refusal if he ever wanted to sell her.

In 1957 my father bought Kings Farm, Tannington, which stood down a lane a long way off the road, and as there was no water or electricity laid on at the house, the buildings were of no use to him. Our relationship had improved somewhat and I suspect that it was an effort to get me away from horse dealing that prompted him to offer me the house and buildings rent free. I had by now met the girl I was going to marry and I decided to take a more reasonable attitude to life. I accepted my father's offer and for the next two years raised pigs and chickens at Kings Farm. It was hard graft carrying enough water out of the pond for 400 pigs and 600 chickens and there was no time for hunting. In the spring of 1959 I bought Glebe Farm, Badingham, and, having married Sheila and after a short honeymoon, took possession on 11th October. This was a small farm of 30 acres but the lack of land did not matter as I intended to keep intensive pigs, a profitable enterprise at the time. The lack of hunting over the previous two years was soon to change and the pattern of my life for the next 35 years was set. By coincidence, the chestnut mare Blaze came on the market and, the original buyer honouring his promise, I bought her back for £55 and started to hunt again with the Easton.

At this time the Master of the Easton was Captain Peter Bernard who hunted the hounds with Ernie Nunn whipping in into him as kennel huntsman, and Fred Ling as amateur whip. Fate was kind to the Easton when it decreed that Peter should be born ten minutes after his brother who later became the Earl of Bandon. If Peter had been in line to succeed to the title and estates he would never have been in a position to take on the Easton Harriers. His grandmother owned and lived at By The Crossways, Kelsale, near Saxmundham in Suffolk which was to become his home from just before he took on the Easton Harriers until his death in March 1977. It is amusing to recall him showing me where his grandmother had paid to have the road moved as she objected to being looked at in her garden. Captain Bernard was one of those people who stand out in a crowd. He had tufts of hair on his cheek bones and bushy eyebrows below which his eyes could express fierce anger or, far more often, twinkling humour and wit. He was perfect material to be a Master of Hounds as there was an aura and natural dignity about him that commanded instant respect from friends and strangers alike. At a meet farmers and farmworkers alike regarded him with a reverence that was akin to that given to royalty and he would always make a point of speaking to everyone in the pub. He had a great sense of humour and would crack jokes and tell stories, often against himself, and once he began to tell these stories you could hear a pin drop in the pub.

Captain Bernard in later years

Church Farm, Saxtead. Alfred was really the horseman of the family and always had methods of curing horses of most ailments and bad habits. He, and his wife Bessie and daughter Anne, always hunted during the winter, showing Hackneys in the summer. Alfred was at one time Honorary Secretary to the Easton. Alfred retired from farming and became landlord of Glemham Crown, eventually parting from his wife and returning to Church Farm where he kept Captain Bernard's horse at livery. Alfred's brother Herbert kept hunting well into my Mastership and always held to the very old custom of having two reins on his snaffle bit. Herbert was one of the Easton's greatest characters. Mr Pepper from Benhall was a perfect example of a real old-fashioned type of hunting farmer. He bred his own hunter on the farm and always hacked to meets when hounds were in his area. He continued to hack even after horsebox trailers became common.

Ernie Nunn was in his late sixties and was highly respected owing to his 56 years of experience, having started his work in hunt service in 1903 aged 12 years. Ernie's first nine years service were with the Suffolk Staghounds but in 1912, aged 21, he moved to the Essex and Suffolk Foxhounds. He would occasionally speak with passionate pride of how important it was to be brought up in hunt service in the old fashioned way, starting at the bottom of the ladder and working upwards. He began as kennel boy doing the lowest of jobs, progressed to riding second horse, then whipping in as Second and then First Whip, before finally reaching the coveted position of carrying the horn as a professional huntsman.

Most of the Easton members seemed to me to be rather grand and 'out of the top drawer'. Those who where not from old families were respected people of consequence in the area, such as doctors, vets, solicitors, and accountants. Most of the larger farmers, whether tenants or owners, used to hunt regularly before the war but had stopped during the urgency of food production and had not started again afterwards. Nevertheless, these farmers still gave the hunt their full support and encouraged their neighbours to do the same.

The best known of the farming families that continued to hunt were the Breese brothers from

Doctor Hutt from Debenham would always hack to meets, usually in the company of Mrs Payne from White Hall, Debenham, and would combine business with pleasure, calling on one or two patients on the way to the meet and some more on the way home. On the days when Mrs Payne did not come it was a common sight to see the Doctor's horse tied to a cottage gate. A verse from the famous hunting song, *We'll All Go A-Hunting Today*, could have been written for him.

> *"There's a Doctor in boots,*
> *With a breakfast that suits,*
> *Of home brewed ale and good beef.*
> *To his patients in bed,*
> *'I have come,' he said,*
> *'To console you in hope of relief.'*
> *To the poor his advice gives away;*
> *To the rich he prescribes and takes pay;*
> *But to each one he said ,*
> *'You will shortly be dead*
> *If you don't go a-hunting today'".*

The Coddenham vet Mr Leason and his wife were always out on Mondays which were their nearest meets. They both enjoyed a drink, especially Mrs Leason, and there was one memorable occasion when she came out of the pub, mounted and called out to her husband,

'Oh darling, I didn't know you'd bought me a new bridle.'

'I haven't,' came the reply. 'You're on somebody else's horse'.

Mr Schreiber from Marlesford Hall always reminded me of a cavalry officer as he looked so dignified on a horse. He was often out with his daughter, Clare, and on occasion with his son, Mark. Another member was our local M.P., Sir Harwood Harrison. Lady Harrison hunted regularly, Sir Harwood occasionally, and their son and daughter also came out. Sir Harwood was waiting at the church gate to shake hands with Sheila and me on our wedding day, 3rd October 1959. The Easton also had a number of prominent lady members: the Honourable Mrs Judith Bull, a formidable character who was held in great respect and later became Vice Chairman: Barbara Buller, who kept a riding school at Grundisburgh: and Pam Spiller who was always great fun and came from great hunting stock as she is descended from the legendary Squire Farquharson who hunted the whole of Dorset at his own expense for over fifty years. A full collection of 'Hunting Types' always features 'The Man Who Never Jumps'.

John Capon

Mrs Gooch, from Tannington Hall, was the Easton's 'Lady Who Never Jumps'. She had an uncanny knack of being in the right place and, whenever we crossed the road, Mrs Gooch would be sitting quietly on her horse, every bit as much in touch with hounds as the rest of the field. I have often come to the road, bleeding profusely from scratches torn by brambles when bursting through the tall hedges called 'bullfinches', to find Mrs Gooch waiting serenely, with information on how far the hare was ahead of hounds, or if a fresh hare had intervened.

Mrs Irene Freeman hunted in style, arriving at the meets in her delightful old custom-made horsebox. Her groom would get her horse out and put on the sidesaddle, and his last duty was to draw the curtain across the window in the rear door of the box in case

Mrs Freeman wished to use the commode which was fitted inside. Mrs Freeman looked very elegant on her sidesaddle but she had one peculiarity as she was a great smoker and had cut a hole in her veil so as to be able still to smoke. It was a constant wonder to me that I would be torn and bleeding after bursting through thick bullfinches yet Mrs Freeman would arrive a few minutes later with her veil still in place.

The only other member at that time with whom I had anything in common in terms of age and background was John Capon. He was also a farmer's son of my age, and there was probably a thirty-year gap between us and the next youngest member of the field. In later years John was to be my Meets Secretary.

Nearly everyone hacked to meets in those days and the conviviality of the meets, usually at pubs, was possible because there would always be a crowd of retired farmworkers and unemployed there, both to enjoy the atmosphere and in the hope of a good tip, usually half a crown (2s. 6d.), for holding a horse. The only alternative to hacking to meets was to hire a lorry for the day from Hatcher, the local contractor at Framlingham. The hire charge for the day was £5. One day Captain Bernard had hired two lorries, one for hounds and one for hunt horses, to go to the meet at Thorndon Black Horse. As was his custom he left some money for the landlord 'to look after the drivers'. The drivers had orders to move their lorries to Rishangles Lodge by 2 o'clock, which is where the Master always liked to finish the day as it was the home of a great sportsman, Jack Edwards, and the Master was sure to be invited in for some tea, followed by large whiskies. The two lorry drivers were given a very large whisky each and we can only assume that they had had a good party in the pub as these two drinks rendered them both impossibly drunk. The Master had to telephone for two more drivers but went to the Hatchers office early next morning, honourably took the blame for their condition, and asked that they should not be sacked. The drivers stayed with the firm until they retired and every employee of Hatchers, and many besides, regarded Captain Bernard as a hero.

In those days, membership of the local hunt was considered almost as a warranty of good character. When ordinary people were describing someone unknown to the other party, I have often heard the phrase, 'Well, he go a' hunting', as if this was proof of his good standing. The dignity of the hunt was of paramount importance. In spite of having enjoyed themselves in the pub prior to hunting, everything was carried out with the utmost decorum. The atmosphere of the Easton Harriers at that time is accurately portrayed in Surtees' account of the Goose and Dumpling Hunt in his novel *Hawbuck Grange*.

A great deal of the country was poorly farmed. The fields were undrained and so wet that they were unsuitable for winter wheat. At the beginning of the season they were mostly still stubble, some of which was so wet that I needed to dismount and lead off. The stubbles gradually became fewer as the winter ploughing progressed and it was every farmer's aim to be completely ploughed by Christmas. One-way ploughs had not yet been invented and all ploughing was 'stetch work'. This meant that there would be perhaps 20 furrows all lying in one direction, then an open furrow and another 20 furrows lying in the other direction. The open furrows were only 4 inches deep and had solid bottoms; they led right across the field and were approximately 10 yards or so apart. This meant that a number of horses could cross over the middle of a ploughed field in comparative ease. Such was the decorum that if two horses came towards the same furrow from different directions the senior of the two riders would expect to go first. I quickly learned to avoid that particular problem and would find a different route as most of the members preferred to cross country at a sedate trot. If these furrows were known to hold a lot of water, the farmer would send a man to dig 'a water furrow', using a spade to dig a little drain to allow the water to flow into the ditch. It was the greatest sin to allow a horse's feet to spoil one of these drains and I remember reading in an old book where a Master had wished 'hell and damnation' to men who rode in water furrows. Water furrows are still dug and spoiling them is now just as much a sin as in the old days, although the plough now is twelve inches deep rather than four inches.

The arable fields were very small compared with today, anything from three to twelve acres, and surrounded by huge hedges, often 20 feet high and 15 feet or more wide, usually including a ditch. During a run, perhaps twenty or thirty of these 'bullfinches' would have to be negotiated. Usually there were

only certain places where it was possible to burst through and, if one had a good eye for country and could remember where these 'crossing places' were, it was possible to get to hounds before one's rivals. An intelligent hunter of a few seasons soon learned where they were. Cantering along a headland furrow with hounds speaking on the other side of the hedge, the horse would slow down and dive into the hedge at the correct place. Sometimes it was not possible to cross through directly and another manoeuvre had to be carried out, needing a handy horse to creep down into the ditch bottom and move along until it was possible to climb out on the other side.

Another aspect of the huge hedges was that it was seldom possible to see hounds and followers needed to rely on the cry to keep in touch with them. On a good scenting day this necessitated pushing on hard across country if you were to keep within earshot. The huntsman and whipper-in did this as best they could, leaving the field to come on at a pace that suited them. Whilst the thickness of the hedges and their close proximity made riding across country difficult, they had one very good point in that they obliged the hounds to hunt every yard of a run. Wherever a hare was found she was never far from a hedge into which she would disappear and from then on hounds were 'brought to their noses' and had to hunt every inch of the line until they either fresh found her, killed her, or lost her. There is still a tiny part of the old style of country preserved at Wilby Hall where the gallant sportsman, Alec Comins, would not allow any fields to be amalgamated but even here it is not quite the same as the hedges have never been neglected enough to get thick and wide at the base.

Quite soon after I started to hunt regularly in 1959 I began to help by whipping-in. Although I did not realize it at the time the hounds were unbelievably wild and unmanageable. I accepted this as normal because I had no knowledge of any other hunts and I just assumed that this was how hounds behaved. We could hack them along roads because of the high, thick, hedges, but at any gateway or gap in the hedge they would break away and could only be turned back by the whipper-in galloping to their heads and cracking his whip, and even then they would dodge round him and keep going if they possibly could. Even where there was no gap some of the hounds would stand up on their hind legs to look across the adjacent field, probably 'winding' the scent of a hare. The worst offender was a bitch called Carbine who would jump up into the air with all four feet off the road.

My job, when on the road, was to overtake hounds and position myself in open gateways and with liberal use of my whip prevent them breaking through and this was how we proceeded along the road with me always overtaking hounds and getting forward to the next open gateway. This task was only possible as three-quarters of the gateways into arable fields still had gates on them that were kept shut, although at this time livestock was seldom driven loose along the road. The greatest problem on the road was where the roadside hedges had been cut down to the ground. The only thing possible to do was to ride alongside hounds between them and the open space. This was often not enough and they would break away either in front of me or behind or both at once. The whole performance was a nightmare and, looking back, it is hard for me to believe just how wild they were so I know how difficult it must be to imagine the scene.

The wildness of the pack was in some part due to, and certainly encouraged by, the abundance of hares at the time. Hounds only needed to go a hundred yards or so before putting up a hare, which is of course the reason why they were to keen to break away from the road. Hunting would have been impossible, as every hound could have had a hare each to hunt, had it not been a hare's instinct to sit tight in her form until she is forced to move. Nevertheless, with this quantity of hares, hounds did split quite often and as they were so unbiddable this involved some fast gallops to get to their heads and turn them back. Even when this was achieved, the odds were that they would start a fresh hare on their way back and the whole operation would start again.

It was during Captain Bernard's twelfth season (1958-1959) that the issue had become insoluble. The Master was too busy to go to the kennels to exercise hounds and had delegated his groom, Ernie Head, to exercise them. Head was not a huntservant and had never had anything to do with hounds; he was a hopeless whipper-in and altogether too slow on the uptake to prevent hounds slipping away. The hounds had become unruly but the situation became unredeemable as a result of an accident to Ernie Nunn which happened at the same time. As Captain Bernard and Ernie were hacking to a meet, a hare crossed the road just in front of them and quite naturally hounds took off after it. Ernie went to jump the ditch to go to stop them but his horse slipped and fell into the ditch bottom, trapping Ernie underneath it and breaking his leg. The Master was the only other person there so he had to ride off to the nearest farm for help to lift off the horse and to telephone for an ambulance. During what must have been a considerable time hounds were doing just what ever they wanted amongst the abundant hares and loose poultry, (every farm had chickens running loose in the farmyard at this time). It was never going to be possible to treat them like a normal pack from that moment.

With my first hand experience of what it was like then, combined with the knowledge I now have after hunting the harriers for 21 seasons, I can clearly see what went wrong all those years ago. Captain Bernard was a first class Master but he made one very serious mistake and that was to decide to hunt hounds himself. I am totally convinced that if he had let Ernie hunt hounds and either whipped-in himself or employed someone to do it, hounds would never have gone as wild as they did.

To be a good huntsman, either as an amateur or as a professional, above all things the hounds must love you and want to be with you in preference to anyone else. For hounds to love you above all others is a gift and I call it a gift because no amount of money or time can get it for you if hounds do not take to you of their own accord. This is especially noticeable when an amateur hunts hounds and they take to him. Although the kennel huntsman has fed and looked after them and been with them for most of the day, they will completely ignore him when the amateur huntsman is present and get very excited as soon as they know he is in the kennel yard even before they can see him. This is why I am convinced that this vital bond is a gift.

Without the bond of love between hounds and the huntsman it is impossible to hunt hounds in the true sense of the word and it all becomes a sham. Worse still, and this is what caused all the trouble in the Easton, it is impossible to whip-in effectively if hounds do not love the huntsman. A huntsman never uses his whip on his hounds; that is the whipper-in's job and, moreover, hounds should never be hit while they are close to the huntsman. They should always feel that there is a safe haven when they are close to him. Whenever they are in trouble or the whipper-in is after them, they should head straightaway for the love and safety of their huntsman as instinctively as a child would run to its mother in time of trouble. It is extremely difficult to whip-in if hounds have no regard for the huntsman as, if hounds treat the huntsman with the same indifference as any other member of the field, they have no one to turn to in time of trouble and no one to go back to when they are berated for some misdeed.

The situation was very difficult for Ernie who, with all his experience at whipping-in and hunting hounds, knew the score exactly and acted as so many professionals have done before and are still doing, that is, to cover up as best he could for the inability of his Master to hunt hounds. When hounds split and Ernie went with one half and got them stopped he could not crack his whip and cry, 'Get away back to him, get away back', as the hounds, as far as they were concerned, had no one to go back to as they were already with the man they loved. After he had stopped them, Ernie had to ride back to the Master bringing the hounds with him. Fred Ling and myself, as amateur whippers-in, had a similar problem. All we could do was to stop them and hope that Ernie was in sight so he could call to them and they would have someone that they actually wanted to go to.

Ernie was approaching seventy and not so quick as he used to be, and I think that he had rather lost heart and had become resigned to the situation. Captain Bernard would send him off to 'bring hounds back' as opposed to whipping-in in the normal sense and with the high hedges he would soon be out of sight and seize the opportunity to find the nearest pub and have a couple of whiskies before finding hounds. The Master would often send John Capon or myself, the 'youngsters', with Ernie on these jaunts and we would have to wait at the pub while he had his whiskies and then be sworn to secrecy not to let the Master know that he had stopped. We went with Ernie so that, in a sense, we could whip-in to him; when we had pushed the stray hounds back to him, he would hack back to the Master with them. Looking back on it all I realize what a terrible fiasco it all was.

During the season 1959–60 (my first as amateur whip) hounds eventually became too wild to hack to meets. Captain Bernard discussed with Ernie whether they ought to resign. Ernie said he would like to go on for one more season to reach his seventieth birthday but could only do so if Fred Ling, who lived quite close to the kennels at Wickham Market, would agree to help him whip-in and to bring hounds to the meet in his lorry. Fred agreed to this and they carried on for one more season (1960–61), the horses either being hacked to the meets by the groom, Head, or boxed by the contractor Hatcher if the meet was too distant, but early in the season the Master and the Kennel Huntsman tended their resignations for the end of that season 30th April 1961. Fred Ling, who had played a vital role not only as amateur whip but also transporting hounds to the meets in his lorry free of charge, decided to give up hunting at the same time.

Advertisements for a Master were placed in the *East Anglian Daily Times* and the *Horse & Hound* but there were no replies. The Committee eventually realized that there would be no Master forthcoming and they would have to run the hunt themselves. The unenviable position of having no Master would come to be fully appreciated over the next two seasons. Captain Bernard, who had just relinquished the responsibility of Mastership with a sigh of relief, found himself feeling duty bound to immediately take on most of the burden of keeping the Easton Harriers going. He offered to head a small management committee who would engage a professional huntsman to hunt hounds for the coming season. An advertisement was placed in *Horse & Hound* and, from the eleven applicants, three were thought to be promising enough for an interview. Almost all interviews are given at the kennels as it gives the huntsman a chance to look around the kennels and his wife to see if she is happy with the house. These interviews are kept to a minimum as the Master (or Committee in this case) are expected to reimburse the hunt servant for his travelling expenses. In the end just two were interviewed, N Osborne from the Romney Marsh Foxhounds and Nick Brooks from the South Herefordshire Foxhounds, and the latter was unanimously selected. The terms were wages of £9 per week with house rent free, free electricity and two tons of coal per year, and all the kennel perquisites. These 'perks' were traditionally part of the huntsman or kennel huntsman's income over and above his wage and consisted of the sale of hides, offal, and bones. The exact amount of this income was always kept a strict secret with the huntsman declaring that it was very little and no Master anywhere in the country was ever allowed to know how much it was. There was a good reason for the security as this income was never declared to the taxman. The Inland Revenue caught up with this dodge about half way through my Mastership and huntsmen all over the UK were obliged to declare it. The Revenue wrote to me with a considerable adjustment to the code number for the PAYE and the increased amount of the weekly tax gave me a fair idea of what the Revenue thought the perks were worth.

The engagement of Brooks involved a great deal of expense for the hunt. It was traditional for the Master (or Committee, in this instance) to pay his removal costs, and to provide him with a new hat, coat, two pairs of breeches and a pair of boots (which he is entitled to keep even if he leaves at the end of one season), but Brooks stipulated that the green coat should be made by Bernard Wetherall, a top class hunt tailor. The hunt also agreed to do considerable work on the huntsman's famous round house at the kennels, to install a lavatory and a bath with hot running water and to redecorate it. This was not unreasonable as it replaced the one installed in 1947 (at a cost of £36 10*s.*) in the shed opposite the back door of the house which was simply a bath beside a brick copper with a wooden partition around it. When a bath was needed the copper had to be filled with pails of water and the fire lit underneath and stoked up until it boiled. Meanwhile, cold water was put into the bath and the boiling water was added to obtain the desired temperature. It is to be hoped that the little fire underneath the copper raised the temperature slightly as there was little in the way of insulation in the shed and I have stood many a time to contemplate the gales which must have whistled through the spaces between the tiles! One had to be tough in those days and I would guess the baths were not often taken especially as all the dirty water had to be pailed out afterwards and poured into the drain.

The Committee decided that a presentation should be made to the retiring Master and kennel huntsman and an appeal limited to five guineas was made. This limit is indicative of the popularity of these two men as the subscription for a complete season's hunting was only three guineas. Judith Bull offered to organise this, saying that the Master had hinted that he would like a radiogram and Sylvia Moye would like a chiming clock. Sylvia was Ernie Nunn's niece and lived at the kennels. She was a great help with the kennel work, which was probably why Ernie could go on until he was seventy. The presentations were made at Mrs Bull's home, Park Farm, Grundisburgh. The Master received his radiogram and Sylvia her chiming clock and the balance of the money went to Ernie.

The Committee realized that it must do something to raise money for the expense of running the hunt now there was no Master. From my later experience I would estimate that Captain Bernard had put in at least as much of his own money as the hunt's guarantee of £800. The Committee had been, of course, quite happy with this arrangement and so were the members as, with the Master's huge input and transfers from the point-to-point account and profits from the ball and the dance, they had been hunting for much less than a quarter of what it actually cost to run the hunt.

The Master's role, and the question of the guarantee, has its origins in the history of hunting. In the early days a gentlemen in an area kept a pack of hounds at his own expense and asked his friends and neighbours to join him. In the case of the Easton it was the Duke of Hamilton who owned the hounds although they were, of course, then called the Hamilton Harriers. The size and grandeur of the pack depended on how wealthy the master was and the extent of his estates, and those who were privileged to follow hounds did so at no expense to themselves. As time passed many of the landowners found that they were unable to afford to continue with this practice. In these circumstances, it was common for the followers to get together and suggest that they help with the expenses. The most important person amongst the followers would approach the Master and tell him that the followers had agreed that, between them, they would 'guarantee' to give him a certain amount each season if he would continue to hunt the country. If the Master agreed to this proposal it was the beginning of hunts as we now know them, the Master receiving a 'guarantee' and the 'subscribers' assisting financially. It is important to emphasise that the guarantee was intended only to help defray the expenses. The style and excellence of the hunt reflected how much the Master was dipping into his own pocket, but the Master was really the 'Master' because he was paying out of his own money and the Committee merely subsidised his expenses.

This is the old way, the original way, but now there are many variations of this. In some cases, the Committee will additionally buy the horses, or the lorry, or the corn for the horses, or the huntsman's clothes, or will pay for vaccinating the puppies, or a variety of other expensive items. It is a question how far this development can be taken before a Master becomes merely an 'Acting Master' who simply 'manages the shop' at home, doing all the organisation and the PR work in visiting farmers and so forth, but sending all the bills to the Honorary Secretary. An Acting Master has to limit his expenditure to that agreed by the Committee who might, for example, tell him that he can only breed from one bitch to save the expense of the vaccines. Although he might know that this is wrong and that the quality of the pack will deteriorate, he has to go along with their decision. The Committee can put an upper limit on how much could be paid for a horse and the Acting Master can be frustrated at seeing his huntsman unable to do his job properly as he is inadequately mounted. He is, therefore, severely limited in his ability to conduct the hunt. Likewise, there are difficulties in a Mastership where the Committee pays for some of the things needed as the Master will then to this certain extent have his hands tied. It would be much better to increase the level of the guarantee to enable the Master to buy his own things and to really be able to run the hunt as he thinks it should be run.

In the spring of 1961, the Easton Committee and members realised with shock that there was going to be no one to 'carry the can' and they would actually have to pay all the bills themselves for the first time. They had never stooped so low as to think of running any fund raising events other than the annual Ball, and the proposal of Alan Bridgford that they run a draw on the Cheltenham Gold Cup was met with gasps of surprise and horror. However, it was agreed that it should go ahead and a subcommittee of Alan Bridgford, Fred Ling, and myself were appointed to run one for the 1961 race. I put every effort into selling the sixpenny tickets and sold £63 worth, over 2,500 tickets or the equivalent of 20 subscriptions.

There was another more genteel suggestion that a cocktail party be held and this was left to the ladies of the Committee to organise. They invited my wife, Sheila, to join them and help with the running of the party. They all made trays of canapés and collected many good prizes for the tombola. Although the older members called it a cocktail party, in fact champagne was served and we were lucky enough to be supplied with Moet et Chandon champagne by John Cobbold, son of the ex-Master Lady Blanche, at the lowest possible price. He charged us a guinea a bottle and we sold the tickets at a guinea each, serving the champagne freely from six o'clock until half past seven, and making the profit on the tombola. This inaugural party was the forerunner of what was to become an annual Easton Harriers institution, looked forward to by hundreds of people from the end of one party until the next.

The Committee had agreed that certain people should each do a part of what had been the Master's duty. Alan Bridgford was in charge of the southern half of the country, hunted on Mondays, and was responsible for visiting farmers and arranging meets. Terence Saffell was to do the same for the northern half of the country hunted on Thursdays. Historically the Easton did not hunt on Saturdays, as it was market day at Framlingham. Mrs. Kingston-Smith and myself were to be whippers-in and Mrs Bull to be in charge of the kennels. There were other people with other duties and as a plan it looked as if it might work but in practice it was a shambles. Very little was done as everyone thought that someone else had done it or would do it. I am indebted to Linda Lancaster who told me about this little verse which I think says it all.

I'M ON A COMMITTEE

Oh give me your pity; I'm on a committee
Which means that, from morning to night,
We attend and amend and contend and defend
Without a conclusion in sight.
We confer and concur, we defer and demur
And reiterate all of our thoughts
We revise the agenda with frequent addenda
And consider a load of reports.
We compose and propose, we support and oppose
And the points of procedure are fun.
But although various notions are brought up as motions
There's terrible little gets done.
We resolve and absolve, but never dissolve
Since it's out of the question for us.
What a shattering pity to end our committee –
Where else could we make such a fuss?

The biggest problem was, of course, the hounds. The wildness was by now ingrained in them and they would be constantly on the lookout for somewhere to break; an open gate into a garden would be enough for the worst. Captain Bernard had put down a number of hounds at the end of his Mastership, those that he and Ernie thought were the ringleaders, and the Committee, in its naivety, thought that a brand new professional huntsman would effect a miraculous cure of the rest. Fortunately Nick Brooks was a good hound man and definitely had that gift that is essential for a good huntsman. Hounds quickly came to love him and Mrs Kingston-Smith and I went to kennels almost every morning all summer to 'walk out' the hounds, i.e. give them their daily exercise along the roads. Very gradually most of the hounds became steadier and, by keeping the worst ones coupled up to a steady one, we managed to get them home again most days. The worst spot was always Pound Corner in the village, only a hundred yards or so from the kennels gate, and a place where the road widened. When Captain Bernard had them they would always break away there and rush the last few yards to the kennels which was not only very undesirable but also extremely dangerous with the traffic coming through the village. As we approached Pound Corner, Betty Kingston-Smith would stay behind while I got to their heads and would do my best not to let them pass me, although not always successfully. They would be bouncing up and baying and I can still vividly recall the eyes of the worst of them, much like the glass eyes of a doll only more shiny. The worst of them would make a break past me and the reach of my whip and race back to the kennels. Brooks insisted that the gate was shut behind us as we went out and when we were past the wide part and he felt he could hold them up himself, I would go to the hounds waiting at the gate and send them back to him. This advice was sound and after some months with nifty use of the whip we could get them home without any slipping away. It is difficult to imagine just how wild they were; it was just as if they were insane. The summer gradually wore on, walking out became much easier, and at last the hunting season approached and it was time for mounted hound exercise.

Captain Bernard's groom, Head, had been kept on at 3*s*. 8*d*. per hour part time during the summer and was by now full time with the hunt horses. One horse had been bought by the Committee from the Leicester Sales for £140 and Captain Bernard had lent the Committee one of his horses, a gelding called Regent. The crunch came with the first day's mounted hound exercise. They were beside themselves with excitement and again their eyes showed the wildness. It sends shivers down my spine to remember how their eyes stood out like organ stops and shone like little torches. They remembered every trick. Once out of the village and opposite a fence of barbed wire they just went *en masse*. Almost as one they left the horses and spread out across the field regardless of shouts and calling. They ran amok from nine o'clock when they left the horses until after nine o'clock at night when the last ones were collected.

The telephone was red hot with angry farmers calling the kennels, the ex-Master, or anyone else they knew who was on the Committee. The whole country seemed to be up in arms at once.

The Management Committee met and decided to call the main Committee for an emergency meeting. It is indicative of the state of emergency that it was held on a Sunday night, 17th September 1961, at the Easton White Horse. The Management Committee told the main Committee that it was with great reluctance that they recommended that the whole pack be put down, with the exception of a nucleus of bitches which would be used to breed a new pack and retain all the old Easton bloodlines. These hounds would be used for breeding only and would never leave the kennels. The main Committee discussed the matter fully and both of us amateur whippers-in were consulted on all matters as we had been with hounds all summer. Once having heard all the facts, the Committee realised that there was no alternative but to put down the hounds, otherwise we would have no farmer goodwill and, therefore, no hunting. I quote here from the Minute Book:

'It was proposed by Mr Bridgford and seconded by Mr Harvey that the recommendation of the subcommittee is adopted and be carried out, namely:
(a) That all hounds be destroyed with the exception of the necessary breeding stock to produce a new pack of Easton Harriers.
(b) That a draft pack of fox hounds be obtained as soon as possible in order to be ready for hunting for the coming season.'

This resolution was put to the Committee and carried unanimously. The meeting also decided that the basic number of hounds to be kept in kennel, apart from the breeding stock, should be about sixteen couples and that every effort should be made to obtain a professional whipper-in for the season 1962–3.

The Annual General Meeting was held on 17th October 1961 at the Easton White Horse. This was a stormy meeting indeed; everyone knew that the hounds had been put down as the news had spread like wildfire. Colonel Clarke was very upset and said that such a decision should not have been taken without calling an Extraordinary General Meeting and that there were four ex-Masters in the country who had not been consulted, especially Lady Blanche Cobbold who had kept them going during the war. Lady Blanche's great ally, Captain Marriott, spoke I think with the greatest knowledge as he had

Ivy House, Stradbroke: Jimmy Wickham, JAH, Geoffrey Ingram-Smith, Herbert Breeze (standing)

hunted hounds for Lady Blanche. I personally think that he knew in his heart that the right decision had been made but he agreed with the others that such a radical decision should not have been made without a general meeting. Captain Marriott stated that foxhounds were undesirable to hunt the hare and that a pack of harriers should be got together as quickly as possible and offered £50 to buy a good stallion hound. There had been some very unfair criticism made of Brooks' ability with hounds, as often is the case when people do not know the facts. These were squashed by Colonel Howe who said, in no uncertain terms, that it was not the fault of Brooks, because the wildness happened long before he came.

The greatest shame of all was that Lady Blanche could never bring herself to forgive Captain Bernard for putting down the hounds. I am sure she thought of them as just very naughty and that some good whipping-in would have cured them, but I know she cannot possibly have imagined just how bad they were as she, along with all the famous Masters in the UK, would never have experienced hounds as wild as these were. It was so very sad that it should have come to this end, as we all owe her such a debt of gratitude. The Easton Harriers would not have survived the war without her Mastership. Unfortunately, when I became Master I was slightly tarred with the same brush but I tried very hard to heal the rift and, to my great delight, in my later years she invited me to hold a lawn meet at Glemham Hall.

Drafts of hounds were obtained and we started the season with a right motley pack. There were some big beagles, a few harriers, and fox hounds from various packs, some of which were broken-coated and looked like otterhounds. Much more importantly we had six couple of puppies to enter which were the last to be bred from Captain Bernard's Mastership and were the first step in the reconstruction of the Easton Harriers proper. This very mixed bunch of hounds took instantly to Brooks. They knitted themselves together into a handy pack and hunted beautifully. Over the years I have heard of other examples of this amazing phenomenon, a pack of hounds thrown together, usually other people's cast-offs, that have come together and hunted as one. In my own experience it was some years later before the Easton Harriers again worked so well together. This new pack hunting so well gave us all such wonderful fun. I deliberately use the word 'fun' because it now all seemed to *be* fun. When the huntsman blew his horn the hounds actually went to him. The old system of galloping to

their heads to stop them was over and we could relax and really enjoy ourselves.

At a meeting of the main Committee in January 1962 it was announced that Mrs Kingston-Smith did not wish to continue to whip-in after the end of the season. I was asked if I would carry on as amateur whip and I said that I would. The meeting was told that two advertisements had been put in the *Horse & Hound* for a Master or Joint Masters but there had been only one reply. This was from the Reverend Wheeler who was rector of Steeple Bumpstead but his acceptance of the Mastership would depend on his bishop agreeing to find him a parish within the Easton country. His application was not taken seriously for the feeling of the meeting was that, on a rector's stipend, he would be unable to help the hunt financially. With no likelihood of a Master it was proposed that the hunt ought to have a professional whip who would also groom the horses. The Management committee were empowered to engage such a person at no more than £10 per week, plus accommodation which would be Pound Cottage, recently vacated by Head. At the next meeting it was stated that D J Pledge had been engaged at a wage of £9 per week and a promise that a lavatory would be installed in Pound Cottage. It is amusing to look back to those times when both hunt servants had only accepted the position on condition that a lavatory was installed in their houses; little did they know that their future Master did not have one. The only lavatory we had at Glebe Farm was an Elsan bucket in an old pantry and a bath beside it where the water had to be pailed into it and out, as it had no waste pipe. I often used to wonder if I was the only Master of a mounted pack in 1963 that did not have a flush lavatory.

With a professional whipper-in as well as a professional huntsman at the kennels, I did not need to go to the kennels every day, so I was able to concentrate more on my business. I made sure, though, that I did go to the kennels often enough to learn the names of the young entry (last years puppies) and all looked set fair for a good start to the 1962–3 seasons with two professionals in kennel and a keen, but 'green', amateur whipper-in. The subscriptions were to remain the same but changes were proposed for the caps; these were settled at 15*s*. for non-members and 7*s*. 6*d*. for Pony Club members, and for the first time field money to be paid by subscribers at 2*s*. 6*d*. per day. This field money, often mistakenly called the daily cap, was fair and still is very fair as the more sport one has the more one supports the hunt. It was hoped that the financial affairs would improve. A cocktail party at Marlesford Hall was discussed, and the Ball at Cockfield Hall, Yoxford. Sheila and I also volunteered to run a tote lottery and this was gratefully accepted.

As so often happens, things did not go as well as hoped and we had more difficulties with Brooks. Brooks, although a very good hound man was as 'tricky as a wagon load of monkeys'. During his first season he resigned after a few weeks saying that he could not manage on the agreed wage. This was an unheard of thing as huntservants are generally honourable and keep their word but he knew that, with no Master, he could set one person off against another. He telephoned Captain Bernard late at night beseeching him to use his influence to keep him out of court for the honour of the hunt as he had been caught poaching pheasants. His misdeeds and cunning acts of outwitting the Committee for his own ends were numerous. This first crisis was resolved by agreeing to pay Mrs Brooks £2 10s. a week for her part-time help.

Brooks developed an even worse problem that could not be overcome. It would be kind to say that, during his first season, Brooks was not bold across country. At the start of his second, his lack of nerve was much more evident although, to give him his fair due, his problem was with our big blind ditches. There was no lack of nerve when he was faced with a good gate. Our motley pack were hunting beautifully but there were inevitably some splits as there were still too many hares. Pledge or I would be off to stop them but as soon as they had been stopped they would return to their beloved huntsman who was perhaps a quarter of a mile or so behind the main pack. Pledge and I were often in a position to go on with the main pack and, if only one whipper-in was needed, Pledge, as the professional, would attend to the problem. This often left me alone with the main pack and, as the saying goes, 'it is an ill wind that blows no-one any good'. Although I did not realise it, I was learning how to hunt a pack of hounds. When Brooks appeared, he hunted them until again left behind at a big place. When I was alone with the pack I did not attempt to 'hunt them', that is, to cast them at a check or anything like that, but nevertheless I was watching them cast themselves and learnt a lot from observation. I was becoming more and more fond of hounds and hunting and the welfare of the Easton Harriers was foremost in my mind. Sheila and I helped enthusiastically with all the money-making events.

Advertisements were again placed in *Horse & Hound* for a Master or Masters for the season 1963–4.

It was essential that a Master was appointed as the hunt certainly could not continue in its present state. There were serious problems with lots of the farmers as the Committee system did not work at all well, many farmers were not notified and, much worse, they had no Master to go to with a complaint, just a faceless Committee. Torn between the knowledge that I certainly could not afford to be Master and the wellbeing of the hunt, I applied for the Mastership and another application was received from Mr Tim Finch, a member of the neighbouring Waveney Harriers. At the Committee meeting called to discuss the applications on 19th December 1962, I was asked to leave the room while the level of guarantee was discussed. It had been conceded that a guarantee of £1,800 per year could be offered to an incoming Master and this was the figure I had in mind when I applied for the Mastership. This was formally proposed by Mrs Bull but Mr James Aldous proposed an amendment that the offer was reduced to £1,500 and this was carried.

When I was called back into the room and offered the £1,500 I declined. Taking on the Mastership would be a tremendous open-handed commitment; I was prepared to risk it at £1,800 but not at £1,500. The reduction was equal to nine months wages for a man. There would be two wages to find for the year, as well as coal and electricity for the kennels, horses to buy for the hunt staff and all the costs of keeping them, hounds to breed and the cost of inoculation of the puppies and countless more expenses, many of which I did not yet know.

Following my refusal to accept the offered guarantee it was resolved to write to Mr Finch to offer him the same guarantee and if he refused, which he very sensibly did, the hunt should continue as before. Farmer troubles were increasing, both from getting out of the notified draw onto land where no permission had been granted and from not remembering the places that they had agreed to keep clear of because of shooting. Almost a third of the farmers were already refusing us permission, and while there was no Master the number would only increase. Two months later, at a Committee Meeting on 12th February 1963, on an impetuous and stupid impulse, I offered to take the hounds on at the offered guarantee of £1,500, although I knew I could not afford it. By doing so, I was giving in to the weight of personal pressure. Long before I had written my letter of application, I had nursed this mad impulse to take on the Mastership. It was constantly in my thoughts and I just could not stop thinking about it. I have heard clergymen tell of how they had felt a calling to serve God and that they had left a well paid job to become a priest. What I felt was similar as I just could not get it out of my mind.

It was pointed out to me at this meeting on 12th February that it was now too late to give notice to the hunt servants as, by tradition, notice has to be given by 31st January. This meant that I would be obliged to take on Brooks and Pledge or the Committee would be held in breach of contract. I was asked to leave the room while this was discussed and there must have been many doubts as, even with their backs against the wall, only seven of the Committee voted for me, the rest abstaining.

In the end, Pledge left of his own accord and Brooks stayed on, although I would have much preferred it to have been the other way round. I advertised for a whipper-in and groom and engaged a young man called

Terry Badger who moved into Pound Cottage. The scene was thus set for my Mastership, a professional huntsman, good with hounds but lacking in nerve, and a young whipper-in who would also double up as a groom to the hunt horses.

When I next saw my father I told him that I had taken on the Easton Harriers.

'What does that mean?' he asked.

'It means that I am going to be the Master.'

'You damned idiot,' he replied. 'You know you can't afford it. Don't you know that Masters of Hounds should have their living come by post.'

I also had to break the news to Sheila. She took it quite calmly and just remarked that she supposed that she would never be able to eat fish and chips out of the paper again.

The Easton Harriers at Framlingham College. Ernie Nunn, Captain Bernard (Master), Herbert Breeze, Michael Harrison.

CHAPTER 2

MY FIRST SEASON 1963–4

The first official engagement of my Mastership was the Peterborough Hound Show, which is the premier hound show in this country and, many would say, in the world. The Easton had always shown hounds there and I think they hold a record amongst Harriers for being the pack to show for more consecutive years than any other pack. The top showing packs would have suffered an enforced break when their Masters were asked to judge but, in the case of the Easton, Captain Bernard had retired from the Mastership for several seasons before he was invited to judge so the Easton could still show, and continued to do so every year, without a break, until after my Mastership when one show was missed.

As this was my first season, Sheila and I went with Captain Bernard and his wife, Ursula, who invited us to join them and stay at the Bridge Hotel, Huntingdon, the night before. The Captain, of course, was still particularly interested as all the hounds showing had been bred by him but prizes were few, with Patrick[62] being second in the entered dog class and Primrose[63] first in the entered bitch class. The dams of both of these were part of the nucleus of bitches kept for breeding when the rest of the pack was put down and they were sired by a Cambridgeshire Harrier doghound. There were three bitches in whelp when I took on the hounds and they whelped soon after I took over. The breeding of them had been agreed between Captain Bernard and Brooks, and although I had very little knowledge at that time, I am sure I would not have had the same combination. All three litters were sired by Cambridgeshire Plumpton[61]. He was the stallion hound bought with the £50 pledged by Captain Marriott at the AGM after the pack had been put down. Two of the bitches were pure Harriers but the other was South Herefordshire Tangle[61], a foxhound bitch who had been drafted to us. It seems strange that they chose a foxhound to breed from when we desperately wanted to breed up a pack of pure Harriers. The reason, I imagine, was that she was a superb hare hunter. When I hunted hounds I learned to love her dearly and she was definitely the best hound I have ever had. She produced three dogs and four bitches and each were later to be used as brood bitches or stallion hounds. Because these were half foxhound they had to be registered in the appendix but the next generation would be allowed back into the studbook proper.

In general terms, it is a very bad idea to cross foxhounds with harriers for two reasons. First, a harrier's height must not exceed 21 inches at the shoulder and the cross, naturally, tends to increase height. The second reason is far more important, and that is their mental attitude and how they behave at a check. The natural instinct of a foxhound at a check is to cast themselves forward, swinging from side to side but a hare hound should always immediately cast himself back at a check, as a hare will most likely have doubled back on her tracks. The foxhound instinct tends to be dominant when crossed with a harrier and is carried on through the first generation and often even into the second. It is, therefore, most undesirable to have some cross bred hounds as with their variable mental attitudes they will not hunt as a pack and some will be casting forwards and some backwards. An additional problem with the habit of casting forward is the likelihood of putting up a fresh hare which, in turn, tends to encourage the offending hounds in their undesirable habit. Tangle had none of these usual tendencies. She would always cast back and had an uncanny knack of hitting off the line after a check. Her progeny in their first season tended to cast forward at first but soon learned to cast back and were exceedingly good, hunting a hare with great style.

The question of hounds' abilities in casting was becoming increasingly important to me as I could see the nature of the country changing. My father was a leading light in the prevailing fashion of making big fields and other farmers were following suit. All over the Easton country hedges and ditches were disappearing and the blissful days of hunting in tiny fields were ending. The Government was giving large grants for land improvement, for the removal of hedges and ditches but especially for land drainage. As more fields became drained so more fields were drilled with winter wheat and I could foresee that there would eventually be large fields of a hundred acres or more drilled with winter wheat and this would make it very difficult to hunt hounds. Generally, it was still possible in the 1960s to keep somewhere near hounds but, if they checked in the middle of a large wheat field away from me, I found they would tend to come looking for me instead of concentrating on casting themselves. This situation and the prospect of it rapidly becoming worse caused me great concern and I realised that we must breed hounds that would hunt on their own but without being wild and too undisciplined.

John and Elizabeth Graham entertained generously at Brundish Manor and, as the conversation at their dinner parties was usually dominated by hunting, this gave me an opportunity to air my concerns about the future of hunting in this area, in particular getting the hounds to be more independent. John Graham, being far more worldly than me, told me of the Windermere Harriers in the Lake District which, since they hunted in the fells, must of necessity be totally independent. As the port decanter continued its rounds it was decided that we would go up to the Lake District after Christmas so I could see the Windermere for myself. I telephoned the Master, John Bulman, and explained that I was looking for a stallion hound that would breed independence into my hounds. John Graham, Sheila, and I set off in January to coincide with their Hunt Ball, although we had been given strict instructions from John Bulman not to bring 'any of your fancy southern clothes', which had bitterly disappointed Sheila.

Having never been further north than Thetford, I was overjoyed at our first sight of 'mountains' in the Yorkshire Dales. We found our way to the Windermere kennels at Dungeon Ghyll and, after looking at hounds, we had tea with John Bulman and his parents at the Dungeon Ghyll Hotel. The hounds had not impressed me, being all types and sizes with a few beagles mixed in. There was little of the original Windermere blood and they did not have good conformation. The idea of introducing Windermere blood into the Easton did not now seem such a good one, but our second reason for the trip was the Hunt Ball and at six o'clock we followed John Bulman and his wife in his van to the Plough Inn at Selside. There was a light covering of snow on the ground and, with the steep hills and John's fast driving, we arrived quite terrified. The Inn was full of genuine country folk and the atmosphere was electric. I heard my first ever hunting song followed by another, before we trooped out on the Master's instructions, to the village hall full of trestle tables laden with ham, pickles, and cakes.

After we had done justice to it and the catering ladies had been thanked by John Bulman, we returned to the pub where the singing started in earnest. A man stood on a beer crate and sang '*The Place Where the Old Horse Died*', a moment I shall remember all my life. The Master then ushered us back across to the Village Hall where the dancing took place and, as the men far out-numbered the ladies, Sheila never sat

down. The atmosphere was stirring: shepherd's sticks stood in corners and inquisitive collie dogs would peep round the door to be met with a 'Get back' from their owners. The evening seem to fly by and after most people had left, a privileged few, including us as the Master's guests, retired to the kitchen at the back of the hall for more drinking. Beer bottles were produced and tops removed and handed round.

Sheila must have looked taken aback as I heard John Bulman say, 'Nay, lads, nay. You cannot expect Mrs Harvey to drink out of a bottle'. After only a slight pause, a cracked cup with no handle was produced for Sheila to drink from.

This little party lasted for another hour or so. Every now and again a bottle was mysteriously put behind the curtain and years later I discovered they were for the policeman outside. It was an unforgettable night and one that was to alter my life forever as I became firmly hooked on singing hunting songs from then on. The problem of breeding hounds to suit our developing country was left for me to deal with.

Harvest in the autumn of 1963 was finished quite early and I was itching to get started with hunting. Terry Badger had been exercising the horses since early September and they were fit and ready to go. Mounted hound exercise had been such a joy compared with the hell that we had experienced just two seasons ago. I had not been able to join them on exercise during harvest as I was busy doing my own harvest work. Although I only had thirty acres of my own, four of which were down to sugar beet, I still had a very busy harvest as I needed a lot of straw for my intensive pigs and this had to come from other farms and be carted and stacked at Glebe Farm. In fact, Sheila and I were working so hard on our less than satisfactory home that we completely forgot about my first AGM as Master and Major Clay had to ring to remind us.

It was very dry and the ground rock hard; Brooks and I had frequent discussions about when we could start with Brooks stating quite firmly that it would be too hard and would damage the hounds' feet. Looking back on it after all these years I think it was perhaps more to do with his nerves and the blindness of the ditches at this time of the year. In latter years I learned to overcome this problem by hunting in large fields of sugar beet, which did not harm the hounds feet.

Although conditions had not improved, a start had to be made and the first early morning was held at my home, Glebe Farm, Badingham, on 12th October. There was little or no scent so the young entry had no opportunity to learn about hunting. I cannot remember what damage was done to hounds' feet but by starting late we certainly had not lost any opportunity to educate the young entry; they could not learn from the old hounds as even they could not hunt more than a few hundred yards.

I held the second early morning at Brook Farm, Kettleburgh, as it was traditional to do so early in the season; Mr Gordon Clarke made us very welcome. Mr Clarke was one of the farmers who had stopped hunting in the War and had not started again; he was a keen horseman and one of a long list of good horsemen who had owned Brook Farm. His predecessor, Jack Kemp, had hosted the Point-to-Point there in 1939, and my good friend Maurice Scott has carried on the list of good horsemen owners. Although there were only eight early mornings, the conditions and the scent did not improve at all. These eight days were only made memorable by the fact that John Capon's wife Ann had her first day out when hounds met at their Thickthorn Farm, Horham, and that young Roger Lintott was blooded on his first day when hounds met at his parents' Upper Grove Farm, Rendham.

It stayed dry and scentless and every day was as poor as the one before. Brooks was very depressed and miserable and in low spirits as we hacked to the Market Hill, Framlingham for the Opening Meet on 31st October 1963. There was a large crowd waiting and a mounted field of seventeen, which

Daughter Bridget with JAH Opening Meet 1963

was considered quite satisfactory at that time. My wife, Sheila, was not amongst the seventeen mounted as she was in hospital having just produced my second daughter, Judith. Our eldest daughter, two-year-old Bridget, was being looked after by my mother who brought her down to Framlingham and I lifted her up and sat her on the pommel of my saddle for the obligatory photograph.

The following Monday coincided with half-term and I was very pleased to see 38 children out but, sadly, the poor scenting conditions continued and I could not give them a very good day. Conditions had improved by 18th November when we met at Gosbeck Greyhound. It was very wet and with the rain came improved scent. Hounds could really hunt for the first time and this raised the morale of both Brooks and me and we were both pleased to see that

the young hounds that we had out were 'entering' and not keeping with their huntsman.

The finances of the Hunt were very shaky and I was desperate to get things on a better footing. I had been taken to one side and told by several influential members that, now I was Master, I could not have anything to do with fund-raising as it was beneath the dignity of the Master and the prestige of the Easton would be damaged. I hate to be deterred from anything I want to do, so I devised a way of fund-raising that would be within the Master's dignity, namely to have a drag hunt to go out on Saturdays. As the drag days would be outside the terms of my guarantee with the Harriers, which stipulated that

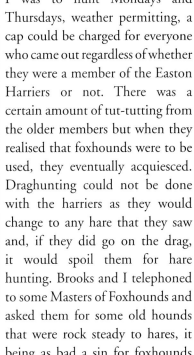

I was to hunt Mondays and Thursdays, weather permitting, a cap could be charged for everyone who came out regardless of whether they were a member of the Easton Harriers or not. There was a certain amount of tut-tutting from the older members but when they realised that foxhounds were to be used, they eventually acquiesced. Draghunting could not be done with the harriers as they would change to any hare that they saw and, if they did go on the drag, it would spoil them for hare hunting. Brooks and I telephoned to some Masters of Foxhounds and asked them for some old hounds that were rock steady to hares, it being as bad a sin for foxhounds to hunt hares as it is for harriers to hunt rabbits. We received drafts from a few packs, some of which were not suitable, and settled to keep about 5½ couple of really steady old foxhounds.

I did not know how to run a drag hunt but I knew whom to ask. I had read a book called *Opium and other Scents* written by Mr Springfield, an ex-Master of the Easton, who had spent many years in Shanghai where he had hunted a drag pack. He strongly advised that the only drag mixture that hounds would really run on, was porcupine droppings marinated in brown bears' urine. I telephoned Colchester Zoo and asked if they could sell me the aforementioned ingredients but the telephone was slammed down. Not to be deterred, I jumped into the car and drove to the Zoo with Chris Bigden, who had agreed to be my drag layer. The Zoo was in its very early days and the owner was in the kiosk taking the entrance money. When we introduced ourselves and said that we were the ones who had asked for porcupine droppings and brown bears' urine, he apologised for slamming down the phone and when we explained our unusual request he told us that he had recently been subjected to a number of practical jokes and naturally assumed this was another, but he agreed to try to supply our wants. Two weeks later he telephoned to say that it was too difficult to collect these items and that he was sorry not to be able to help. I then did what I ought to have done in the first place and telephoned the Master of the Cambridge University Drag to ask what they used and I was told foxes' urine from London Zoo. I telephoned for this and a gallon was immediately sent by train to Ipswich Station, costing £3 delivered. This seemed very expensive as £3 would have bought 24 gallons of petrol.

Chris Bigden had come to Suffolk in the early Sixties with a great desire to hunt and as he and his wife, Sara, lived only a mile or so from Glebe Farm we soon became good friends. Chris' only knowledge of hunting was from seeing sets of hunting prints which nearly always show hard men jumping over terrifying obstacles. This is exactly how Chris rode across country; the bigger the jump the faster he rode at it, and his lean blood horse Nutty was just as game. Chris was often on the floor and sometimes both horse and rider would be down together. His riding was so desperate that I would sometimes send him home but it made not the slightest difference. In later seasons I offered to pay his subscription to both the Essex and Suffolk Foxhounds and the Waveney if he would promise not to come out with the Easton.

Chris was to be mounted on Nutty to lay the drag and first he tried well-soaked rags on the end of a cord. This was not entirely successful as the rags bounced off the ground too much and did not leave a satisfactory 'line'. The second attempt was to add a few links of chain to the end of the cord. This kept the rags on the ground but made his arms ache and also got caught in roots and other obstacles. The third idea was to ask his wife to sew sponges on to overreach boots and the fox's urine to be squirted on to the sponges when necessary from a Fairy Liquid bottle. This worked well and if the sponges came off, Chris would squirt a little onto Nutty's back fetlocks and the hounds would hunt just as well. Occasionally, Chris could not lay the drag and I would ask someone else to do it and it was very noticeable that without Nutty the hounds did not go nearly as well. At first I thought that perhaps temporary drag-layers were squeamish about squirting the offensive liquid on as

often as they ought but this was not the case. I first realised the true reason when the drag course ended by going round three sides of a large field. When the hounds caught sight of Nutty they left the line and cut across to him, standing around baying at him, as staghounds do when they have their stag at bay. After a while, it was only necessary to put a little mixture on Nutty's legs for them to hunt him. They were definitely hunting Nutty and would, in the end, hardly go at all for another horse.

There were three particular drags which remain in my memory. One was the meet at Grundisburgh Dog when it became known that the course would include the senior hunter trial course at Rookery Farm. This caused a record turnout of sixty-two people and caps amounted to £22. The second was a meet at Kesgrave Bell and the course was round and about the heathland which was not built up in those days. In one place there was a long track bounded by high gorse on either side. Chris and I thought it would be fun to build some jumps across it but we put far too many and far too close. The older members of the Harriers had decided to come to this meet confident in the knowledge that there were no ditches at Martlesham, so it would be easy going but were caught unawares and went flat out into the line of jumps. Their horses hardly had time to land before they were going over the next one. It was the end of the run so I was waiting at the end with the hounds and could clearly hear the shrieks of the ladies as they bucketed over the jumps. They were all rather pleased with themselves afterwards and the track was christened the 'Valley of Death'. The third meet was at Hasketon Turk's Head and the course included part of the Point-to-Point course. It was a day of thick fog and it would certainly not have been possible to hunt normally but with a large field, all eager to go, I decided to risk it. After all, I knew where I was going. I laid hounds on to the line and they had settled to a good pace when the first Point-to-Point fence loomed out of the fog. I was somewhat apprehensive about it but sailed over safely and the next two. Then a terrible thing happened. I was just about to take off at the open ditch fence when Chris sailed over it towards me from the other side. How he missed me I do not know. He had become disorientated in the fog and on seeing a fence thought he was back on track.

Although my first priority in introducing the draghunting was to raise funds for the Hunt, it had three other benefits, most importantly with the farmers. At this time many farmers had turned against the Hunt and access to their farms was forbidden but when planning the course of the drag, I would boldly ask a farmer who had refused the Harriers if I could 'just go along the furrow' of a certain field, or 'just across' a certain meadow. When they expostulated that I could not possibly be sure of where hounds would go I could reply that I could, because of the drag, and that we would keep exactly to where I had asked, and then I usually received permission. After two seasons of this, most of the farmers had relaxed and would let me go with the Harriers as well. The second benefit was to get a lot of young people out with hounds to enjoy hunting, even if it was only with the drag. The previous image of the Easton with its staid members going in stately procession steadily across the country did not encourage the young to come out hunting. They found the speed of the drag and the number of jumps very exciting and, after I finished with the drag after two seasons, most of them kept hunting with the Harriers. The third advantage was that I hunted the draghounds myself, an elementary introduction prior to hunting the harriers myself after my first season as Master.

There were two reasons why I had to give up the drag. By the end of the second season, Nutty had become too old and worn out to carry on and by this time the hounds would not really go with any enthusiasm if another horse was used. More important, perhaps, was the time aspect. It took up most of two days a week, one to walk and plan the course and the other to hunt the hounds. With a further two days to hunt with the Harriers, I was giving up four working days which was far too much. Chris and I had great fun with the drag. The day before a meet Chris would walk around the course with me and memorise the route. We usually did this in the morning and were sometimes asked in for lunch, especially at Grundisburgh where the Saffells were always most hospitable. On one occasion we were invited in for tea by Mrs Schreiber at Marlesford Hall. This was served in the drawing room with the finest china and we both felt embarrassingly scruffy in our everyday clothes, but Mrs Schreiber insisted that we were not to fuss. Mr Schreiber was a Trustee of the Easton Harriers at that time and Clare, their daughter, hunted regularly. Once, after walking the course, Chris suggested we went into Ipswich for a meal and to my great surprise suggested that we went into a Chinese restaurant, which was the first one to open in Ipswich. It was a great culinary adventure for me but I soon realised that I loved it and we went far too often. Neither of us could afford such luxuries and we felt very guilty about doing so as, not only were we spending money, but also losing time at work.

The draghunting took a great deal of time to run but it was a good fundraiser. We hunted eleven times in each of the two seasons and at some meets the caps would amount to £15 or more. All expenses were born out of my own pocket so everything raised went to Hunt funds. The cap for the first season was only 5s. but, even at this low rate, the season raised £98, the equivalent of thirty farmers' subscriptions at three guineas or twelve members paying the full subscription of seven guineas. In the second season the caps were increased to 7s. 6d. for children and 10s. for adults and raised £130, equivalent to thirteen farmers' or nine full subscriptions at the new rates of seven guineas and fifteen guineas respectively.

My first season as Master was more turbulent than I would have wished: I had trouble with the old members, trouble with the Norfolk and Suffolk Foxhounds, and an unpleasant and heated AGM.

The trouble with the old members was, to a degree, understandable, but yet very difficult and embarrassing for me to handle. Here was I, a young man in his early twenties, being always correctly addressed as Master by an experienced field of long-standing members, mostly two generations older than me. It was a complete role reversal as for years I had addressed most of the field formally and with the respect due to the age difference. The real trouble lay in their inability to adapt to the changing nature of the country. Farming patterns were changing and more winter wheat was being planted, perhaps as much as 20% at some meets. Now, with around 80% of any country down to winter wheat, this seems laughable but it was a serious problem. It simply did not occur to the older members to detour slightly from the direct line to avoid these fields, even though it was comparatively easy with plenty of cartways and tracks and the other fields as stubble or plough. Some would make an attempt to ride round the edge, although still well away from the hedges; others would ride right across the middle.

This, I knew, must stop or we would lose the goodwill of even more farmers and it would have been impossible to hunt with any fewer farmers' co-operation, as already around a third were writing to say that they did not want us on their land. This very high proportion was due to a variety of reasons, but the principal one was the bad feeling left over from when the hounds were out of control in the late 1950s with the additional ongoing aggravation of the thoughtless damage caused by some of the members. Some farmers, of course, were irreconcilable. I worked hard to win round the opinion of farmers towards the

Easton Harriers and over the seasons had great success until out of a total of 860 farmers, only fourteen refused permission to hunt. One of these was Dickie Bird Whiting at Stonewall Farm, Earl Soham, who farmed with his brother and both men were of a rather dour disposition. Over the years I occasionally saw one of them in a pub and would always buy him a glass of beer and have a chat. On one of my many visits to them at Stonewall Farm, I found the two brothers mucking out a yard by hand and while I was there, it came on to heavy rain so I sheltered with them and eventually managed to find out why they were so opposed to the Easton Harriers. In the late 1920s they had been cutting a lovely field of clover to make 'stuver', a Suffolk name for hay made from clover which is very nutritious but the clipper broke because the ground was very rough because members of the Easton had ridden over the clover ley in a wet time, leaving deep hoof prints which had now been baked hard by the sun. There was a delay of two days in obtaining the necessary part to repair the clipper and before they were able to cut the remainder of the field it came on to prolonged rain and the crop was ruined. The first few cuts before the clipper broke had been made and carted in fine condition and the loss of a fine crop was rightly blamed on the Easton Harriers. The sins of those thoughtless members were still getting us banned over forty years later and I never could win them round.

Another reason behind farmers' hostility was the high-handed attitude of the Norwich Staghounds who traditionally met in Easton Harriers country four times a year at Debenham, Eye, Laxfield, and Saxtead. This pack hunted carted deer which means that two deer were brought to the meet in a trailer and one of these was turned off and hunted until brought to bay, caught, and put back into its trailer. If the first one did not go very far then the second one was used. These stag hunts were usually fast and furious and since no one had any idea where the stag would choose to run, it was impossible to notify any farmers that they were coming with the exception of the farmer who gave the turn off. Most of the farmers hated the staghounds as all the followers rode furiously across country with no time for explanation or courtesies, as it was common for these runs to be over twenty miles and if anyone stopped to explain, they would never get on terms with hounds again. The policy of the staghounds was to pay for any damage and to pay very handsomely but this did not really work as most of the farmers would not write to claim but just accept the damage and harbour a grudge. Unfortunately, to a high

percentage of farmers, a hunt was just a hunt and the Easton Harriers would be tarred with the same brush and be barred for damage done by the staghounds.

To help alleviate these problems, I decided to write a letter to all the members explaining how I felt they ought to behave towards the farmers and, in particular, to avoid wheat and rape *completely*, going round by adjacent ploughed land. In my innocence I worded my letter 'to avoid wheatfields and beware of rape in the stubble' which caused considerable teasing. Moreover, on the very day that most of them opened the letter, the hounds met at Cretingham Bell and we spent a large part of the day on Dennis Wilson's land. He, being very keen on hunting, was following on foot but spent all day shouting to hunt staff to gallop across the middle of the wheat and, to make matters worse, insisted that the members rode round the edge of the wheat saying loudly that, 'Of course, it did no harm'. Dennis Wilson's views were not shared by most of his fellow farmers and this well-meant enthusiasm I could have done without as it certainly did not endorse what I had stated to be the farmers' feelings in my letter.

The staghounds were disbanded the season before I became Master, but, instead of making life easier for me, it made it worse, much worse. Henry Bothway, the last Master and huntsman of the staghounds decided to form a pack of foxhounds in their place. He then registered all the country that the old staghounds hunted as the country of the new Norfolk and Suffolk Foxhounds. This comprised all the Dunston Harriers, Waveney Harriers, and Easton Harriers countries although the only time this area had been hunted by foxhounds was for a few years a century earlier. The Easton Harriers had never shared their country with foxhounds but, as foxhounds normally take precedence over harehounds, this meant that if the registration was allowed to pass unchallenged I would have to ask Mr Bothway's permission for every meet of our season, even for a meet at our own kennels. The hierarchy of the Dunston Harriers were well disposed towards the new foxhounds so did not object, but the Easton and the Waveney objected very strongly.

This was a battle I could well have done without. Again I was pitted against my elders and began to wish that I had never taken on the Mastership as it involved all these unpleasant matters, but I had some strong allies. My great mentor, Captain Bernard, supported me wholeheartedly and equally determined was Lord Somerleyton, Master of the Waveney. A long and bitter struggle ensued until the Masters of Foxhounds Association decided to hold a tribunal in

London, presided over by Lord Halifax. I was quite terrified at the thought of having to appear before a bench of famous Masters and beseeched Captain Bernard to do it for me. He quite rightly refused saying that I was the Master and must do it, but that he would come with me. The Masters of the Norfolk and Suffolk Fox Hounds and the Dunston Harriers put their case forward first and then it was the turn of the Easton and the Waveney. I made my case on the basis that the Easton farmers would not tolerate two mounted packs crossing their land and also explained how much shooting there was and that, while harriers can avoid the coverts, foxhounds have to draw them and that would not suit syndicate shoots. It took a lot of courage but I also made a point of how much the staghounds had been disliked and resented in the country and that the foxhounds had the same Masters and members and this would cause friction. Lord Somerleyton then made very similar points to my own but delivered them with considerably more eloquence than my stumbling submission. We made hunting history on that day as the tribunal found in our favour and harriers took precedence over foxhounds for the first time ever.

The hearing had been very tense and heated and at one moment the Honourable Charles Fellowes said: 'What! Foxhounds meet at the invitation of Harriers? Never!' He was so worked up that he was frothing through his moustache and his body shook with emotion as he said the words. I am eternally grateful that Captain Bernard came with me and stood beside me while I gave evidence, as I desperately needed his reassurance. I think we had quite a few whiskies on the train coming home.

The last of the main difficulties of my first season was the AGM which, naively, I had believed would be plain sailing. Being terribly self-conscious, I was dreading making my first Master's Report in front of my peers and betters for, although I was now the Master, I still felt decidedly intimidated when confronted by them all. This, however, was only a personal problem and the main one was the level of subscription. Although I had been told very clearly that the financial affairs of the hunt were not part of the Master's mandate, I could easily see that no proposals for an increase in subscriptions would come to the floor. I had made my views known at a Committee Meeting on 10th March 1964 when, to a shocked Committee, I had proposed that the farmers' subscriptions be raised from three guineas to ten guineas and ordinary subscriptions from seven guineas to fifteen guineas. This proposal was discussed and passed subject to ratification at the

AGM. The AGM was held at the Crown & Anchor, Framlingham, on 28th May (1964). According to the Minutes, 'After some discussion it was resolved to accept the Committee's recommendations regarding the increase in subscriptions, with the addition that there should be a family subscription for ordinary subscribers of 30 guineas and for farmers of 20 guineas.'

This was somewhat understated as 'some discussion' was an uproar. I have never seen so many people on their feet at an AGM. There were heated speeches as to how long certain families had been supporters of the Easton and how this unreasonable increase in subscriptions would sever these ancient ties. Others used the line of 'how much they loved their hunting but would not any longer be able to enjoy their sport'. It was even suggested by some that this AGM might not accept the Committee's recommendation on the level of subscription. Captain Bernard, the Chairman, then pointed out that if an AGM did not accept the proposals from the Committee it amounted to a vote of no confidence and the Committee must all resign. This threat, delivered as only he could, had the effect of calming the meeting and the proposals were duly carried. I have often said, partly in jest but nevertheless truly, that a Master's main purpose is to make unpopular decisions as the members make the popular ones for themselves.

The meeting closed on a more gratifying note with the report from Major Clay, the Secretary, who sent out the cards to farmers asking their permission to hunt. He said that it had been much easier to arrange fixtures with a Master than it had been with a Committee and that relations with farmers were much improved.

Meanwhile, the business of the hunt went on and my first season as Master provided the usual range of memorable events in the hunting field. Scent improved although some days were very poor and others were very good. There were still far too many hares but we had lots of fun. Altogether the Harriers hunted on forty-five days and killed 49½ brace, although I suspect that this figure was rather questionable as Brooks was rather 'elastic' about his numbers. We saw a white hare go into kale at Cretingham and, although we drew it thoroughly, it was not seen again. The day from Debenham Lion on 2nd December was of personal importance to me because, for the first time, I watched hounds hunt a hare in a classical figure of eight, killing her on the same seat as she was found, the total distance of both circles being 4–4½ miles. The meet on 30th December was cancelled in respect of the death of Mr Alan Bridgford. He had been a great supporter of the Easton and his daughter, Gay, continued the tradition, being an excellent member for the whole of my Mastership.

On a day of bitter cold weather after the meet at Stradbroke Hempsheaf, Brooks lost his horn after an hour's hunting. We all spread out looking for it but it could not be found. Captain Bernard remonstrated angrily with Brooks who replied, 'Well, sir. It's cold enough for anyone to lose the horn.' This amused the Captain and Brooks managed the rest of the short day without one.

The future looked good when seventy-one children attended the children's meet at Henley, Cross Keys. The children all followed me with mistaken trust across what looked like a neglected meadow but I soon found my horse floundering in boggy ground and there were empty saddles galore. To make the fiasco worse I became entangled in a collapsed barbed wire fence on the far side. There was a field of thirty for the lawn meet at my family home, Braiseworth Hall,

Captain Bernard (on the grey) still hunting in the late 1970s

Tannington, and soon after moving off, Major Clay and Chris Bigden both had their horses in the bottom of a ditch at the same time. The meet at Rendham White Horse, on 20th January was particularly jovial and we moved off in high spirits. Scent was good and, with hounds flying and the adrenaline running high, we passed through the farm yard at Rendham Hall. The owner, Mr Tommy Jack, had stopped work to watch us cross his farm and began to run to open a gate for me.

'Don't worry Mr Jack, I can jump it', I cried, and jumped out of the farm yard and sailed away across the meadows in the wake of my flying hounds.

With never a check they went over the top onto Mr Mellors' land and a huge gate on an uphill slope loomed up. I knew that Tommy Jack was still watching and felt I had to have a go at it. Noddy, the big horse I was riding, was a very bold 'lepper' and went at it willingly but just hit the top. Knowing that the hinge had been bent, Chris Bigden and I went back that night to repair it by torchlight and I was shocked to see that the hinge was above my shoulder. It is wonderful what adrenaline will do; I would not

have jumped it in cold blood for £100 and I don't think Noddy would have faced it without the cry of hounds in front. These nightly repair jobs were part of the campaign to woo back the farmers. Chris would nearly always come with me and we would walk across fields loaded with pieces of wood, nails, and hammers, wondering if we would be arrested as poachers by an observant bobby.

The meet at Glemham Crown on 27th January 1964 was a milestone in my life as I hunted the harriers for the first time. I cannot remember why Brooks could not hunt them; perhaps he was on an interview or trial for his next position with the Carmarthenshire Foxhounds. Tim Toller was to whip-in to me and I unboxed at his home, Walnut Tree Farm, Benhall. I wanted to hack the short distance to the meet so hounds would be aware that Brooks was not there and settle down with me. We hacked through Harrow Lane then turned off near the waterworks and went across country on a footpath, dismounting to lead over a narrow wooden bridge, and arrived at the meet without experiencing any difficulties. Tim was wearing the green coat that Captain Bernard had given him and was well qualified to whip-in having done five seasons with Captain Bernard and several seasons with the Sproughton Foot Beagles before that.

Tim recalled to me a story of when Mr Springfield was hunting hounds and had forgotten his false teeth. This meant, of course, that he could not blow the horn. 'Springie' sent back to Easton for his teeth but, in the meantime, instructed Tim Toller to blow the horn for him, giving him strict orders to 'keep in his pocket', *i.e.* be near enough to blow when told to. Tim would whip-in to Ernie Nunn if Captain Bernard was away and remembered that, as they hacked home, Ernie would blow his horn when about half a mile short of the kennels. The other hounds in kennel would hear and start baying frantically which was the signal for Mrs Nunn to put the kettle on and the groom to be in attendance ready to take the horses. I had forgotten all about this old practice, although I used to do it myself in my first seasons until I had a lorry.

I had a bout of influenza in early February so my wife acted as Field Master on 3rd and 6th February and had the distinction of marking a hare to ground in a gateway pipe. The Waveney Harriers invited us to meet at Fressingfield and hounds ran so fast and straight that at one point I had lost them. From our own 'home' meet at I found myself in the position of having to make a wide detour from the direct line. Seeing a lady in her garden I explained my predicament and asked her permission to take a short cut by jumping into her garden and walking out into the road the other side. Permission was readily granted, but just after landing, her husband came out of the house and tore me off a strip, not knowing that I had asked permission. The last meet of the season was at Dennington Queen on 2nd March so it must have been an early spring.

One of my major initiatives during my first season was to establish the Supporters Club. I advertised in *The East Anglian Daily Times* that anyone interested in forming the club should attend a meeting at my home on 4th March. Seventeen people attended, it was decided that they should form the first committee, and the Supporters Club was born. By the time of the Easton Harriers AGM on 28th May, we had one hundred and seventy five members and the club has never looked back since.

I was president of the Club and as such attended all the Committee meetings and became deeply involved in everything that was planned. One of my suggestions was that the Club should revive the Opening Meet Dance, which the Easton had traditionally held before the War. Captain Bernard offered his home for the event and it was held there for many seasons. He always wore a marvellous old smoking jacket with elaborate frogging down the front. It was at one of these dances that I last saw the old Captain do one of his party pieces. He would dance with a lady who did not know his reputation and then suddenly stop and freeze in an upright position as though he had had a seizure. Then, still stiff, he would fall over backwards not bending at all, even when he hit the floor still managing to keep a rigid look on his face. He would lie still for about half a minute and then jump up laughing.

These little dances were great fun and always quickly sold out. The Captain set a limit of eighty guests but this was sometimes stretched to one hundred and thirty and once even to one hundred and forty. He would say to us that we were not to think he had not noticed, but he always took it in good part.

Although it was unusual for the Supporters Club to hold events that required dinner jackets, I suggested that we did on this occasion as it allowed the girls to dress up and I loved to see them all in their lovely dresses. The invitations were printed to read 'Dress black tie' and at the first dance a farmer who did not understand the terminology literally came in his best suit with a black funeral tie.

I was invited to the lunch which preceded the AGM of the Masters of Harriers & Beagles Association and felt quite excited, wondering whom I would meet. I had decided to hunt hounds the next season so I would need a horn and made use of my trip to London to go to Swain & Adeney in Piccadilly to buy one. I was shown a selection of six and taken downstairs to a storeroom to try them. What a terrible embarrassment it was, as I unsuccessfully tried to blow them all with the impassive employee gravely handing me one after another. I felt so disconcerted that I bought all six at £3 each and spent the next year practising every day, often while I was driving my pick-up around, until eventually I could get a note out of one, although it took more than a year. Leaving Swain & Adeney, I hailed a taxi and, with my best effort at a cultured voice, said, 'The United Hunts' Club please'. The taxi driver was very chatty and we got into a conversation. After a while he suddenly said, 'How far from Denmark Green were you born?' I laughed and said: 'About 12 miles'. I had, during the conversation, obviously relaxed back into my normal way of speaking and he had easily recognised my accent as he had been evacuated to Diss during the War and lived on Denmark Green.

I had taken steps to have the Easton Harriers country officially registered for the first time with the Masters of Harriers and Beagles Association. Until then, the question of boundaries was somewhat vague. In the old days the predecessors of the Waveney Harriers was a private pack belonging to and hunted by Lord Stradbroke, and known as the Henham Harriers after Lord Stradbroke's seat. The country of the Henham Harriers naturally contained all of the Stradbroke estate which extended down to, and including parts of, Badingham, Bruisyard, and Dennington, as far as Tannington Lodge. The Easton country included all of Laxfield, Syleham, and Fressingfield so the vague boundary formed a huge 'S' bend. The Waveney had not hunted the southern part of their country for some years so I drew a boundary that I thought was more sensible, taking Bruisyard, Badingham, Dennington, and Tannington for the Easton and giving Fressingfield, Syleham, and part of Laxfield to the Waveney. I thought it best to use easily defined boundaries so decided on the River Min from the coast to Yoxford, then the A1120 to Emmett's Shop in Peasenhall, Heveningham Long Lane to Ubbeston, the

B1117 through Laxfield Street to Stradbroke, then the B1118 to Oakley. The northern boundary then took the line of the A140 to Ipswich and finally the A14 to Felixstowe. I was not sure what the Waveney reaction would be to my rather bold approach and was pleased when Captain Bernard offered his staunch support to the radical proposal. The outcome was that the Captain invited the Waveney Master, Colonel Mike Tomkin, to come to his home and after a few drinks the maps were spread out and the boundaries signed, with both Mike Tomkin and I signing in various places along the clearly marked boundary. The Foxhound Masters also signed the southern boundary with the proviso that Barham and Coddenham was still to be hunted by the Essex and Suffolk Foxhounds as well as the Easton as had formerly been the case. I was very pleased with myself for achieving this formally signed boundary and duly registered it with the Keeper of the Map at the Masters of Harriers & Beagles Association.

Chris Bigden laying drag in fog – see page 18

Drawn by Jason Gathorne-Hardy

The last significant event of my first season was my introduction to French hunting. John Graham of Brundish Manor was a great veneur and had somewhat taken me under his wing. Over various good dinner parties, he taught me a great deal about the style in which a hare should be hunted and about doubles and how old hounds would learn to cut the double, and many more points of venery that I have never forgotten. He had a suggestion to make when I wanted to draft some hounds, for various reasons but mostly because they were horse-shy after being jumped on or ridden over. John had a long standing friend in France who was looking for some English

harriers and as they hunt in forests the horse-shyness would not effect them as the horses would seldom be near them. He asked if I would like to let his friend have them and then suggested that I go with him to take the 2½ couple to France where he would introduce me to French hunting. I was very excited, as my only experience of going abroad was a day-trip to Holland with the National Farmers' Union. We went in my pick-up truck with a detachable roof on top for the hounds and had terrible trouble with the French Customs who wanted to charge us tax on the imported hounds. In England it is generally considered ungentlemanly to charge any money for draft hounds on the principle that Masters only draft hounds that they do not want due to some fault. John's French seemed to me to be quite good but to explain 'English gentlemanly behaviour' to French Custom officials, especially that 'five dogs', 'five beautiful pedigree dogs', were given free, was very difficult. John argued his point for hours but eventually won and we were able to carry on.

I shall never be able to repay the debt of gratitude that I owe John for introducing me to his friend, George Lamiot, who lived in Evreux in Normandy. George was considerably older than me and was another great veneur. I have always said that I have learned more about venery in one evening spent beside his fire, than in several seasons hunting my own hounds. George and I became great friends, bound together by our mutual love of venery and I would sit for hours, often into the early morning, listening and absorbing all that he told me.

CHAPTER 3

FIRST MASTERSHIP 1964–68

My second season saw great changes, most importantly that I had decided I would hunt hounds myself which entailed a complete change of hunt staff.

I had advertised for a kennel huntsman and selected Fred Hargreaves as a likely candidate for the post. He came on trial to whip-in at Thorndon Black Horse on 30th January and soon afterwards accepted my offer. All hunt servants change jobs on 1st May each year and it is only in very exceptional circumstances that this is not the case such as the death of a huntsman which might entail a new one arriving mid-season. May Day of 1964, then, saw Brooks depart from Easton with his wife and furniture bound for the Carmarthenshire Foxhounds, and Fred Hargreaves arrive with his wife, son and furniture from the Whaddon Chase Foxhounds which had recently amalgamated with the Bicester because the Bicester had lost a great deal of their country to Milton Keynes. Terry Badger also moved out of Pound Cottage to go to the Albrighton Woodland Foxhounds as Fred would whip in to me. The difference between a huntsman and a kennel huntsman is not always clearly understood. The duties are exactly the same in kennel. They are responsible for the running of the kennels, the cleanliness, the collection of fallen stock from farms, the skinning, and the feeding of hounds. Feeding hounds is a great skill because if all the hounds were simply allowed to help themselves there would be grossly fat ones and very thin ones. The skill is standing at the door of the feed yard and 'drawing' hounds in one at a time, starting with the fussy feeders who just pick and lick and look for some delicate morsel and to leave them for a while, then draw in the next most fussy ones and so on until the gluttons are let in at the end. Sometimes there seems to be very little left for them but nevertheless they always look in good condition. The main difference between a huntsman and a kennel huntsman is that a huntsman hunts hounds and carries the horn on hunting days whilst a kennel huntsman whips in to an amateur huntsman. The term amateur huntsman simply means that that person is not paid for his services. Mostly, but not always, an amateur huntsman is the Master or Joint Master. A person paid for his services is a hunt servant and those who are not are amateurs and this has nothing to do with how good or bad they are at their job.

Fred Hargreaves was a true professional and had been brought up through the old hard school. He knew his job thoroughly and we were to have many happy seasons together. Mrs Hargreaves was equally committed to the task in hand and cheerfully dealt with the endless telephone calls from farmers who wanted fallen stock collected. She was superb with the whelps, both when they were born and especially at weaning time and she reared them all successfully. She also went far beyond the call of duty and would baby-sit my two daughters at the kennels while Sheila hunted. I would leave Glebe Farm in the pickup with Sheila and the two little ones in the front and the pram in the back, arrive at the kennels and unload the children and the pram. When Fred, Sheila, and I were mounted, Mrs Hargreaves would let the hounds out and we would hack to the meet.

I had one parting shot from Brooks which hit me below the belt. He had gone away and left an unpaid bill for his car at Neslings Garage in Wickham Market for £33. I paid it to keep the good name of the hunt but it was a hard blow as it represented a month's wages and I was already putting in a lot of my own money into the hunt, which I could not afford.

Fred Hargreaves showed hounds at my second Peterborough Show and we had some successes with Plausible[64] being first in the unentered dog hound class, Patrick[62] third in the stallion hound class, and Villager[63] and Viceroy[63] won the Lady Cook Cup for the best couple of dog hounds. Plausible then went on to become Reserve Champion, but he was later exported to Pennsylvania to Tony Garvin of the Springtown Harriers. We had one prize among the bitches with Premium[63] being second in the under 19 inches class. The Lady Cook Cup was large and was rather a problem to us at Glebe Farm for security reasons; the doorframes were so rotten that it was pointless locking the door as the hasp just pulled out of the rotten wood. Sheila overcame this problem when we went out by hiding it in the washing machine under some dirty washing. Although later we did a great deal of work to the house, we never locked our door for the eight years that we were at Glebe Farm.

The season started with the first early morning hunt on 21st September and Mr 'Hubby' Bloomfield had invited us to meet at Poplar Farm, Cretingham. The ground was rock hard and to save the jarring of the hunters' legs on this hard ground, Fred and I rode little cobs from Mr Diaper's riding school in Dovercourt. Hiring cobs from 50 miles away might seem odd, but this connection had begun in my dealing days. Soon after I was married and was still horse dealing, I bought a donkey which my wife's little sister, Rita, then aged about five, fell in love with. She rode it about the orchard and wanted to keep it. Sheila was very keen that she should have the donkey so I weakened and said that she could providing I got back the £8 I had paid for it. I then advertised the donkey for hire at 30s. per week and received lots of telephone calls, one of which was from Mr Diaper who said he would have it for the whole of the summer holidays. So the £8 was recovered, the donkey was Rita's and stayed with us until its death, but the deal gave me the idea to ask Charlie Diaper if he wanted any ponies on hire. He jumped at the idea and a price of £3 per week was settled. This sideline business grew and in the next summer I had about thirty cobs and ponies on hire to him at Dovercourt.

Rita on the donkey

Thus it was that I had access to cobs on which to start the season; mine was called Sovereign. The dry conditions proved scentless and this state continued until the middle of October. The second meet of the year was held in accordance with tradition, at Brook Farm, Kettleburgh, but it was the third of these early meets, held at my home, Glebe Farm, on 26th September, that was most memorable, for three reasons. Rita, now grown out of her donkey, had her first morning's hunting on her new pony, Pip, and also Fred Hargreaves' son, John, aged nine, had his first morning's hunting. The third aspect was typical of the atmosphere of the Easton Harriers. At a party the night before, when the drinks were flowing, my friend Ernie Calver said how much he envied us who went hunting and how he had always wanted to ride to hounds since the days when he boxed the Breese family to meets.

On the spur of the moment I said, 'Well, you can if you like. My old mare Blaze is on the meadow and she will look after you. Be at my house in the morning at six o'clock'.

Blaze was now retired and was in foal, had no shoes on, and had not been ridden since the previous season. I never expected the offer to be taken up and had quite forgotten about the remark but when I came out of

the house in the morning, Ernie was standing in the yard.

Although somewhat taken aback, I said, 'You mean to go then?' and he said, 'Well you said that I could'.

I got the old mare from the meadow, put on her saddle and bridle, gave Ernie a leg on and we were away with hounds. The old mare was used to being with hounds and as Ernie could not ride at all she stayed with the hounds and me. How he did not fall off I shall never know but I would think he was saved by the combination of hanging onto the mane and the non-existent scent, which ensured a gentle morning. He came out on the old mare four more times and then kept hunting until after my Mastership and he, and his wife Mary, were always willing to help with any fundraising efforts.

No one came out for the meet at Church Farm, Saxtead, but we had an excellent morning 'rabbit breaking' as there were lots of old meadows with thick hedges and an abundance of rabbits. I wanted to obtain, and later on did achieve, an instant obedience to my call of 'Ware rabbit!' and for hounds to stop dead at the command. By the Opening Meet I wanted my young hounds to know the difference between a rabbit and a hare and to understand what a terrible sin it was to chase rabbits. With no one out, it meant Fred and I could go round all the meadows finding as many rabbits as possible and stopping the hounds as it is the only way to teach them. One cannot simply show them a video.

The meet at Thickthorn Farm was thrilling for me as, even with the bad scent, hounds hit off a drag and slowly kept on it until they finally dragged right up to their hare after two miles and put her off her seat. A drag in this sense is not an artificial trail laid as in drag hunting but the scent of a hare which has passed some time before and has not been seen by the hounds or the humans. It is usually where a hare has been feeding in the early morning, prior to laying up in her seat (or form) for the day.

On 15th October scent was suddenly there. Hounds ran really well at Dennington Lodge and the damp conditions continued. Mrs Webster from Easton Hall had her first morning's hunting when the meet was at the kennels and five days later, on 24th October, when we met for the second time at Brook Farm, it was to be a very special day for five children. These five children worked very hard at the riding school at Dovercourt where I had all the ponies on hire and I had promised them a day's hunting at the end of the summer. They were very excited and thoroughly enjoyed the day, each one riding their personal favourite pony or cob that I had brought from the riding school.

The last early morning was at Captain Bernard's, By the Crossways, at Kelsale, on 2nd November and two days later I received a lovely letter from Ernie Nunn, our ex-Kennel Huntsman, which pleased me greatly as I had such respect for him and still have his spurs on my office wall. In contrast to this lovely letter, I was to receive a reprimand from Captain Charles Marriott, an ex-Master of the Easton who had served for two seasons and would have probably gone on longer but for an unfortunate event which entailed his honourable resignation. Captain Marriott took a great interest in me during my first few seasons and, as he was an ex-Master, I treated him with all due respect. He was rather eccentric and openly admitted that he had never done a day's work in his life. He lived at Sandpit Farm, Bruisyard, which was only two miles from my home at Glebe Farm. He was quite fierce and bellowed his instructions to whomever, not mincing his words regardless of whom he upset.

One evening the telephone rang and Sheila answered. I saw her face fall and her hand begin to tremble and with a faltering voice, she said, 'It's Captain Marriott for you.'

I took the receiver and started to say 'Hello' when a great bellow came from the other end. 'Harvey! Get down here!' and the line disconnected.

Sheila was standing nearby and looking very worried.

'Whatever is the matter? What has happened?'

'I don't know but he wants to see me. I'd better go down.'

Here I was, not only being treated like the lowest form of serf but also scuttling to do as I was bid, even though I was Master.

I drove down to Sandpit Farm and knocked at the door. Mrs Marriott answered and showed me into his study. The Captain was sitting in his armchair with a revolving circular bookcase in front of him and he growled at me to sit down. His hand went into the two sections of the bookcase that I could not see and there was a clinking sound as he poured me a large whiskey.

'Now look here Harvey, I've been watching you and you're no damn good. I have my doubts that you will ever make a Master'.

'Oh dear sir. What have I done wrong?'

'Well damn it Harvey, to start with you can't even drink. You don't know how to drink, and I'm telling you this Harvey, if you want to be a Master of Hounds, you must drink and drink with the men. Do you know what I mean, Harvey? Lead from the front. *Always* lead from the front.'

I cannot remember the rest of the evening except that I went home more than slightly the worse for wear. There were several more of these sessions and Sheila began to refuse to answer the telephone after six o'clock in case it was him.

On another occasion he nearly burst my eardrums with his, 'Get down here, Harvey!' This time it was about horn blowing and after some whiskies he got up out of his chair, took the horn from the mantelpiece and said we had better go through to the drawing room so as not to upset Ruby, his wife. He blew several calls not very well as he was out of practice but I quickly said I thought I knew them all and thanked him, much preferring to go back to the study and listen to his tales of the old days.

There was another evening when I was summoned to take instruction about using the whip. After hearing of all the times when he had seen me use my whip incorrectly, and several whiskies later, he rose from his armchair and went towards the door. He took a whip from the entrance hall and we went outside where he climbed onto the mounting block to get a height above ground as if he were on a horse. He then showed the principles of how to make a whip crack and in particular the wrist movement and then he put it into practice.

'Stand well back!' he commanded, and proceeded to try to crack the whip but it had not been cleaned for years and was far too stiff. I can still taste the little stones that got into my mouth as the thong hit the gravel time and time again.

'Have you got that, Harvey? Have you got that?'

'Oh yes sir. I can see the knack of it now.'

I would have told him any fib to get him down from that mounting block.

The Opening Meet was on 5th November and there were thirty mounted, nearly double the previous year, which pleased me as things were looking up. Amongst the mounted field were John Graham and George Lamiot, my new found French friend, who had asked if there were any more of these good harriers to draft. John had invited him over and had asked me to mount him so I lent him a horse called Paddy who was very safe over blind ditches. We moved off to draw Mr Larter's farm and, as usual, stopped to raise our hats towards his bedroom window, as he was now bedridden. Before he was confined to the house, he would follow us enthusiastically in his Model-T Ford. We continued to raise our hats to his window for many years after his death in respect to his memory.

We soon found a hare, which immediately made for the Pageant Field, the sports ground in the town, with hounds close behind. I galloped back along the road towards Framlingham and stopped hounds at Jeffreson's Well, well into the town, but the hare carried on, going down Castle Street and Church Street on to the Market Hill which she decided to go right round, close in front of Barclays Bank, Durrants the Butchers, past Lloyds bank and up Church Lane and into the churchyard. I had all these details from people who had been to the opening meet and were now shopping.

Our second hare ran a more conventional line but a most embarrassing thing happened as Paddy bucked George off. I rode back to apologise but tried to pass it off lightly by shaking his hand and saying, 'Thank you for that George. He only does that once a season and now I know it won't be me.' A very good run redeemed the situation and took us nearly to my house at Badingham. George later returned to France taking a couple of hounds with him, Tarnish and Valerie.

George and John were together responsible for a small experiment I tried with hound breeding. Over many good dinner parties with John Graham, I was learning more and more about venery. One of the things John talked about, and also lent me books to read about, was the old Southern Harriers of two or three centuries earlier which, although as high as a foxhound, would hunt a hare very slowly, allowing it plenty of time to make complicated doubles which, in turn, slowed down the hounds even more. This type of hunting would not suit our modern followers who want to ride across country but the followers of long ago days delighted in the venery, watching their hounds unravel the complicated doubles and revelling in their wonderful cry. John Graham wanted to breed hounds which would hunt like this and then hunt them on foot. To this end he tried crossing bloodhound bitches with a French Gascon-Saintongeois dog and George Lamiot sent him one called Musketeer. He had to come through quarantine so it was an expensive experiment, but it worked, and a small pack was bred and kennelled at his home, Brundish Manor. These hunted in the most delightful way, with tremendous cry but very slowly, perfect for following on foot.

I was most impressed with the cry of the French hounds so I decided that, since he was here, I would try using Musketeer on a couple of Easton bitches as an experiment to get that lovely cry into the harriers. My intention was to keep breeding back to pure harriers and hopefully to keep the good cry. There was a tremendous upheaval amongst the old members who thought this experiment was dreadful and appealed to the Chairman, Captain Bernard, to stop me doing so. He knew that I had bred more than enough bitches to pure harriers and that this was only an experiment so he told them that I was Master and that he would not interfere. Some of the members turned very cold towards John, wishing that this outsider, who had moved from the Waveney country, would not influence a young Master with his outlandish ideas.

Aside from this exotic experiment, the season continued in the traditional manner, the first Monday meet being at Debach Post. This meet was confusing as the 'Post' was actually a signpost at a T-junction, not a pub like all the other Easton meets. Mr French, our host farmer, would bring a basket with a bottle of whisky for the men and a bottle of sherry for the ladies. As the years went on, he became more and more shaky and, when pouring drinks in his usual generous style, would spill more than reached the inside of the glass. I can remember so much whisky running down the inside of my sleeve that my elbow was wet. On this occasion, the ground was so hard and dry on rough, ploughed land, that I had to blow for home at one o'clock as some hounds were getting very sore.

On 16th November I halved a gate on Mr Wilson's land and had to pay the traditional five guineas, although by then the price of a new gate was something more like twelve guineas. In fact, I broke a gate in the same place four years' running so I was pleased that it was never replaced with a new one otherwise it would have broken me in both meanings of the word.

On Monday 30th November, John Graham had another French visitor, M. Ghee, and again I was asked to mount him and let him have Paddy who did not buck off the visitor this time. The meet was at Ashbocking Nelson and there was a hard frost. I did not want to cancel as we had our visitor so we went to the meet and decided to wait for the frost to go out. During the long wait, a tremendous party ensued and the atmosphere was electric; once or twice I went out and tested the ground but it was still too hard. The fun of the party made me not want to go out for the third time so I asked Fred Hargreaves to go and look.

He was reluctant. 'Oh dear, sir, you can't expect a hunt servant to make such a difficult decision.'

'All right', I said, much to the amusement to all those present. 'Go and bring a clod in here and I will make the decision.'

Fred arrived with a large clod and I placed it on the bar and poked it with my finger.

'It's still too hard. We can't go yet,' I declared.

The party continued and rounds of drinks kept coming until about half an hour later someone asked me if I thought there was any chance that we would be going. I went up to the clod, still sitting on the bar, and gave it another poke with my finger.

'Yes', I replied, 'The frost is going out nicely. We can go now!'

Of course, it was the warmth in the bar that had softened the clod and when I rode out onto the first plough to draw, the shoes of my horse rang out like steel to steel. The alcohol and the adrenaline of the party drained away from me in seconds as I realised that I definitely should not have moved off. I was about to shout to Fred to send hounds back to me when up jumped a hare and we were away. There were twenty-eight out and what a run we had. The scent was so good that the hare did not have time to double and ran without a check to beyond Crowfield Rose where we managed to stop hounds and hacked back through the lanes. Miraculously, no one had a fall and no harm came from the foolhardy fun. The Frenchman was most impressed at the exceptional bravery of the English!

That was the first day of a memorable week as I had decided I would like to try to hunt every day for a week. As no pack hunted on a Friday, I changed the Easton meet from Thursday to Friday. After Monday with the Harriers at Ashbocking, I had Tuesday with the Suffolk Foxhounds at Preston Bells, Wednesday with the Waveney Harriers at White House Farm, Frostenden, Thursday with the Essex and Suffolk Foxhounds at Barham Sorrel Horse, Friday with the Easton again at Monk Soham Oak, and Saturday with the Drag. Unfortunately the meets on Wednesday, Friday, and Saturday all had to be cancelled due to frost so this ambition failed miserably.

I decided to have a day with the Cambridgeshire Harriers and on 8th December set off with Chris and Sara Bigden, Terence Saffell, and Christine Dickinson. The meet was at the Flint Cross Roads at Heydon and Mrs Gingell, the Master, welcomed us warmly and introduced us to the farmer over whose land we would be hunting. He insisted that we join the other Cambridgeshire members for tea when we finished hunting which we gratefully accepted.

Mrs Gingell moved off to draw asking me to ride with her. The farmer stopped back to speak to his wife and then cantered to catch up with us up a grass track so smooth it was almost lawn-like, but his horse put its foot through into a rabbit burrow and came down. A message quickly came up to Mrs Gingell that the fall was serious and not long after another message came to say that he was dead. He had broken his neck. I have always thought that he stopped to tell his wife that he had invited five extra for tea. What an awful accident to be killed in sight of one's own home and on such a smooth track. We had come out full of eager anticipation and went home in sorrow and in low spirits.

During this season I was beginning to win back farmers' support and over a hundred farmers who had banned the hunt would now allow me to go. In this I was greatly helped by being my father's son. He was well-known and highly respected by almost all farmers, but also, by belonging to a local farming family, I was one of them, and not some outsider they knew nothing about. At first a lot of farmers just agreed to let me and my whipper-in go if hounds should cross their land but not the field, but this was usually only the thin end of the wedge, and gradually permission was given for the field to go as well. This was in no small measure due to the fact that I had appointed Terence Saffell to be Field Master. His brief was to be as strict as was necessary to ensure that no damage was done and his bellow could be heard for miles when anyone was seen to infringe the rules.

Because it is so traditional to hunt, some people do not always realise how generous the farmers are to

Terence and Marion Saffell leading the field
Photograph kindly loaned by John Finch

allow us access to their farms on hunting days. I used to give a lot of hunting lectures and to emphasise this point, I would ask the audience what they would say if the secretary of a motor cycle club knocked on their door and asked for permission to ride round their gardens saying, 'Be a good sport, we will be careful to keep on the paths and won't ride over your flower beds'. That is, I think, a more or less fair parallel to draw and it made the audience think again about the privilege they receive by the farmers' generosity.

I had the necessary gift with hounds and loved hunting them, I had good horses, and I had a first class kennel huntsman in Fred Hargreaves. Although outwardly things were going really well, a great black cloud hung over me which spoiled the enjoyment of what I was achieving. The trouble, of course, was money. The guarantee of £1,500 was crippling me. I had built new piggeries at Glebe Farm and was heavily overdrawn and, as if matters were not bad enough, my new bank manager was an ex-RSPCA man and whenever I requested to increase my overdraft, he would ask how much was I putting into the hunt as he understood from his colleagues that Masters were expected to subsidise the Hunt heavily. I became very fed up with his attitude and asked my father if he thought that a bank manager should make these sorts of remarks. I also said that I had taken as much hindrance from him as I could stand and was thinking of changing banks.

'Well, boy,' my father replied, 'If you move, so will I', and with that all the Harvey accounts were moved from Lloyds to Barclays, where they still are.

With my heart in my boots, I wrote to the Committee to say that I could not carry on at a guarantee of £1,500. It is a little difficult for a Master to work out how much it costs him to be Master when he keeps all the horses at the kennels. At this time, if I were not Master, the most I would have kept would be a horse for myself and one for my wife. Rightly or wrongly, I considered that the cost of keeping my personal horses at kennels was more than justified by the amount of time I put in to Hunt affairs. This involved travelling from Badingham to the kennels to walk out seven days a week during the summer, visiting and talking to farmers, working on the social fundraising events, and so on, which, at that time, would have averaged between 30-35 hours a week. In later seasons this rose to well above 40 hours per week. In financial terms, I counted all the expenses of hunting: what I paid out in wages for the Kennel Huntsman and grooms, garage bills for the hunt van used to collect flesh and for the lorry used for the horses (bought in my second season), vets' bills both for horses and hounds, clothes bought for hunt servants (boots, breeches, coats, gloves, hats, etc.), the expense of the Puppy Show and Puppy Walkers' Dinners, and buying the horses. I calculated that I had been putting in approximately £1,200 of my own money, over and above the guarantee of £1,500. This compared with the total subscription income of £822 4s 6d a year.

The Committee and the members seemed not to want to know of this financial problem. They took the attitude that if they kept quiet the problem would go away and thought that making up this terrible shortfall was just part of the Master's duties. After all, Masters always had. My predecessor, Captain Bernard, was a wealthy man and put in each year more of his own money than he received in guarantee, i.e. the Hunt paid less than half of the expenses of running the Hunt. Before Captain Bernard, Lady Blanche Cobbold was also in a position to subsidise the Hunt even more and kept them going during the War on a pittance. Nevertheless, the Committee that had been far from unanimous in electing me as Master must have had a considerable change of heart and thought that I was doing a good job. They instructed the Honorary Secretary, John Moyle to try to prevent me from resigning and eventually increased the guarantee by £900 which went a long way to alleviate the deficit.

What made all the financial worry worthwhile, of course, was the hunting but there were occasions when I could not even have that. I took a horse called Joker to the Leicester Sales on 16th December and, although he was sold, I could not get home because of terrible thick fog. I telephoned Fred to tell him that he would have to hunt hounds at Kenton Crown, as I would not be home in time. He told me afterwards that he panicked about it and had someone let the hounds out of the hound van directly on to the first draw because he thought that, if he let the hounds out at the meet, they would not have stayed with him but would have gone looking for me.

But this was an isolated incident and mostly I could revel in the joy of my first season of actively hunting my hounds. On Boxing Day there was deep snow but I decided to go out on foot and drew the field just behind The Saxtead Volunteer. The first hare we found made straight for the green, turned right and ran past the front of the pub, then across the road towards Saxtead church, a most unusual line but one that pleased the large crowd. We gave a lawn meet at Glebe Farm on 31st December and there was a mounted field of forty but Mrs Sims' horse falling into a ditch, and afterwards having to be put down, sadly marred the day. We had an exceptional day on 11th January from Monk Soham Oak when we enjoyed a three miles straight hunt from Chicken Alley to beyond Bedingfield church on a Jack hare. Another very good day was at Southolt Plough on 18th January when hounds ran hard all day with Sheila going very well on her new hunter, Lucy. We marked one hare to ground in a drainpipe where it was left, in accordance with the rules of the Masters of Harriers & Beagles Association.

When the Cambridgeshire Harriers met by invitation at Debenham Cherry Tree on 21st January there were three ex-Masters of the Easton out, Mr Springfield and Captains Marriott and Bernard. Hounds ran with a good cry but we were short of country as Mr Knowland of Crows Hall decided that hounds were getting his Jersey herd too excited. The abiding personal memory of the day was of sheer terror at the behaviour of my big, weight-carrying hunter, Noddy, at one point. We had come to a very difficult ditch with a high, thick, hedge and I asked him to jump at the only possible place which was where there was a very narrow sleeper bridge. Noddy misunderstood the command and proceeded to mince slowly across the bridge, with me expecting to crash into the bottom of the deep ditch at any moment. Somehow he got to the other side but I shall never know how. Later on we settled into a regular pattern of the Cambridgeshire coming to us one year and the Easton going to them the next and having a party each time after hunting.

I cancelled the drag hunt on 30th January in respect of Sir Winston Churchill's funeral and spent the day watching it on television. Two days later the meet was at Easton White Horse; it was damp and still, scent was very good, and hounds simply flew. For a while I encouraged Sheila to come with me on her Lucy and was delighted to see how well she was going on her new horse as she sailed over two sets of rails and three gates. She had dropped back into the field when she had a crashing fall. Her horse's foot had gone through into a rabbit hole and they landed in a crumpled heap. I was some way off and thoughts of the Cambridgeshire man filled my head. I was very relieved when someone helped her up, very muddy but otherwise sound, as was Lucy.

Sheila and I loved parties of every description and we went to most Hunt Balls but made a special point of going to the Norfolk and Suffolk Foxhounds Ball to show that I was not holding a grudge against them following the bitter row we had had. During the Ball

I said to Sheila that I would like to invite them to hunt in our country and would she mind if it was a lawn meet at Glebe Farm. I could see the Master, Mr Henry Bothway, sitting at his table, so went across and shook hands with him and was invited to sit down. This was quite something since the last time we had seen each other was at the tribunal in London. I asked him if he would like to bring his hounds into the Easton country for a lawn meet at my home and he readily accepted my offer. The date was fixed for 3rd February and, because it was after the shooting season, I could get permission to draw the woods. Although it took a lot of time, I visited every farmer and made arrangements to draw every wood from Badingham to Saxmundham. The great day arrived and we were well stocked up with whisky and gin and sausage rolls but I had got it all wrong because they all wanted port and cherry brandy. We first drew the Bruisyard Big Wood, then all the others, and were still drawing at dusk before hacking back to Glebe Farm in the gathering gloom of a winter's night. It had been a blank day but we livened it up by asking Henry and Mrs Bothway to stay for dinner. Mrs Bothway had been the wife of Sheila's doctor who lived in Earl Soham but had lost her heart to Henry as he rode fearlessly after his staghounds.

The following day the Waveney Harriers came for an invitation meet at Dennington Queen, which attracted a joint field of over forty mounted. The Bedfield Crown meet provided us with another travelling Jack which was found on Chandos Farm, Worlingworth, and took us to the far side of Saxtead. It was not the distance that made this outstanding but the speed: hounds never paused and it was a case of sit down and gallop all the way for the few of us who kept up with hounds. We had a great deal of fun on 18th February after the meet at Kelsale Eight Bells. Hounds ran towards Middleton Green and into country where there were very small meadows and jumpable fences. The scent was good and the hares obliged and criss-crossed this area from every possible angle so we had maximum fun and called the area 'our little Leicestershire'. There was one anxious moment when hounds were running towards the railway line and I could hear a train coming. I had to get to them but between them and me was a horrible drop fence. I had to jump it but in the morning Paddy had two strained tendons which was probably caused by the desperate leap.

We were struck by disease when the meet at Braiseworth Hall, Tannington, was cancelled because of swine fever, as was the Waveney invitation for us to meet at The Swan, Fressingfield, but we had one last good day from the Hare and Hounds at Framlingham. We finished up in Tannington but we were one hound light. The missing hounds was, appropriately, Vagabond and I blew and blew for him all the way back to Framlingham but he did not appear. His eventual recovery is an interesting tale of hound psychology. After taking the rest of the pack back to the kennels, I spent a long time in the early evening blowing for him, and then went out again just before dawn. At last I saw him behind Church Farm, Saxtead. He was on the far side of a field and when I called his name he bolted off as though I had shot him with an airgun. I tried several more times but each time with the same result. I walked back to Herbert Breese at Church Farm and telephoned Fred and told him to bring some hounds.

'We don't need them, sir. I can catch him,' Fred replied.

I said: 'All very well if you can, but bring a few couple with you in any case.'

Fred arrived and we both set off across the fields until we saw Vagabond, but as soon as Fred called his name he disappeared, just as he had done with me. We walked back to fetch the hounds and walked from field to field, luckily without putting up a hare, until we saw him again. The hounds with us also saw him and I said to them, 'Run on'. They went across to him, I then called them back to me and he came with them. Then the odd thing happened. He came out ahead of the others and galloped up to me making funny little noises, jumping up at me repeatedly with his stern beating frantically. He was jumping up as high as my shoulder and licking my face and he kept doing it continually until we were back at Church Farm and put them into the van. I was full of emotion about how pleased he was to see me and had allowed him to plaster me with wet mud as I would certainly not have stopped him from showing his joy at finding me. The lesson learned from this is that some hounds, although not all, completely lose their confidence when they are alone and must be shown the utmost patience and understanding. I sensed enough to tell Fred to bring the hounds but I did not expect the profound effect it would have.

Colonel Brian Gooch invited us to meet at Tannington Hall for our last meet on 11th March but it was so dry that dust was blowing and the scent predictably bad. Hounds had hunted on eighteen early mornings before the Opening Meet and thirty-one times during the season proper with seven cancelled

for various reasons: swine fever, Sir Winston's funeral, snow, and frost.

1965–66

My third season started officially on 1st May 1965 and the summer passed in the usual routine of breaking the puppies and walking out, before the tempo starts to increase in the late summer with hound exercise, then early morning hunting with the first meets at dawn then getting later and later through October leading up to the Opening Meet around 1st November. The summer highlights were Peterborough Hound Show and the Puppy Show.

The hunt was spared the expense and inconvenience of keeping the puppies during their first year by the custom of keen supporters taking one or two puppies each. They were returned to the kennels in the spring when they were a year old to be walked out with the rest of the pack during the summer before being entered in the autumn but the Puppy Show in the summer was the hunt's opportunity to thank the walkers. It was a great social occasion, an opportunity for the members to meet during the non-hunting months of the summer, and Masters of other packs were invited to judge the puppies. Everyone dressed elegantly, the men in suits or blazers with either Panamas or bowler hats and the ladies in their summer frocks and lovely hats. During Captain Bernard's Mastership the shows were held at his house and were very grand affairs. The silver spoons presented to every puppy walker were from Garrard's of Regent Street, jewellers to the royal family for at least a century, and each was engraved with the hunt button on the handle and the name of the hound inside the bowl. The presentations were followed by tea, served by Captain Bernard's housekeeper, Ruth. Certain guests were invited to use the breakfast cups and as amateur whip, I was allowed one. The size of the cup was important because whisky was added in proportion to the contents, so the larger the cup the more whisky one had in the tea.

The tradition of the shows being held at the Master's home gave me a serious problem when I became Master as my home at Glebe Farm was very primitive and, without even a flush lavatory, it was naturally impossible for me to hold a puppy show there. To overcome this problem I asked my parents if I could hold the puppy show at Braiseworth Hall, Tannington, where the gardens were beautiful, there were large lawns and it was perfect for such a show. The ring was constructed of neat wooden hurdles and rows of chairs were placed around. I thought that the tennis court would be an ideal place to hold the hounds between classes as it was surrounded by a high fence of wire netting and, with a proper gate, it would be easy to draw the hounds out in the correct order. Fred had the hounds in mint condition and the sun shone and it was baking hot. When all the guests arrived, they stood around chatting before the judging began. Everything seemed to be just right and I was feeling very proud. I knew that the tea would be first class and I really felt that this puppy show would compare very favourably with those of my predecessor.

Parading hounds at the Framlingham Show

Disaster struck. Mrs Freeman walked up to the tennis court to look at the hounds with her terriers on a lead, all the hounds came across to look at the terriers and put their front feet on the wire netting, this caused the wire netting to open at the bottom, and all of them escaped. As it was so hot, they immediately jumped into the moat and swam around before climbing out covered in black mud and slime. They then proceeded to run joyfully amongst all the assembled guests, shaking themselves vigorously and covering everyone with stinking black mud. The scene was one of unimaginable horror with screaming ladies fleeing in all directions and men looking down despairingly at their trousers and jackets. The wretched hounds were compounding the problem by brushing past trouser legs and frocks, then jumping up and placing two slimy paws on a lady's dress or smart blazer. Hounds thought the fleeing ladies just wanted to play with them so frisked alongside then jumping up as soon as one of them stopped. Fred and I were catching hounds and putting them back in the tennis court as fast as we could, both plastered with mud and stinking like polecats. The British stiff upper lip came into play and the judging continued as if nothing had happened but it was quite difficult to draw hounds in the correct order as they were practically unrecognisable with their white patches covered up and the ladies watched the judging in their mud-splattered frocks and beautiful hats, their faces decorated with a few spots of mud. So much for my proud thoughts earlier; pride comes before a fall and this was quite some fall!

The Easton had always paraded at Framlingham Show and I did for the first few seasons of my Mastership but it was such a trouble to get two horses up from grass, just to parade for a few minutes, and I was always so rushed as I was usually stewarding the driving classes and would have to rush down to the Hare and Hounds to change into my hunting clothes, that in the end I found it all too difficult and told the show committee that I did not wish to parade. They were disappointed but understood. The Show was held in the Castle Meadow and in Captain Bernard's time, some of his pals decided to lay a drag out of the ring, into the castle moat, right round the castle and back into the ring, but luckily for the Captain the hounds ignored the drag.

The last annual highlight of the summer was Peterborough Hound Show. After my first season when Sheila and I stayed with Captain and Mrs Bernard, we always stayed at the Haycock Hotel at Wansford for the night before and the night after the show and, for many years, this was a special treat as it was our only holiday. It was a great extravagance to stay for two nights as it cost £12, plus the cost of dinner. The hotel in those days was slightly scruffy and one had the feeling it would have been unwise to take down the pictures, as they appeared to be holding up the wallpaper. The bedrooms did not have *en suite* bathrooms but, just across the landing, were the most delightful old-fashioned bathrooms with huge cast iron baths, standing on claw feet, sporting enormous brass taps. We always had the Lincoln Room with a large four-poster bed and would book it for the next year as we settled the bill. The hotel guests were mostly Masters of Hounds and hunt officials and the bar was, of course, packed with these characters, many of whom had their hounds kennelled in the loose boxes in the stable yard. There were hunting prints in every room and with the fabulous characters and the background sound of baying hounds, the atmosphere was pure magic. Breakfast on the morning of the show was unforgettable with over half of the people at the tables already dressed in their hunting liveries. We would take a more leisurely leave after breakfast as the kennel huntsman was bringing up our hounds and we would meet them at the show. Sheila would be wearing a very smart hat and I would be in my best suit with bowler hat. Wherever one looked there were gentlemen in bowler hats and ladies in their best. The whole scene was one of tremendous dignity and tradition and we felt proud to be part of it. I would have gone to any lengths to do the thing properly but it was not until years later that I realised that I had, for several years, been committing a serious *faux pas* in the question of dress. My best suit was of brown tweed so I wore brown brogue shoes but it is definitely *de rigueur* to wear black shoes if one wears a black bowler. I had no idea about this, as I had not been brought up in a family who wore bowlers.

Peterborough was great fun but I never thought of it from one year to the next and it never affected the breeding of the Easton Harriers. To me, it was just a pleasant day out, to enjoy the atmosphere and to meet all the friends from the year before. It was disappointing for the kennel huntsman not to win a few rosettes but it did not bother me. I bred hounds to hunt, fifty to sixty days a season, not to show for just one day. Far too many Masters were sending their bitches to the Peterborough Champion dog with no knowledge of how he worked or, indeed, if he worked at all. I knew of one well-known pack that kept a winning dog just for Peterborough and he never went out of the kennel except to show. The result of this foolishness was that the working qualities of these packs went steadily downhill. My policy was to enter hounds in every class at Peterborough and simply take the best we had. Our best were exactly like the Easton champions of the 1950s, but the modern idea was for a racier, lighter type of hound that could gallop. I disapprove of harehounds being too fast as it does not give the hare a chance to make all her wonderful doubles and the beauty of a hare hunt is lost. I drafted many a good hound for being too fast.

Peterborough and the Puppy Show were the social highlights of the summer but the normal routine was walking out the hounds every day, although this was enlivened to begin with by breaking the puppies. This was done by linking a puppy to an older hound with a 'pair of couples', two leather collars joined together by a short length of chain. This was always a fraught time. The main problem was they often became tangled up with six or even eight hounds all knotted together by their couples. It was the kennel huntsman's job to untangle them while I walked slowly on because if I stopped hounds would start milling around me and in no time there would be more entanglements. Another

problem occurred when a coupled pair decided to gallop past me and one went one side of me and one the other, the chain hitting me behind the knees and bringing me crashing to the ground. We always breathed a sigh of relief when we could dispense with them as all the problems were magnified by the fact that I was breeding so many puppies and starting them off all at once. At any one time there would be up to thirty hounds with a puppy coupled to it. As well as teaching the puppies to respond to verbal commands, such as to get to the side of the road when a car comes along, the most important lesson is that of 'riot' and I used to spend all summer trying to get amongst as many forms of riot, i.e. any form of animal life that they must not chase, as I could. The residents of Easton were very helpful and would exercise their dogs at the same time as we walked out. At first, the young entry would be straining at their couples with their hackles up, dragging the older hound out into the road in their determination to get at the 'cur dog', an ancient phrase in hound language meaning any dog that is not a hound. Gradually they learned to ignore cur dogs but once off the couples they would sometimes find the temptation too much and would need a severe reprimand. We were also lucky in that we had a fearless cat in kennels that would just sit and scratch the nose of any hound that came too near. Most helpful of all were our great supporters the Kerr family of Easton Farm Park who allowed us free access at any time to the park where there was every form of riot: loose chickens and ducks, frisky goats and sheep and large Highland cattle, among others. This was the most important lesson of their lives and usually by July we could walk through the Farm Park with all the hounds loose running well ahead of us with complete confidence that they would be completely steady to whatever riot they met. This gave us a great feeling of achievement although, puppies being puppies, they might still be tempted to chase a cat or chicken, or run across the road to sniff at a pet dog on the pavement, but a single stern reprimand of 'Have a care! Shame on you!' would be enough to make them push into the middle of the pack with embarrassment.

I walked hounds out at nine o'clock seven days a week throughout the summer and once all the puppies were off couples it was a real joy to do so. I really believe that hounds reflect the thoughts and feelings of their huntsman. I was young, full of fun, and enjoying every minute of life, and I really loved my hounds. This feeling of exuberance reflected in the hounds and they would play and skip around me like lambs in the spring. They would run well ahead of us on the road and every now and again one would come galloping back and take a flying leap and lick my face. Tangle's offspring were both very naughty and very loving at the same time. They just could not resist galloping through a gateway, into a field, completing a small circle and galloping back to the road. This in itself was of no harm but had to be corrected in case the circles became larger and larger so occasionally Fred would correct an offender with a real cut of his whip but it worried it not a jot. Without even dropping its stern it

Hounds on the fallen tree in the meadow near the kennels

would gallop straight up and lick my face two or three times consecutively as if to say, 'He needn't think I'm worried about that!' Sometimes we would just go into the meadow next to the kennels and let them play. Tangle's offspring would usually begin the games by starting to gallop in circles 'throwing their tongues' which had the effect of making all but the older hounds join in the fun. The meadow at that time was divided into three parts by dykes and when the games were going well, Tangle's brood would take off and gallop right round the whole meadow taking the dykes in their stride and throwing their tongues just as if they were really hunting. When they had had enough of playing and were hot, the leaders would gallop back to where Fred and I stood under a tree by the river, and pour over the edge of the bank into the river, six or eight abreast, with the others close behind, like a blanket of hounds in mid-air. After drinking their fill, they would gallop along the river bed and disappear around a corner, turn round and come rushing back, perhaps six or seven abreast with the water flying up, climb out and shake the water all over us. With the games over, they would lie down or wander about, or more interestingly, eat the earth at one particular place where a hole had developed because of this habit as they would bite lumps off the side or scratch soil from the bottom and eat it. Old Ernie Nunn told me that hounds had done this at the some place for all the fourteen seasons he was at the Easton. Some days they would ignore the hole and on others be fighting each other to get at it. I can only assume that it must have contained some mineral which they needed from time to time. I trusted the hounds explicitly and never had

a moment's worry when they galloped away from me. It caused me much amusement when we had a visiting Master or huntsman to see the worried expression on their faces when the hounds took off for one of their gallops. Fred and I were a little worried as to whether we ought to allow them to throw their tongues in these games because it might lead to them becoming babblers when it came to hunting but we decided to risk it and we made the right decision as there was never any babbling in the hunting field.

Hound exercise was different to the 'walking out' of the summer as the huntsman and staff are mounted and it takes longer. Its purpose is to get the hounds fit and to get the young entry used to seeing their huntsman on a horse but I used to do much of our hound exercise on bicycles, gradually increasing the distance each day. We always observed the old custom of wearing white kennel coats and a bowler hat when on hound exercise.

The next stage of training was the early mornings to teach the young entry, the puppies from the year before, to hunt. A young hound is 'unentered' until he can use his nose and follow the line of a hare; once he can use his nose and speak to the line he is said to have entered. Some hounds enter in the first months or so, others take a long time and I have known a hound not to enter until its second season but those that are slow to enter often turn out to be the best. How good the pack is in years to come will depend on how well they are taught. On the first day, when the old hounds found a line and hunted it, the young entry would keep close to me, looking up at me with puzzled expressions on their faces and clearly wondering why the hounds were not being rated or punished for chasing the hare. By quietly encouraging them to go, they gradually learned that these hares were things they were allowed to hunt. The final hurdle, which we always hoped would be the last, was when they saw a rabbit. Off they would go in great glee and could not understand why the old hounds did not come with them. When they were severely rated by the whipper-in for chasing rabbits they would come back to the pack looking rather confused. Hare and rabbit look similar but they have quite different scents and by the time of the opening meet, one shout of 'Ware rabbit' was enough to stop them.

This formative time in the life of the young hounds is critical as, if things go wrong, they can be spoiled permanently. In particular, they could still be a little apprehensive about horses as we had only the few days 'hound exercise' with horses before starting to hunt. The worst thing that could happen to them would be to get kicked or galloped over by a horse out of control on the stubbles. Another ever-present problem would be a young hound struggling out of a blind ditch only to be jumped on as it reached the top on the other side. It is clearly vital, therefore, that during this period of intensive training they are exposed only to horses, and thus the riders, that the Master can trust. Quietness is also essential for the young entry to learn from the older hounds and a chattering field, especially the fair sex with high-pitched voices, is very distracting. How I cringe when I hear people saying that they will take their young horses out to school it at an early morning. Early mornings are no place to school a horse. They are solely to school hounds. The subscription entitled the member to hunt on any hunting day from the Opening Meet until the end of the season but it did *not* entitle him to hunt before the Opening Meet so hunting on early mornings was strictly by the Master's invitation only. The first few mornings I would have only my kennel huntsman and amateur whip out with me. Then I would invite perhaps two or three members to come out, people I could depend on to have their horses well under control and to keep well back from hounds, never closer than a hundred yards. I would hunt three mornings a week, occasionally four, and as the young hounds entered I would gradually invite more and more members. There was considerable, although mostly good-hearted, jealousy about the order in which they were invited.

The invitation, once given, was for the remainder of the early mornings, and as I invited more and more people, I gradually met at later times. If the sun allowed, I would work backwards from the Opening Meet with the meets at ten o'clock the week before, nine o'clock the week before that, and so on but, if the autumn was hot and dry, the meets would have to remain at eight o'clock. The last week before the Opening Meet was always advertised and open to all and no caps were taken, but we saw so many people during that free week that we never saw again that, in later seasons, I told the cappers to take a cap for that week.

In this season, 1965–6, we enjoyed Peterborough as much as ever but it was not a good year for the Easton and we won only two rosettes; Patrick[62] was third in the stallion hound class, and Sanguine[63] was third in the unentered bitches. Hunting started on 15th September and we met on a lay-by in Tannington at 5 o'clock with 25½ couple. I had misjudged the time of dawn and we were forced to wait for enough light. Hares seemed very scarce and we drew for 2½ hours before finding, then soon caught it. Five days later we met again on the same lay-by at 6 o'clock. I believed it was very important to meet at dawn in the autumn as, once the sun comes up, scent evaporates and it is time to go home. This was another point of venery I had learned from John Graham and the books he had lent me, that the packs of the old Southern hounds had always met at dawn so they could follow the drag of a hare right up to where she had settled for the day. Unfortunately, on this day we found no hares at all, not at all what I needed for my young entry.

The third early morning was very eventful. Tony Garvin, the Master of the Springtown Harriers in Pennsylvania, had arrived in England some days earlier and was visiting harrier kennels looking for a draft of English harriers to send back to America. He telephoned me to ask if he could visit our kennels and I invited him to stay with us at Glebe Farm. Over dinner he told us about the other kennels he had visited and what hounds he had liked, and his shock at the high price one Master had suggested for a draft. Whilst drafts between English Masters are almost always free, it is quite in order to charge whatever price one can get for hounds going abroad, although I never asked anything for the hounds which I drafted to George Lamiot in France.

Tony Garvin readily took up my offer of a mount and rode Sheila's mare, Lucy, but it was one of those days when things just go wrong. The old horsebox that dear old Mrs Freeman had let me have very cheaply, broke down in Framlingham so we had no horses until seven o'clock. We had not long moved off when a row broke out between a certain young thruster and his girl friend and in his rage he brandished his whip in the air. Wishing to end this embarrassing scene, she tore off down the side of a sugar beet field but he, not going to let the quarrel end like that, set off after her, still brandishing his whip. After a while it seemed to end peacefully but some time later the same maiden, perhaps still slightly flustered, let her horse go too fast on the road and it slipped down and cut both its knees. Fred was riding Boniface, usually a really good horse with hounds, who on this occasion kicked a hound in the face; some of the best horses do not like hounds in sugar beet. To try to redeem our reputation with our distinguished visitor from America we came out of the beet and hunted in the open and had two good little hunts, killing both hares. I presented the mask to Tony and later sent it, on his behalf, to Roland Ward, the London taxidermist.

At breakfast, after hunting, Tony said, 'Well, Tony, I think you about the calmest guy I have ever seen. Your lorry breaks down and your horses are not at the meet, one of your members chases a lady with his whip, you have a hound kicked and a horse down on the road, and then you have two lovely and successful hunts one after the other and you never turn a hair. Gee, man, you are some cool guy.' By the time breakfast was over Sheila had worked out who the couple were who had quarrelled.

Tony and I then went to look round the kennels. I thought he would like to see a typical English puppy walker so took him to Beryl Leman at Ashfield Lodge. Beryl, closely attended by her Alsatian, produced two puppies, both looking very well (in fact, too well; they were grossly

Fred Hargreaves

Photograph kindly loaned by John Hargreaves

fat). After ten minutes or so we left to go to the kennels and I told him the story behind Beryl's glass eye. While milking one day, the cow had tossed its head and its horn hooked out her eye. With her eye in her hand she then walked right up the fields to where George Emeny was ploughing with a pair of horses and she asked him to come home and finish the milking. She then walked back, got out her car and drove herself to the doctor in Earl Soham, still holding her eye cupped in her hand.

Tony did not seem to give this interesting tale the attention it deserved. Just before I had started, he had said something about a German shepherd but I took no notice as I was not interested in shepherds in Germany and, anyway, I had difficulty understanding all he said because of his accent. At every slight pause in the story, he would again say 'German Shepherd' but still I took no notice. After all, we all have our funny ways. When I had eventually finished the story,

he put his hand under his thigh and brought it out covered with blood.

'What's that?' I said. 'What's happened?'

'It was the German shepherd, it nipped me as we came out of the gate.'

'Oh', I said, thinking quickly. 'You mean Beryl's dog?'

'Yes', he said. 'I keep trying to tell you.'

Until then, I had never heard of a dog called a German Shepherd as we always called them Alsatians. Once we arrived at the kennels, Mrs Hargreaves provided the necessary and he disappeared into the lavatory to dress his wounded thigh.

The rest of the early morning hunting was quite normal, except for the day I included the French hound Musketeer for the meet at Hoo House on 7th October. I had chosen this meet as being close to the kennels if things went wrong. Musketeer hunted very well and it was a joy to hear his lovely voice but there were serious problems. Being early in the season, I had been asked to avoid certain coverts so as not to disturb the pheasants but Musketeer was the most headstrong hound I had ever seen and there was absolutely no stopping him if he was on the line. I got so fed up with him that when I was near Abbey Farm, I jumped off and caught him and shut him in the bull pen (without the bull). I had broken the long tradition of the second meet being at Brook Farm by starting hunting in the sugar beet at Tannington but did meet there on 23rd October and the five girls again came from Dovercourt.

The Opening Meet was, as always, on the Market Hill, Framlingham, on Thursday 4th November 1965. By tradition, the Easton Opening Meet is always been held on the first Thursday in November except when the last day of October is a Thursday. The second Thursday was always at Worlingworth Swan and at the Swan meet this season Chris Bigden bought a horse. In his usual impetuous style, he asked my permission to hunt in civvies and rode his new horse all day in his ordinary clothes. The pub was packed full of locals and they included Ky Lawes who used to drive a steam engine for my father and grandfather.

Miss Barbara Carter, a local farmer, would always be there, with her Earl Haig box and, although all of us had already bought our poppies and worn them at the Opening Meet, we had to buy a second one for Miss Carter. Every year she would formally give the 'turn off'. We would move off from the pub and follow her home. Then she would walk out to the edge of a ploughed field and say, 'There you are gentlemen' and we, with our hats in our hand, would thank her as we passed. This 'turn off' seems a local term and John Graham always said he believed it was connected to the carted stag hunts. Whoever gave the 'turn off', i.e. the farm that was used for the first draw, was thought of as a sporting person and rather special. The Suffolk farm workers used the term slightly differently and if the meet was to be at, say, Worlingworth Swan, they would say, 'The hounds turn off at the Swan next Thursday'. I was always told that, if hounds were running, the huntsman and whip could lawfully follow their hounds across forbidden land as long as the quarry had been found on property where permission had been granted. Perhaps this was another reason the 'turn off' was held so important.

Another character who was always at the Swan meet was Alec Abbott of Red House Farm. Alec was one of the last of the farmers who could still tell the huntsman exactly where a hare would be sitting. After we moved off, Alec would go home and walk up his fields and when I got there he would say, 'Old Sally, she'll be sitting about 150 yards from that bush'. The hare would always be exactly where he said. Sam Whiting, on the other hand, was an 'Artful Dodger'. He would come to me at meets saying 'I have seen a hare on a seat as I come and can put you right on to her when you turn off.' It cost me a few pints to learn that there was never one there.

It was a day of torrential rain but the hunting was excellent and after one kill, I blooded Ernie Calver. After hunting we went back inside the Swan and a great party broke out; I can still see the hunt coats hanging on the back of chairs with the water running out of them all over the brick floor.

Unfortunately, my diary records very little for the third season so I am reduced to memory alone for a few facts. One very sad memory needs no diary entry to remind me: the death of Ann Daniel. Although her husband Commander Daniel did not hunt, Ann and her children were usually out as often as possible, often twice a week. The meet was at Grundisburgh Dog on 28th February 1966, and a large part of the day was to be spent on the estate of Lord Cranworth of Grundisburgh Hall. Lord Cranworth's sister, Mrs

Judith Bull, lived at Park Farm, Grundisburgh, and was a great supporter of the Easton. There was no room for boxes in the village, so we always unboxed at Park Farm and hacked down for the meet and, as we were asked in for drinks before unboxing and for refreshments after hunting, this meet was a peculiar mixture of a lawn meet and a pub meet. On this day Mrs Bull's horse was lame so I lent her one called Embassy. Judith Bull and Ann Daniel were great friends and when Judith heard that Ann was not intending to come on that day, she telephoned her to say that she must make an effort to get there as she did not want her friend to miss 'her' meet. We had been hunting for an hour or so and had had one good little run, when I decided to go to a fresh draw. I was trotting along with the field following when the accident occurred. I cannot remember if it was a rabbit hole or if the horse crossed its legs, but Mrs Daniel's horse went down and somersaulted over. The pommel of the saddle crushed her skull and I think death was instantaneous. Poor Mrs Bull could never forgive herself for persuading Ann to come on that day, and often mentioned it.

An important change was made in the staff at the kennels during this season. The horses were all kept there but I had difficulty in getting grooms who were suitable and reliable. The worst case which was when I had a girl who had a flat at Whitton Lodge, on the far side of Ipswich, and used to come in by bus. Peggy Jenkins, who lived across the river from the kennels at Four Bridges, was a real godsend as she would help out with the horses whenever I was let down by girl grooms. This brief period is the only time I had unreliable girls as I have otherwise found them to be very loyal to me and to the horses in their charge. I advertised for a groom and one of the applicants was an oldish man from Beccles called Johnson. We spoke on the telephone and arranged for him to come to Glebe Farm for an interview on a Sunday. When he arrived I found that he had cycled the twenty miles from Beccles and was quite prepared to cycle on to Easton. I insisted that he left his cycle at Badingham and drove him over to Easton in my pickup to show him the job. Johnson was an old fashioned farm worker who had been a horseman all his life until tractors took over. He was just the type I had been brought up with and we understood each other perfectly. He had never been with light horses but I set him on at a wage of £11 to do the job seven days a week with no overtime but with Pound Cottage, rent-free. He would do all the stable work and a girl would do the exercising. The condition of employment was that at the end of the season I would 'stand him off', stop paying him, until the horses came in again in the autumn. He was quite content with these conditions as he could get casual work, such as hoeing sugar beet, during the summer. At the end of the season I duly stood him off and about a month later I saw him on the road and stopped to speak to him. I was rather concerned as he had married for a second time and had a wife and several children to keep.

'How are you doing, Johnson? Are you managing all right?'

'Yes, thank you sir,' he replied. 'I'm half a crown a week better off than when I worked for you'.

He had been unable to find a job and was drawing dole money. I have never forgotten this as I had been paying him considerably more than a farm worker's basic pay because he did weekend work. How demoralising for a man to be better off on the dole than in a good full time job. Johnson, being the sort of man he was, did not stay on the dole a day longer than he had to and took on all sorts of work during the summer.

I had seven or more horses at the kennels, Sheila's hunter Lucy, two for me, two for the kennel huntsman, a spare one and a courtesy horse. Fred used to hear through the hunt servants' grapevine, and I would hear at dinner parties, how some of my neighbours had cancelled meets because 'the huntsman's horse was lame'. As the term 'the' huntsman's horse was used, it implied that he had only the one off which to hunt hounds. As Master, I would have been very ashamed and embarrassed if a situation like this happened at the Easton. Fred and I had two horses each with a spare that either of us could ride. This, I found, was perfect and the system worked very well. It is my belief that a huntsman showing good sport and crossing a lot of country with long days cannot use the same horse two days a week in our heavy country, although a horse can do three days a fortnight and thus it was that I could hunt the Drag on Saturdays with no extra horses. Our days with the Harriers were Monday and Thursday and the Drag on Saturday and this was ideal for the hunt horses as they could work on a rota, Horse A doing Monday and Saturday in the first week and only Thursday in the second week, Horse B doing Thursday in the first week and Monday and Saturday of the second week. In this way the horses were always iron fit and there was plenty left at the end of the day if hounds had a sharp hunt, as is often the case. Another practice in some hunts is to mount the whipper-in on a cheap horse. Nothing could be more wrong as a whipper-in, however good he is, can

only be as good as the horse he is riding and he should always be mounted on the best that is affordable.

We had a spare horse in case of injury or to be a courtesy horse. The courtesy horse would be lent to anyone who would directly or indirectly help the hunt in some way, for instance the local policeman and vet, a farmer who fancied an occasional day, a farmer's son or daughter who could ride but had no horse, or someone visiting a farmer. The Easton were never required to use this horse for the vet as our vet was Major Hugh Clay, our Honorary Secretary, who always had his own horse and did not charge the hunt for his services, only for the cost of the drugs and inoculations used. Our courtesy horse was a little dun coloured cob called Coffee Cream who could equally well carry a large child or a fourteen stone man. He was ideal in many ways but he would occasionally tip off his casual rider. This was not intentional but he was clever, as little cobs so often are, and had a neat way of jumping ditches so he landed at a right angle in the furrow on the other side. As this involved twisting in mid air it was very unseating for the unwary. The surfeit of horses gave me another small source of income as I would hire out the spare one and Coffee Cream when they were not needed for their respective duties. I charged £3 per day, which I reckoned paid the cost of their food for a week.

An important part of the improving prospects of the Hunt was that there were lots of new people coming out hunting but among them was Barry Hood from Sproughton. He was a horse dealer and fattened pigs on swill from Ipswich. He was very keen to whip-in so I started to allow him to help in small ways. He very soon became reasonably good and was quick when needed, such as to stop hounds when they divided. The older members did not like to see him in such a prominent position and did not hesitate to tell me so. Judith Bull was the most vociferous in this matter, telling me quite bluntly that he was 'the wrong type' and that she had 'seen his type before' and it had always led to trouble, and asking me to stop letting him whip-in. I took no notice of her advice thinking that it was just a case of incompatible class distinction. I felt that hunting should be open for all and everyone should be welcome to follow hounds. I was later bitterly to regret not taking her advice.

During my third season (1965–6) the Dunston Harriers disbanded and I was given the pick of their hounds. I took four couple of entered and one and a half of unentered thinking that an infusion of new blood would be beneficial but I was not very impressed with this draft and only bred from one of them, a bitch called Joyful[64] who I put to a dog called Merlin[67] who was a quarter French. My policy was to breed far more bitches than were needed to sustain the size of the pack, keep only the best of the puppies and draft the rest to other packs. I made my choice in two stages, first on grounds of looks before they were entered and then on grounds of their work. I would keep all the puppies until they were at least a year old and then after the Puppy Show I would draft those that were too big or too small, or had a 'gay stern', i.e. a curly tail, or any other conformation fault. I did this before I entered them as 'Sod's Law' would ensure that the worst lookers were also the best to hunt and I would have been tempted to keep them. I had no difficulty in finding hunts to take my drafts as I was offering hounds for free, already inoculated and broken from all forms of riot. The Jersey Drag or the Clifton Foot Harriers would take all my small ones and the Waveney Harriers or the Ross Harriers would take the bigger ones. The rest were entered and then I would draft more during their first or second seasons for faults in their work.

Hounds at Easton Park gates

They might be too shy or too fast, have a squeaky voice or be mute and run without speaking at all, or, worst of all, be too excitable and not stop when the other hounds checked but just gallop on without the scent. The hounds that survived this great drafting procedure were the very tops. They were a huntsman's dream, thinking alike and casting themselves together, swinging this way and that like a flock of birds.

Unfortunately, the procedure caused me some difficulties because of the tradition of 'puppy walking' as every walker naturally thought of their particular puppy as a star and feelings were hurt if it was drafted. The Supporters Club helped me out of this particular difficulty by buying a piece of ground next to the grass yard. The ground was completely overgrown and gangs of members hacked and cut and burned until we had it cleared when it proved to be the old sewer beds built for Easton Park, the former home of the Duke of Hamilton. To our great surprise, we found a good red brick building in the centre of this piece of land which had housed the pump for the sewer. Ernie Nunn told me that, although he had been kennel huntsman for fourteen seasons, he had never seen this building. The grass yard fence ran along two sides of the new piece of land so there were only two sides left for us to fence and we did this with galvanised iron sheets which had been used as lining for Nissen huts. These were very cheap and had to be painted with black bitumen on both sides before they were erected. We used them instead of wire netting because one of the sides to be fenced ran along the bottom of gardens and I thought that if the hounds could see the people in their gardens, they would bay at them. We also put in a concrete path round the inside of the fence to stop the hounds digging they way out.

The new exercise yard solved my problem with the puppy walkers because I could rear the puppies at the kennels instead of putting them out to walk. It was a revolutionary step and the first season I put half the puppies out to walk with the best walkers and kept the other half in the new grass yard. When we came to break them the next spring, the half we had kept in kennel were much easier to handle. There were no other drawbacks that I could see so after that I stopped using puppy walkers altogether. This was a great shame in some ways as it had always been a traditional part of the Hunt's make-up and, in fact, for hundreds of years hunts could not survive without good walkers. Prior to the modern vaccines it would have been impossible to rear puppies at the kennels as they would not have survived the 6–20 week stage of their life and it was also important that they be reared on a farm so that they saw loose chickens and ducks and farm livestock and were taught to leave them alone. With breeding so many puppies, it had always been very difficult for me to find enough puppy walkers for them all and a 'poor walk', where they spent all day shut in a loose box, was no good at all.

The season ended on Wednesday 9th March, with a hunt breakfast and lawn meet at my home. This meet was on a Wednesday so as not to clash with the Hunters' Improvement Society's stallion show at Newmarket the next day. We had hunted on fifty-one days and killed 31½ brace of hares with three days being lost through snow and frost. During my

Mastership I recorded as kills only hares which had been caught after good hunts and not others killed easily, for instance one 'chopped' in her form or one that was clearly sick and killed in the first ditch. All these I used to call 'unfortunate accidents', but it is surprising how many hunts count every hare killed as part of their tally, no matter how caught.

Two days later, on Friday 11th March 1966, we went to France to stay with George Lamiot at Evreux. It was arranged that the next day, the Saturday, George's daughter Marie Noel would take Sheila shopping in Paris and I could go hunting with a roe deer pack, which hunted in the Forêt de Senonches. The Master, the Comte de Flandres, made me very welcome on two counts, first because any friend of the famous George Lamiot was welcome but, more importantly, because I was a hare hunter. All French huntsmen acknowledge that a hare is the most difficult animal to hunt and hare hunters are held in high esteem. We had a very interesting 5½ hour hunt; it was very hot and dry and scent predictably poor, but during the whole of this long hunt hounds stuck to their original buck. It ended with the Master walking bent double following the slot marks of the buck but lost even this last hope when we came to a rocky track. George and I were invited to stay for the hunt dinner in a large hunting lodge kept up in the forest just for their hunt dinners once a week. It was a long room with a huge log fire at both ends, a long table and masses of trophies hanging on the walls. All the members were wearing their elaborate hunt coats and the atmosphere was magical. Unfortunately, I had a bad attack of asthma and told George that I would go and sit in his car but he would not hear of me doing this and drove me home so we both missed the dinner. I have always regretted it but, as asthma inhalers had not then been invented, there was no alternative.

The Comte de Flandres later asked me to write an article about hare hunting in England for the French magazine *La Venerie* so I wrote it in English and he translated it into French. George Lamiot had made John Graham and me members of the Société de

Miss Carter giving the "turn-off" – see page 38

Drawn by Jason Gathorne-Hardy

Venerie in France so we received the monthly copies of the magazine. Major Clay saw the magazine on my kitchen table, picked it up and saw my article and asked if he could borrow it to read. Unbeknown to me, he was going to dinner that night with Mr Irvine, my long-suffering French master at school. He showed the article to Mr Irvine with some remark about how well he had taught me French but, after reading a few paragraphs, he looked Hugh Clay straight in the eye and said, 'Harvey definitely did not write this!'

On the Monday we were to hunt fox with George Lamiot and his harriers and I was really looking forward to this as they were almost all my Easton Harrier drafts. Sheila and I were to be the only ones mounted, other than George who was hunting hounds. This was strictly a private pack so George could invite whomever he pleased to hunt and this day was to be just for us. He wanted to hunt fox so I was given instructions to blow my 'funny little English horn' three times for a fox and four times for a boar. We drew and drew until half past three and then I heard hounds speak for the first time. There was a great crashing sound in the undergrowth and I thought 'boar'. It crossed right in front of me with my little harriers in full cry not far behind it and I blew my horn four times.

George came flying up on his trotter exclaiming, 'You have played a horrid joke on your old friend, you blew four times for a boar!' but I assured him that they really were hunting a boar. It was very late in the day to start a boar hunt, but I was really excited with my beloved little harriers going like demons after their boar. Sheila and I set off after George but after a mile or two we came to a very steep drop and Sheila would not ride down it. I urged her, begged her, swore at her, yelled at her, but to no avail. What could I do? I could not leave her alone in the forest as she would never find her way back to the meet and would get absolutely lost wandering all night in the forest. I sat and listened to the cry of the harriers disappearing into the distance, then turned and went back to the meet, and boxed up the horses. I was livid but, after sitting in the car fuming for an hour and a half when, suddenly, I heard hounds' voices. I got out of the car and listened. It was definitely my harriers I could hear so I quickly got my horse out and was away and soon up behind them. We had an hour or more of furious riding as they were really flying, finding a stinking boar very easy to hunt after the delicate scent of a hare. Eventually, George regretfully told me to get ahead and stop them as it was, by now, very dark and I rode back to the meet in a much better humour.

Two days later I had an enjoyable day in the Forêt de Bord Louviers with M. Jean Ferjoux's Staghounds and had the hounds all to myself for half an hour just before the stag was taken. The meet was unforgettable; everything in French hunting is generally done in great style but today's meet was just the opposite. The meet was in a large broiler hut with firm chicken muck about a foot deep all over the floor and, while eats and drinks were handed round, the Master's wife was sitting on a chicken crate in the middle of it all, breast-feeding her baby. The next day, Thursday, George took us to see the Rally Taillis-Tayout and I had the pleasure of meeting Jean Bocquillon again. Sheila rode again and we had a fair day but scent was very difficult under the hot sun and we did not take our buck. We drove to Boulogne that night and George came to England with us, taking back with him some more harriers, Tantalus, Tartar, Muffler, and Vagabond.

1966–7

My fourth season started on 8th September with a meet at Chandos Farm, Worlingworth, at half past five to hunt in 90 acres of sugar beet. We brought every hound possible, thirty-one couple, and there were just four of us mounted, myself hunting hounds with Fred Hargreaves and two amateur whippers-in, Geoffrey Ingram-Smith and Barry Hood, and Ernie Calver on foot. We had met slightly early and had to wait a few minutes until there was enough light. While we sat there in the gloom, Geoffrey made his famous remark: 'Well, gentlemen. Here we sit, waiting for the season to start.'

The scent was very poor but we had one little hunt when a hare came out of the beet just in front of hounds, and ran a lap of Bull's Hall stubbles before returning to the beet. Mulberry, a French cross, was missing at the end, but I found her later. These early mornings were particularly interesting for me as I was entering the first cross French hounds for the first time. They entered very well, with lovely voices, but they were very temperamental, shy, and difficult to

handle. John Graham was out most mornings and on 19th September had with him Mr Eric Furness, Master of the Peak Bloodhounds in Derbyshire. By the end of September all the young ones were going well and not hanging around me, but I suspected that the High Peak draft, which had arrived the previous spring and which were very excitable and unsteady, were inclined to babble. One particular morning I decided that I should keep a close eye on these hounds and, pushing on hard across country to keep near them, ended up in a deep ditch. It was entirely my own fault as I was riding Noddy, a very reliable horse of some seasons, but he did rely on a tap on the ribs with the whip and a 'hup' when expected to take off. With concentrating so hard watching the High Peak hounds, I forgot to apply the 'aids' and into the ditch we went. The draft was easy to watch as they were black and tan like all the High Peak pack as any puppy born with white on it was drafted. The Weston Harriers in Somerset were the same and both packs were very beautiful and left a lasting impression, but it must have been very difficult to learn their names with no distinctive white mark to go by. Quite soon I decided that there definitely was a tendency to babble so in the middle of October I drafted four couple to Major Riley for his drag hunt on Jersey which would suit them better.

On 1st October hounds met at Upper Grove Farm, Rendham, at half past six and our hosts' son, Roger Lintott, joined us on his pony. The day was more or less scentless except when we were on the large acreage of dairy grass belonging to Mr Jack of Rendham Hall. Hounds could and did run well whenever the hare crossed the grass and this was quite enough to get Chris Bigden wound up. He went at a fair sized hedge and cleared it but hit a wire fence on the other side and both he and Nutty somersaulted. Not long after, we had another good spin across the grass and Chris and John Capon both squared up to a good hedge and sailed over it side by side. It was very pretty to watch as it a hedge between meadows is so rarely found in the Easton country.

Two days later we met at Ashfield Place at seven o'clock. The owner, Dr Mills, and her farm manager, Ian Robinson, both hunted and we had the best hunting so far. Unfortunately, the field became too excited and at one point failed to stop at a check and galloped right through my hounds. I was livid with rage and cursed terribly and sent Chris Bigden home as I suspected he was the ringleader. Mrs Ponsonby, who lived at Hill Farm, next door to the meet, had written to say that she did not want us on her land but during the day we slipped up and rode across a very rough piece of grass, usually cut once a year. This was about fifty yards wide but she complained and when I went to see her I received a real rocket. She could not have been more fierce if the whole field had gone across the middle of a wheat field. Four weeks later she telephoned me to ask if I could find or lend horses for her two sons to hunt on Boxing Day.

On 6th October the Saffell family were hosts to us at Rookery Farm and we had an experimental day, leaving at home the fastest and the slowest hounds and the High Peak draft. The eighteen couple hunted beautifully together and an excellent breakfast ended the morning. We had another outstanding day on 8th October when hounds came to my home, Glebe Farm, Badingham, at seven o'clock. The scent was very good and we had a very fast hunt to Low Farm, Ubbeston, and back again with barely a check, and caught our hare. The horses were a little blown as I drew Badingham Hall but hounds started to speak on a line, hunting slowly for a little while, and then the pack split. One half went towards Boats Hall which we had been asked to avoid because of shooting, so I went with the other half knowing that Fred would stop the others long before they got to the shooting coverts. All the field, except my little sister-in-law eleven-year-old Rita, went with Fred so Rita and I were alone with our half-pack which flew across to the main A1120 road, ran parallel to it to Peasenhall, then across to Ubbeston and circled round before running back to the area where we had found her. The ditches were very big and blind and were taken at a gallop. An overgrown lane barred our way but I just plunged into it, somehow got out the other side and kicked on again. After the lane I looked back to see if Rita was still on board but she was coming on like a good 'un. Our private hunt lasted an hour and a half, mostly at galloping speed, and I wrote in my diary that it was, 'the fastest hunt I have ever had with the Easton Harriers. I have not ridden across Suffolk like this since the old staghound days.'

On 11th October we went to our great supporter, Herbert Bloomfield, at Poplar Farm Cretingham, at eight o'clock. John Graham had bought a new horse and put it up at the kennels the night before and hacked on with us to the meet to settle it down. The day was moderate but there was one interesting incident. Hounds had seriously overrun the line but Mulberry, the young French cross bitch, stopped and turned with the line, speaking with her lovely deep voice. The whole pack turned as one and flew to her at such a rate that they collided with her, knocking her into some nettles, and scaring her so much that she was very timid for the rest of the day.

In the afternoon of the same day, John Graham brought his pack of French cross bloodhounds to a meet at my home at three o'clock. He drew at Peasenhall Manor and put a hare away from the same seat as I had found one on the previous Saturday. She started to run exactly as the one that I hunted on Saturday and at a check I suggested that John cast his hounds in the direction that mine had gone. This happened several times with me suggesting that he tried 'near that oak tree' or 'through that gap'.

John was most impressed. 'Tony,' he said, 'I have always thought you were quite a good huntsman, but this is just brilliant. It's uncanny how you instinctively know just where to cast.'

I was grinning to myself, knowing that this game could not go on much longer and soon his hounds checked again. He looked at me for more guidance but I had to say, 'Sorry, John, this is where my hounds lost the line on Saturday.'

It was a really good joke and we had many laughs about it later. This hare, who was christened Monty, became quite infamous. We both hunted her for the next three seasons; she was always found in the same place, always ran the same line, and was always lost in the same place. I would never consider doing anything unsporting but now I wish I had put someone there to see exactly what she did each time to outwit us. It would have been nice to know, even though we would not have acted on the information. Of course, as each year came round, I did not expect to find the same hare on the same seat, otherwise I might have thought of positioning someone.

That evening I sat at our round dinner table in Glebe Farm with six men and Sheila to enjoy the annual tradition of eating a Michaelmas Goose together. The guests were John Graham, Ernie Calver, Chris Bigden, Geoffrey Ingram-Smith, and John Parker. I gave the ancient toast with the goose course: 'He who eats goose on Michaelmas Day, shan't money lack his debts to pay.' This was the perfect way to end a lovely day: hunting in the morning, hunting in the afternoon, and dinner amongst one's closest friends at night: just my sort of day.

On 27th October, the meet was at Great Lodge, Framlingham, and as usual hounds ran into the big wood and spent about an hour hunting round and round with a glorious cry. From where I stood watching, I could see the hunted hare going round inside the wood often only about ten yards behind the last hound having almost lapped the pack. Later in the day, two hares were chopped but the hounds were disinterested and showed no inclination to break them up. Barry Hood jumped off his horse, hung them on his saddle and afterwards gave them to Sheila who subsequently turned them into delicious jugged hare.

The last early morning was on 29th October at Earl Soham Falcon, and it was a great day. The scent was very good and hounds ran hard all morning and at one point marked their hare to ground in a gateway pipe where we left her. We found another hare and ran a fast line to Bedfield and back when the hare passed through a very thick hedge onto Saxtead Green. When I got round this hedge and onto the Green, I could see Beryl Leman in trencher-fed style calling to a hound that she had walked. She was trying to get it onto the line of the hare that she had seen crossing the Green. I laid hounds onto the line and they ran over a lovely line of fences behind The Cedars and over the main A1120. Three of us jumped a gate off the main road into Mr Wolton's sow meadow and hounds finally lost the line behind the Volunteer Inn. This, of course, called for a brief interval at the ''Teers' which turned out not to be quite so brief as intended. We had one more hunt after we left the Volunteer and I noted that some usually quiet individuals had been transformed during

Jean Bocquillon and Ernie Calver
Photograph kindly loaned by John Finch

the interval into thrusters. I feared for my hounds and the end result was three broken gates!

Two days later, on 31st October, I was in France with Sheila and Christine Dickinson to stay with Jean Bocquillon, at the Ferme du Grande Logis at Baron in Oise. We had gone to see their Opening Meet, known as the St Hubert after the patron saint of hunting. The day started with the St Hubert Mass and, as a hare hunter, I was given the great honour of being placed second in the procession going into church. It was a wonderful sight to see all the members of the hunt in the church with their elaborate hunt coats. On either side of the altar, were two boys, each about twelve years old: one was in riding clothes and held a hound on a lead and the other was a choirboy in his robes holding a tray of buns for the Mass. As the service went on, each boy became bored with the proceedings and gazed around, looking up at the roof, and losing concentration on what they were doing.

The old hound on the lead was gradually pulling closer and closer to the tray of buns and the boy with the tray was allowing it to tip down so the contents were almost sliding off. It was hilarious to watch as, at times, the hound's nose was only a foot or so away from the tray. Just in time, the boys regained their concentration and disaster was averted.

Despite this humorous aspect, the atmosphere within the church was electric and listening to the trompes being blown caused every hair on my head to prickle and stand up. When we came out of church there was a huge crowd of people waiting and the whole pack was blessed amidst much blowing of trompes. They blew the fanfare of *Le Lièvre* (The Hare) in my honour and I had to take off my hat and stand to attention whilst it was played. Christine and I rode Jean's horses and Sheila had a hireling. It was a very long day and after some very good hunting the roe deer was taken at six o'clock. The *curée* was held at a chateau nearby and went on for an hour or so, well into the dark with the scene lit up by car lights. The *curée* is a trompe blowing ceremony in which the whole account of the day's hunting is told by the blowing of successive tunes, each one of which describes part of the hunt. After the *curée* we all went to the house of Jean's brother Pierre for a buffet party. Pierre had recently married an English girl, Bridget, and the party was partly a hunt dinner and partly a wedding reception. There were about 170 people there and more blowing of horns with the blowers standing in stages up the wide staircase. When the blowers came down, Sheila decided this was a good moment to visit the ladies room. Quickly she sped upstairs, rounded a corner, and found herself face to face with a fully-grown boar, stuffed and standing naturally with its huge tusks gleaming through its black hairs. Altogether it was a memorable party.

On the morning of the Easton's Opening Meet, on Thursday 3rd November (1966) I was still feeling very weak from the 'flu but telephoned Fred to bring hounds to just outside Framlingham and then hacked in with them. We were greeted by a really good crowd of supporters and there were about thirty mounted. These included three strangers who were later to become known as the Three Musketeers. We moved off, paying our usual respects to Mr Larter by raising our hats to his window, and found our first hare quite quickly. The scent was good and some fast gallops followed. At one time, the three strangers all galloped at a gateway abreast and, needless to say, one of them was knocked into the ditch, which happened to be a very deep one. One really good run took us to Colston Hall, Badingham, and back again with Captain Marriott viewing her on her way back going into some rushes where she was lost. There were an unusual amount of empty saddles which perhaps was in some part due to the pace. The three strangers got into another muddle, galloping on a long stubble field which ran into a narrow point at the end. As they were out of control, at least one of the horses could not stop and ended up in a very muddy pond.

I blew for home at half past three having chopped 1½ brace and killed 1½ brace after really good hunts. I had kept going with help from a few offered flasks and the good day must have cured the 'flu as a party of us went to dinner at Framlingham Crown, the party including John and Ann Capon, Terence and Marion Saffell, Christine Dickinson and her friend Liz Mitchell, Geoffrey and Monica Ingram-Smith, Robert and Ann Hawes, and Ernie and Mary Calver, as well as Sheila and I.

We had one major change this season and this was in the hunting days. Since there was no longer any drag to hunt on Saturdays, I decided to hunt the Harriers on Saturdays instead. My agreement said that I should hunt on every Monday and Thursday, weather permitting, but I changed it without official permission from the committee and said I would hunt as many Mondays as I could get country for, which was very few before Christmas because of shooting.

The second meet of the official season, therefore, came on Saturday 5th November and we met at Swilland Half Moon. We unboxed at the Saffells at Rookery Farm, Grundisburgh, and hacked to the meet, and again there were over thirty mounted. Hares were difficult to find and every one that was found was chopped although I tried to prevent this by cracking my whip to alert the hares. It was a miserable, disappointing day and I blew for home at half past one, hacking back to Rookery Farm for lunch which was the best part of the day. Afterwards we all set off to build a big bonfire ready for the Supporters Club Firework Party.

The following Thursday there were only eight mounted followers for the Worlingworth Swan meet but every one of us had a fall, some more than once, including myself who was trying a new horse. There was one curious incident during the day. The line ran through a dry pond and as hounds, racing along in full cry, took it down into the pond, suddenly chickens flew out in all directions. As I came past I could see that there was a chicken hut in the bottom of the pond. On our return to the meet, a lady arrived holding a dead chicken which, she claimed, had been killed by my hounds. I said that I was confident that my hounds would not kill a chicken and indeed there was not a mark on it. Ernie Calver who was a poultry dealer came to the rescue and said that it would have died of a heart attack when the hounds rushed through the dry pond. She was asking £2 for it but Ernie said it was not worth more than £1. Nevertheless, I paid her £2 for it and she went to go away with the chicken and my money.

'Hold on!' I said. 'Where are you going with the chicken?'

'I'm going to cook it for my husband's Sunday lunch', she replied.

'Well', I said. 'I don't mind paying you double what it's worth but I think I ought to have it.'

'Oh,' she said. 'All right then,' and left.

On the second Saturday we had a good day from a meet at Ashfield Place with began with a few little hunts. During this time my young sister-in-law Rita followed us over a gate but her pony only got half way over and for a while rocked back and forth like a rocking horse with either its front legs on the ground or its hind ones! Somehow it eventually got off unharmed. The last hunt was very fast and took in most of Ashfield and back across to Cretingham; I was the only one to be up with hounds at the end with the others coming up one by one. The cry was so good it could be heard miles away.

The following Thursday saw us at the Laxfield Royal Oak and Captain Marriott joined us mounted but he could not get his horse over the ditches very well so we did not see much of him. One of those embarrassing incidents which are always waiting for the unwary happened to me. I was galloping through the meadows at Laxfield House past a shepherd's hut when the shepherd, Royden Chenery, suddenly appeared in the doorway of the hut. My horse Paddy shied so violently that I came off and landed in a puddle much to the amusement of the shepherd.

On Saturday 19th November, we had a fright in the kennel when a young hound lost consciousness after feeding. Fred rushed it to the vet and it recovered but, when he returned, he found Tatler also unconscious and sadly Tatler died. The cause was traced to a calf which had been killed by the vet giving it a treble dose of anaesthetic. Tatler died because he had eaten the heart.

My grandmother used to say 'Love will take you further than gunpowder can blow you' and the blossoming courtship between Sheila's friend Christine Dickinson and my French friend, Jean Bocquillon, brought him to England once more. I lent him my horse Noddy and he joined us at the Eye White Lion meet, causing quite a sensation by blowing his trompe in the town. During the day a hare took us on an unusual line and hounds drove on so fast that we almost lost them but, luckily, they turned and we got on terms with them again and raced on. Ernie Calver and myself both fell at a bad place leaving John Capon the only person to be up with hounds at the end of this hunt.

The Easton Ball was held on 25th November at Hintlesham Hall, by kind permission of Mr Stokes, who made a small charge for the use of his beautiful home. His brother was the (Labour) Member of Parliament for Ipswich at this time. To be able to hold our Ball there we had to obtain permission from the Essex and Suffolk Foxhounds as the Rules of Hunting state that one Hunt cannot hold fund-raising events in another Hunt's country without obtaining permission. The Essex & Suffolk had held their Ball there earlier so we were able to just follow them and do the same as they did. Mrs Bull, Mrs Daniels, and Sheila went to make the arrangements with Mr Stokes and agreed to have the same band and the same caterer. There were 275 present and when the ball was in full swing Mr Stokes came round the tables telling people how wicked they were to hunt 'little foxes'. Later on, there was a power cut and the lights all went out, but the band were able to keep playing by candlelight as in those days they did not need power for their instruments. Eventually we all did the Post Horn Gallop, then stood for the National Anthem, and the ball was finished. As people were crowding down the stairs, Chris decided to slide down the banisters and managed to allow his feet to make a direct hit on a lady's bottom, which had the effect of lifting her off the last two steps into the crowd below. Luckily no one was hurt but, as Master, I was very embarrassed and pretended he was nothing to do with me, even though he and Sara would be coming home with us.

The meet at Dennington Queen, on 1st December, was notable for almost gale-force winds, and an instance of the almost incredible properties of scent. I saw hounds running in full cry at least two hundred yards downwind of where the hare had actually run.

What an amazing thing scent is; a hare running at full speed leaves a tiny scent behind it, and yet the scent can be blown two hundred yards and remain intact.

Through my friendship with John Graham, I had met Eric Furness who was owner, Master and Huntsman of the Peak Bloodhounds in Derbyshire. I had instantly liked him and invited him to bring his bloodhounds to hunt in the Easton country. The bloodhounds hunted 'the clean boot', the natural scent of a man (as long as he is not wearing rubber footwear as this impairs the scent). The meet was advertised for Debenham Cherry Tree and I planned to take a line to Saxtead Green where we could stop at The Volunteer, while the second runner got a good start and then take a second line back to Winston Hall, just outside Debenham.

The whole affair started to get out of hand as soon as the meet was advertised; it attracted unbelievable media attention and, in the end, both the local television companies sent crews, plus all the local and seven national newspapers. The day started with an excellent hunt breakfast with John and Elizabeth Graham at Brundish Manor, and then we went on to Debenham to find it packed with people; we could hardly fight our way through the crowd to get to the pub. There were reporters everywhere, firing questions at Eric and I, and Eric was getting very angry. He hated reporters because they always asked the same questions, something along the lines, 'Is hunting a running man good sport?' to which Eric had to answer 'yes' otherwise he would not be doing it. The next question was always: 'If this is such good sport why can't people do this instead of fox hunting?' The subject being too big even to try to explain the difference, he would just clam up and try to ignore them.

Eventually it was time to move off and we went to the turn-off point where the first runner had left his handkerchief on a stick. All the hounds immediately ran to the stick and had a good sniff at the handkerchief and then set off. The crowd had somehow discovered the line we would be taking; there were people swarming all over the line with cameras and there was even one man with a pet bloodhound on a lead trying to hunt the line. To make matters worse, we had set the runner off far too early so the scent was rather light and, with all the distraction, we made very slow progress for the first few miles. Meanwhile, Sheila was quietly making her way home to Badingham unaware that a convoy of cars was following her nearly all the way as many people had assumed that, as my wife, she would know where to go. We eventually arrived on Saxtead Green where the hounds identified Tom Dent, the runner, and licked him all over. This part of the hunt is vitally important as the hounds must find, and identify, the person who they have been hunting so for them the hunt is completed. This is because they are 'de change', and will not change from the scent of the man whose scent they have identified on the handkerchief which is of the utmost importance as endless trouble would be caused if hounds were likely to change to the scent of a casual passer-by who happened to walk near the line.

We were mortified to find that we could not stop at The Volunteer for a drink or two, as planned, because the second runner had been gone for nearly two hours. Again the hounds sniffed the handkerchief and we were away. I wrote in my diary: '*The second hunt was the very essence of perfect hound-work with them taking the line back to Winston Hall on their own (with no help) two hours behind their quarry*'. When we arrived at Winston Hall, the runner was sitting on top of a straw stack with the hounds all around the bottom of the ladder, baying. He had, of course, been told to stand still and let them lick him and identify him but, as he stood listening to their booming voices coming up from the meadows, he had lost his nerve and bolted up the thatching ladder. It looked such a comical sight to see a great, burly Scot sitting up there and not daring to come down, but it makes no difference how big you are if you think you are going to be eaten. Eventually, after a lot of pleading and assurances, he came down to be licked all over and the run was finished. This second run had made all the aggravation of the earlier part of the day pale into insignificance; it was pure magic to see how well the hounds could hunt a line which was two hours old, and it was also a joy for riding across country.

The day ended with a dinner at the Homersfield Black Swan whose reputation at that time was second to none. What a day it had been, lovely hunt breakfast, gross aggravation from reporters and public alike, pet bloodhound owner on the line, a blissful second run, the amusing sight of the burly Scot on top of the stack, and a really good dinner in grand company to end the day.

There was such good scent after the meet at Stradbroke White Hart on 8th December that the first hare hardly turned at all and ran alongside the river until she was eventually lost in some bramble bushes. The wet conditions which gave us such good scent had filled the ditches so that most had to be taken at the gallop. Other hares gave us good hunts with the last one swimming the river below Thickthorn Farm

with all 17½ couple of hounds swimming after her and speaking at the same time. It was a lovely sight and they hunted on and eventually killed their hare. Those of us who were brave enough to jump the river were rewarded with refreshments at Thickthorn Farm, John Capon's home.

I left the Easton to have a day with John Graham's hounds on 9th December at Caxton Marsh in Norfolk. They hunted the marshes beautifully and after about one and a half hours on the same hare there was a very serious check. John pricked his hare and, bending double, followed her pad marks along a stretch of sandy soil with just one hound, Tanner, a Scarteen hound from Ireland, able to speak to the line. At the end of the sand, all the hounds spoke again and went on but eventually lost their line. I had read about this pricking in books about old-time hare-hunting and was thrilled to see it for myself for the first time. A week later I had another unforgettable day with John's hounds in the Norfolk marshes. Geoffrey Ingram-Smith and I travelled with him in his Land Rover with the hound trailer behind and crossed the River Yare on the chain ferry at Reedham. We then caught the train and, with a couple of hounds each, sat in the guards van until we came to the Berney Arms Inn which is about six miles from any road. We hunted for a few hours, and then caught the train back to Reedham and put the hounds into their hound van. John insisted that we stop for 'tea' at the Poringland Dove, which was kept by a brilliant horseman, Fred Elby. John's idea of 'tea' consisted of three double brandies and one cup of tea. We went home very happy and Geoffrey and I shared a bottle of champagne with Sheila as we told her of our adventures before going to a Supporters Club Meeting. It was just as well that the breathalyser was not used in those days.

The extremely wet weather continued and one good day came after another. The meet at Rendham White Horse on 22nd December was especially good as it was one of those where lots of farmers came and the atmosphere in the pub was electric. We moved off and found a hare in the first field, and then it started to snow lightly. As I blew them away, I had to tuck my head down to keep the snow out of my eyes. When I looked up there was a little hedge in front of me so I gave Noddy a boot in the ribs and he hopped over it, only to stop dead on the other side when he saw fast flowing water. This shot me right out of the saddle and I found my neck between his ears and my chin on his brow band. I struggled to get back into the saddle but the old horse just kept putting his head lower and lower. I stood no chance of saving my dignity and slid over his head into the raging torrent below. Somehow, I managed to twist in mid air so I landed on my feet with the bridle in my hand and the reins still round Noddy's neck. The combined length of rein and bridle just allowed me to climb out on the far side and then I called to Noddy and he heaved himself over to me. I quickly put the bridle back on and was away to where I thought hounds would be. I found them and had them to myself for a while until the others caught up The most embarrassing part was that, as it was only three days before Christmas, the children were home for Christmas holidays and as I stood in the water, there was a whole row of little faces grinning down at me. Debbie Saffell later made a splendid drawing of the scene which I kept for many years.

A great party developed in the pub afterwards. The landlady was a great character and extremely flirtatious but she may have gone too far when she said to Graham Croll, 'Well, you can have me, if you can catch me.' Graham bounded over the bar and chased her through the kitchen and we last saw her running past the front of the pub into the car park. The mark on the bar counter where Graham's spurs had gouged out a large piece remained for many years.

There was another good day on Christmas Eve from Debenham Red Lion, with the first hare giving us such a good hunt over some really big country that I needed to change horses. Marion Saffell lent me her Charity and her son, Nick, rode my Paddy quietly for an hour or so. We were unable to hunt on Boxing Day due to a very hard frost but we met nevertheless, and took 17½ couple of selected hounds, the largest and the smallest being left in kennel. The end result was a pack that were as like as peas in a pod and I was very proud of them. We paraded in front of a huge crowd at The Saxtead Volunteer and the police estimated that there were about three hundred cars on the Green. We stayed with hounds until one o'clock and then sent hounds and horses home. I had a quick drink with Ernie Calver and both he and I went to lunch with Herbert Breese at Church Farm.

Dear old Herbert, in his usual style, said everything twice: 'Now then you boys, now then you boys.

Come back to Church Farm, come back to Church Farm. I got some beef a month old, I got some beef a month old. Ordered it to be hung at Ray Kent's on 24th November, I ordered it to be hung at Ray Kent's on 24th November'.[1]

Herbert's kitchen was delightful with an old high-backed settle curving round the table. It was very cosy with Ernie and I sitting on it, a drink in our hand, while Herbert produced the remains of the joint and carved us a generous amount. It was indeed very good. When we had finished, Herbert said, 'Mince pies you boys, mince pies you boys' and put a plateful on the table in front of us and disappeared.

Ernie and I took one each and were eating it when he returned with a bottle in his hand and, quite crossly, he said: 'Now boys! Oh dear, oh dear! Don't you know how to eat a mince pie? How have you been brought up?'

He carefully lifted the top off a couple of pies and poured in a little brandy, then brought the cream jug and poured in a little cream, and then, with something of a flourish, replaced the lids.

'Now boys, now boys! They are ready to eat, they are ready to eat!'

After our mince pies he produced old photographs of the harriers in his father's time and we had a lovely hour or so listening to his stories of the old days. One of them was about his father riding round his farm one day and catching the local poacher setting his snare on a well-used hare run. This poacher was well-known in the neighbourhood and more or less tolerated by the farmers but, on seeing him, Mr Breese became very angry.

'Blast you, Ned. I don't mind you having a few rabbits, but it's a rotten trick to snare a hare. Don't you know the Harriers meet at mine next Thursday?'

Old Ned looked up and said, 'Don't you worry about that, Mr Breese. You'll find a hare on this here field next Thursday and, what's more, she'll run back to yours.'

Graham Croll, Geoffrey Ingram-Smith, John Capon and Ernie Calver, in France

Photograph kindly loaned by John Finch

---

[1] Ray Kent was the Framlingham butcher

When the great day arrived with the expected crowd and after all had been entertained, hounds moved off to draw. The meadow in front of the house sloped away offering a clear view of the arable field beyond, close to where Ned had been caught. Hounds found their hare where the old poacher had said it would be, and it ran straight towards the house. Undeterred, she ran through the sixty or so people watching on foot and went straight up to the front door, still standing open. As she reached the door she turned sharp left and ran round the end of the house but the hounds, bringing a strong line up to the door, went straight on into the house and proceeded to devour joints of beef and ham that were waiting for the hunting tea.

Back in the 1966–67 season, I had a joint meet with John Graham's hounds on 27th December, each of us bringing two couple of hounds. I chose my best hound, Tangle, with Vivid, Hector, and Brenda and took them in the boot of my car to the meet at Dennington Hall. It was still freezing and the scent was very poor. We had great difficulty in finding a hare but did manage a hunt at the end of the day with Tangle putting them right at checks so I was well pleased and the honour of the Easton Harriers was upheld, even if Tangle was a foxhound. When I got home, Jean Bocquillon was there, having come from France that morning. His courtship of Christine Dickinson was in earnest and he had come to stay with us for a while. As he had missed the 'important' joint meet, I thought he ought to have a private day so on the next day I fetched the same two couple and we hunted from Glebe Farm. Jean and I walked out on to my wheat field and soon found and had a delightful one and a half hours of slow hunting around Bruisyard and Badingham before stopping for lunch. It was the greatest fun to be walking alongside such a famous veneur and to hear his comments and observations at each check, even though the frost persisted and scent was still poor.

The following day, which was Thursday 29th December, we gave a lawn meet at Glebe Farm, in honour of Jean's visit, which began with a hunt breakfast for ten people at Glebe Farm. I lent Jean my good horse Noddy and I rode Paddy, Sheila had her Lucy, and Christine had Duffus, a beautiful show hunter that she eventually took to France after her marriage to Jean, and hunted in France for many seasons. There were over forty mounted when we went to draw, the frost had finally given over and the scent was surprisingly good. I viewed a hare away, quietly laid hounds on the line, and we had a classic hunt in a large figure-of-eight before a serious check. I

was convinced that she had clapped down somewhere near and persevered trying to find her, perhaps for rather too long as some members of the field started to drift back to the meet. John Graham was one of these but as he rode away he noticed the marks of a hare going over a sand heap off the road into a field. He rode back to me and delighted me by saying, 'Master, I have pricked your hare.'

I took hounds along the main road to where he had seen the prick marks and the hounds roared over the sand heap and went on for three fields before catching their hare. Although the horses had nearly had enough, I could not bear to waste the brilliant scent so drew again and had another great hunt but lost our hare. I then hacked back to Glebe Farm, tired but exhilarated but as I came into the yard I could hear music coming from the house and found John Graham's horse in an empty pig-sty. When I walked into the house there was such a party going on, empty champagne bottles were standing around, and those who had supposedly 'gone home' early were dancing on the drawing room carpet, still wearing their boots and spurs. Sheila was dancing with John Graham and Chris Bigden with Clare Schreiber, and there were others I forget now, but there was a sharp contrast with those of us who had stayed with hounds and had come in for soup.

The fun continued as there was a Hunt Dinner that night at Framlingham Crown which went on until the early hours, but we hunted again the next day with John Graham's hounds at Flixton Buck. Jean Bocquillon and I were lucky to watch a hare make her doubles and stood still to watch hounds work it out. As usual, hunting alternated with social events and we went home to change into our dinner jackets to enjoy one of the excellent dinners at Brundish Manor before a ball at Framlingham College. Sadly we did not hunt the next day due to frost, otherwise I would have hunted six days running, but we did have a good party at Glebe Farm to conclude Jean's visit to England.

Seventy children were out for the Children's Meet at Ashbocking Nelson but a wind frost had started to blow and I had to stop at one o'clock as the ground was getting very hard wherever the wind caught it. We lost the next three meets due to frost but managed to meet on 12th January at Dennington Bell. At one point, when I was drawing towards Sunflower Farm, I rashly offered a guinea to anyone who would jump an enormous ditch ahead of us. John Capon and Geoffrey Ingram-Smith instantly took me up and jumped it, so then I felt I had to as well, and my little joke cost me £2 2s 0d. Earlier in the day we had jumped a fair sized hedge on Major Rous' land, behind Dennington Hall, and by the time the field had finished, it was in a sorry state. Chris Bigden and I went back after tea and carried posts and rails cross-country to do the necessary repairs.

Soon after this Terence Saffell, Geoffrey Ingram-Smith, Ernie Calver and I visited the Lakes again and I was privileged to watch what must be the most perfect day's hare hunting I am ever likely to see. After a fairly good day with the Easton at Wilby Swan we went home quickly, changed and started off at five in the afternoon, stopping at the Haycock at Wansford for the first night. We arrived in the Lakes the next afternoon and went straight to the kennels of the Windermere Harriers at the Dungeon Ghyll Hotel where we had tea with Mr and Mrs Bulman, the Master's parents. I can still clearly remember the taste of the wonderful Cumberland rum butter left over from Christmas. We then went to the Britannia Inn where we were booked in to stay. This was very convenient as the Windermere singsong was to be held there that night.

After dinner I asked for a glass of milk and explained that these Lakeland men could really drink and that I was taking a safety precaution. The others followed my example and later we moved into the bar to find that John Bulman, the Master, was already in with his huge piano accordion. Soon the bar was packed and the singing began and the atmosphere was terrific with good Lakeland songs well sung. The four of us drank round for round with the locals but did not really get going and we sat on a long settle as boring as four old maids. Towards the end of the long evening, for it was well into the early hours, the others said to me that they did not think much of my milk idea and if I wanted to do it again, I could do it on my own.

The next morning we had hardly finished our breakfast when the Coniston Foxhounds were outside the door of the Britannia at nine o'clock. We watched them move off to draw and then went to the meet of the Windermere Harriers at Gate Ghyll at ten o'clock. John Bulman was hunting hounds and he advised me to walk up to the fell wall which, he explained, was the highest one that runs horizontally around the fell. Ernie and Geoffrey had vowed and declared that they were going to keep with the Master all day.

'Why shouldn't we?' they said. 'If he only walks, of course we can keep up with him.' I knew better having been in the Lakes once before.

Terence and I did as the Master advised and had a perfect view. We watched hounds draw and find with the hare easily out-stripping the harriers up the fellside. My eyes then were like a hawk and I could see the hare most of the time, looking back to watch the hounds following her line. It was all so perfect that it is impossible to describe all that it meant to me and it would have been an ideal time to teach someone all there is to know about hare-hunting. I could see her going through a hole in the wall and then come back through another hole higher up. I watched as she stopped to listen how far back the hounds were, and then perform a classic double with the three large jumps. The hounds, although nothing to look at, were excellent and worked out every ruse and double that she had made. The best moment of my hare-hunting life was still to come as I watched a hare make a five-point double in clear view on the fellside right opposite Terence and me. If the line of scent had been visible, it would have looked like the outstretched fingers of a human hand. She ran from the 'wrist' to a point, then returned along the same line to the wrist, then ran out again to another point and returned, repeating this five times before running back down the 'forearm' and then jumping sideways several times to break the line. The excitement brought me out in goose pimples as I waited for hounds to reach the spot. They ran up one finger of the multiple double, checked at the end, cast themselves, hunted the line of another finger, and ran back to the wrist, repeating this until, after ten minutes or so, they eventually made a very wide cast and hit off the line where she had finished her jumps. They went on to kill their hare.

I could not contain myself behind the fell wall any longer and joined John Bulman as he drew again, noticing that Ernie and Geoffrey had given up following him after a gallant effort. As we walked, John was pointing out various hounds and talking about their respective expertise when up jumped a hare out of some rushes. In his lovely Lakeland accent he said, 'Now Tony, I think I know her. Would you like to see a hare go to ground?'

Of course I replied that I would and he told me to go to a gryke in the rocks, pointing up the fellside.

'What's a gryke?' I asked, and he explained that it was a crack or split, and made sure that I knew which one he meant. Hounds were running in the distance as I climbed up and stood downwind of the gryke. I stood there for what seemed ages and the cry of the hounds became very faint. I was beginning to think that it could not have been the right hare and was just about to move when she came leisurely into view. She stopped about two yards or so from the gryke and sat up on her hind legs with one ear turned back to listen for hounds. The cry became louder and louder as the hounds came nearer but she still sat unconcerned as if nothing was happening and then, when the first hound came into view, she just calmly popped into the safety of the rocks. I felt as if I was floating away in ecstasy. The culminating moment of the most perfect day's hare-hunting was to listen to hounds marking her to ground.

Driving home to Suffolk the four of us were talking about how enjoyable the singing had been and I said how much I would like to get it started in the Easton. Ernie said, 'It's no good you talking like that. Who amongst the Easton people would sing a song? No one except maybe you, if you'd had a few drinks.'

Once back in Suffolk we waxed lyrical about the lovely songs, especially *The Place Where The Old Horse Died*. The Breese brothers told us that they knew of these songs and that they used to be sung in the Easton Harriers but the singing tradition had died out during the War. After a Supporters Club meeting, Ernie Calver and I called into the Hare and Hounds in Framlingham, a great meeting place for all countrymen where the landlord, Jimmy Finbow, was well liked and respected, and got into conversation with Herbert Breese, asking him for more details about the singing of hunting songs. He told us that he had the music sheets for some songs amongst which, he thought, was *The Place Where The Old Horse Died*. The upshot of the conversation was that, at closing time, Herbert suggested that we went home with him to Church Farm and he would find the song sheets and play the tunes. After pouring us a drink each, he went to the piano, lifted up the lid and brought out a handful of music sheets.

As he sorted through the sheets he was muttering to himself, 'Hmm, hmm, the mice have been at the music. Hmm, hmm, the mice have been at the music' and from where we sat we could clearly see the signs of many hours of nibbling. All this seemed very funny to us 'youngsters' and we grinned at each other and started to giggle quietly. He eventually found the song sheet with the words and music for *The Place Where The Old Horse Died*. It was beautifully produced and had in full colour on the cover a picture of a huntsman and horse jumping a gate.

With a few more 'Hmm, hmm's and 'There it is. There it is'-es, he placed the music with due reverence on the front of the piano and settled himself on the stool. I do not know how long it had been since he last played the piano, I imagine several years, but he did his best and strummed out the tune in a rather jerky, stiff-fingered fashion. Ernie and I were watching in amazement as neither of us had any idea

that he could play when suddenly a mouse popped out of the open piano onto the lid and began to run from side to side until it eventually jumped off. We were already in a frivolous mood and this was just too much. We dissolved into uncontrollable giggles. We tried to suppress our amusement, as we did not want Herbert to think we were laughing at his piano-playing efforts. We may have succeeded if more and more mice had not kept popping out and leaping off the end of the lid. Herbert was staring so intently at the music that he did not notice the mice just in front of him and this, of course, made it all the funnier. There is nothing more difficult than trying to stop a fit of the giggles. Just as we had almost succeeded in controlling ourselves, a little half-grown black mouse hopped out which kept running from side to side but dare not jump off. Neither of us will ever forget that little black mouse.

Putting all thoughts of mice to one side, that evening started the revival of singing in the Easton Harriers as I borrowed the sheets, copied out the words and learned my first few hunting songs. It was not long before the Easton was famed for its singing. My enthusiasm was catching and gradually more and more members learnt songs and even the most self-conscious person would sing, recite or tell a joke. At one of the best hunt dinners I can remember, fourteen members of the thirty-three at the table gave a rendering of their particular party piece.

The run of good scenting days continued and a great day followed the meet at Charsfield Horseshoes on 30th January with a succession of excellent hunts, the last of which was very fast and we could only just keep up with hounds. I recorded in my diary that this was perhaps the best hunt of the season and, when hounds killed their hare, I presented pads to Judy Sims, Peggy Jenkins, Geoffrey Ingram-Smith, and Jimmy Fitzroy, and the pate to Barry Hood. I found myself with an ill horse at Monk Soham Oak on 2nd February and borrowed Red Buck from John Capon, while he took my Paddy back to the meet then went home and brought another horse for me. Red Buck was considered the best hunter in the Easton Harriers and I had the great pleasure of sailing over a gate out of Hungers Green, Bedfield, during a good run where hounds had taken the line through a flock of chickens with never a second look at the fluttering, squawking fowl. This pleased me greatly as we had a lot of young hounds out.

The meet at Debenham Cherry Tree on 4th February was put back to one o'clock because of frost but scent was exceptionally good and hounds just flew all day.

At one point, having dropped onto a road, I came up behind a bus and, nervous that I would lose hounds, I overtook it, much to the amusement of the passengers. As I was catching up, I saw the hunted hare coming back towards me, so I stopped to watch her and saw her swim across a moat into the meadow beyond. This saved her scut as hounds declined to swim and left the line. I did not cast them in the meadow beyond the moat where I knew she had gone because my policy was to help my hounds as little as possible. This caused them to hunt better and better by themselves and it was pure joy to watch them casting themselves in ever widening circles when they checked in the middle of a large wheat field.

Later in the day there was a very fast hunt and, as my horse was fading under me, I changed onto Geoffrey Ingram-Smith's horse, Surprise Packet, and he took mine back to the meet. At the end of this tremendous run, hounds caught their hare and Surprise Packet was, indeed, surprised! Nobody was in sight as the pace and length of the run had left everyone way behind. My bladder was nearly bursting and, without a moment's thought, I stood up in my stirrups to have a 'huntsman's pee'. This was a new experience for Surprise Packet and he snorted and turned away from the flow. I took a tight hold of him and this caused him to wheel round on the spot, which, in turn, caused the flow to make a wider arc, thus compounding the problem. Geoffrey was obviously a gentleman! The rest of the field eventually arrived on flagging horses, declaring that this hunt had been the fastest they had ever remembered and the day ended with the Supporters Club Cheese and Wine Party at Hasketon Manor, the home of Sir Harwood and Lady Harrison.

On Saturday 11th February (1967) the Pentagon authorised the grounding of all U.S. planes within Europe so that the Easton Harriers could accept an invitation to meet at the Officers' Club at the US Airforce Base at Bentwaters. I was never clear why it affected the whole of Europe, but was told that it did. The American officers asked me who else they should invite and I suggested it would be nice to invite all the farmers over whose land we would hunt that day. The farmers, car and foot followers, and about fifty mounted followers were wonderfully well entertained in the Officers' Club, before moving off to draw on the edge of the airfield. Hounds feathered along a line into a small copse and seven fallow deer emerged and skipped and hopped amongst hounds whose only reaction was complete surprise and bewilderment.

Sadly, it was an indifferent day's hunting, the best part of which was the meet and the tea afterwards.

I left Suffolk the following day to hunt in France, leaving Fred Hargreaves to hunt hounds at Brandeston Queen on the Monday. The day, as far as I could ascertain, was chiefly marked by the number of people who fell, among them the huntsman (Fred), the whipper-in (Barry Hood), the Field Master (Terence Saffell), an ex-Master (Captain Bernard), and Louis Borrett who had travelled over one hundred miles to hunt. Geoffrey Ingram-Smith accompanied me to France and we motored to Dover, caught the ferry and then the train to Paris. Jean Bocquillon met us at the station and, on the way home, called at the kennels of the Marquis de Raule to show us his staghounds. On Monday we had an interesting day with Jean's hounds hunting roe deer, but the scent was very poor, the day being saved by an excellent dinner in the evening. The next day we were invited to hunt with Monique de Rothschild's boar hounds but unfortunately we had a blank day at the end of which we went into a village café for a meal. As we were looking at the menus, Mme de Rothschild asked us what we would like.

With a mischievous grin on his face, Jean said, 'As we have seen none yet today, perhaps a little pork?'

Madame grabbed his wrist and kicked his bottom all round the café, much to the amusement of Geoffrey and myself and the other customers.

I returned to England on Wednesday ready to hunt hounds on Thursday 16th February, the first time hounds had ever met at the Peasenhall Swan. This caused quite a stir in the village and there was a good crowd to see us move off. During the day we found our old friend, the hare we called Monty, but she was headed and took a different course from her usual run which spoiled the fun for me. On the following Saturday the meet was at Bruisyard Butcher's Arms at one o'clock to allow time for the 'bone' to come out of the ground. The first hare provided a good run through the marshes and low meadows, then crossed over Colston Hall to my home, Glebe Farm, where the line was lost. I blew my horn to summon Sheila to the door and she supplied us all with a quick noggin. We drew again and had a good run back towards the meet, crossing the grassland at Bruisyard Hall, where John Capon and Terence Saffell jumped a huge gate closely followed by Nick Saffell, aged about twelve years, on his pony, the rest of us choosing to decline.

We had a busy day after a lawn meet at Marlesford Hall and killed a well-hunted hare in the cart shed at Moat Farm, Parham. Years later, another hare saved her scut by jumping up into a cart in the same shed:

I would not have known about her if the owner, John Gray, had not come across her after we had gone. Why hares should choose to go into this particular shed is a mystery as they hardly ever enter a building.

Apart from one day spoiled by gale winds, good sport continued until the fateful meet at Framlingham College on 6th March, when I committed a terrible *faux pas*. I always followed the old tradition of meeting at twelve o'clock in March, but forgot to tell the Headmaster. It was one of the most embarrassing situations of my Mastership, as the Headmaster had assembled the whole school outside to watch the meet at eleven o'clock. We were never again invited to meet at the College.

The penultimate day of the season was held on a Wednesday as the Stallion Show at Newmarket was the next day. It therefore coincided with my birthday. The meet was rather riotous with most people in the pub well before eleven o'clock. There was plenty of singing and merry-making and the atmosphere was made very special for me as both Ernie Nunn, the old Kennel Huntsman, and Captain Bernard, my old Master, was there. When we eventually came out of the pub at twelve-thirty, I was confronted by Major Cleeve from Eye who had been mounted since eleven-thirty and was looking very cross indeed. The Major never came into the pub at meets and usually just rode around until we came out, occasionally rapping on the window which his whip.

'Good morning, Major,' I said cheerfully. 'I'm sorry we are rather late, but it is my birthday.'

'Oh is it Master?' he replied, very frostily. 'I'm glad you only have one a year.'

After a fair day's sport I drew for home at three o'clock and the party continued in the evening at the Hare and Hounds in Framlingham with over fifteen members present. Two days later we had our last day on 10th March: the meet was at Braiseworth Hall, Tannington, and, in very heavy rain, we had a fairly good day covering a lot of country. A hunt dinner at Scole Inn officially ended the season.

We had hunted on sixty three days with one day lost through wet and three through snow and frost. This proved to be a record, although I tried very hard to beat it, I never managed again to hunt on sixty-three days in one season. Since my first nervous day with the drag, I had now hunted hounds one hundred and ninety eight times.

I had just finished a tremendously good season and things were going really well for the Easton Harriers. I had put a lot of time and effort into trying to improve farmer relations and this was at last beginning to pay dividends. The great improvement was due to the good offices of Terence Saffell as Field Master, and the fact that I always knew whose farm I was on and could remember and respect the individual farmer's wishes. In my efforts at winning back farmers' support, I never lost sight of how fortunate I was to be my father's son.

The social life of the hunt was excellent with lots of private dinner parties and hunt dinners. The hunt dinners were of two varieties: ones that I organised in advance by telephone and, far more often, others that were on the spur of the moment. The latter were usually for the last people left in the pub after hunting and, as these late stayers were inevitably the most fun, these impromptu dinners could be uproarious. The organised dinners were held at Framlingham Crown and, as I always insisted on one long table, numbers were restricted to thirty-three and places were in great demand. I had to work out a formula so that all members would be invited on a rota system. Since it was the performers, people who would sing, recite or tell a joke, who made the atmosphere so very special, they were invited to every dinner, with the other members in turn, which roughly worked out to be alternate dinners. I had a large book with the members' names and telephone numbers down the side and columns headed with the date of each dinner, and I would put a tick or cross in each square according to their answer. This personal record proved very useful to me as the great demand for an invitation sometimes caused some bitterness from those who thought they were discriminated against. With the book, I could just look up their name and tell them when they had been last invited or whether they had declined an invitation, and soothe their ruffled feathers. There was very little unrest amongst the members during my Mastership, apart from the pecking order for dinner invitations. I deliberately did not choose a larger venue for the dinners as I felt that, if it were too large, it would spoil the atmosphere.

The hunt dinners were always held on a Thursday night after hunting and the atmosphere was wonderful as the adrenaline would still be flowing after a good day's sport. There was one slight drawback for me personally as the lorry came to collect my fat pigs on a Friday morning at four in the morning and the dinners often went on until one o'clock but the loss of sleep was nothing compared with the fun we had. The spirit was such within the hunt that I have known all the guests stay at the table for two hours after the last drink was served at midnight. Often the only way to end the dinners was for me to sing the very sad song, *The Place Where The Old Horse Died*, which was miserable enough to dampen even the highest spirit.

We were such good customers at the Crown Hotel in Framlingham that the manager would not let the bedrooms above the dining room when he knew there was going to be a hunt dinner. One dinner, before he learnt to leave the rooms empty, I went out of the dining room to find three couples sitting on the stairs looking into the dining room through an internal window. I apologised to them for keeping them awake but they waved the apology aside, declaring that they were thoroughly enjoying themselves and had never seen anything like it.

1967–68

We started to walk out the young hounds on couples on 11th March, the morning after the last day's hunting of the 1966–67 season, and all 10½ couple were going off couples by 29th March, which was incredibly quick as it usually took three to four times longer than this. Although Fred was not keen on showing he had the hounds looking at their finest for Peterborough but with the usual small success. Banish[67] was third in the unentered bitch class and Banish[67] and her sister Bashful[67] were third in the couples' class. The long distance courtship between my French friend, Jean Bocquillon, and Sheila's friend Christine Dickinson, culminated in their marriage during the summer of 1967 and Sheila was delighted that Christine asked if she could be married from our home at Glebe Farm, Badingham. The service was at Badingham church with the French guests forming a guard of honour with their trompes, as the bride and groom walked down the path to the horse and landau that I had provided to take them to Framlingham Crown Hotel for the reception. As the landau drew up to the door the French hunting guests blew their trompes and,

Showing at Peterborough

as the haunting sound echoed throughout the town, every shop and even the bank emptied as customers and staff alike hurried onto the Market Hill to find the source of this evocative music.

The first meet of the season 1967–68 was on Thursday, 14th September in sugar beet at Tannington

at six o'clock with only myself, Fred, and the amateur whipper-in, Geoffrey Ingram-Smith. No matter how early the meet, Geoffrey was always there which was highly commendable as he came fifteen miles or so from Bromeswell, and even more commendable on the part of his wife, Monica, who would have been up very early to give the horse his breakfast.

The early morning meets went off splendidly, all the young hounds entered and were going well in time for the Opening Meet. Before that day came I had moved from Glebe Farm, our home for eight years, to Tannington Hall. Ill health caused Colonel Gooch to sell the Hall and my father bought it and offered to rent the house and farm buildings to me. I inspected the buildings and found that, with extensive repairs and alterations, I would be able to keep four times as many pigs as I presently had at Badingham. With the sale of Glebe Farm, I would be able to capitalise the venture, so I agreed a rent with my father and we moved into Tannington Hall on 12th October 1967. Our furniture from Glebe Farm looked ridiculously sparse in the large house but it was adequate until we could add to it.

The £900 rise in the guarantee had eased the crippling financial burden but I was still putting far more of my own money into the hunt than I could afford. Time, of course, is also money and I was devoting more time to hunt affairs than I could spare and this had to be made up by working the early mornings and after tea. Many is the time I have done repairs in the dark with a tilley lantern or weighed pigs in the evening, but I felt I was carrying out the duties and responsibilities of the Mastership as well as I possibly could. There were more than enough good horses that could really do their job and Fred and myself could always be up with hounds. Good grooms ensured that the horses were beautifully turned out for every meet as well as being superbly fit. Fred and myself were always immaculately turned out in white Bedford-cord breeches and properly valeted green coats, all tailor-made by Bernard Weatherall in London. We both had two green coats, with the oldest one being used for early mornings and very wet days. Our leather boots were made to measure by Lobbs or, latterly, Charles

Smith of Northampton. Hats were made by Locks of St James although I did have a hunt servant who asked if his could be made by Patey.

The hounds I had bred were now in their third season and approaching peak performance. The pack was going better than ever and I was really at one with them. I never lied to them so they trusted me implicitly whenever I helped them. If I doubled the horn they would fly to me, every hound coming to me as eagerly as if they were hunting a strong scent, and if I capped them on they would sweep forward under my cap, confident of finding the line there. I would also cap them on to encourage them to take the line over a bad scenting field and, however faint or catchy the scent, they would persevere as long as I had the cap in my hand. My special favourite, Tangle, the foxhound bitch, was outstanding. Often she could hunt when all the others could not and she would fresh find a hunted hare time and time again. On one occasion hounds had checked after a good run and cast themselves to no avail but Tangle, who had not cast herself with the others, was feathering along a line to one side. I left her to her own devices for a while and she painstakingly feathered along the line for a few more fields, her stern showing more excitement at times than others, but the other hounds just followed her, unable to help. I had a large mounted field behind me and the day was cold so reluctantly I decided that I ought to draw again. I blew for hounds and Tangle stopped her feathering, lifted her head to look at me and, without moving, just spoke to me twice, loudly, then resumed her feathering. As clear as day, she had said to me, 'Leave me alone, I know what I'm doing'. A few moments later, she fresh found her hare which they went on to catch.

Although the policy of breeding far more hounds than were needed and then drafting vigorously was a very expensive one because of the high cost of vaccinations, it was also proving to be very successful as the hounds that were retained were first-class in their work and were also uniform in size and conformation. Moreover, the quality of their work was in general appreciated by the field as, although we all thoroughly enjoyed the meets and the camaraderie that went with them, once we moved off the hunting was taken very seriously and pure venery was the order of the day.

The Opening Meet was on Thursday, 2nd November, and a large mounted field gathered on the Market Hill to receive the traditional stirrup cup, provided by the Crown Hotel. The scent was very good and an excellent day was had by all. The best run took us past Oakenhill Hall, crossing over the River Alde, up and over Colston Hall, turning just short of Glebe Farm, from which I had so recently moved and ended up just behind the White Horse Inn. The run was very fast. All ditches were taken at a canter and a stile on an uphill bank had to be jumped to gain access to Colston Hall land. About half the field managed this jump and were well-pleased with themselves as it was quite formidable.

Fred, my kennel huntsman, was unable to be at Worlingworth Swan on Saturday 4th November, so I fetched hounds from Easton, and Jimmy Fitzroy whipped into me. The day was completely scentless with high winds and heavy rain so, after one and a half hours, we returned to The Swan, very cold and soaking wet. One of the members came up to me with a twinkle in his eye and asked if we were wet and cold enough to deserve brandy and ginger? I said I thought we were and our spirits were soon restored with much merry making and singing. Crawford Stopher, a jack-of-all-trades who often did casual work for me, very wisely offered to take hounds back to Easton which left me to enjoy the party. The camaraderie amongst the members of the Easton Harriers was such that they could turn even a cold, wet, scentless day to advantage and end up going home very happy.

The heavy rain continued for several days causing the cancellation of the next meet so it was a week later when we were next able to hunt at Laxfield. Still we were unlucky because there was a blue haze which always means poor scent and we had no good hunts but there were abundant hares which always obliged by crossing the meadows at Laxfield House. This meant that the field had ample opportunities to jump gates and post and rails, which was some compensation for the lack of a good run.

On Saturday 11th November hounds met at Tannington Horseshoes, which was now my local since our move to the Hall a month earlier. This meet was memorable for the first hare which jumped up in the middle of hounds and ran over their backs to get away. She made for some ploughed land but hit the first furrow at top speed, flew five feet up into the air, then dropped motionless to the ground, having presumably broken her neck. I felt very sorry for her as she deserved to get away after that miraculous start. Hounds met at Wilby Swan on Thursday 16th November, and with a fair scent we had a really good day. At one point Major Cleeve attempted to follow me over a gate but his horse did not rise at all and he broke the gate in half. Mary Calver had invited us all into the Old Rectory for tea, which turned out to be steak and kidney pie and we all went home in high spirits. This would not have been the case had we known that it was to be our last day for three months, owing to an outbreak of foot and mouth disease.

As if this bad news was not bad enough, much worse was to come. The increased guarantee which had eased my financial troubles was proving very difficult for the hunt to raise and Jimmy Fitzroy, who had been a member for five seasons and occasionally whipped-in to me when needed, warned me that Barry Hood had been saying that I was making a profit from running the hunt from the guarantee of £2,400, and that he would take over the Mastership with a guarantee of £1,200. I remembered Judith Bull's stern warning about letting Barry whip in as 'his sort would always let you down'. How I wished I had listened to those wise words but now the harm had been done and it was too late. Five committee members met Barry at an unofficial meeting and I felt I should have to resign but, fearful of over-reacting, I confirmed this with Captain Bernard, Chairman and experienced ex-Master, before the next Committee Meeting on 28th November. At this meeting the issue of selling Pound Cottage was discussed but John Moyle, the Honorary Secretary, said that the decision should be postponed until after a special meeting had been called to discuss the question of the guarantee. I felt this was my opportunity to resign and took it. If Barry thought that this cleared the way for him to take on the Mastership, he could not have been more wrong as the angry feeling against him for having caused this unpleasant trouble was so strong that he would never have been considered for the Mastership. It was agreed that the next meeting be held on 11th December at the Crown & Anchor in Framlingham at eight o'clock. I wrote my official letter of resignation with great sadness and also gave Fred Hargreaves notice that his employment with me would end on 30th April.

The outbreak of foot and mouth disease meant there would be no hunting in the foreseeable future so I decided to 'let hounds down' and went back to the summer routine of walking out every morning. It was usual for us to go into the round house for coffee after walking out and Fred would occasionally ask me if I really meant to give up. He was sure I would change my mind. I always gave him the same answer, that I had no choice and could not reconsider.

I deliberately did not attend the meeting on 11th December but according to the minutes:

> 'A letter from Mr. Harvey resigning
> the Mastership as from the 1st May 1968
> was read. Mr Moyle said that the total
> liquid resources of the Hunt amounted to approximately £1500, and there was a further £1200 to pay the Master before the end of this Season. The most optimistic forecast of income for the next Season would not permit a guarantee of more than £1600. It was proposed by Miss Leman and seconded by Mr. Hood that the guarantee for next Season be fixed at £1600. It was proposed by Mr Kingston Smith seconded by Major Clay and carried that Mr Harvey should be asked whether he would be prepared to carry on next Season with a guarantee of £1600, either by himself or with a joint Master or Masters, hunting two days a week and keeping fourteen couple of hounds in kennel. If he declined an advertisement for a Master or Masters to be put in Horse & Hound. It was suggested by Mr Capon that next Season we should Hunt on Mondays and Thursdays and Thursdays and Saturdays in alternate weeks. The question of Pound Cottage was to be left in abeyance for the time being. Mr Capon informed the meeting that the Hunt Ball had been fixed for the 22nd February 1968 at the Orwell Hotel, Felixstowe. It was decided to hold a further committee meeting on the 1st Monday in February.'

As Barry Hood had been proposing to take on the Mastership at £1,200, I am sure he was very pleased to second the proposal of £1,600. I was also interested to see that the committee thought it possible to run a hunt with only 14 couples of hounds. I took it as a great compliment that it was the two most senior members of the committee who proposed and seconded that I should be asked to carry on, even though they must have known that I could not.

I attended the next committee meeting on 9th February at The Conservative Club in Framlingham and there were seventeen committee members present. An application for sole Mastership had been received from the Hon. James Fitzroy, and for Joint Mastership from Mr Terence Saffell and Mr Ian Finch. I knew beforehand about both applications as they had all first checked to make sure that I would not change my mind. The applicants were interviewed in turn by the committee and in both cases they stated that it was their intention to ask my present kennel huntsman to stay on as huntsman. When the last applicant had left the room, the Chairman explained the procedure and that a secret vote would be taken. The applicants were called back into the room and Jimmy Fitzroy was told that the committee would recommend to a general meeting that he be appointed as Master, with a guarantee of £1,600. The general meeting held on 26th February accepted the committee's recommendation and Jimmy was officially appointed as Master to take over on lst May 1968. Jimmy was, according to my father's theory, ideally suited to the position as he actually did have his living 'come by post' and, without the burden of having to earn a living, he would have ample time for the many duties of Mastership. Jimmy was bred to be a sporting gentleman as his father, Lord Southampton, had been a Master of Foxhounds, as had many of his forebears.

Hunting resumed after a lapse of three months on 10th February with hounds meeting at Shrublands Farm, Badingham. This farm was on the opposite side of the road to Glebe Farm, which I had recently vacated and was owned by Robert and Ann Hawes. Ann was an enthusiastic follower of the Easton and always ready to help out in an emergency. An unusual day followed with very heavy-going and an excellent scent. I viewed the first hare away from Badingham Old Hall, quietly laid hounds on the line and they settled and just flew. I was never within a field of them and the Field Master and members were a field or so behind me. Hounds ran at this pace for about forty minutes then had their first serious check on the field where I had first seen her stealing away. I saw a hare moving slowly on the far side of the field and mistakenly thought it to be the hunted hare. I cast the hounds very quietly and slowly in that direction and they hit off the line and again were so fast that I had a job to keep them in sight. I had thought that the horses might have lost a little of their fitness and had my two girl grooms, Sally and Denise, following on the road with second horses. Never have I made a better decision than that, and when hounds caught this second hare, Fred Hargreaves and I changed onto our second horses, using the 'huntsman's change'. With our very tired and blown horses on their way home, we drew again and, for the third time, I was able to lay them on the line of a hare I had seen go away. We were very glad of our fresh horses as hounds continued to run at this breakneck pace, the hares having to cover a lot of country as they had little time to double. After having no hunting for three months, the field were reluctant to give up and stretched back for a mile or so behind hounds, the horses in varying degrees of tiredness and many reduced to a walk. Many were no doubt hoping that hounds would turn and they would again be in the thick of the action. The day was unusual in three respects: first, that my kennel huntsman and I had second horses: second, that hounds had hunted all day and had never once seen a hare: and third, that hounds had not been excitable and inclined to over-run as I had expected after such a long break.

This brilliant day emphasised how deplorable my situation was and I could not bear to think of being parted from these first-class hounds. The day had proved that my breeding policy, although very expensive, was right and I had a pack of hounds that was second to none. They went brilliantly for me and, more often, completely unaided. Out of a deep depression at the thought of having to give up such hounds came an idea. Could I re-start the Dunston Harriers and take some of my hounds with me? I immediately found an old copy of Baily's Hunting Directory and looked up who was chairman of the Dunston at the time they disbanded. I made contact with him and was asked to lunch to discuss the proposal. I made it clear to him that I had five adequate horses and could easily bring enough good and steady hounds to form the nucleus of a new pack. I left his lunch table with the assurance that he would call together the old committee and discuss the proposal. The news spread very quickly and the Easton's Master-elect, Jimmy Fitzroy, went to the Chairman, Captain Bernard, and asked him to stop me taking any hounds to the Dunston, as he feared I would take all the best ones. Captain Bernard immediately contacted me and said that he had told Jimmy that he was confident I would not do anything to harm the Easton and, in any case, he could not alter what was in the Mastership agreement. I had 36½ couple in kennel and my Mastership agreement with the Easton stated that I must leave a minimum of 14 couple in kennel at the end of my term of office. In no circumstances would I have left them with so few hounds but I could nevertheless take with me a balanced draft of hounds of all ages which would be an excellent foundation for a new pack. I was on tenterhooks for a few weeks while waiting to hear from the former Dunston Chairman as to the result of the meeting but while they decided to reform the Dunston they appointed Robert Bothway to be the Master. I was bitterly disappointed but I could understand their reasoning as Robert's father, Henry, had been Master and huntsman of the old Norwich Staghounds and, after that, the Norfolk and Suffolk Foxhounds, and when I got over my initial disappointment I contacted

Robert to ask if he would like a draft of hounds which he readily accepted. This again brought some anxiety from Jimmy but I assured him I would leave him with a good balanced pack of all ages, free from all faults, level and all suitable to breed from. I drafted 3 couple to the Dunston, which I was later to have the pleasure of seeing in the field, and 8½ couple of small ones to the Clifton Foot Harriers, the last ones going on 28th April, two days before my Mastership ended, and also lent them Sapper as a stallion hound. Very reluctantly I decided that the French cross hounds should be put down. They were a joy to listen to with their lovely deep voices but they were still temperamental, shy and difficult to handle. I left the new Master with a balanced pack of 20½ couple of first-class hounds.

After that brilliant day at Badingham there were only eleven more days to the end of the season. These eleven days were all very good with the meet at Stradbroke Hempsheaf on 22nd February proving to be another outstanding day. It began with an exceptional hunt of an hour and ten minutes which showed every aspect of hare-hunting it its best and I was so thrilled with it that I kept the pate for myself and presented pads to Captain Bernard, Major Cleeve, Ernie Calver, and Hugh Clay. I cannot remember why but I had no whipper-in for the meet at Framlingham Hare and Hounds on 24th February but, with Philip Underwood visiting from the Suffolk Foxhounds, I was put to the test to show good sport. Everything went like clockwork, including taking hounds over the Market Hill on a Saturday, market day, and we had a grand day with lots of fun. Otley White Hart on Monday 26th February provided another good

Herbert Breese's Golden Meet

day and just as I wanted to go home a hare, probably a travelling Jack, jumped up and it was forty minutes later before anyone could get near enough to hounds to stop them.

A very special meet was the Golden Meet of Herbert Breese, who had been a member of the Easton for fifty seasons, at his local pub, the Saxtead Volunteer, on 29th February. The news of this special meet travelled far and wide and many of his old friends were there,

including Henry Bothway, whose carted staghounds had often turned off at Church Farm after meeting at the Volunteer. The *East Anglian Daily Times* sent a reporter and a photographer to record the event and a large photograph appeared in the paper in the following day. As to be expected, there was a great party at the meet, which had been advertised for a quarter to eleven to allow more time for 'partifying'. There were a great many characters I had not seen for years and the atmosphere was electric. Through the window I saw Miss Wolton standing outside and as I knew she would love to hear the songs I went outside and invited her in. At first she was horrified at the thought saying that she had never been in a public house but, when I told her there were lots of other ladies in there and that I was going to sing some hunting songs, she weakened and I was able to persuade her to stand just inside the door.

I sang *Drink Puppy Drink* first as it was Herbert's favourite, followed by *The Ballad of the Easton Harriers* which was a song I had written myself. Later on I sang another well-known old favourite, *The Holcombe Song*, the tune of which I had borrowed for *The Ballad of the Easton Harriers*. The choruses were sung with such gusto that it could have lifted the roof off the pub. Last of all I sang a song which I had specially written for the occasion and which encompassed stories from Herbert and about Herbert himself. Some of the verses had taken me several weeks to write as it involved a long and complicated story. Herbert and his father were riding one day and called at the Dennington Queen for a drink. A man in the pub remarked about a tremendous leap that Herbert's father had taken a few days before whilst out hunting with the Easton Harriers and Herbert's father remarked that the horse had ploughed half an acre of land in the morning before it went hunting. It would have been one of a pair of horses on the plough and an acre was considered to be a good day's work. There must have been enough scepticism shown to anger Mr Breese and prompt him to make this open wager to anyone in the pub who wished to take him up, a bet for £10 that the mare would plough half an acre, be at the meet at one o'clock and then to follow in the huntsman's footsteps wherever he went for the rest of the day, then be put into a cart and driven for ten miles in under an hour. She must have been an outstanding mare because the bet had the effect of silencing any 'doubting Thomas' as no one dared to take up the wager. When I did eventually get all the relevant information into a verse I was very pleased with myself.

We eventually moved off at a quarter past twelve after one and a half hours of the best camaraderie one could imagine, even with the Easton Harriers. There was a French visitor, Jean Carnois, and goodness knows what he thought if this was his first experience of an English meet. The scent was fairly good and just right for our French visitor to see hounds working at their best. Afterwards he told me how much he had enjoyed the venery and how impressed he was with the way that my hounds persevered on a difficult scent. We had been one hound light for about an hour when I decided to blow for home and I hoped the missing hound, Tassle, would pitch up at the meet. The landlord, John Keeble, was looking through the window indicating for us to go round to the back door of the pub. This always happened as no landlord ever asked for an extension to be open after two o'clock when we returned even though the subterfuge was a complete nonsense. Any policeman would know exactly where we were as all the lorries and trailers had their ramps up with the horses inside and no one to be seen. We had a marvellous relationship with the police who never troubled us and we, in turn, never caused them any problems. However, the effect of creeping in through the back door, which often meant through the kitchen of the pub, created an immediate atmosphere of naughty schoolboys and every drink tasted all the better for it. Pubs in Suffolk did not provide food in those days but we were so hungry that we persuaded John to give us some bread and cheese. This quickly disappeared and I asked if there was anything else and he went away and came back with a turkey carcass which he unceremoniously dumped on the counter. 'There you are together, 'haps you'll be satisfied when you've eat me out of house and hoom!' When we left the pub I was so exhilarated that I challenged Jean Carnois to jump for the honour of France. John Keeble kept geese and to keep them out of his backyard he had puts sheets of galvanised iron across as a barrier. We both, of course, were in our leather hunting boots but set off and cleared the sheets of tin so the honour of

both our countries was upheld, amidst great cheers and clapping from the others.

Tassle was still not back so I asked Fred Hargreaves if he would look for her that night as I had the dinner to go to. The special dinner for the Golden Meet was held at Wickham Market White Hart with many of Herbert's old friends present. I made a speech in honour of the occasion and was then asked to sing the Golden Meet song again. The whole evening was delightful and passed far too quickly. During the evening I telephoned the kennels to be told that Fred had been unable to find Tassle so next morning I returned to the meet just before daybreak and set off to walk over the draw. I walked and called and blew my horn and eventually came across her dead in a snare. She was a daughter of my wonderful bitch Tangle. I put her across my back and carried her to the road near White House Farm, Dennington, then fetched my pick-up and came back to collect her. What a sad ending to what had been such an unforgettable day. The landowner was, and is, a very good sportsman, and had been at the meet the day before. He was very upset when he heard of the incident and said that he always shut up his snares when we were in the area. The difficulty had arisen because we had run well out of our draw and he was not expecting us.

When I next saw Miss Wolton, the lady I had persuaded to go into the pub for the first time, she was very excited and said how much she had enjoyed herself. She was a daughter of Plant Wolton who had been a tenant of the Duke of Hamilton at Grove Farm, Easton, a regular follower of the Hamilton Harriers, forerunner of the Easton, and somewhat of a favourite of the Duchess. Miss Wolton told me that, as he could not afford to mount all his children, he would show no favouritism so none of them followed hounds on horseback. She had been passionately fond of hunting all of her life and now in her mid-sixties would follow the Easton on her lovely old 'sit up and beg' bicycle with laces in the rear mudguards to keep ladies dresses clear of the spokes. Miss Wolton astounded John Graham when she met him with his bloodhound-cross French hounds, as she stopped her bicycle and hopped off to enquire if they were Dumfriesshire Foxhounds. John was speechless that this little spinster lady, living in Tannington, would have ever heard of the Dumfriesshire Foxhounds but the Duke of Hamilton had estates in Scotland and she had gone up there to work as a governess in her young days and used to follow the Dumfriesshire Foxhounds. The Dumfriesshire is a unique pack, bred by the Buchanan-Jardine family for generations, based on the first cross French/Bloodhound, thus the similarity in looks that she recognised. It was small wonder that she was reluctant to venture into the pub as she told me that, in her young days, even when there was a lawn meet, the men all went into the dining room and the ladies into the drawing room and they did not mix while they enjoyed their pre-hunting drinks.

There is another little tale which involves Miss Wolton. Colin Plumbe and I had been friends since I first met him when I went for the first time to hunt in the Lake District and he was the amateur whipper-in to the Windermere Harriers. He has come down to Suffolk and stayed with me every year since and always presents a silver coaster with the hunt button engraved on it, the set to be held by the Master as long as he is in office. He always came to church with me and I would go early as I had my church warden's duties to attend to. On one such Sunday, whilst I was lighting the candles on the altar, the next person to arrive was Miss Wolton who went into great detail about a wonderful hunt she had witnessed from her bicycle and how sharp the hounds had turned at such-and-such a double. Colin was listening in amazement as this prototype Victorian spinster extolled the virtues of the Easton. She had just finished her story when Canon Donnan walked in and I re-introduced Colin to him, 'Oh yes', he said, 'you are a hunting friend of Tony's aren't you? I would dearly love to hunt but I am afraid I would fall off the jumps, but I do send my girl groom out and I follow by car.' The next one to arrive was Mr Davy from Wood Farm, Tannington, who straight away asked me where hounds were the day before, for he could clearly hear them as he stood in his garden. We worked out that they would have been about three to three and a half miles away at that time. It pleased me no end that he should have, unwittingly, have praised the good cry of my hounds in front of Colin. We came out of church and went directly to Brundish Crown for a pre-lunch drink. Colin's wife, Tizza, was doing the horses from yesterday's hunting so she wasn't able to join us but a few hunting people came in and Colin remarked how lovely it was to be in Suffolk again amongst real, country people and went on to tell them how impressed he was with the pro-hunting congregation in the church.

The next day's hunting after the Golden Meet was expected to be rather an anti-climax. The meet was at Dennington Queen on 2nd March and it was bright sunshine and very dry and the scent was predictably poor. After trying to hunt on Dennington Hall land I decided it would be a much better idea to stop for a 'lunch break'. We were not very far from Dennington Bell so we went there and, of course, had a few rounds of drinks whilst eating all their picked eggs, crisps, chocolate, nuts, cheese biscuits and whatever else they had. The sun had gone in and I thought it time to draw again. My hounds had the same thought as, although they had stayed quietly by me outside the pub, they now began to bay. Two brilliant hunts followed the 'lunch break' with the scent now quite good and it was very late when I blew for home. During the last hunt I lamed my horse and borrowed Terence Saffell's to finish the day, Marion Saffell kindly volunteering to walk mine back to the meet.

Our French visitor, Jean Carnois joined us again on 4th March at Easton White Horse, a picture postcard setting for a meet. There was no scent at all on the plough but the hounds could scream along the low meadows and marshes. Twice the hare swam the River Deben and each time I thought I would lose hounds as it was a long way round but both times she was kind to me and swam back over to my side. I had 18½ couple out and the cry was just out of this world. I was delighted to think that the Frenchman was witnessing all of this. We gave a dinner party at Tannington Hall that night in his honour with Rosie Spragg to partner him, and Terence and Marion Saffell, Jimmy and Nona Shand, Geoffrey and Monica Ingram-Smith, and Geoffrey and Julie Hennessy.

The penultimate meet was at Kenton Crown but it was spoiled by gale force winds. I did try to hunt but it was hopeless and we finished after an hour or so. The next day was 8th March which was my thirty-first birthday and Sheila gave me a party at Tannington Hall. During the evening I had an

S. Calver, Marion Safell, Gordon Grover, Jeffrey and Gill Bowden

unexpected presentation, a lovely surprise and all the more special as it was from the Hennessy family thanking me for all the fun they had had with the Easton Harriers. Geoffrey, standing beside his lovely wife, made a most eloquent speech before giving me the Munnings print which has hung above my bedside table ever since.

Saturday 9th March was my last day hunting hounds and the meet was at Debenham Cherry Tree. The atmosphere in the pub was not quite the same as usual and we moved off more or less on time and drew a ley on Winston Hall. This farm was always a good place to find a hare and we found straight away but after a few fields found ourselves in a field where it seemed there were more hares than hounds. After getting hounds together again, I drew in a different place and we had several more little hunts, which gave the field lots of galloping through the lovely meadows at Winston Hall. There were no good hunts but sport was much better than the average end of season March day. We put the hounds and horses away and, as I was walking towards the pub, I met Ernie Calver. I pulled my horn out of my coat and held it out to him saying, 'You take this as I shall never need it again.' I had hunted hounds 219 times.

This had been a dreadful season, one that I would not wish on my worst enemy. The worst part was my enforced resignation bringing with it all the heartache of knowing that I would be parted from the hounds. This was closely followed by the foot and mouth outbreak that stopped hunting for three months and had the effect of making matters much worse for me. Walking out with hounds every day from the kennels gave me more time to reflect and intensified my happiness.

I finished the season on a much brighter note with four days' hunting in France staying with my great mentor, George Lamiot. Before my arrival he had telephoned some Masters to arrange my hunting schedule and he later told me that the Comte Jacques de Flandres had changed the date of his meet to accommodate my visit. I felt both embarrassed and highly honoured at this great compliment. My first day was with his hounds, the Equipage du Rochard, and the meet was in the Forêt de Breteuil. I rode a horse called Ouistit lent to me by my host. The scent was as poor as one could expect for 19th March but hounds persevered and, after a long and difficult check in the middle, went on to kill their buck at the Rond d'Aumote, after a hunt of 2¾ hours. The next day was with the staghounds, the Equipage Normand Picardie, who met in the Forêt de Bord Louviers. Again, my

host lent me a horse, an old black trotter which was mostly ridden by George's son, Jean Lamiot. The day started well for me as I was honoured by being asked to be present at the 'Rapport' when the harbourer tells the Master and prominent members his knowledge of the age and location of various deer. I could not understand much of what was said, except for the hunting terms. The rest of the day went very badly. The Master was in a terrible temper, the whipper-in was continually flogging hounds, and even the local blacksmith was on foot with a whip. One member was so ignorant that he told me, in all seriousness, that at least ten stags were needed for a good days' sport. I was thoroughly disgusted with all I saw and was glad when home was blown but the day ended on a better note with Jean Lamiot's sister and her husband, taking us to dinner at the Restaurant de St. Hubert. I ate frogs legs for the first time and thoroughly enjoyed them.

The next morning, after an early start and a long drive, I was privileged to hunt again with the Picardie Valois and the meet was in the Forêt de Compiègne at the Points de Roi. I now considered the Master, Jean Bocquillon, a very good friend and he showed that this feeling was mutual first by again lending me his good horse, and secondly by inviting me to ride up with him as he hunted hounds. I was very impressed by his ability to hunt hounds and their love for him and how much they wanted to please him. I had never seen the like before and the combination of them hunting independently, far from him, and the handiness with which he could cast them, left a lasting impression on my mind. It was twenty-five to thirty years later when I again saw this expertise, but this time in the United Kingdom. To see a huntsman in the field with this skill can turn a moderate day into pure joy just by watching a gifted huntsman make his art look so easy. Unfortunately, I tried to be too clever and, getting lost, went back to the meet and then followed with George Lamiot in his car. At a very difficult check, the hounds caught sight of the Forester (harbourer) and they ran up to him in full cry. Jean later explained to me that the hounds always associate the Forester with a find. He was very cross and scolded them and they hung down their sterns and looked very ashamed. It had been a great treat to see a first class huntsman with his hounds so full of life and happiness and just longing to please him.

Two days later I was with Jean again and he lent me the same horse. It was a very poor day as we drew for 3½ hours and did not find. We had been drawing in the Forêt St Laurent and the people who owned the forest gave a dinner that night. Sometimes a day that starts off badly will just continue that way and the whole excellent dinner was completely ruined by the local mayor who never stopped talking and butted in to everyone's conversation. The last day of our visit was Sunday 24th March, and Jean, Christine, Sheila, and myself all went to church at Chantilly, before having lunch with Jean's parents. After lunch we visited the National Stud at Compiègne.

CHAPTER 4

NOT MASTER: SEASONS 1968–71

1968–9

After my return to England the next official hunting fixture was the Peterborough Hound Show in July and, although I was no longer Master, I still attended because all the hounds shown were bred by me. The only success we had was with Progress[66] who was second in the entered bitch class and third in the brood bitch class. I did not feel at all disappointed as the entered bitch class is the most difficult to win, so to come second is very rewarding.

The summer of 1968 seemed very strange as for five years I had been accustomed to going to the kennels every day. When my term of Mastership was drawing to a close, I ought to have put down dear old Tangle as she was too old to do another season but I just could not contemplate such a thing. Instead of doing my painful duty, I decided to break the rules of hunting and bring her to Tannington for her old age. I asked the new Master, Jimmy Fitzroy, if he would keep her in the pack for the summer and this he agreed to do. I could hardly wait for the corn to be cut so I would be able to start hunting with my private pack of one hound. I fetched her from the kennels on 5th September 1969 and put her in her kennel with only my old lurcher dog to keep her company. Most hounds who have been in a pack environment all their life would not have settled down, but she did so without any apparent pining for the other hounds.

The first two times I hunted her were very unsuccessful as there was a blue haze and scent was predictably poor, but on the third outing we had a great hunt with Tangle working out some doubles in fine style. The next day Sheila brought her poodle along to help draw and we had another good hunt. I was too busy to take her out again for a few days but then decided to try her in the dark and drove around the stubbles until my lights picked up a hare. I let her out and laid her on the line. She hunted this hare for an hour and twenty minutes with no help from me. I caught her up and returned to where I had left the van and as I drove home I noticed the smoke from the cottage fires was coming out of the chimney and straight down to the road, a sure sign of a very good scent.

I was so excited about this great hunt that I wanted to go again the next evening but it had rained heavily all day so I would be unable to drive on the stubble as my van did not have four-wheel drive. I decided to try to ride and rang Ernie Calver to come with me. We rode our horses to the field and Sheila brought Tangle down in the van. We soon found and had an hour and a half with conditions so black we could hardly see each other unless we were almost touching. The old bitch's voice kept us in touch with her and, luckily, the hare did not go far out but kept circling around the two hundred acre field. I began to get very worried about stopping her but at last I caught sight of her, leapt off and grabbed her, and led her to the lane but I decided it was far too dangerous to take her home by road, so shut her up in a farm building. We walked our horses homeward up the lane, discussing what fun it had been and how stupid we were to be out on such a pitch-black night. Tangle took strong exception to being abandoned in a farm shed and set up howling in the most dismal, wolf-like fashion. The lane was only tarred as far as the farm buildings so we were somewhat surprised to hear a car coming towards us. When it had passed us we looked back and saw the silhouette of a couple sitting very close together with his arm around her. Tangle stopped howling when she heard the car so all was quiet when the car stopped and the lights went out but, after a few minutes, the old bitch started up again. The car leaped into life and roared back up the lane past us. Again we could see the silhouette but this time the occupants were far apart! We laughed and thought that love-making would not be on the agenda that night. The poor couple must have been terrified as it was a god-forsaken ghostly cry and we could still hear her when we got off our horses outside the Hall, a good two miles from where we had left her. We returned in the van to collect her and that ended an unforgettable night.

One afternoon my eldest daughter Bridget, who was then seven, asked if she could come with me and watch Tangle hunt. I did not think she would be able to keep up so I decided to try to hunt with Tangle on a long lunge line but it was not successful as she refused to speak when on the lunge. I had to let her loose but Bridget held my hand and we managed to keep up with her. It was the most perfect way for a child to learn about hunting as there were no distractions and she had the opportunity to ask me first-hand what was happening.

'Why is Tangle making that funny noise, Daddy?'

'Well, it is to tell me that she can smell where the hare has gone.'

'Why has she stopped making that noise?'

'It's because she can't smell the hare any more and she's not sure where it's gone.'

'So is that the end of the hunt?'

'No, I don't think so, watch how she is going in all different directions. She is smelling in all the places where she thinks the hare may have gone.'

'Oh Daddy, she's found which way it went 'cos she's making that noise again.'

Gradually the terminology improved until she was using the correct words, like 'Tangle is speaking', or 'in full cry', casting, checks, and so on. She soon became terribly interested in how the hares confused Tangle and why they kept twisting and turning. Some lucky sightings of a hare doing some sharp turns and then watching to see Tangle overrun a little and cast back to regain the line, all helped to teach her about hunting.

One day when Tangle had been hunting for half an hour or so, a hare came into the same field as us and Bridget asked if it was the one that Tangle was hunting. I replied that I thought it probably was but I was not sure and we must keep our eyes on it. The hare ran along the side of the field into the corner, then stopped and sat up.

'Why is she doing that, Daddy?'

'Well, I think she's the hunted hare and she's listening to hear how far Tangle is behind.'

'Oh Daddy, look! She's going back the same way as she came.'

'Keep your eyes on her, Bridget. Watch her very closely.'

The hare ran back on her line for about a hundred yards or so, then sprang into the ditch.

'Why did she do that, Daddy?'

'Well, it is all part of her plan to confuse Tangle and to put her off the scent.'

Tangle then appeared and slowly hunted the line along the edge of the field until she passed the place where the hare had sprung into the ditch but, after about twenty yards, she stopped.

'Why has she stopped, Daddy? The line went right up to the corner.'

'Tangle is very clever and knows that, because the scent is suddenly much stronger, it means that the hare has doubled back.'

The old bitch cast herself out into the field, in classic style, but as she had not found the line, she went along the headland grass and found the spot where the hare had landed, and hunted on.

'Now Bridget, I must explain to you that you have just seen the most beautiful part of a hare-hunt. It is called 'cutting the double'. Usually, only old hounds are clever enough to do this and it means that they realise that the scent is twice as strong because the hare has doubled back. If there had been younger hounds with Tangle they would have hunted on right into the corner because they had not yet learned to recognise the double scent. It usually takes about five seasons for them to learn and some never do learn.'

Eventually Bridget understood how the line could be moved by the wind and spoiled by muck or sprays. Having her with me gave me tremendous pleasure, especially as she grasped the real points of venery so quickly

Various people would come out with me. Nona and Jimmy Shand on one occasion, and Herbert and Alfred Breese on another. One of the most remarkable hunts with Tangle was when Geoffrey and Julie Hennessy came with me and she hunted a hare all around Tannington, covering almost all of the parish, including through my parents' garden. We followed this hunt in my guests' Land Rover until finally we stopped her near the Horseshoes pub and went back to the Hall for a supper of Shepherd's Pie, kindly brought by my guests.

The longest hunt I ever had with Tangle was with Jimmy Fitzroy, the new Master. Usually I just wanted an hour or so before supper or the pub but on this occasion there was no time restriction and Jimmy was as keen as me. The hunting was slow but fascinating and we let the old bitch hunt on and on for hours until at one point, when she was taking the line within twenty yards or so of the van, she just stopped hunting, looked across at the van, and walked slowly to it. The door of the van had somehow been left open and when we got there we found her sitting on the front seat. She had hunted herself to a standstill.

During this first summer at Tannington Hall, I had decided to renew all the plumbing in the piggeries and to bring a fresh supply to each building in a trench thirty inches deep to avoid freezing in bad winters. I did all the plumbing myself and consequently was in a trench connecting up lengths of pipe when I had an important visitor. I looked up to see a pair of highly-polished brown boots and leggings and instantly knew that it was Major Hugh Clay, my vet and one of the hunt secretaries, who was standing beside the trench.

I was rather taken aback and must have looked surprised as he said, 'I'm sorry to arrive unexpectedly but I would like a few words with you.' I climbed out of the trench and he came directly to the point and asked me if I would take on the Mastership of the hounds again. I pointed out that they already had a Master who was contracted until the following May and he explained that the senior members of the committee were becoming very anxious about whether the new Master was up to the job in hand and had sufficient decorum to carry it through. In short, he had been asked to approach me to see if I would take on the hounds again and, if I agreed, they would call a committee meeting and propose a vote of no confidence in the new Master. He told me that he had been authorised to offer the original guarantee of £2,400 and they would find the money from somewhere. My immediate thought was that Jimmy Fitzroy had been a true friend and I said that I could not accept the proposal as it would be like stabbing him in the back. Hugh asked me if I was sure that I would not reconsider. I said that my answer was final, Hugh left, and I dropped back into my trench.

It was an unsettled summer for the Easton Harriers as there were two further matters of unrest. The least important was the hunting days and those who favoured hunting on Wednesday and Saturday decided that, with a new Master, this was the time to try for a change. A General Meeting was called for 12th August 1968 at the Conservative Club in Framlingham to discuss the matter and the voting was ten in favour of Wednesday/Saturday and fourteen in favour of Thursday/Saturday, so the hunting days stayed as they were. Much more serious was the question of who was to hunt hounds and whether Fred Hargreaves was to be the huntsman or not. When the new Master had taken office he had said he would like to retain Fred to hunt hounds and Fred was, of course, delighted as it is every kennel huntsman's dream to graduate eventually to the position of huntsman. Jimmy Fitzroy had subsequently decided that *he* would like to hunt hounds himself, not appreciating that a Master's agreement with a hunt servant is binding and should not be altered for the duration of that season. Fred was justifiably upset and set about enlisting all the support he could get. There were strong feelings amongst the members that the Master had seriously wronged him and an Extraordinary General Meeting was called to meet at the Conservative Club in Framlingham on 9th September to try to sort out the matter. Once the Master realised the seriousness of what he had done he immediately backed down and said that Fred could hunt hounds so the meeting seemed rather pointless but it did clear the air as rumours and counter rumours had been flying around. As Chairman, Captain Bernard was quite angry and told the meeting that the members should be loyal to their Master and if they had any complaints, these must be brought directly

to him. I witnessed all these matters first hand as ex-Masters are usually asked to serve on the committee.

Eventually the long summer passed and hunting at last began. When we had moved to Tannington Hall where there was plenty of stabling, I had asked Sheila if two girl grooms could live in. She agreed and they had their meals, two rooms in the house, and wages of £3 and £2 per week, respectively. With enormous breakfasts and dinners, they lived like lords and soon found they had put on a stone or two in weight. Even after I resigned the Mastership, I wanted to keep on these first class grooms, despite the extra work for my long-suffering wife. She agreed and, as I had not sold my best horses, I had plenty of horsepower and often lent horses to people who needed a mount. My first mounted day's hunting was with the Easton who met at Tannington Hall on 24th October 1968 at nine o'clock. Fred hunted hounds very well and we had a busy morning with one very good hunt to Dennington and back again.

On 26th October I went to the opening meet of the new Dunston Harriers given by the Master, Robert Bothway, at his home, The Poplars, Wreningham. There were ninety-six mounted and over two hundred on foot. I rode Stonebow and lent Paddy to John Parker, but it was to be a poor scenting day with blue haze hanging in the distance. Home was blown at four o'clock and the day ended with a hunting tea. During tea, the Master's father, Henry, insisted I go back to the Grange for a drink with him on the way home. I had thought it a great shame that the new Dunston had decided to wear red coats and Henry agreed with me and told me that he had offered to pay for new green coats. Hare hunting livery is traditionally green, except for rare and historical reasons, such as the Holcombe Harriers, who pleased King John so much that he said they were to wear his livery forever.

The Easton Opening Meet was on 7th November and we had a cracking good day with one embarrassing moment when I had occasion to sweep off my hat and apologise to my ex-kennel huntsman for being on the line. It was the cause of much merriment amongst the field as standing on the line with me, ex-Master and huntsman of the Easton, were Robert Bothway, current Master of the Dunston, and Desmond Longe, Chairman of the Waveney Harriers. I had brought three horses to the meet as I mounted Hugh Clay and Ann Hawes. The day ended with a lovely, intimate opening meet dance at Captain Bernard's home, By the Crossways, Kelsale.

I settled down to a pattern of hunting with the Dunston on Tuesdays and Saturdays and the Easton on Thursdays and I enjoyed good days with both packs. I had great pleasure in watching the Dunston hunt as I could see how my draft from the Easton compared with the hounds from other packs. They showed to their best advantage when the scent was poor. The Dunston huntsman was Ralph Baines who had been kennel huntsman to the Norfolk and Suffolk Foxhounds and, before that, the Norwich Staghounds. He adapted to hunting hare very well and would keep on the line of the hunted hare and often fresh found her. The subscription to the Dunston was £35 but I subscribed £100 and, partly because of this and partly as an ex-Master wearing a green coat, I was allowed the privilege of taking my own line and not having to stay behind the Field Master. This privilege was even greater as it was extended to include whomever I had taken with me and I often took a guest, mostly one of the fair sex, and often provided them with a horse.

Fred Hargreaves continued to show good sport with the Easton. The Christmas Eve meet at Wilby Swan was great fun, even though the Master was in a very bad mood. Alec Comins, who owned the hunting paradise otherwise known as Wilby Hall, actually came into the pub which was unheard of previously. The atmosphere was terrific, and culminated in me betting Chris Bigden a pound that he could not, successfully, jump a ditch sitting behind his saddle. I lost the bet.

Boxing Day proved to be eventful with one part very untypical of the Easton. I could not forgive Barry Hood for his part in causing my resignation and there was considerable hostility between us. Apparently, during the day, I had made a disparaging remark about his horse and he took great exception to this. As I was now free from responsibility I had accepted Herbert Breese's invitation to stop for half-time drinks and a light lunch at Church Farm, along with Sue Gooderham, Captain Marriott, Captain Bernard, and Ernie Calver. The 'light lunch' consisted mostly of whisky with a few of Herbert's special mince pies and went on for quite a time so we decided it was no good looking for hounds again and hacked back to the meet. I put my horse away in the trailer and then saw Barry Hood walking towards me with a full pint of beer. I momentarily thought that he had brought it as a peace offering, but as soon as he reached me he threw it in my face and tried to provoke me to fight. I have always kept well away from any fighting and certainly was not going to disgrace the name of the Easton by brawling on a village green in my hunt coat. He was so frustrated by my refusal to fight, that he grabbed the front of my coat and jerked three

buttons off, bringing little tufts of green material with them. After this I managed to get into my van and quickly reversed with him trying to open the door and as I drove off he went sprawling on the grass. During this rumpus, he had repeatedly said that he had an invitation to Herbert Breese's for tea. Why he kept saying this, I was not sure but I thought that if I went straight home, as I had intended, it would imply that I was afraid, so I changed my mind and returned to Church Farm. I found Herbert Breese still busily entertaining various people with mostly liquid tea and he was very pleased to see me back again so soon. I was singing a song when Barry walked in and his anger seemed to have burnt itself out. I soon went home feeling that I had made my point and joined Sheila in the last minute preparations for a dinner party and the day ended on a much more pleasant note.

Good sport continued and on 1st February hounds met at my local, Tannington Three Horseshoes, for the last time as the pub was soon to be closed. The day was memorable for two reasons: first, that it was my daughter Bridget's debut mounted in the hunting field on a pony called Midnight and, secondly, for an après chasse party which got rather out of hand. The first hunt took us in a huge circle and hounds killed near the meet. The second hunt took us across World's End Farm with good riding on grass and stubbles. The third run went past the meet and parallel to the road where I live. I was cantering along the roadside furrow, concentrating on the hound work and not thinking about my riding, but Paddy obviously had his mind on other things because, when we came to the gateway opposite to the drive down to the stables, he ducked out to go home. This caught me so much by surprise that I ended up shooting over his shoulder into the ditch bottom with Paddy disappearing towards the stable. No harm was done and we were soon re-united and finished the run, although my daughter thought it was capital fun that Daddy had fallen off. At half past one the Master declared that his horse was tired and the vet had said that it must have a short day, and he was going home. I rode Paddy back to the stables and drove my van up to the pub to dispense hospitality for the last time in my local. People drifted away until only a few were left and I was ready to buy another round and asked the Master what he would like.

He said he would like a pint of bitter but I was in a very naughty mood and said: 'You are a foreigner, from Yorkshire, and now you live in Suffolk, you ought to have a Suffolk drink, a John Turner'. This is a pint of mild beer reinforced with a shot of gin.

He agreed, and I bought a round for all four of us. The Master thought John Turners were very good and promptly bought another round and the other two followed suit. By the time we had had four each, we were past caring and all of us bought another round, while I was telling tales of the famous Tom Read who lived at Tannington Grange, just down the road. Mr Read's meets were renowned for his John Turners and the large lunch that he provided for the Hunt in the middle of the day.

This story led me to say that I had always wanted to emulate him and stop for lunch and then hunt again afterwards. This, in turn, naturally led us to try to persuade the Master to get hounds out and hunt again. He was showing token reluctance so another John Turner was quickly bought and he soon acquiesced. I said I would telephone for a fresh horse to be brought up but the redoubtable Stopher was in the pub and, as he was courting one of the grooms, he offered to take a message to the stables. Geoffrey Ingram-Smith mounted

John Finch and Ernie Calver

from the ramp and promptly fell off the other side and re-mounted amidst much laughter from the locals and us. When we were all mounted Stopher let out the hounds and we went into a nearby field to draw, found at once and had a sharp little run. The serious troubles began when hounds checked and I heard a yell from behind and turned to see Geoffrey sitting under his horse's neck holding the reins in his hands. The hounds hit off the line again and were away with the Master trotting, slowly, after them. Etiquette prevented me from overtaking him, but I was afraid of losing hounds, so I gave his horse a few flicks of my whip. One of these flicks missed the horse and touched the Master in the back. The Master then realised what I had been doing and flew into a temper and tried to hit me with his whip. This gave me a very good reason to forget about the etiquette and I kicked on and was soon with hounds. The Master, still very angry, gave chase but I had a fresh horse and his was spent so we were soon parted. When I got to hounds

they were checked and I looked back to see the Master lying over backwards trying to blow his horn, but it was mostly bubbles that were coming out.

The situation was in one way very funny but, at the time, it had the opposite effect on me and I became very worried about the likelihood of an accident and someone getting hurt. Another great concern was that if my father should come along and see us in this state as he was a strict teetotaller and he would not have been amused. With horror I realised that it was all my fault and I was responsible for this fiasco, so I spoke to Ernie Calver and asked him to push hounds on to me and I would take them home. The hounds, of course, still knew me and were willing to come with me so we managed to get them back to the Hall safely.

I jumped off my horse and, asking Ernie to hold it, walked into the stables to put the hounds into a loose box. As I was doing this, the Master came in and helped with the last few who were reluctant to be shut up. We walked back outside to see Ernie Calver sitting on the ground, holding the reins of all three horses. I knew that all of them were far too tight to drive home, so decided to ask Sheila to sober them up.

As we walked across to the Hall we were confronted by a very vicious swan that the former owners had left behind and we dodged around to keep out of its reach. The Master thought this was very funny.

'Surely you're not frightened of a swan,' he said and walked right up to it and took hold of it just below its head and lifted it up. It did not even flap. Apparently there is a nerve at the top of the neck which when nipped, totally immobilises the bird.

Still laughing at us he said, 'Watch, I can even ride it,' and he pretended to put it between his legs as he carried it to the moat.

Fred Hargreaves was very cross when he collected the hounds and, for some reason, immediately laid the blame on me.

'Really, sir. I thought you of all people would have known better. What a carry on. What a time on a Saturday night to have to turn out to collect hounds.

I didn't think you would do this to me, sir. You were always so considerate when I worked for you.'

I just could not think why he automatically laid the blame at my door.

I was fortunate that the meet at Southolt Plough coincided with my birthday on 8th March. This meet was always very special, with most of the farmers coming, often with their wives, and the atmosphere was convivial. The Master's lorry broke down so he and hounds were very late arriving. He had telephoned to say what had happened which immediately triggered off a singing session and it was quite late when hounds eventually arrived. The hunting was very good but I had a serious mishap when a bank gave way and my horse Stonebow fell on his back in a huge ditch. Luckily the ditch was so wide that he was able, with help, to get up but he had knocked off his chestnut and there was blood everywhere. I had taken Embassy for Captain Bernard to ride but he had chosen not to for some reason and Vickie Hayward-Lonsdale had ridden him at a moment's notice. This was very lucky for me, for she took Stonebow back to the meet and I finished the day on Embassy. The *après chasse* was so good so I did not get home until six o'clock.

The last day of the season was at Wilby Swan on 20th March and it was especially memorable as it was the last time that Fred Hargreaves would hunt hounds. Fred had made a very good job of hunting hounds but the Master had given notice of his intention to hunt hounds himself the following season so Fred had decided to hand in his resignation and was going to become the landlord of the Dennington Bell. I was very sad to see him leave hunt service as he was the archetypal hunt servant, having come up through the old hard school and had served under famous Masters and huntsmen. A collection was made for a testimonial to Fred and Mrs Hargreaves and, Fred having chosen a new saddle and Mrs Hargreaves a handbag, these were presented to them by Captain Bernard in a ceremony at the Bell on 6th August 1970.

The season ended with a dinner at Framlingham Crown and the hotel surprised us by producing a large gateau with a hunting scene on the top. Before it was cut it was carried round the table with due ceremony for all to admire. After the gateau there were jokes and songs by Ernie Calver and I, followed by Mary Calver who sang a very good song, which she had written herself.

Season 1969–70

Things started to go wrong from the start. I anticipated that the Master, Jimmy Fitzroy, would be an excellent man with hounds as he had been a successful gun dog trainer so I assumed that hounds would naturally take to him but it is simply a question of luck whether hounds take to you or not and Jimmy did not have the luck. No man could have tried harder than he did. He had a private income so had plenty of time to devote to hounds and he spent many hours with them in kennel, walking around the grass yard throwing cubes of cooked liver to them, but once outside the kennel gate they treated him like a stranger, and showed complete indifference as to whether they walked in the same direction as him. It was a terrible shame. He had advertised for a new kennel huntsmen and had selected a man called Dyer to succeed Fred Hargreaves. He moved into the famous round house on lst May 1969 but proved to be the opposite of his predecessor, rough and noisy, and most members considered him to be very uncouth. Moreover, he was a very hard man to hounds and used the whip to excess.

For the hounds, walking out with Dyer and the Master was the complete reverse of walking out with Fred and me. Just a few words from Fred were enough to correct any waywardness and they would always jump up and try to lick my face and frolic around us like lambs in the spring, but now they were with a bullying brute and a stranger as, despite spending many hours with them, the Master was unable to establish the vital rapport. They were really terrified of Dyer and I can remember seeing them, at the following Opening Meet, cringing up against the wall of The Crown Hotel, some climbing over others, as they tried to avoid the thong of his whip. The situation was made worse because neither the huntsman nor the whip knew the hounds' names properly. During his first season as Master, Jimmy should have learned the hounds' names from Fred, but he used to get an awful lot of them wrong and then told Dyer the wrong names. As they no longer loved their huntsman and were terrified of the whipper-in, it was not long before they began to get into the bad habits of their forebears in the 1950s and then the vicious circle began. It was only a few months before some hounds started to break away when on exercise and go off hunting by themselves. This behaviour is very contagious so the Master started to walk out only on the roads very close to Easton where there were thick clipped hedges, avoiding the temptation of open fields but restricting the amount of exercise and this only aggravated the problem. Last year's puppies, this year's young entry, were learning bad habits right from the start. Another development which was a bad omen for the future was that the Master decided to ride with Dyer as he went on his rounds picking up fallen stock. He thought that this would give him an opportunity to meet the farmers but it also gave opportunities for heavy drinking and Dyer and his Master would be seen holding each other's arms to steady themselves as they walked back to the flesh wagon.

The season started off with a long period of almost non-existent scent, the worst I have ever known. This was most unfortunate for a Master hunting hounds for the first time but there was nothing he could do except wait for better times to come. Scent returned on 13th November when hounds met at Laxfield Oak. Dyer was so noisy and rough with hounds at the meet that I found it extremely embarrassing and moved out of earshot. We eventually had some fairly good sport although Dyer managing to smash a set of rails at Laxfield House.

On 11th December hounds met at Rendham White Horse and we had a wonderful day with one particularly good hunt in a large circle and returning to the field where she was found but here a fresh hare intervened, thus spoiling the hunt. Chris Bigden won another one pound bet by jumping a ditch facing backwards. The Master was so thrilled with this, his first really good day, that he continued the celebrations long after we had left the meet, finishing up at the White Hart in Wickham Market. The landlord telephoned Mrs Fitzroy to ask her to collect him but when she arrived he refused to get into the car, saying that he had been in the open air all day, hunting his hounds, and would ride home on the top of it. Pam knew it was no good trying to reason with him so she agreed and set off to drive carefully down the A12 on her way home to Tunstall with Jimmy on the roof of the car, blowing his horn! Once off the main road, it would appear that she stopped being quite so careful and, at a sharp bend, Jimmy shot off the roof onto the roadside. Being a natural countryman, he recognised where he was and started to walk home by a short cut through the forest.

Après chasse amusements come in many guises and while the Master was enjoying his version, another Easton member had other ideas and had taken his girl friend into the forest. He thought he heard a hunting horn but put it down to imagination running riot after such a good day's hunting. Soon afterwards, he heard it again, much louder and clearer this time. He quickly disentangled himself from his girlfriend and started up the car thinking they should drive quickly

away. He switched on his lights and, to his horror, he saw his Master, horn in hand, stumbling along the forest rides towards them. Knowing that the Master was nearly home, he decided that discretion was the better part of valour, and quickly drove away and, as far as I know, the Master never knew whose lights had dazzled him in the forest.

Although this incident had its various amusing sides, there were many other such incidents of the Master boozing until late at night while still in his hunt coat which, by the time they had been repeated several times, were magnified enough to cause serious concern to the committee. I was again approached and asked if I would take on the hounds again, but again I declined. No one in the hunt knew how terribly hurt I had been when I resigned and I could not resume the Mastership while the rebels were still on the committee. The committee decided to advertise for a new Master but at a meeting held on 6th February at the Conservative Club, Framlingham, it was reported that the only application received was from Mr Fitzroy. The Master, knowing the depth of feeling against his kennel huntsman, had given an assurance in his application for re-election that Dyer would be replaced. The Chairman, realising that it would be a foregone conclusion that Mr Fitzroy would be re-elected, had called a special general meeting for half past eight on the same night, when members were told that the committee recommended that the Honourable James Fitzroy be re-appointed as Master at a guarantee of £2,000 a year. This proposal was carried and Jimmy Fitzroy was on course for his third season.

We had spent Christmas with Christine and Jean Bocquillon in France and had plenty of opportunity to hunt, so I missed some of the Easton season. Sheila's hunting had been interrupted for two years due to the arrival of our third daughter, Charlotte, in April 1969, but it was resumed on 15th January (1970) at the meet at Stradbroke White Hart. My diary briefly records 'that she went well'. Another laconic entry records that Dyer was not out at Eye White Lion on 22nd January because he had fallen into the sea. Gordon Grover had opened up this new draw for us in country around his farm at Yaxley and we had a fair day but on the way back to the meet at the end of the day the whole pack just left the Master and crossed several fields before they could be made to come back. Twice this happened and it grieved me terribly, as we were now back in the same state as the terrible times of the latter seasons of Captain Bernard and Ernie Nunn in the 1950s. Sue Gooderham opened up another new draw for the Easton around the Iken area and hounds met at her husband's pub, The Plough & Sail, at Snape, on 7th February. All the farmers came to the meet and it was a very pleasant change to have grass tracks to ride on in this light-soil part of the Easton country. I was going to lend my best horse Stonebow to Ken Duke from Iken Hall but he was, unfortunately, indisposed with influenza.

I had asked the Master if I could invite the Dunston Harriers for a meet at Tannington Hall and this was arranged for 12th February. It was freezing hard when I went to bed and snowing when I woke up but somehow I felt that we would be able to hunt and telephoned the reluctant Masters to persuade them to come. We had to wait for some time for the 'bone', i.e. frost, to go out of the ground which, of course, meant that a great party was soon in full swing. The meet was being recorded for a South African radio station and I hope they mentioned that this was not a typical one. The frost would not oblige

Mary Garton, Gill Bowden, Jeffrey Bowden, S. Calver, Rosie Spragg, Heather Prescott

but the bottles did and went their rounds. Songs were sung and jokes were told. Robert Bothway and Miles Stimpson were the visiting Masters and had brought most of the Dunston members with them. The dining room was packed and the atmosphere was magical. After two hours of partifying, I said that I thought it was fit to go. Robert Bothway agreed with me but Miles Stimpson made a formal declaration that he did not and left to go home. He was quite right as it was hardly fit to go but no one else was in a mood to care. Hounds were running well when we came to Fenton's Farm and into a large meadow with a neat, clipped hedge on the far side. As one, the field spread out and took it abreast but to my horror I saw there was wheat on the far side and by the time forty-odd horses had pulled up and turned back to the edge, the field was in a terrible mess. Ernie Calver fell off and hitched a ride, Gretna Green style, behind Gordon Grover and, although he was holding around Gordon's waist, he still couldn't balance and the end result was that he fell off again taking Gordon with him. Both were re-united with their horses and carried on hunting. Everyone came into the Hall afterwards where Sheila

had baked lots of bread rolls and made gallons of soups and this was eagerly consumed. People went home earlier than usual, as we were to meet later in the evening for a joint hunt dinner.

I had chosen Eye White Lion for the dinner as it would be easy for the Dunston members to find. Twelve from each hunt were invited and we all met promptly at half past seven. Dinner was not served until nine o'clock, followed by the usual singing and tales. The singing session was excellent with contributions from both hunts but an extraordinary thing happened that I shall never forget. We discovered later that Ernie Calver had been concussed but during the evening he sang five songs which were other people's songs to which he had never learnt the words, yet he sang them word perfect. It has continued to amaze me just how much our minds store of which we are completely unaware. The Dunston reciprocated by inviting the Easton to meet at Tivetshall Station on 3rd March. We were all ushered upstairs into the clubroom where the Dunston dispensed unlimited hospitality to their guests. The hunting was moderate with hardly any scent due to a strong March wind and a light covering of snow. Chris Bigden provided the only excitement of the day when he went to jump a wide ditch, well filled with water. Unfortunately, the bank gave way as he took off and his horse was almost completely submerged and he himself up to his waist. Both hunts met in the evening at the Park Hotel in Diss for a dinner dance which was highly successful with good support from both hunts.

Sue and George Gooderham, Sue Clough, and Mary and Ernie Calver joined Sheila and I for our annual pilgrimage to the Lake District. We enjoyed the Windermere Harriers dinner dance on the Friday night and the joint meet of the Windermere Harriers and the Blackcombe Beagles on the Saturday. This joint meet was always great fun, with the harriers sometimes mixing well with the beagles and sometimes not. Following hunting, the tea and singing was always held in a large room upstairs at the Pennington Arms in Ravenglass, where a huge pan of 'tatie pot' would be bubbling on the stove. I replied to the toast to the visitors and we were reluctant to leave but we had dinner booked early at the Skelwith Bridge Hotel, followed by a singing session at the Britannia Inn. My diary notes that Friday night concluded at four o'clock and Saturday night at three o'clock, so as usual we made our way home on Sunday deliriously happy but very tired.

The Easton had their last meet at Peasenhall Swan on 19th March where hunting was better than could be expected for an end of season day. This season saw the loss of two long-standing, and highly-respected, committee members: Mrs Judith Bull, who had been Vice Chairman, and John Moyle, who had been Honorary Secretary for nineteen years and had carried a heavy load during the years when there was no Master.

I organised an End-of-Season dinner at Framlingham Crown which turned out to be the best so far because of the number of people spontaneously getting up to contribute to the enjoyment of the evening. The atmosphere was so good that no one left the table until two o'clock. The manager later told me that he had seen his residents, sitting on the stairs 'goggle-eyed and unable to speak' as they watched and listened through the internal window. He also told me that his auditors had queried the account for that evening, as the drink bill was two-thirds more than the cost of the meal.

Season 1970–71

The Master selected Bernard Needham as his new kennel huntsman and he and his wife Isobel moved into the round house on 1st May 1970. Bernard was a very different type to Dyer, very professional, and whenever I saw him during the summer I was impressed with the quiet way he handled hounds. Jimmy Fitzroy had been re-appointed as Master with a revised guarantee of £2,000 and this extra money had to be raised. At a committee meeting I said that, if we left things as they were, there would be a serious deficit in the accounts presented at next year's AGM and proposed doubling the subscription from £25 to £50. After discussion, this was adopted. The AGM was held at the Conservative Club, Framlingham, on 2nd October and accepted the committee's recommendation for the new level of subscriptions, which were: members £50, family £75, farmers £40, farmer family £60, 16–21 £20, under 16s £1. Hunting days were again discussed and it was decided by fourteen votes to nine to continue hunting on Mondays and Thursdays. The Master reported that he thought it had been a good season with very few days lost through bad weather and that he had bred six couple of puppies.

The season started on 23rd September with a meet at Valley Farm, Ubbeston, at nine o'clock, a much later hour than usual. There was a fairly good scent, although it was sunny and hot. Bernard Needham whipped-in very professionally and my first impressions of him were confirmed. Three days later hounds met at Thickthorn Farm, Horham, which was owned by John Capon who was the new secretary for meets. The Master was at his worst, doing far too much holloaing and cheering, and had his hounds heads up all morning. Bernard Needham looked on in dismay and appeared so down-hearted I felt he was about to cry. The Opening Meet was on 29th October with approximately thirty people mounted and a good crowd on the Market Hill. The hunting was moderate and following was almost impossible as all the draw was drilled with winter wheat. The highlight of the day was the dance at Captain Bernard's home during the evening. This was run by the Supporters Club and was supposed to be for members only and limited to eighty people but there were, in fact, over a hundred people.

On 19th November, hounds met at Laxfield Royal Oak and really good hunting followed, mostly around Laxfield House where our enjoyment was increased by all the grass and jumpable gates. Everyone arrived in high spirits for a hunt dinner during the evening at Framlingham Crown. Mary and Ernie Calver started off the singing followed by Geoffrey Hennessy, my wife Sheila, Peter Sillars, Judith Hale and, of course, myself. I was still hunting two days a week with the Dunston and having great sport with hare hunting at its best. One day in particular was very eventful when a hare entered a market garden with hounds close behind. The owner shot the hare but not before hounds had made a real mess of his neat garden. It was one of those days when I was very pleased not to be Master.

The Easton Master did a 'Lord Scamperdale' on us at Eye on 3rd December and slipped quietly out of the pub and moved off before any of us had realised. Riding out of Eye we could hear hounds before we could see them and it was one of those good scenting days when hounds just flew. By half past two every horse had had enough and 'Home' was blown early. This suited me as I was to go to an evening bloodstock sale at Newmarket. I was intending to produce quality hunters by crossing Cleveland Bay mares with a throroughbred stallion and returned home with one called Double Bleep.

The hunting was poor and hares difficult to find when we next met at Worlingworth Swan. Yvonne Sharpe came with me and rode Sheila's little mare Lucy. There was not the usual party afterwards with only one song from Arthur Cornish and this was spoiled as his false teeth kept falling down. The next night, the Sharpes, Hennessys, Shands, and Bigdens, joined us at the Dunston Harriers' Hunt Ball in the Norwood Rooms in Norwich. At this same ball, a year earlier, we had our first introduction to a discothèque but it had been very gentle and sweet with a Mickey Mouse film showing on the ceiling. This year's shocking modern disco was more like the present day and I took each of the ladies in our party into the disco to experience this musical revolution, although another reason may have been the two delectable girls, one black and one white, dancing in the middle of the room, each on her own pedestal.

The next morning's hunting was very exciting but the best part, for me, was that during a conversation with the Waveney Harriers' Chairman, Desmond Longe, he promised to include me in his spring visit to the staghounds on Exmoor. I took Ernie Calver to hunt with the Suffolk Foxhounds on 22nd December. He was featured on television that night drinking his glass of port and that was about the most exciting part of an uneventful day as we stood outside a covert for two hours, followed by ten minutes of hunting.

The Easton's Christmas Eve meet was at Southolt Plough with the usual good meet and mishaps to follow. Graham Croll managed to get submerged in one ditch and although soaked, he hunted on until both he and Chris Bigden landed in another deep ditch at the same time. Quite a few of us dined that night at Framlingham Crown followed by a singing session in the Hare and Hounds. Boxing Day was very peaceful with a huge crowd and I again stopped for lunch with Herbert Breese at Church Farm where I enjoyed his beef, which had been hung for a month, served with homemade horseradish. Like a model husband I went home early as we had the in-laws coming for dinner.

After Christmas we flew to France, taking Ernie and Mary Calver with us. Although there was a frost we managed to hunt on the first day amidst incredibly beautiful scenery, with black and white hounds looking particularly impressive against a light covering of snow. The hunt dinner was in a restaurant in the forest with the steak being cooked over an open fire on a grid. Spontaneous dancing followed with us all still in our hunt coats with boots and spurs. More snow

fell overnight which prevented any more hunting as there is a French law that prohibits hunting when the quarry's tracks can be clearly seen in the snow on the grounds of sportsmanship. As there was no hunting I was roped in to judge a local pony club show on one day and on another, we visited the Musée de Chasse in Paris. There were grand dinner parties each evening with roast wild boar and venison and all the excitement of French cooking. Ernie had been thrilled with the hunting on the first day and both he and Mary were absolutely loving the social side. To see them enjoying themselves as much as Sheila and I had on our first visits gave me the idea to invite the members of Jean Bocquillon's pack, the Picardie Valois, to England to hunt with the Easton Harriers in the hope that the invitation might be reciprocated. Before this came to fruition, I was away again as on Sunday 24th January Stanley Tompkins and I drove up to Lancashire with two horses each to hunt with the north-western harrier packs. Little did I think that this trip was the first of many 'hunting jollies' by which I would eventually hunt with every pack in Great Britain.

My first Easton meet after our return from France was at Earl Soham Falcon and the Master managed to upset the notorious Whiting brothers from Stonewall Farm who had never allowed the Easton permission to hunt on their land. I had shown Jimmy where their land was and how to avoid it but he just deliberately rode out on a clover ley saying 'What difference does it make when he won't have us anyway'. One of the Whitings went home and fetched his gun and shot the hunted hare, then started to walk towards Jimmy. This had the desired effect and the Master suddenly fully understood the situation. No one realised the significance of a visitor from the Blankney Foxhounds when hounds met at Rendham White Horse on 11th February although my diary records with two exclamation marks that the Master went straight home after hunting. The Easton Point-to-Point races were two days later with four horses running in the Members' Race. Geoffrey Ingram-Smith won with Tony Gower's horses second and third and Graham Croll failing to finish having parted from his horse at the open ditch. In the Master's tent after the racing had finished, Jimmy Fitzroy told Captain Bernard that he was resigning to take on the Mastership of the Blankney Foxhounds and the significance of the visitor at Rendham, who had come to watch him in the field, was revealed. The Master's immediate departure after hunting was either because he wanted to make a good impression or because the visitor was going to Jimmy's home for further discussions. It was rather bad form to give his resignation after the traditional date of 1st February as it left the Easton with little time to find a new Master.

At this time I was serving on the committee of the Masters of Harriers and Beagles Association and early in the week following Jimmy's resignation I travelled up to London to attend a committee meeting at the Cavalry Club. Captain Bernard was also on the committee and, as a past Chairman of the Association, still held considerable sway. During pre-lunch drinks he gathered a bevy of the great and the good around me and, in front of all these senior Masters, he beseeched me to take on the Easton Harriers once again. Before I could answer, he went on along the lines of that 'in life one sometimes has to put one's personal feelings behind one and think of the common good.' Under such pressure, and in such august company, I gave in and said that I would.

An Easton Harriers' committee meeting was held at the Conservative Club in Framlingham on 19th February 1971 and the Master's untimely resignation was discussed. It was generally thought that, at such short notice, the best plan of action would be to try to find an Acting Master. Major Hugh Clay interrupted these thoughts by proposing that I should be asked to take on the Mastership at a guarantee of £2,400, the figure at the time I resigned, but I declined the proposal at this figure. There was more discussion during which Chris Bigden and Graham Croll both offered to guarantee the bank account for a sum of £200 each and, after these assurances, I was offered a guarantee of £2,600 which I accepted. The entry in my diary reads simply: *'19th Feb, Con Club. I took on the Mastership (very reluctantly).'*

On the following Monday the meet was at Saxtead Volunteer and, after a very good hunt, the hare was lost in my parents' garden at Braiseworth Hall. The gardener later told me that she had entered the moat and hidden in some rushes. We were able to hunt at Kelsale on 1st March, although there was a long snowstorm. I was delighted when my daughter Bridget squared-up to a her first really thick 'bullfinch' hedge and crashed through, albeit that she was nearly dragged off her pony by the thorns. The day ended with tea at Captain Bernard's home, By the Crossways, Kelsale. His teas were notorious whether after hunting or at the puppy shows which used to be held there when he was Master. There would be plenty to eat but the main point of interest was the huge breakfast cups, many of them with two handles. The Captain was a splendid host and continually went round pouring

whisky into the tea. It was great fun for me because, as I graduated from being a member to a amateur whip, I had a larger cup until, as Master, he would insist that I had the largest of all.

The meet at Brundish Crown on Thursday 4th March 1971 was cancelled due to frost but I managed to get a partial day's hunting the next day with the Dunston from the meet at Burston Crown. They were hunting on a Friday because of Point-to-Pointing on the Saturday but conditions were so bad I am surprised they met at all. By one o'clock the 'bone' had not gone out of the ground and the Master and huntsman wanted to go home but I persuaded them to wait a little longer as I wanted to sing them a song which I had written for the occasion of their Tramps Ball in Wreningham Village Hall but had not been able to sing then. When I eventually managed to make the premiere, Robert Bothway, the Dunston Master, followed suit and sang another. This triggered off a party and the poor landlady brought out every piece of food she had in the pub. This was such a departure from the norm as the Dunston meets were normally staid and rather formal in comparison with the Easton. We finally moved off at three o'clock and had a wonderful hunt, fresh finding our hare twice and eventually killed her after a hunt of over an hour. I arrived home deliriously happy at six o'clock and, after a quick bath, went to dinner at Framlingham Crown to make arrangements for the End of Season hunt dinner.

Desmond Longe, chairman of the Waveney, was as good as his word and had made arrangements for me to hunt with the staghounds on Exmoor. I travelled down on 25th March with two horses and Rita, my young sister-in-law, to groom for me. I hunted with two stag packs, the Devon & Somerset, and the Quantock, three packs of foxhounds, and the Minehead Harriers. I was quite amazed at the rugged terrain and how the hunt staff and followers rode down hills which seemed impossibly steep to me. Although both of my horses had had a busy season and were very fit, they both, in turn, were so stiff after their first day on the steep hills, that they could hardly move and I needed to chase them up the road with my whip to get them loosened up.

Although I had been reluctant to take on the Easton Mastership again, once committed I was keen to make a start and I preferred not to have to wait until after 1st May to begin breeding the next year's entry so I asked Jimmy Fitzroy's permission to discuss an early start to the breeding programme with his kennel huntsman and permission was readily given. I had for some time been thinking that the Easton hounds were a little light on 'cry' and I wanted to try to breed more cry and, if possible, more depth into their voices. I had discussed this with John Loy, Master of the Rockwood Harriers, whom I had come to know well through meeting regularly at Peterborough Hound Show. He was of a similar mind to me as we both valued good venery above all other aspects of hunting. Consequently, on the way home from our annual pilgrimage to the Lake District, this time with the Shands, Tompkins, and Calvers, we called at the Rockwood kennels at Blacker Farm, Emley, near Huddersfield in Yorkshire to select a stallion hound. After close inspection of the doghounds available, I settled on one called Pickwick and said I would collect him in the near future. Following a general meeting on 17th March which officially accepted me as Master, I drove back to Yorkshire the next day to collect Pickwick, returning the same afternoon to attend the End of Season dinner which went off with the usual gusto. I also brought home another stallion hound called Landlord whom I used on a few bitches with good results but his one drawback was that he was very quarrelsome in kennels. I had no hesitation in keeping on Bernard Needham as I had always liked what I had seen of his work and was sure we could work well together. His name was added to my wages book on 1st May 1971 and his wages set so that he had £15 a week clear after deducting his National Insurance stamp. The two girl grooms each had £5 per week 'all found'. Thus my responsibilities had begun again and my carefree days were over for many seasons to come.

CHAPTER 5

SECOND MASTERSHIP 1971–5

I had taken the hounds on for my second term of Mastership on the understanding that I would hunt hounds and this meant that I resumed walking out on a daily basis during the summer. It alarmed me to see just how wild the hounds had become, not quite so bad as the terrible days of the Fifties, but bad enough to present a very serious problem. Bernard Needham was a good hound man and we managed to walk out by the usual tactic of keeping on roads with thick hedges on each side until we came to a meadow near Letheringham Water Mill, where we could allow them a little freedom. It was very upsetting for me to find just how bad a state the hounds were in, the wild staring eyes consistently looking for a means of escape. I was very grateful that Bernard had done one season with the previous Master and knew just how bad they were. I dread to think what it would have been like if I had started with a new kennel huntsman.

I had only been away from hounds for three seasons so all hounds of four seasons or more already knew me and it was not surprising that it was with these older hounds that I first managed to regain some rapport but I was taken aback, and slightly ashamed, when I realised that I had forgotten their names. After walking out for a few weeks and getting more used to each individual hound, some names were beginning to come back to me, but often they were not the same as Bernard was using. There was one bitch in particular who I thought was Pickle but Bernard called her something else. I would walk alongside her and say, 'Pickle, Pickle,' but there was no response. I discussed this predicament with Bernard and suggested that I ask Fred Hargreaves, my old kennel huntsman, to walk out with us, as he would be more likely to remember their names as he was with them one more season after I resigned. On his retirement, Fred had become the landlord of the Dennington Bell so it was no hardship for me to go and see him.

His first reaction was very negative. 'Oh no, sir. I won't interfere in another man's work. It wouldn't be right.'

I said: 'Fred, you're talking nonsense. It's not Needham's fault if his Master taught him the wrong names. And anyway, you owe it to me to help me start off right.'

After a few more half-hearted refusals, he gave in and agreed to help. As we walked along with hounds, I said, 'What's the name of the bitch in front of you?'

'Pickle,' he said, and the bitch immediately looked round and waved her stern. I think it must have been his Yorkshire accent and the particular way that he pronounced the word Pickle that made the bitch respond. Fred walked out a few more times and we sorted out all the wrong names but more problems arose when we studied the last two season's breeding as, by using the wrong names, they had unwittingly bred dogs and bitches that were far too closely related.

As the months went by I gradually built up a better relationship with the hounds and we could walk out further afield, until towards the end of August, I felt confident enough to go on hound exercise using bicycles. Most of the hounds had lost the wildness and had relaxed into that playful, happy, loving relationship that I so desired in a pack that I was going to handle in the field. There were still a few that would have been away across the stubble but, with the combination of Bernard's expertise and the fact that I would peddle as fast as I could past open, tempting spaces, we managed to complete hound exercise without any mishaps.

I had decided to keep all the horses at Tannington Hall and employed two girl grooms. Rita, my wife's little sister, had left school and she and Milly Griffiths lived in the Hall and made an excellent job of turning out six hunters.

The first early morning was at the Hall on Thursday, 16th September, at six o'clock. I drew a large sugar beet

Bernard Needham

Photograph kindly loaned by John Finch

field that held several leverets which would not leave the beet and, remarkably, the hounds kept together for most of the time. It was an early morning with special interest for me as not only had I the young entry to watch but also the stallion hound that I had borrowed from the Rockwood. I had so trusted John Loy's word regarding the hunting ability of Pickwick that I had used him on seven of my Easton bitches. To use an unproven stallion hound on so many bitches was at best a gamble, and at worst utter foolishness, but this first early morning proved that my gamble had paid off as Pickwick, as well as having a lovely deep voice, was also outstandingly good in his work although a little independent. In general, conditions were unfavourable for scent as it had not rained for over a month but, nevertheless, hounds could hunt as long as the dew remained on the leaves of the sugar beet. My daughter Bridget was unable to enjoy any long runs as the leverets turned in very small circles in the beet which meant it was a case of sitting still and watching.

We hunted three times a week, always in sugar beet, but had some excitement on Tuesday 28th September when a strong hare went out of the beet and across to Oak Farm, Worlingworth, through the churchyard and the rectory garden before coming away to Wood Farm where we lost the line. I was very pleased to think that I had a sporting rector in Bill Donnan and he would have been delighted to

Michaelmas Goose Dinner: from left to right, JAH, John Graham, John Capon, Geoffrey Ingram-Smith, Chris Bigden, and Ernie Calver

hear hounds running through his garden. We were almost an hour before finding a hare on 4th October. This was not surprising as this sugar beet field had been drawn on eight earlier occasions. When we did find, it was an old hare which circled the beet for sometime until her line was lost. I decided it was time to go home and came out onto the road when the thing I had been dreading happened. Hounds just left me and flashed across a stubble. Bernard had quite a job to stop them but managed to do so before they put up a hare. I was very disappointed that this had happened as, although they had been breaking away from Jimmy Fitzroy for the past two seasons, I had hoped that this bad behaviour was now behind them.

I can only assume that they were still excited after the good hunt in the beet and just could not resist it. I do not think they ever did it again and it was very, very fortunate that they did not put up a hare as it could have become an ongoing and worsening problem until it was as bad as the terrible times in the 1950s.

On 11th October we met at Tannington Hall for the last early morning in sugar beet but it did not turn out that way at all. The first hare took us out of the beet to Tannington Lodge across Fenton's Farm to Dennington Lodge, where she was caught. In the field was an American friend of Sue Gooderham from the Bentwaters air base and, when hounds killed, Sue told me that Bud would like to be blooded. I did so and later, when he had enjoyed one of Sheila's hunt breakfasts, he made a speech to thank me very much for the 'rabbit's foot'. It had become an annual tradition for me to hold a Michaelmas Goose Dinner on the old date, i.e. 11th October, which I believe only East Anglia still recognises. I had invited nine guests, all self-employed men: Jimmy Shand, Peter Sillars, Geoffrey Ingram-Smith, John Capon, Terence Saffell, Chris Bigden, Ernie Calver, Graham Croll, and Bill Wilson. We had seven courses of soup, sole, goose, pudding, Scotch woodcock, cheese, and fruit. During the evening the ten of us managed to consume with ease two bottles of whisky, one gin, one sherry, two Chablis, three claret, three champagne and two port. When I had finished recording these details in my diary, I was moved to conclude with '. . . and a perfect wife for a cook!' A hunt breakfast and a seven-course dinner on the same day is quite a feat for any lady to achieve.

The morning at Thickthorn Farm on 14th October, was absolutely scentless and the only bright moment was watching Stanley Tompkins jump the river in fine style at a fast canter. I was late arriving at the meet on 21st October at Great Lodge, Framlingham: this had never happened before and it brought bad luck as Graham Croll's horse died under him. The carcass went to the kennels, where it was found that its lungs had haemorrhaged. This same night a special hunt dinner had been planned to say goodbye to Mr & Mrs

Magoni who had been managing the Framlingham Crown Hotel for some time and had been especially supportive of the Easton Harriers. The atmosphere was not as good as usual, owing to Graham losing his horse, but I did propose a toast to the Magonis and, later in the evening, another to Rozzie Mackman and Peter Theobald who were to be married on the following Saturday, when I had the pleasure of driving them to the church in a Victoria. Problems arose at Poplar Farm, Cretingham, on 25th October when a senior member of the hunt led a group of children along the edge of some wheat and the owner, Mr Lindeman, became quite upset. I went to see him afterwards and he was demanding compensation but I left him with the understanding that he would ring me again just before harvest when we could ascertain the amount of damage. Fortunately, I did not hear from him again.

Forty-five horses assembled on the Market Hill, Framlingham, on 4th November for the Opening Meet and it was a reasonably good day. John Capon and myself had spent most of the Sunday before putting up some hunt jumps at Oakenhill Hall. The hares obliged and ran in the right directions so we were able to jump them several times. The day ended with the traditional Opening Meet Dance at Captain Bernard's home with about one hundred people present. It was as good as ever with that special atmosphere that By The Crossways always generated. Two days later at Charsfield hares proved very difficult to find and, when found, ran immediately to the fields of blackcurrants which had the effect of stopping hounds dead in their tracks as the smell of blackcurrants is so strong that it immediately kills any scent. I blew for home at half past three as I was thinking about the excellent tea that was waiting for us at Pear Tree Farm where the Hennessy family entertained us so well for so many years.

John Parker from Wingfield brought a large party of children to the meet at Debach Post on 8th November, but the day was spoiled when Terence Saffell's old horse Rudy died under Barbara Buller. There were so many hares at the Worlingworth Swan meet on 11th November that the day was ruined, in complete contrast to two days later at Henley Cross Keys when we had a blank day. Torrential rain soon soaked us all at Laxfield on 18th November, but no one cared as hounds just flew and we crossed a lot of country around Laxfield House and across to Brundish Crown. Hot toddies in the King's Head soon warmed us up and we all went home in high spirits, especially the Master.

At the Clopton Crown meet on 22nd November I was delighted to see an Irish Catholic priest sitting on his horse outside the pub. I was told he was Father O'Leary from Bentwaters airfield and tried to persuade him to come into the pub but he refused that and the offer of a drink. I particularly noticed his breeches, which were black and had little covered buttons close together from the knee to the ankle. At that time Charsfield still had some thick bullfinches and hounds were running beautifully when I came to one that was particularly thick. I knew that the ditch was wide and deep on the other side and rode up and down this hedge looking for a place where it would be possible to break through. With this delay, hounds were getting out of earshot and, in desperation, I burst through with a terrible crashing, tearing sound, and landed safely on the other side, to find the good Father sitting quietly on his grey cob. I was in some agitation and when the Father pointed across country, I took off in that direction. I reached the top of a small incline and thought I just caught sight of a hound disappearing in the distance. I galloped to the spot where I last saw it and still could not see or hear hounds, so stopped my blowing horse and listened. The field came up in ones and twos, according to how good their horses were, all having enjoyed a fabulous gallop and some dismounted to give their horses a rest while we listened.

The good Father was the last to arrive on his puffing cob and immediately rode up to me to say, 'I'm thinking I made a terrible mistake. I pointed in the direction that your hare had gone. Your hounds were in the opposite direction!'

I was soon re-united with my hounds but the story gathered much in the telling and was a huge joke for many a season.

Colin and Tizza Plumbe arrived on 24th November for their annual visit. Tizza had brought her hunter Huffus and Colin a pair of strong fell boots. They hunted with me at Hoxne Grapes the following day and during a great hunt a terrible thing happened. I was keeping up with hounds as well as I could by cutting corners when I heard the awful cry of a hound in pain. I galloped to the spot to find Prettylass hooked like a fish on a long wire with a hook at the end which had gone into her stomach. She was racing round and round in an arc at the extent of the wire, in great pain and extreme agitation at being left behind. In this sort of situation hounds are very dangerous and will bite anyone who tries to help them. I ran the thong of my whip through the keeper to form a noose and placed it round her neck which enabled me to keep her head and teeth away from me while I unhooked her. I wondered if she would try to bite me when I let her go but she just took off across country to join the other hounds.

Colin had his first day of mounted hunting at Otley White Hart on Saturday 27th November. At a check Terence Saffell asked him how he was getting on and Colin replied that he thought he was getting on rather well.

Terence said, ' You won't be for much longer unless you tighten your girth,' and Colin then tightened the girth by six holes.

The Plumbes stayed on and had a day with the Dunston Harriers on Tuesday. I took the horses home so that they could have a hunting tea with Stanley Tompkins, who then persuaded them to go with him to a boxing banquet in Norwich, so it was quite late by the time they came home.

My idea for a 'French exchange' visit had been enthusiastically received by the Easton members, certain of whom had agreed to host a couple of the visitors in their homes, and plans were laid. First, of course, was the official invitation to all members of the Picardie Valois and then many letters and telephone calls followed, as it was important to suit the guests to their hosts as well as possible. Some of the hosts spoke no French at all, others had sufficient to get by, and a few were fluent, and there was a similar range of English-speaking ability among the guests but as well as thinking about the language abilities we tried to put like-

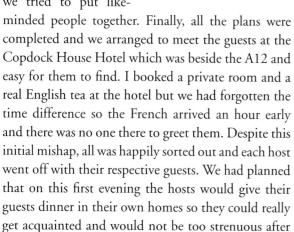
The French visitors in England

minded people together. Finally, all the plans were completed and we arranged to meet the guests at the Copdock House Hotel which was beside the A12 and easy for them to find. I booked a private room and a real English tea at the hotel but we had forgotten the time difference so the French arrived an hour early and there was no one there to greet them. Despite this initial mishap, all was happily sorted out and each host went off with their respective guests. We had planned that on this first evening the hosts would give their guests dinner in their own homes so they could really get acquainted and would not be too strenuous after the long journey.

The hosts and guests were:

Hugh & Joy Clay	Mme Eugene
John & Veronica Parker	M & Mme Baldert
Terence & Marion Saffell	M Jean Courbain
John & Ann Capon	M & Mme Meignon
Stanley Tompkins	M & Mme Reims
Peter & Jill Sillars	M & Mme Dettolle
Bill & Angela Rix	M & Mme Peters
Graham & Judy Croll	M & Mme Poire
Bill & Jill Wilson	M Jean Pierre Poire (brother to above)
Robert & Ann Hawes	M Varenne
Tony & Sheila Harvey	M & Mme Bocquillon (Master)

Because English hunting is so different to French hunting I had naturally given a great deal of thought to making it as easy as possible for the visitors. The most important problem was that it is most unusual to jump anything at all in the hunting field in France and the visitors were naturally very apprehensive of what would be expected of them. Their only knowledge of English hunting was sets of hunting prints that always portray the most terrifying obstacles. Because I knew that this anxiety would exist, I suggested that it would be the decent thing for hosts to mount their guests on their own horses and ride the hirelings themselves. This suggestion was not unanimously accepted at first but materialised in the end.

The second decision was to select a good meet and one that would be typically English. I eventually chose Dennington Queen as the villages square, surrounded by the pub, the church and the shop, seemed to me to provide a really English ambience. On the morning of 9th December people began to arrive at around half past ten and before eleven o'clock the pub was bursting at the seams. The news of the French visit had spread all over East Anglia and there were visitors from the Sproughton Foot Beagles, the Dunston Harriers, the

Suffolk Foxhounds, the Essex and Suffolk Foxhounds, the Waveney Harriers, and probably others that I did not know about. Without any request the meet was policed very efficiently and the officers ensured that all visitors parked on the roadside, thus leaving the pub yard for the boxes but even so when it was time to move off the pub yard was so crowded with spectators that it was difficult to lower the ramps of the horseboxes. Six of the French men had brought their trompes and decided to blow when about half of the horses were unboxed. Absolute chaos ensued as all the English horses wheeled round to face the music. Dozens of people were knocked over; Beryl Webster needed two stitches in her head; one horse decided on desperate measures and jumped over the drawbar of a trailer which was still attached to the car; another horse froze and stood trembling at the top of the ramp with his eyes out like organ stops. Eventually, everyone was mounted but I was still worried that our English horses might buck when the French horns were blown loudly from right behind their ears. I need not have concerned myself as they behaved perfectly and we moved off at a walk with the six men blowing the 'Marche de Venerie', the traditional tune played when moving off. I looked behind me and it was a most wonderful sight. Terence Saffell was leading the field, closely followed by the six blowers, their French hunt coats resplendent in gold braid and their brass trompes glinting in the sunlight. Behind the blowers came the mounted field, numbering about seventy or so, against the backdrop of Dennington church and the village. The scene is etched in my memory and the atmosphere was such that the hair stood up on the back of my neck, as I am sure it did for many of the participants.

I went directly to a willow tree behind Jackson's Farm where there was usually a hare on her seat and she obliged by being 'at home'. We were away at once and ran to a huge kale field at Laxfield where I gave her best as it would have been too difficult to get her away. In the next draw two hares got up at the same time and ran parallel to each other for a time, then parted. Pickwick, as independent as always, went away on one hare and the rest of the pack on the other. I went with the main pack, telling Bernard to leave Pickwick to his own devices. We ran for forty minutes and then had a serious check. I was about to help hounds when they heard Pickwick speaking on his private hunt. I had picked him for his very deep and powerful voice which he passed on to his offspring, thus greatly improving the cry of the Easton hounds, and although he had been in the

Easton pack for less than three months, the other hounds already trusted him and flew to his well-known voice. All the hounds joined him and went on eventually to kill his hare. I then took the now united pack back to where we had lost our original hare and was busy casting them where I thought she may have gone, when Pickwick hit off a line. Slowly he hunted it, sometimes speaking, sometimes only feathering, and took the line for two fields, then fresh found the hare and they ran on and killed her in the open after two more fields. This hare was, without doubt, the one that the main pack had originally been hunting and this display of venery pleased the French visitors enormously. I asked Bernard to cut off two pads for presentation and the guests were just starting to blow *La Mort* when a hare jumped up and we were away. This ran to Sunflower Wood where she was lost. I asked Bernard to hold hounds up whilst I presented the two pads, one to M. Varenne, who had his own pack of harriers in France, and the other to Martine Poire. While I was presenting the pads, *La Mort* was blown without interruption and sounded magical on the edge of the wood.

I decided to have one more hunt so drew again and we were soon away. It was not long before we came to a very bad, blind, and hairy ditch. It was a hellish place and I did not like the look of it at all but what was I to do? The Frenchmen were behind me and the honour of England was at stake. I was riding my Paddy who was a brilliant ditch jumper but somehow we both finished up in the ditch. As Paddy and I were struggling in the bottom, I looked up and saw Geoffrey Ingram-Smith jump right over the top of us, but Paddy was as nimble as a cat and we were soon out. Terence Saffell and Robert Bothway both fell at different places in the same ditch but at least, between the three of us, we had made clear places to jump. The French visitors sailed over triumphantly, enormously pleased that they had succeeded where we had failed, and I am sure they dined out on this story for years.

The hunted hare was running towards Laxfield House and, after taking us across some lovely country, again made for Sunflower Wood. Hounds ran round the wood a couple of times and I thought that this was my moment to go home. I went to the road to find the eighty-year-old Ernie Nunn, who had been kennel huntsman to Captain Bernard for fourteen seasons, standing there. As I blew for hounds, Ernie asked if I would like him to 'cope' for them which he did with magical ringing tones, as only a true professional can. I blew less than I normally would have done, just so that I could enjoy listening to Ernie's voice. It was a very emotional moment for me, to see this grand old hunt servant, under whose watchful eye I had started to whip-in, coping for my hounds. The tears welled up in my eyes and ran down my cheeks and I had to use my handkerchief to dry my face before I could thank him and ride away. I expect that this was the last time he ever coped for hounds.

There was a hunt dinner at Framlingham Crown to round off the day and this went with even more zeal and enthusiasm than usual. In addition to all the hosts and the guests, there were Nona and Jimmy Shand, Julie and Geoffrey Hennessy with their French friend Odile Buton, Mary & Ernie Calver and Gerald Ashley-Cooper. The chef at The Crown was on his mettle and we started off with smoked salmon, followed by soup, beautiful pink lamb, and then the Chef's special hunting gateau decorated with hounds and horses which he proudly presented to all the guests before cutting. A magnificent mature and creamy Stilton concluded the meal. The singing of hunting songs in the customary way would have been rather one-sided but the Easton Harriers, as always, rose to the occasion and both surprised and delighted their Master. Peter Sillars sang his French version of *Ilkley Moor bar 'tat*, Geoffrey Ingram-Smith followed with a French version of *Take the yellow handkerchief in remembrance of me*, Jimmy Shand and myself then sang English songs, and then Geoffrey Hennessy gave another translated song. This special effort from the Easton members really set the spirit for the rest of the evening and it was tit for tat, with Englishmen and Frenchmen performing in turn. The atmosphere was unsurpassable.

The programme for Friday was coursing in the morning, followed by lunch, and in the afternoon the ladies were to visit the hairdressers ready for the Dunston Ball in the evening while the men could do as they wished. The coursing started at eleven o'clock and was particularly interesting for the French guests as, I believe, it is illegal in France. The coursing was very good and when we were just about to stop for lunch, two vanloads of men and greyhounds arrived from Wolverhampton so I invited them to join us for lunch in the Hall. Sheila had cooked two huge joints of salt beef and plenty of soup. The soup was very welcome and I carved the salt beef and the ladies put it into baps. The French were completely mystified by the salt beef and thought it was some kind of ham. After lunch we coursed again with the Wolverhampton gang on another part of the farm. This was unplanned but I could not send them back without a course when they had come so far.

John Capon had arranged a coach to take us to the Dunston ball and the Norwood Rooms looked lovely with plenty of flowers on the tables and pedestals. The French guests had taken their trompes with them and I had arranged for them to blow during the band interval. When the trompe blowers walked onto the dance floor the band struck up with the French national anthem and everyone stood up. This gesture particularly impressed and pleased our guests as they told us that French people hardly ever stand up for their own national anthem. There were sixty-three of us in our Easton party and we had a fabulous time.

I had arranged for the visitors to be able to see two packs from the same meet on the Saturday, having persuaded the Sproughton Foot Beagles to meet at the Finborough Chestnut at half past one, following the meet of the Suffolk Foxhounds at eleven o'clock. Christine Bocquillon and Michel Peters decided to ride to the foxhounds but the rest of us followed by car, then returned for the beagle meet. On their second hare hounds ran a lovely line round rolling country so we could see all of the hound work from the vantage points. There was then a very difficult check but Jean Bocquillon, who was not far from me, bent double with his trompe sticking up on his back and started to walk slowly up a track. He was staring at the ground and was following imprints of the hunted hare's toenails. I went across to him and he asked if he should tell the huntsman. I said just to raise his hat, but before he could do so hounds hit off the line and hunted past us without our help. This delighted us both and persuaded us to give the Master our heartiest congratulations.

The hosts were to dine their guests before joining us at nine o'clock, at the Hall, for a farewell champagne cocktail party. We joined the Capons and Saffells and dined at the Occold Country Club but the service was so slow that we had to leave immediately after the main course to be home in time to receive our guests. Everyone was a little tired and jaded and, as a result, the party was somewhat subdued in comparison with earlier evenings but the evening finished with a trompe blowing session in the courtyard, which awoke and alarmed all of Tannington and half of Brundish. So ended a very successful visit. Our guests had been well looked after and they were impressed with the venery they had seen from the Easton and the Sproughton Foot, although they had not seen enough of the Suffolk Foxhounds to give an opinion. The social side of the visit had been a great success and friendships were forged which were to last for many years to come.

It was an enormous anticlimax when only five people turned out for the meet at Debenham Lion on the following Monday: two Saffells, Shirley Smith with a friend, and Jean Balch, a local farmer's wife who was out for the first time. The Children's Meet was held at Helmingham Hall on 21st December with a good turnout of over fifty ponies. Helmingham is the ideal spot for a children's meet as there is plenty of room in the park to unbox and the children love riding over the drawbridge into the courtyard. The first hare was caught very easily, probably because it was already injured, perhaps by a car. The second hare left it a fraction too late to go away and received a little nip from a hound but after this rude awakening she was not going to dally and went away at a great pace and straight for several miles. The children were stretched back as far as the eye could see when, luckily, she decided to return in the direction of Helmingham and we managed to gather most of the children together again.

Helmingham Hall – hounds on the bridge

There were fifty-six people mounted for the Christmas Eve meet at Badingham White Horse, including a number of strangers who may have come from the Essex and Suffolk who had yellow jaundice in their hounds and had stopped hunting. It was a lucky day for me; each hare ran a convenient line where it was possible for us all to be up with hounds, and they ran hard all day, most of the time unaided. I was delighted as this was just the sort of hunting that I wanted the foxhunting visitors to see. Even my dour kennel huntsman, Bernard Needham, was moved to comment on how well they had gone. There were only six horses left in the field when I blew for home at a quarter to three. The pub had obtained an extension until four o'clock and all the rooms were packed with hunting people and locals. I made sure I was home in reasonable time as we were going to the Saffells, so a good day's hunting ended just as it should, with a good dinner party with friends.

On Boxing Day I always unboxed with Herbert Breese at Church Farm and hacked to the meet. This gave the hounds a chance to empty and settle down a little before their long wait. I always liked to arrive at the meet by eleven o'clock and did not move off until midday so that everyone had an ample opportunity to see hounds and to renew old acquaintances. A huge crowd greeted us when we arrived at the meet, cars were parked from Saxtead Lodge to beyond Soham Gates and every road leading off the green was lined with cars. I stood with hounds on a little area of grass in front of the pub and the public were round the edge of it. This was ideal for me as I could move from side to side to greet people whom I knew and answer questions from members of the public. Marion Saffell and Sue Gooderham positioned themselves at the bottom of the green so as to be able to count the horses and made it between seventy-five and eighty.

The first hunt was hopeless with people and cars everywhere the hare tried to go so I went to World's End Farm and found a really good hare. She crossed the Tannington road and ran on without doubling, skirting the edge of Bedfield to Mr Nesling's at Wood Farm, Worlingworth. The slightest check occurred here and then hounds ran on to Ducks Paddle at Tannington, then swung left to Worlingworth Hall before swinging right-handed across to Wilby Green. This entire hunt had been at racing pace with no real check as she had no time for doubles. It was a case of really sitting down and riding across country, taking every obstacle just as it came. I looked back from time to time and could see horses and riders stretched out for a mile and a half behind me. I had as much as I could do to keep hounds in sight and my horse Stonebow was really blown. As we approached Wilby Green he was reduced to a trot and, as I was so near home, I thought I had better get a fresh horse. I blew my horn and when Rita ran out of the stable I shouted to her to saddle Paddy. By the time I got to the stable she had him saddled and outside ready. I did a quick 'huntsman's change' and galloped off up the road, overtaking an unbroken line of cars as I went. I had last seen hounds entering Wilby Green and, as I turned towards it, I could see Bernard hacking towards me with hounds. I have a small meadow on that corner so I asked one of the car followers to open the gate and went in to allow the horses to catch up. Bernard dismounted from Shamara to ease her and help her get her wind back. When about twenty or so horses had caught up, I decided that Brundish Crown would be a much better place to wait, so we hacked up the road for half-time drinks.

Outside the pub I was accused by several people of having laid a drag and the more I protested my innocence, the more they were sure of my guilt. Geoffrey Clarke, with a twinkle in his eye, asked how it was that, if it was not a drag, I could have arranged to have a fresh horse ready. I thought it best to leave the subject and let them believe what they liked. It certainly was a most unusual run, but not a drag and if I *had* laid a drag it would have been over much easier country to cross.

Blown horses and exhilarated riders continued to catch up, all congratulating themselves on having completed the run. There must have been about two hundred people outside the crown and Bernard and I were receiving many compliments, many of which were contained inside a Paris goblet.

Geoffrey Clarke then asked if I would do him a favour. His eighty-year-old mother, whose husband Hugh had been Honorary Secretary to the Easton for many years, lived just down the road at the Grove. She had loved hunting when she was young and used to go across country like the very devil, but now she was ill and not likely to live much longer. He asked me to take hounds down to the Grove so she could see them one more time from her bedroom window before she died. Naturally, I did as he asked, took hounds down the road then stood with them in front of the house and blew my horn long and loud. Two people helped her to the window and we swept off our hats. She tried to wave to us but someone had to help her lift her arm. I blew again and hounds looked up me and bayed frantically. That visit revived her spirits so much that she ate some tea that night and ate well the next day and was well enough to come downstairs again. She completely recovered and lived for seventeen more years.

> *'There's only one cure for malady sure*
> *That washes the heart to the core.*
> *'Tis the sound of the horn, on a fine hunting morn*
> *What'ere the heart wish for more.*
> *It turneth the grim into gay*
> *Makes pain unto pleasure give way*
> *Turns the old into young*
> *And the weak into strong*
> *If they all go a 'hunting today.'*

After this, I went through the meadows behind The Grove but, finding the gate shut, jumped it into the first draw. A hare was soon found which ran to Fenton's Farm, Dennington, where Paddy completely ran out of steam. Sue Gooderham came to my rescue, as she had done so many times before, lending me her Robin and taking Paddy home who was later found to be ill and was unfit to hunt for some time.

Mrs Shand-Kydd invited us to a lawn meet at Hoxne Old Rectory on New Years Day 1972 and what a lawn meet it turned out to be. She had invited the entire village and this made for a very special atmosphere for the twenty-six of us who were mounted. I arrived with a bad hangover from the previous evening but large glasses of cherry brandy quickly cured the problem. This day was to be very special as I would experience a most extraordinary aspect of hound behaviour. The first two hunts were quite average then hounds settled to their third hare and really pushed on across the airfield into Hoxne and right-handed to Park Farm and back to Thorpe Hall. I was a field or so behind them for most of this cracking hunt and when I caught up they had checked on a very heavily mucked field. As my horse needed some time to get his wind, I just walked across it thinking to cast hounds on the far side. Among them were two brothers entered that season, Hero and Hector. Hero had entered quite soon, as did all the other young hounds with the exception of Hector who spent most of his time under my left stirrup; if a hare was found right in front of me, he would run with the other hounds for a hundred yards or so and then turn back to me. As I was slowly walking my horse across the deep muck, I came across a narrow strip about eighteen inches wide that was clear of muck and had been missed by the spreader. Hector left me and started to feather down this strip, then spoke with a very deep voice. I just could not believe my eyes: this seemingly useless hound was actually doing something and doing it in the most difficult circumstances. Then another amazing thing happened as the whole pack flew back to Hector's voice. A pack will always fly to the voice of a trusted old hound, but here they were doing it to an unentered hound who had never spoken before. For the rest of his long life, Hector would never hunt properly and would always be under my left stirrup but, at any difficult check, or when the hare had run the road, he would leave me, put them right and, as soon as they began to run again, he would return to me. My next kennel huntsman, Jim Wickham, and I used to call him 'The Specialist'. The lazy old devil 'hunted' for two seasons longer than his good brother Hero who had worn himself out with hard work. Not one of the many huntsmen with whom I have discussed this over the years had ever heard of anything like it.

Fog ruined the day at Kenton Crown on 6th January 1972 and the only highlight was when my daughter Bridget sang two songs in the pub, *Paddy Stole the Rope* and *Two Convicts*. A reporter from *The Diss Chronicle* was present and there was a picture of her on her pony Jemima in the next edition. We held the hunt ball for 330 people at Orwell Park, Nacton, on Friday 7th January and most of were feeling the effects the next morning for the meet at Worlingworth Swan. Poor hunting followed with lines everywhere as there was a big shoot at Bedingfield Hall and the hares had all moved across the land that we were drawing. One good hunt ended the day with hounds hunting their hare through the gardens at Dovermoor and across the old railway line. I went home from there to find the Swan packed with a merry crowd waiting for us to return. The après hunt party was so good that I agreed to meet Stanley Tompkins for dinner at the Scole Inn.

The next day of interest was our invitation to meet in the Waveney country. The meet was at Chestnut Tree Farm, at St Cross, and our hosts, Ivor and Mrs Constance, gave us a right royal welcome. They were very generous with both food and drink but it was not their fault that I managed to fall off at the meet. As I was mounting Paddy, Bernard noticed that I had left his tail bandage on and just as I was swinging my leg over Paddy's back, Bernard grabbed his tail to pull off the bandage. This startled him and he turned quickly, throwing me to the feet of some passing Waveney dignitaries. This unpromising start did not spoil the day and hounds ran hard all day. It is every huntsman's dream to have a good day when visiting another country but this was an absolutely fabulous day. I took the hounds to draw and once they had found I more or less just rode at the head of the field. At each check they cast themselves in a small circle, then a larger one, until they hit off the line again. When I blew for them, they came right away and even the most stubborn doghounds came at once. The first time this happened, Bernard was near me and I whispered to him, 'They are putting on their party manners today.' A classic hunt ended the day with one large circle, back to the field where she was found. Hounds feathered about and fresh found her again and ran in another circle in the opposite direction back to the original field. She was fresh found for the second time from the original seat where we had first found her. This time she ran straight and we had our work cut out to keep hounds within earshot. We finally got to hounds where they had checked and thought it was best to go home. The only person to finish this hunt apart from myself and Bernard Needham was Geoffrey Ingram-Smith, with no one else even in sight. A huge tea was waiting for us at Chestnut Farm with endless cups of tea, suitably laced with whisky by Ivor. Bernard and I discussed the day on the way home, especially about how obedient the hounds had been to the horn and laughed about their 'party manners'. We thought it was just our good luck that they had behaved like that in front of our hosts but, in the seasons to come, I noticed that they were always the same when out of their own country. It was another interesting aspect of hound behaviour.

The meet at Badingham White Horse on 15th January was notable for the fact that I had my first ride on Shamara, a bay mare lent to me by the Youngman family of Charsfield, great supporters of the Easton. Little did I know that I would hunt her for about the next ten seasons. We had a fairly good day but most of us were thinking ahead and looking forward to the next week, the return visit to France.

Much cross-Channel planning had again taken place and it was settled that we would travel to France on Monday 17th January. Robert Bothway and Stanley & Kathleen Tompkins caught the train at Norwich, and John and Sara Capon, Ernie and Mary Calver, Shirley and Chris Smith, Jill Sillars, Sue Clough, Ann Hawes, Geoffrey Ingram-Smith, Sheila and I joined them, boarding the same train at Ipswich. One of the group mentioned that it was Geoffrey's birthday so a party started at once which caused a small delay at Colchester while British Rail

In France   Photograph kindly loaned by John Finch

found extra supplies of whisky. We would certainly have missed our flight had Sheila not taken us firmly in hand. Graham Croll joined us at the airport and when we arrived in France our hosts were waiting to take us to their homes. Robert Bothway, John and Sara Capon, Sheila and I, all stayed with our good friends Jean and Christine Bocquillon at the Ferme du Grand Logis at Baron. This was a large and delightful farmhouse where our host was born and lived ever since and now shared happily with his English wife who had hunted for many years with the Easton prior to her marriage. That evening we all dined with Jean-Louis and Claudine Meignon and enjoyed a crab starter in the most wonderful sauce, followed by roe deer venison fit for a king. After dinner we watched his ciné film of their visit to England, showing both the hunting and the coursing.

The English visitors were somewhat surprised by the amount of handshaking at the meet on the first day, Tuesday 18th January, with our host's own roe deer hounds, the Picardie Valois, at St Jean aux Bois in the Forêt de Compiègne. My horse was called Mickey and was lent to me by Michel Peters. Jean Bocquillon invited Robert Bothway and myself to hear the *Rapport* which was a great honour. I felt sorry for Jean as there

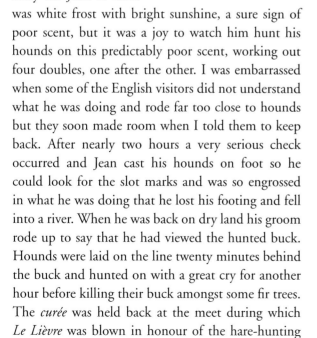

In France   Photograph kindly loaned by John Finch

was white frost with bright sunshine, a sure sign of poor scent, but it was a joy to watch him hunt his hounds on this predictably poor scent, working out four doubles, one after the other. I was embarrassed when some of the English visitors did not understand what he was doing and rode far too close to hounds but they soon made room when I told them to keep back. After nearly two hours a very serious check occurred and Jean cast his hounds on foot so he could look for the slot marks and was so engrossed in what he was doing that he lost his footing and fell into a river. When he was back on dry land his groom rode up to say that he had viewed the hunted buck. Hounds were laid on the line twenty minutes behind the buck and hunted on with a great cry for another hour before killing their buck amongst some fir trees. The *curée* was held back at the meet during which *Le Lièvre* was blown in honour of the hare-hunting

visitors. Robert Bothway and I stood to attention with our hats by our side.

The dinner that night was held at Batigny and the atmosphere was beyond my wildest dreams. The French had been really bitten by the singing bug and had found old books containing hunting songs to go with the trompe tunes. They started off by singing Happy Birthday to Geoffrey in French and then we responded in English. A huge cake was ceremoniously paraded during the singing. I cannot remember how many French people sang but I did record the English efforts. The first was myself, followed by Mary Calver, then Geoffrey with his French rendering of *Take the Yellow Handkerchief*. Ernie Calver was next, followed by Robert Bothway, Stanley Tompkins and lastly, Sheila with *If I were a blackbird*. Once back in Baron, Jean and I had a late night look at hounds in kennel and I fell asleep listening to the hounds singing and awoke the next morning to the same glorious sound.

On Wednesday we were to have a day with the Rally Montpleisur Boarhounds in the Forêt de Ourscamps. On the way to the meet we passed another meet and several of our group stopped thinking this was the boarhounds, but it was a meet of Monique de Rothschild's staghounds, La Futaie des Amis, and I had to go back to fetch them. Unfortunately, we were to have a blank day with the Rally Montpleisur and the only excitement was when the boarhounds twice rioted on deer. That evening we were invited to a dinner dance at the Château de Rivencourt, the beautiful home of Jean Varenne who had been one of our visitors in England. There was much laughter and maximum use was made of the bunches of mistletoe which hung in various places. An excellent six-course dinner was followed by dancing and everyone mixed well, with the English ladies delighting in the manners and gallantry of the Frenchmen. Sheila and Christine had worked hard all day to put the finishing touches to the tables and rooms and their efforts were well spent for the whole evening was the greatest fun and ended at four o'clock in the morning.

The following day on the way to the meet we visited the Museum of Venerie at Senlis, which I had seen before, but enjoyed even more the second time. The most remarkable exhibit was the stuffed hound that was in at the kill of 476 stags; he must have had the constitution of an ox. Unfortunately, the hunting was a disaster and was one of the most miserable days I have ever endured. Jean Varenne had a private pack of Porcelain Harriers, called the Chasse de Rivencourt. These hounds were all creamy-white, extremely elegant and beautiful to look at with the most delightfully musical voices. The meet was at the Ferme de Sailleux a Saulchois, on a very cold and very wet morning and the only ones to be mounted were the two visiting Masters of Harriers. We found and went away but

In France   Photograph kindly loaned by John Finch

the hunt was short lived as the hounds were not as good as they looked and the huntsman was not very helpful to them. The day got colder and colder and our friends in their warm cars did not help by asking whether we wished we were ordinary members like them. Robert Bothway had a nice little roan cob but I had a chestnut mare who was a real brute. I had never been so pleased to get off a horse as I was at half past four that day. I was soaked through to my underwear and was shaking with cold. I stood in front of a huge fire and drank six glasses of champagne, one after the other and then began to feel a little more human. A very enjoyable dinner at Baron where we had frogs' legs for a starter ended the day and all of us were in bed by half past ten.

Friday was Sheila's birthday, 21st January, and there was appropriate singing at the breakfast table. Jean Varenne had persuaded Jean Bocquillon to bring his hounds to the Forêt de Bellinglise where, he assured him, there were plenty of roe deer. An Englishwoman, Lyllia Foot, lent me a lovely horse to ride but, unfortunately, we had another blank day. All the French were furious with Jean Varenne for saying there were plenty of buck when there were none. To brighten us up, Baroness Snay invited us into her house for drinks: she was very generous and the gesture certainly worked. We were invited to Chateau Bellinglise for dinner and, as we approached, the magnificence of the floodlit chateau took our breath away. As we went there straight from hunting, changing rooms were

provided for those who had been riding and for the ladies to change from their casual clothes into their beautiful dresses. Everyone enjoyed an amazing eight-course dinner and at the end the lights were dimmed and a birthday cake with twenty-one candles was slowly brought up to the birthday girl. The rooms were truly magnificent with huge chandeliers and fabulous furniture. Impromptu dancing broke out and we danced into the early hours. My wife was the centre of attention, dancing with one Frenchman after another and was having the time of her life when the French gently sat her down on a chair and removed her shoe. She watched intently as they filled it with champagne then each of her admirers drank from it in turn, each one expressing his thoughts in that delightful broken English that women find so irresistible. Towards the end of the evening, I made a speech to thank all our French hosts for their hospitality. Lyllia Foot stood beside me and translated each sentence as I spoke. Lyllia had a very naughty sense of humour and there were outbursts of laughter where I did not intend them to be, so goodness knows what she was actually saying.

The next morning we sadly left our kind friends and flew back from Orly Airport, arriving at Ipswich Station at six o'clock.

The first meet after our return was at Glemham Crown on Monday 24th January and it was a terribly wet day, but the small field of six people included Colonel Allen, his first day with the harriers although he lived next door to them, his garden bordering the grass yard of the kennels. We had a good, but short, day as the conditions were terrible with high winds and torrential rain. Benedict was missing at the end of the day and although Bernard and I spent many hours looking for him, we failed and only found him two days later in Sweffling. We had invited the Dunston for an invitation meet at Eye White Lion but had to cancel owing to floods. I could not contact everyone so I went along to the White Lion to make my apologies in person to Gordon Grover and a few of the Dunston who turned up and then we decided to make the best of a bad job and had lunch together. The joint dinner we had arranged in the White Lion for that night went ahead as planned and fourteen from the Dunston and nineteen from the Easton made up the table. After dinner, the atmosphere was as good as ever, the Dunston joining in the fun and I remember an excellent poem from George Richardson. Sheila and I and six others sang and, later on, I disappeared and came back dressed as a tramp to recite my *The Dunston Harriers Tramp*.

Every huntsman has doubts about certain hounds from time to time but does not often have an opportunity clearly to see those hounds working away from the others. I thought of a plan to overcome this problem and arranged with Bernard that we would each, separately, draw up lists of the bitches and the doghounds in order of their working excellence. When we compared our lists it was interesting that, while they were not of course in exactly the same order, the same names were in the top five or six couple. I then explained to the members that I would be having an experimental day on 3rd February at Thorndon Black Horse, and that they could please themselves if they came as I would be leaving in kennel all my best hounds, the top six couple of each gender on our lists. The idea was to see how the rest would perform which would be fascinating for Bernard and me but not so interesting for others and only six members came out. Ten couple of hounds took to the field, drew well, found, and went away quite satisfactorily but the difference was seen at the first check. It was really funny for Bernard and myself to watch hounds who just stood there waiting for a lead from their elders and betters but after a few feeble and very short hunts, they began to get the message that they must do it themselves. Banish and Bashful, who were Tangle's granddaughters, and Picnic and Sabre really excelled themselves and a really good run ended the day. We did not see any faults that were serious, mostly just youth and inexperience but we considered the exercise had been well worth while.

The meet at Bedfield Crown on 10th February was one I shall never forget. After several good little hunts around Bedfield and Earl Soham, hounds put up a fresh hare on Bob Rumsey's field which took a straight line, parallel to Spring Hill and Ringies Arch, where they crossed the river, and ran on towards Debenham. I had by now realised we were hunting a travelling jack so settled down to really push on across country. Shamara, although an excellent mare, would at times take hold and virtually run away out of control. The excitement of this run put her in this frame of mind but I thought to myself, 'Go, old girl, if that's how

you feel. You'll be glad to stop before this run is over.' Just as I had these thoughts we came to a grass lane and she really set off with a vengeance. To my horror I could see that, further ahead, sugar beet had been carted along this lane and, with the wet weather we had had, I knew there would be deep ruts under the sea of slush. I tried to steady her but she just bored at me and went into the mire at full gallop. Inevitably, she tripped in the submerged ruts and crashed down, sliding along in the slushy mud for some yards. My eyes and mouth were full but I could feel her getting to her feet beside me and then, just as if she had not done enough mischief, she decided to take off after hounds before I could get up. I kept hold of my reins and she dragged me along for about fifty yards or so, before eventually stopping. Being dragged through the slush filled every possible opening and orifice in my clothing with liquid mud: it went up my sleeve, down my neck, between my coat and waistcoat, it even filled the ticket pocket, and about half a pail full went into the hare pocket inside the flap. Worst of all, was the quantity that poured into my breeches from the waistband.

Despite the mud filling my breeches, I mounted as quickly as possible and pushed on after my hounds, finding it very difficult to keep on the saddle as it was so slippery. They had checked just above Debenham and I tried to cast them which was a mistake because, as I was not there to see them check, I could not make a proper decision. I tried to cast them wrongly and it would have been better to leave them to their own devices as some old hounds went back and sorted it out for themselves and hunted on for a few more fields. The line was by now so faint that I had to give the travelling Jack best but then had to face the long hack back to Bedfield. It was a really miserable ride. Not only was I soaked but, as I trotted along, the slush in my breeches went 'plop' every time I touched the saddle and the gallon of slush in the hare pocket kept up the same rhythm. As I met people on the road their reactions varied from horror, if they were strangers, to uncontrollable mirth from those I knew. At last I arrived back at the Crown and, as I was frozen, I decided to have a few whiskies before I went home. In the pub there was the usual gathering of countrymen waiting for our return and, when I walked in, their faces were a picture. They looked so seriously at me, then they looked at each other, and then broke out into helpless laughter, slapping their thighs and tossing their heads in the way that old-fashioned countrymen do. I joined in their laughter, more because of their expressions than anything else. They wanted to know what had happened and most of them knew the place and understood at once. They were really sympathetic about the miserable ride home but, as one of them said, 'Well, bor, I di'nt like to laugh, bein' as you wus the Master, but I just couldn't help myself.'

When I got home I bathed and then tried to valet my coat. In the end I laid it on a piece of concrete and squirted it with a hose. Luckily it was not my best coat as it was rather spoiled and showed the effects of the mud bath for the rest of its life.

The Waveney Point-to-Point was on 12th February so we met at half past nine at Brandeston Queen and had another '2nd XI' day, bringing only 7½ couple of hounds and leaving all the best at home. We had ample opportunity to study each of these and knew them all much better by the time we went home. Beauty was far too excitable and flashy and was put on the list to draft. We had suspected Hotspur of being mute but he went off on a line on his own and passed fairly close to Cliff, who worked for Maurice Scott. I rode across to ask him if the hound had been speaking but before I could say anything he said, 'One of your dogs has been passed here and it was hoolly a'bowyacking.' I was delighted to hear this and Hotspur had redeemed his reputation as 'bowyacking' is Suffolk dialect for the cry of hounds.

At Cretingham Dennis Wilson asked me to draw a wood as he thought he had a fox. Occasionally a farmer would ask me to draw for a fox but I was always reluctant to do so because it meant a change of quarry for my hounds and if I allowed or encouraged them to hunt one such, i.e. a fox, occasionally, they might begin to think it was acceptable to hunt other quarry, such as a deer, or someone's dog. It was very bad for the discipline of hounds and I would only ever pretend to hunt a fox to keep a farmer happy. On this occasion hounds started to feather along a line, but only the Rockwood hounds would speak and this made me sure that it was a fox. Luckily for me, a hare jumped up and we were able to hunt our legitimate quarry.

A red letter day was had from Kenton Crown on 24th February with exceptionally good scent and hounds running hard most of the day. After two and a half hours of good hunting, a travelling Jack was found at Kenton Hall and ran past Kenton church, over the main road, past Fleming's Hall, Southolt church, and Athelington Water Lane, and we finally killed our hunted hare in the field behind Worlingworth Station near Fingal Street after barely a check. Then something happened that I had never seen before or since: scent was so good that hounds hit off the same line and hunted it heel way for nearly two miles, almost back to Southolt church before I could stop them.

Bernard had hunted hounds on 21st February as I was in London for a Masters of Harriers and Beagles Association Meeting and, by all accounts, he gave them a very good day, then he had a day off on Saturday 26th February as it was his parents' Golden Wedding party. The meet was at Kelsale Eight Bells and I unboxed at Captain Bernard's home and hacked down to the village. I was delighted to see Ernie Nunn there and it must have brought back so many happy memories for him to be at his old Master's favourite meet. Hounds ran hard all day but there was not an outstanding hunt. Once again, I enjoyed a delightful tea at By the Crossways and, as a reigning Master, I had the privilege of the large double handled cup, with a generous slug of whisky in the tea. I took hounds back to the kennels, fed them and put them away for the night, before hurrying home for a quick bath and change and then out again to see the Norringtons at the Coddenham Stud. They had been upset when hounds ran too close to their in-foal mares on the previous Monday during my day in London but I left them reasonably happy and then went on directly to the Supporters Club Cheese & Wine party at the home of Mrs Freeman, at Beacon House, Bealings.

We were invited by the Dunston Harriers to meet at Burston Crown on Tuesday 29th February but despite the unusual date it was not a successful day at all. The Dunston field was very badly behaved and some thrusters careered into hounds at a check, more than once. The Easton hounds were used to hunting by themselves without the fear of being trodden on and this rough treatment unnerved them completely and they never settled down again. In the evening twenty from both hunts met for a dinner at the Scole Inn. The meal was good but the dining room was too grand to create the right ambience for singing. Some of the Dunston men told very amusing jokes and we all enjoyed ourselves and had a good time together.

My birthday meet was at Bedfield Crown on 8th March where I was surprised with a lovely present from Stanley and Kathleen Tompkins, an elaborate gold stock pin. We were very naughty about moving off but then had some fair hunting, considering it was March. The best hunt took us to just short of Wilby Green, and on the way back I called at the Hall and blew my horn until Sheila appeared and gave us all another small birthday drink. I took the opportunity to change to a fresh horse to finish the day and, indeed, to finish the season as it was our last meet. A dinner at Framlingham Crown combined the celebrations of my birthday and the end of the season and it was as much fun as usual and went on well into the early hours of Thursday.

We left early the next morning for some hunting in the Lake District. On Friday (10th March) we met with the Coniston Foxhounds and then went to the Windermere dinner and dance at the Belsfield Hotel. On Saturday we hunted with the Windermere Harriers and ten-year-old Bridget went off to walk with the huntsman and whipper-in who was our old friend Colin Plumbe. Sheila became very worried when she had not seen her for an hour or so and needed firm handling, otherwise she would have called out the Mountain Rescue. Bridget returned safely, with hounds and huntsman, having collected as many skulls and rams' horns as she could possibly carry. We all had tea in the Britannia and my daughter delighted her father by singing a song and, on this happy note, my personal hunting season ended.

1972–3

We had 17 couple of well advanced puppies so we started walking out as soon as possible after hunting finished. Having obtained the previous Master's permission to put the bitches to the stallion hounds before my incumbency officially started on 1st May, I had bred seven bitches early the previous year. This was important because, not only did I have my preferred large number from which to draft, but also puppies born in March or early April are a full year old when they are first walked out the following spring and seventeen months old when they first begin to hunt in the autumn. These three months make an enormous difference to their mental attitude and physical strength, as much as the difference between thirteen and seventeen year old teenagers. With 17 couple of puppies, we were walking up the road with 34 couples of an older hound and a puppy. Most sensible huntsmen would have taken this number of puppies in two stages but I preferred to do it all at once and get it over with. It was the usual hell of being tripped up and of groups of hounds getting knotted up in their couples but all went well and by the end of May every puppy was going off couples and behaving reasonably. During the summer I drafted almost half of them to other hunts for the usual reasons, because they were too small, too large, too heavy in the shoulder, too narrow in the chest, or had some other conformation fault. I entered the Easton in every class

at the Peterborough Hound Show but we were always just pipped at the post and failed to win a rosette.

This was a good indicator of the way the season was going to go. The start of the season was delayed because Bernard Needham had influenza but we eventually started on 27th September. The early morning hunting was far from ideal because of the dry conditions and the very wet weather in the early part of the summer. The early summer wet had caused the sugar beet to form huge leaves which were higher than the hounds and crackled and crunched so loudly when hounds passed through them that they could not hear each others' voices, but it had not rained for six weeks and the ground was too hard to hunt in the open. I was disappointed that these bad scenting conditions should coincide with a visit from some Frenchmen. Thierry Clerc came over with his two friends, Arnaud and Patrick, and they stayed with us at Tannington. They watched us try to hunt in the sugar beet on 14th October, then returned for a late breakfast before going off to the Easton Harriers Hunter Trials at Broadwater Park, which they found very interesting. Next on the agenda was the kennels where, after showing them round, I asked Bernard to draw out the hounds that they were taking back to France with them. The draft for France was my old stallion hound, Rockwood Pickwick, who had sired two lots of puppies for us but was now too slow to hunt with us although he could still sire puppies. With him went Patience, Pastime, Passport, Heckler, Hemlock, Solomon, Blazer, and two little whelps Decimal and Delicate. I cannot remember why I parted with these two whelps, as it is a most unusual practice.

Altogether we had eleven early mornings, none of which were much good, with the end result that the young entry knew precious little more by the Opening Meet than they had when we started. On 30th October Benedict died in kennels with yellow jaundice and all the other hounds over three seasons old had to be re-vaccinated. Because of the hard going only thirty-five horses were at the Opening Meet at Framlingham on Thursday 2nd November, hunting was predictably poor, and both hounds and horses were sore when I blew for home. It eventually rained heavily on Tuesday 7th November and when hounds met at Worlingworth Swan two days later, I had high hopes of a good scent, but to no avail. Hounds could hunt no more than a field or two and I was so disappointed that I blew for home at two o'clock. Poor scenting continued and this affected the spirits of every member, especially me, and at a hunt dinner at Framlingham Crown on 16th November there was none of the usual *joie de vivre*. There was worse than mere bad scent and bad spirits on 20th November when, from the meet at Easton White Horse, Helen, a very good bitch, was hit by a van and broke her back.

Things did not improve when the Waveney Harriers came to join us at Hoxne Grapes on 23rd November. At the meet I explained carefully to the Masters and senior members of the visitors that the Easton did not ride on wheat fields at all but went round on the adjoining fields instead, it being possible still to avoid the winter wheat altogether because it was still only 40% of the acreage. The first hare found went away on the opposite side of the field to me so I was well behind my hounds but the visitors, who should

An Opening Meet – outside the Crown Hotel

have waited either for me or my Field Master to go first, immediately set off after hounds. As I hurried along I could see ahead of me various of the Waveney dignitaries jumping into the first wheat field behind hounds, less than ten minutes after they had agreed to avoid them. I could hardly believe my eyes, and to make matters worse, this field belonged to a farmer who did not welcome us but would tolerate us only as long as there was no damage. I was absolutely livid with rage and when I caught up with them I yelled at them with such vigour that it completely shocked the Easton members who had never seen me as angry as that. Apologies were offered and it was all over in a few minutes until the next morning when I had to go and see the farmer concerned. In situations like this, I always went immediately to apologise before the farmer complained, or often before he was aware of the damage, and found it to be the best policy. My excuse was that they were visitors and did not know the rules. His answer was that 'I oughta have left them Norfolk buggers t'other side of the Waveney where they belong and not to ask them again!' I felt quite relieved that I had been let off with this mild rebuke and not banned for future years.

The poor scenting conditions continued with bright sun on most days and often high winds. At Eye on 14th December one farmer rang to say that he did not want us and this had the effect of halving

the draw because, in order to avoid his farm, I could not draw any of his neighbours' land in case a hare found there ran over the barred territory. In my diary that evening, I wrote: '*This is the worst season I can remember for hunting, too dry at first and either hot sun or gale winds almost ever since.*'

Scenting conditions changed precisely during the last hour of hunting from Debenham on 21st December when hounds could really run for the first time this season. This cheered me up no end and it signalled the end of our bad start. We had our 'Christmas Eve' meet on Saturday 23rd at Badingham White Horse. There was always a tremendous atmosphere at this meet, the climax of which was 'drinking the General's health' because General Miller, who lived at the Old Rectory, used to telephone the landlord to tell him to produce a bottle of port for us. The hunting was simply superb, the best a pack of harriers hunting hare could possibly achieve as they ran unaided all day, and I did nothing but observe. I neither offered them any help, nor did they need any. It must have been just as wonderful for the hounds as it was for me as all season they had been trying their hardest every day in dreadful scenting conditions and now for the first time they were able not just to go but really to fly. Towards the end of the day we had a really long run with a hare found on Walnut Tree Farm which ran to Laxfield, turning just short of the village, and coming back over the lovely country at Laxfield House where the hare obliged us by keeping well clear of a flock of sheep. They ran on behind the Bell, almost to Dennington Hall and then left-handed towards Castle Farm, where she beat us and we were obliged to give her best. As people caught up, I enquired if they would like me to draw again but everyone said they were tired and would be glad to stop. Even Bernard pleaded to be allowed to stop as he was 'absolutely done in.'

There had been forty-eight horses at the meet and about twenty finished this day which included my daughter Bridget having her fourth day since breaking up from school. The pub put on a very good tea and the party atmosphere was about to explode into song when I had to leave to take Bridget home. It was generally thought that she was ill but it transpired it was pure exhaustion after such a hard day. At the end of the long hunt she had only three horses ahead of her. The day finished in my favourite way, with a dinner party with friends, on this occasion with Marion and Terence Saffell.

Boxing Day fell on a Tuesday which meant that the horses and ponies had an extra day's well-deserved rest. We unboxed at Church Farm and hacked along the main road and what a sight greeted us as we approached Saxtead Green. It was only a quarter to eleven when we hacked across the Green but already cars were bumper to bumper on every road, both on the Green and on the side roads. The crowd around us at the meet appeared to be twenty or thirty deep and the feeling of support was tremendous. John Keeble, the landlord, sent a large silver cup out to Bernard and I, from which we both drank. Stanley Tompkins was the only other person to bring us a drink so we moved off at midday very sober. There were about seventy-five mounted and the sport to follow was perfect for a Boxing Day: no classic hunts but plenty of twenty minutes or so, mostly over really good country. The adrenaline was running soon after moving off and styles and gates were taken, one after the other. Church Farm was such fun with lots of old meadows and jumpable gates and fences. Bernard jumped a large gate with wire on top of it which I did not fancy, so I took the hedge beside it. One hare took us through the paddocks between Church Farm and the church and hounds were really flying towards Wood Hall. Bernard and I took the hedge and ditch off the road and onto the meadow in front of Church Farm and a really upstanding gate on the other side. We changed hares and the second one brought us back the same way, and we took a hedge and ditch and almost immediately a stream. This caused some fun and there were three horses in the stream and six others down with bowler hats strewn all over the place. I had the fun of jumping the first gate I ever jumped at Trust Farm, Dennington, this time closely followed by my daughter Bridget. Altogether, it was a really great Boxing Day and I was very pleased. We just could not have had more fun whatever we had done. Herbert Breese was on top form and while we were boxing up produced his usual mince pies with brandy which were enjoyed by Monica and Geoffrey Ingram-Smith, Rosie Spragg, and of course, Bridget and me.

The sight of a horse and carriage at the front door greeted the 320 people who came to the hunt ball at Orwell Park, Nacton, on Friday 5th January (1973). The entrance hall had a large fireplace on either side and I obtained permission to have both alight and blazing with logs as people arrived. To the right was the original ballroom and to the left, the dining room. We danced to Claude Cavollotti's Nighttimers, which was a very expensive London band. They were so good that the ballroom was always full and the disco never more than half full. The dining room at Orwell Park was surrounded by gilt mirrors so I decided to have the whole room candlelit, hiring large candelabras from a London firm which were the only lights in the room. The effect was quite outstanding as, not only were the tables dancing with flickering candles but, the scene was reflected in the large mirrors which made the dining room seem even larger. The serving table was across one end. There were two suckling pigs at each end and huge joints of beef and ham with a boar's head raised on a platform for a centrepiece. Six men in white jackets and chef's hats carved the joints which completed the scene. I had given the regular chef at the school full licence to do his best and he thoroughly enjoyed showing off his full talents after a year of school dinners. Tall, elegant gilt chairs were also hired and the whole dining room looked much as it could have done in its heyday, as a private home.

There was no hunting to blow away the cobwebs on the morning after the ball as it was too foggy. New Years Day and 4th January had also been lost to fog but a very good day followed the lawn meet at Horham Old Rectory on 11th January with some long runs, one of which finished just outside Stradbroke. This hunt had brought us across Mr Neville Hadingham's farm with its predominance of grass and good, jumpable hedges. When we killed our hare, I could see that everyone's horse was in need of a blow so I sent Stanley Tompkins and another on ahead into Stradbroke to order a round of drinks at the Hempsheaf. There were only five people left at the end of the day, amongst whom were two youngsters, Harriet Crowther and Alastair Danter, who had both been going really well. Altogether, it was as good a day as anyone could wish for but hunting is a game of contrasts and on Saturday 13th January, when we again met at Badingham White Horse although to draw towards Bruisyard, hares proved difficult to find and the only decent hunt was ruined when a farmer was unsporting enough to shoot our hunted hare. Two days later, I was delighted to see Lord Cranbrook on foot at Glemham Crown. In the best hunt of the day hounds took the line into water, spoke in the water, and then fresh found their hare in some rushes. She got away and deserved to save her scut as she had given us a grand hunt.

On Tuesday 16th January we held a little coursing match at my home under the full moon at eight o'clock in the evening and, after great fun, Stanley Tompkins' greyhound caught one hare. This little sporting occasion was a good prologue to the visit of the Pipewell Beagles at Worlingworth Swan on Wednesday 17th January at twelve-thirty. I had first met the Master, David Reynolds, in the Lake District as we both used to visit at the same time for the end of season hunt and dinner dance. David, never one to hide his light under a bushel, was always telling us how good his beagles were, so I suggested that he proved his point by bringing them into the Easton country for us to see for ourselves. He brought four friends with him and a really good crowd greeted them at the meet which included a large contingent from our own local Sproughton Foot Beagles. Miss Carter gave the turn off as usual but things did not turn out quite as we had hoped. Frank Reeve had asked me to keep well away from his sows on a meadow which is now a housing estate in Worlingworth. The first hare ran directly through the sows with the beagles hunting most beautifully but, not content with that, she circled four more times, each time through the middle of the sows. I told David that, notwithstanding the brilliance of his hounds, he really had to stop them and go elsewhere.

I took him in the direction of Red House Farm, where I knew Alec Abbott would be waiting to show us where old Sally was sitting. As we approached I could see Alec walking towards us and thought this was a good chance to have a joke with David. I told David that he was the farmer he owned the sows and that he had a fierce temper. David tentatively suggested that he should draw elsewhere but I said, 'No, it's your hounds that have been five times through the sows and you must face the music.'

David's face was a picture of surprise when, instead of a thorough telling off about the sows, Alec just raised his hat and gleefully told him where Sally was sitting. One more really good hunt ended the day before we went back to the pub where a good tea was waiting for us. When tea was over about half the people went home but then singing broke out with the Easton and the Pipewell vying with each other to sing the best songs.

Inevitably, a hunt dinner at the Framlingham Crown had been arranged. I did not normally ask my kennel huntsman to hunt dinners, but I did so on this occasion as the Pipewell had theirs with them. At the dinner there were twelve Easton members, twelve Sproughton members, five Pipewell members, and the two kennel huntsmen and their wives. The singing session was the best ever seen at the Crown, with non-stop singing from ten o'clock until midnight. Bernard Needham caused me great surprise when he jumped up and sang a good song. The party broke up about half past midnight and the visitors returned to my home where we congregated round the kitchen table with a bottle or two of wine. This soon prompted the idea that breakfast would be fun and my long-suffering wife once more rose to the occasion and cooked us all eggs and bacon. The visitors eventually collected their hounds from the stables and departed for the long drive back to Northamptonshire at two o'clock in the morning.

Good hunting continued and we had a lot of sport at Eye on 25th January with a good run which took us over Gordon Grover's hunt jumps and then ran into the meres at the edge of the town. These meres were unrideable as the ground was too boggy so I stopped at a vantage point to watch hounds hunt through but a newcomer to the Easton just kept going on and cantered right up to the first dyke. He urged his horse to jump the dyke and it tried but the banks collapsed and it fell into the black mud. It struggled helplessly in the slime while someone galloped to call for help and a breakdown lorry came and lifted it out using its winch. This was all very embarrassing but it was made worse because the rider tried to laugh it off. This newcomer was rumoured to own nightclubs in Norwich and, although it was obvious that he knew nothing about hunting, we had made him welcome as we did all newcomers. He had a smart hunter which he said had been owned by Jimmy Edwards, a well known character and television personality.

At Coddenham two days later I was fortunate enough to be able to watch the curious behaviour of the hunted hare which came up to a pond, stopped to consider for some time, then swam across it and climbed into a clump of rushes. Even more curiously, when I returned home that evening I noticed that my lawn was covered in daisies in full bloom, so mild had the weather been. I had invited the Dunston Harriers for an invitation meet at Rendham White Horse on 1st February but their huntsman, Ralph Baines, was ill. I hunted the Easton hounds instead, all the Dunston members came anyway, and we had the customary joint dinner at Eye White Lion. On 8th February, hounds met at Thorndon and hares were very scarce but Jack Edwards of Rishangles Lodge told me to draw his farm and said he would give £100 to hunt funds if we did not find a hare there. He was a great sportsman, so much so that his sporting prowess made him a legend in his own time; his land duly did hold a hare and we had a good hunt before losing her near Swiss Cottage. Jack always brought out a drink when hounds were near the Lodge and had done so since the beginning of Captain Bernard's Mastership. On the way back I made sure to pass through the yard at the Lodge and, knowing that Captain Bernard had been with Jack for some time, I blew my horn. The two old gentlemen appeared at the front door with a tea trolley loaded with bottles and glasses and started to make their way down the wide path of crazy paving from the front door down to the bridge over the moat where I was waiting with hounds. Both were somewhat unsteadily guiding the tea trolley along the path when disaster struck. A front wheel caught in the crazy paving, the trolley tipped, the opened bottles of whisky and glasses started to fall, but both gentlemen dived for the whisky bottles and saved them in a manner reminiscent of their rugby playing days. Not a drop of whisky was spilled but most of the beautiful cut glass tumblers were smashed. Jack made the best of the situation but he told me later that it had been very expensive to replace the tumblers.

The highlights of the Point-to-Point at Higham on 10th February were that we managed to get all the races sponsored and that there were eleven entries for the Members' Race, and ten actually raced. It was very frosty on 15th February when the meet was at Kelsale so I put the meet back to half past twelve but by half past one there was still no sign that the bone would come out of the ground so, at Sue Gooderham's suggestion, about twenty of us went to Thorpeness to gallop along the beach to Sizewell. I was riding a grey horse called Tojo and I could not get him near the waves, let alone into the sea, until I asked Stanley Tompkins for a lead and soon we were galloping along in the waves. Stanley was a little ahead and further into the sea than me and suddenly his horse hit a submerged breaker and somersaulted over it. When they got to their feet Stanley's bowler hat was bobbing out to sea like a little boat so I held his horse while he waded out, up to his shoulders, to retrieve it. Graham Croll was riding his blood horse well ahead of us and was unaware of the danger until his horse did the same thing. Both men were soaked through and, as Stanley had thirty miles to drive home, Sue Gooderham took them to her home, Snape Bridge House, and found dry clothes for them. Amidst all the excitement, a lady stood quietly watching us. I thought I recognised her and went

across to find out that she was Miss Handley who had taught me at kindergarten thirty-two years earlier.

I spent some time opening up two new draws in areas which, although technically in the Easton Harriers' country, had not been hunted in my memory. The first was for a meet at Knodishall Butchers' Arms and Bill Rix took me round to meet all the farmers, including Mrs Wentworth-Day, who owned the large Blackheath Estate. All went well and everyone said we were welcome to go. The second was a meet at Wetheringsett White Horse and for this one I was helped by Leslie Draper from Gull Farm, Debenham. As we set off together to visit the farms he asked me what I was going to do about all the 'small men', meaning men with farms of under twenty acres of which there were many in that area. I said I would treat them just the same as the big farmers and, after being welcomed by and getting permission from the Kerrs and Alstons, we set off to visit all the others. I insisted that I was introduced to everyone and there were so many that it took another day to complete the exercise but all agreed, some more willingly than others, and if my memory serves me correctly there were twenty-eight names and addresses of farmers to be notified for the Wetheringsett meet. Unfortunately, after all this effort the day from Knodishall was not very successful as it was entirely drilled with wheat and the only highlight was that Ernie Nunn lived there and I had the pleasure of seeing him again. The day from Wetheringsett on 22nd February was much better. The pub was tiny and was soon packed with people and drinks were passed overhead as it was impossible to move. I noted in my diary that the new lavatories were larger than the bar. The hunting was first class and hounds ran hard all day until I was forced to blow for home at a quarter to three as all the horses had had enough. A great party broke out and the singing was especially evocative in the tiny room and, when it was time to go home, John Freeman insisted that we follow him and have more drinks at Red House Farm. Mrs Freeman, who was caught unawares, was not quite in accord with her husband so we drank up and disappeared as suddenly as we came.

At Gosbeck Greyhound two days later Bernard had to stay at home because of pressure of work so Geoffrey Ingram-Smith and Sue Gooderham turned hounds to me in his place. Gosbeck was usually a quiet meet but John Harrington altered its image by singing before and after hunting which put us all in the right mood for the Supporters Club cheese and wine party at Blomvyle Hall, Hacheston, that night. Colin and Wendy Walker's generosity in opening their house to us proved a great attraction and 120 people attended. The Trinity Foot Beagles hunted by invitation at Dennington Hall on Tuesday 27th February but I was, unfortunately, unable to stay too long due to another appointment.

On the following day Colin and Tizza Plumbe arrived for their annual visit bringing a horse each this time as Tizza had managed to convert Colin to hunting on horseback. Their visit had been timed to coincide with Herbert Breese's fifty-fifth year as a member of the Easton and when I had eventually discovered that this would be called his Emerald Meet I arranged for the meet to be at his local, Saxtead Volunteer, on the nearest day to his birthday, Thursday 1st March. The meet was advertised to be at eleven o'clock to move off at half past twelve, and there were several people already there when I arrived at a quarter to eleven. It did not take long to get into the party spirit and the singing was soon in earnest with Geoffrey's accordion and Ben Fletcher's trombone helping to create a wonderful atmosphere. A few of us sang songs before Colin Plumbe sang *The Duke of Buckingham* and then, just before we

JAH leading field across the middle of a plough, so common before the seas of winter wheat

moved off, I sang *The Ballad of Herbert Breese* which I had written for his Golden Meet. Miss Wolton did not require so much persuasion to enter the pub as she had done five years earlier and she stood with Mrs Lee who was headmistress at my kindergarten. As I sang the ballad, Herbert became very emotional and cried openly, and I had to look away or I would have cried too and forgotten the words.

Scent was only moderate at first and several little hunts followed, two of which were through gardens of new houses built in Brandeston. A straight-running hare was found on Brook Farm and it was immediately obvious that scent had improved. This hare took us via West Hill, through Boundary Farm, Earl Soham, past Cretingham Lodge, almost to the village, then she swung left-handed across George Abbott's land, and finally round Grove Farm, now a golf course, to Moat Farm. There was a serious check here which gave the horses a welcome break before she was fresh found, and she then ran back across Grove Farm, swam the River Deben, passed Cretingham village,

to Friday Street and back along the meadows parallel to the river. The scent along these low meadows was such that every hound was speaking in full volume and the cry echoed up from the valley causing the hair to stand up on my neck. She crossed the Brandeston road, near the bridge and there she was lost. She richly deserved to beat us and it had been a wonderful hunt with hounds running unaided throughout. I find it impossible to express on paper the tremendous pleasure that a hunt of this calibre gave me. The only indication I can give is that after a day such as this the adrenaline can still be running two days later. This hare was almost certainly a travelling Jack and once back home in Cretingham had started to circle around in its known territory. It was after five o'clock by the time we had hacked back to Saxtead which meant that there would be no *après chasse* party as a dinner had been arranged.

We had chosen to have the dinner at Eye White Lion because there was a large room there which could be hired for special occasions and so we would be able to accommodate as many members as wished to come and, although it was limited to members and their spouses, sixty-four people sat down to dinner. Brian Bird started the fun when he climbed up a concealed ladder into the minstrels gallery wearing a soldier's metal helmet with the visor down and proceeded to play his accordion. This set the tone for the evening and the merriment was nonstop from then on. All the usual people sang but the highlights were Ann Hawes singing a song she had just written herself, Isobel Needham and Geoffrey Hennessy appearing on the gallery to perform a duet, and Isobel reciting *Albert and the Lion*. I decided to try to end this party on a high note and announced at half past eleven that we would have one more song to wind up the evening but this suggestion was ignored and the party went on until one o'clock in the morning.

I had arranged a coursing match for Colin and Tizza the following morning and fifty-five dogs appeared from all over the country. Amongst the good coursing men were some undesirables who did not catch up their dogs properly after a course, and worse still, some even slipped fresh dogs on tired hares. I was very angry and called a stop to the coursing and told them what I thought of them. Colin and I went duck shooting instead, ending the day with a good dinner at Ernie and Mary Calver's. On the Saturday we met early at Bedfield Crown at half past eight so as to get some hunting before the Waveney Point-to-Point at Higham. There were only twelve out, which included our two visitors, and because she knew the pub would not be open, Julie Hennessy had brought at bottle of port which, once opened, had a very short life. I took only 7½ couple of old hounds and hunted them without a whipper-in and we had quite good sport for a few hours before returning to the meet for toasted sandwiches and a half of bitter before going to the races. After the races John Parker, an Easton member who lived not far from the Higham course, kindly invited us in for champagne and it was the greatest fun, just as I would have wished while the Plumbes were visiting.

We hunted on Monday 5th March at Ashbocking Nelson with the harriers, and the following day with the Sproughton Foot Beagles which brought us to what had to be my birthday meet, although it was a day previous. I wanted to travel to the Lake District on my birthday so hunted from the Debenham Cherry Tree on 7th March. I could only hunt 9½ couple as there was a mysterious throat infection in the kennel and on this hot and sunny day with scent almost nil I could not show good sport. I blew for home, thinking we could have more fun in the pub than in the field, but when we returned it was closed. The members would not let my birthday end on this flat note so we went down the street to the Dove Coffee Shop, an incongruous setting for a lot of people in hunting clothes. Graham Croll would not hear of my birthday meet being without alcohol so he disappeared across the road to a friend of his wife's and returned with two bottles of champagne. We drank the champagne from our coffee cups and the pure ridiculousness of our situation generated such a feeling of fun that Ann Hawes and Colin Plumbe sang. Graham disappeared again and returned with two more bottles of champagne which followed a similar fate to the previous two. Customers coming in to the coffee shop either went straight out again or smiled and joined in the fun. Before we left I asked the owner how much we owed for loss of trade but he declined, saying he had enjoyed it. I promised Graham that I would have the four corks mounted like a real hunting trophy and did so, placing them on an oak shield with the inscription: 'E.H. 7.3.73 Found Flemings Antiques,

3.00pm, killed in Dove Coffee Shop 3.05pm after a quick burst across the street.' The trophy still hangs on my office wall.

We had a very good journey up to the Lake District the next morning, overtaking the Birds and the Calvers and signalling for them to stop at the Haycock Inn at Wansford-in-England for the first of my birthday drinks before going on to The Old Bell at Barnby Moor for lunch. We called at the Greta Bridge for tea and arrived in fine fettle for an evening in the Britannia, where we renewed our friendship with the Pipewell Beaglers. On 9th March we watched the Coniston Foxhounds before going to the Windermere Harriers' Dinner Dance at the Old English Hotel, in Windermere, during which the landlord of the Travellers' Rest at Grasmere invited all the Easton members to visit his pub for an early drink the following morning. I went in with the Windermere Master, John Bulman, but then the landlord, who was notoriously bad tempered, locked the door and refused to let the rest of the group in. Ernie Calver and Brian Bird were hammering on the door and tapping on the window but he still would not let them in. I kept holding up my glass to them as if to drink their health which did not improve their tempers. An hour later we went to the Windermere Harriers meet in Langdale and enjoyed a fantastic day's sport with a good evening's fun to round off the day at the Red Lion in Grasmere.

On 13th March I left home with Stanley Tompkins for another hunting holiday in the West Country. We hunted nine days out of ten, all with different packs and noted that we had these nine days hunting without going in a pub, that there was one day with only men in the field and another day with only women in the field except for ourselves. Stanley drove the whole way home while I sat with pad and pencil and composed *The Ballad of Stanley Tompkins*.

On 18th April I sent a draft of hounds to the Rallye Planquette in France, delivering them to Philip, brother of the Master Count Christian de Langdale, who was in England for the Badminton Horse Trials. I sent Picnic, Taplow, Proxy, Sapphire, and Devious.

In my speech at the AGM on 13th August I reported that there had been sixty days hunting with five days lost for fog and one for frost, and 11½ brace of hares killed. I thanked the farmers for their support and mentioned that of over eight hundred, only twelve now refused us permission. I made a point of saying how much the Ladies' Committee had raised and, later on in the meeting, the Honorary Secretary stated that the ladies of the social committee raised half the income of the hunt. I thanked the Supporters Club for their sterling work which included the planting out of the kennel garden with shrubs and trees, and also the buying of the new van for flesh collection. I congratulated Graham Croll on his appointment as Joint Master to Essex and Suffolk Foxhounds and later on I proposed that Ben Fletcher be appointed as Road Safety Officer and this was passed by the meeting. It had been advised that all hunts should have a R.S.O. as it was important that hunts should be seen to do everything possible to prevent an accident. Ben fulfilled this roll for many seasons and was a familiar figure with his red flag, stopping the traffic when hounds crossed the road. He also had another role which helped me as Master, and that was to make sure that everyone parked neatly and safely at meets. It was just unbelievable how stupid some people could be when parking, the worst being parking a lorry in front of the Fire Station in Debenham, locking the vehicle and riding away for a day's hunting. The Master has to take the blame for these acts of thoughtless stupidity.

1973–74

I started the season with some changes as my new grooms were Delia Andrews and Heather Hamm and poor Heather did not have the best of starts. On Friday 29th September she was exercising my best horse Paddy and cantering him in Kings Farm Lane when he took hold and she could not stop him. He galloped off the grass on to where the lane was being concreted and set his foot down on the edge of the concrete, twisting his fetlock and breaking a bone in his pastern. He had to be put down and I was heartbroken to lose this little horse. I wrote in my diary: '*I think I shall never have the same affinity with another hunter – I have ridden him for eleven seasons and had approximately 400 days hunting. He knew every meet in Easton Harriers country and remembered every crossing place and gap – it was almost possible to hunt hounds with him without reins. A cobby little horse, with a great turn of speed.*'

Early mornings in the sugar beet began on 27th September and we had five mornings in the beet, all from Tannington Hall, the last one on the morning of my Michaelmas Goose Dinner on 11th October. The Hunter Trials were held again at Broadwater Park two days later and the first of the meets in the open being at Church Farm, Saxtead, on 16th October. The young entry killed a chicken at the meet at Poplar Farm, Cretingham, which did not upset the owner, 'Hubby' Bloomfield, half as much as it did me although not enough to stop us enjoying an impromptu hunt

breakfast of beef and beer in the New Bell afterwards. Things became more serious when two days later the young hounds killed three more chickens at Stradbroke. The hare had run straight through some chickens shacking on the stubble which squawked and flew in all directions and were just too tempting for the young hounds. I was very upset because we had never had this sort of trouble before. Bernard went off the next morning and bought some old hens and let them loose at the kennels and this solved the problem. My middle daughter Judith made her debut in the hunting field on her tenth birthday on 27th October at Dennington Queen and enjoyed hunting on our good old pony Jemima. The Sproughton Foot Beagles met at Tannington Hall on the same afternoon and sang 'Happy Birthday' to her at the Beagle tea afterwards.

The Opening Meet was at Framlingham Market Hill on Thursday 1st November and there were about fifty mounted and a good crowd on foot. I lent a horse to Colin Nicholas from New Zealand but hunting was moderate, with most hares going into ditches and either running the ditch bottoms or disappearing. While I found it very frustrating it was also extremely interesting that so many hares should decide to adopt the same tactics on the same day. I had put up some hunt jumps on my meadows at Bruisyard which caused a little fun but it was a very disappointing opening meet. It was redeemed by the usual excellent dance in the evening at the home of Captain Bernard and it was also the prettiest autumn I can ever remember: the leaves were of particularly beautiful colours and remained on the trees for a long time.

The meet at Worlingworth Swan on 8th November 1973 was extremely memorable for me, as it was exactly twenty years since my first ever, nervous, day with the Easton Harriers when I was sixteen years old and, unbeknown to me, Ernie Calver had telephoned lots of the old members and they all turned up at the meet. It was very moving for me to see them all together again after twenty years. Captain Bernard officially proposed my health and the landlord produced a large silver cup, well filled with port and brandy. A photograph was taken of Captain Bernard and I holding the cup in memory of Captain Bernard introducing me to this drink at this meet about eighteen years earlier.

We had the best day so far and had one run to Southolt Park, which gave us an excuse to call at the Plough. The next hare kindly brought us back into Worlingworth to finish the day. I had to hurry away from the pub to attend the presentation to the retiring District Commissioner of our Easton Harriers Pony Club, of which I was *ex officio* the President, but before I left Ernie Calver made me promise to go to the Laxfield King's Head that evening. The Pony Club presentation was made at Woodside, Constitution Hill, Ipswich, the home of Ginger and Bala Paul and I remember that the claret was most delicious, the best I had ever tasted at a stand-up drinks party, but then it was back to Laxfield. When we walked into the King's Head we discovered that the Card Room was full of Easton Harriers members who immediately broke into *For he's a jolly good fellow*. A wonderful supper was produced from somewhere, even though the pub did not do food at that time, and a cake was also produced with twenty candles, one for each year of hunting. A television set was brought out in order that I could see myself on a programme called *Bygones*. I think Ernie Calver and Brian Bird had arranged the evening but I was never officially told so. It ended with Robert and Ann Hawes inviting us back to Redhouse Farm for coffee.

A few days later my spirits had plummeted as, after the meet at Stonham Ten Bells on 10th November, I wrote: '*Wind too strong – sea of wheat and the only way to get anywhere was on the grass lanes. Had one or two little hunts and a good one to finish up with over country towards Pettaugh. Am getting very depressed about the wheat problem – I think the days of a mounted pack are nearly done in the Easton country – perhaps change to foot harriers?*'

Julie Hennessy's bottle of port livened up the Debach Post meet on 12th November but when we moved off hares were difficult to find. Later on, hounds were drawing a plough when two hares and a fox jumped up simultaneously in the middle of a field. The hounds hunted one of the hares but soon crossed the fox line, became confused, and could do very little more. At Hoxne Grapes on 22nd November Graham Croll brought out some friends from Spain, so I was very disappointed that we did not have a good day. It took two hours to find a hare which soon crossed a road

and four hounds were hit by a car. The hounds were unhurt but the car was badly damaged. Michel Peters, one of the Picardie Valois members who had stayed with Sue Gooderham, came to stay with her again and hunted with me at Ashfield Place on 6th December. He saw some good venerie in the middle of the day, with the hare swimming the River Deben three times. A whole party of us went to the Dunston Harriers Ball on Friday, 7th December, and arrived home at four o'clock but I decided to hack the eleven miles to the meet at Dennington Bell the next morning because my lorry had broken down and the cobwebs had been blown away by the time I arrived at the Bell. My companions of the night before were looking very seedy and did not brighten up until they had had an hour or so in the saddle. Bernard hunted hounds on 22nd December, as it was my sister Sarah's wedding day.

Hunting was poor for several days owing to near gale-force winds and the first good day was Christmas Eve when hounds met at Badingham White Horse and we enjoyed the customary bottle of port and drank to the health of General Miller. This year the landlord had kindly donated the bottle to maintain the tradition, as the General had not telephoned his instructions, due perhaps to poor health. Hounds ran hard all day and covered a lot of country, finishing just short of Heveningham church so we had a long hack back to the meet and arrived there after four o'clock. My daughter Bridget had been riding a cob called Amber lent to her by Brian Bird and she was still up with hounds when we finished but the cob had been pulling all day and had fallen several times. When we started to hack home she had difficulty in keeping in the saddle and someone led Amber while another person rode on the other side, gripping her shoulder to keep her upright. There were no cars followers left and we had to ride all the way back in this peculiar manner but still managed to keep up the slow trot called a 'hound jog'. We boxed up and went into the pub and in a few minutes Bridget was asleep on the settle. Several of the ladies were very concerned and suggested that

Geoffrey and Julie Hennessy, noted for their service as cappers and for their hospitality

Photograph kindly loaned by Moggie Austin

I take her home straight away and Monica Ingram-Smith offered me her car. I woke Bridget up but as she walked towards the car she collapsed and had to be carried the rest of the way. When I got home I carried her into the house to her very shocked and scared mother. The doctor was sent for and he said she was concussed and must have struck her head during one of the falls. I returned the car and went in for a quick drink with the members then went to take Amber home to Brian Bird in Laxfield. I had not gone far when I realised that the tail-board of the lorry was down and had to stop to shut it again, thinking that it had not been done up properly. When I reached Brian's I was told, curtly, that they had already fetched Amber home which explained why the ramp had been left undone. It transpired that Brian, unaware of what a long day we had had or that I needed to take Bridget home, had assumed that Amber had been in my lorry for about two hours and had exploded with rage, being well known for his very short temper. However, I thought it rude and very bad form not to have left a message and did not hesitate to tell him so when next we met. It did not make the slightest difference to our friendship and the incident was not mentioned again.

On Boxing Day I hacked the hounds from Church Farm, where I had unboxed as usual, to Saxtead Green on my own as I had been forced to borrow a horse for Bernard from Michael Becher and he had said he would bring it directly to the meet. There was a huge crowd waiting for hounds, estimated by the police as being well over a thousand people, and I felt quite proud riding up with hounds on my own. There were ninety-two horses and, by a curious coincidence, the traditional collection for Bernard's Christmas box was exactly the same from the members as that from the general public. There was always a major problem with hunting at Saxtead in that there was a water-course running between the meadows belonging to Mr Last at World's End Farm, and those of Herbert Breese at Church Farm which was fenced with barbed wire on both sides and consequently impossible to cross for a long stretch. I asked and received permission to take down a section of the wire on either side and to build a huge 'tiger trap' over the watercourse. I built it of very strong timber and it was a formidable jump for when hounds were running and not for play. On this Boxing Day, I had intended to give the field a 'jolly' through Herbert Breese's meadows and one of his men, Jack Bloomfield, had built jumps in all the gateways with bushes. I told a few people of my intention to fool around for a while but, as I went to

the place where I was going to start the jolly, hounds hit off a strong line. Every hound was speaking and I could not possibly think of having Bernard stop them, just for a jolly. They were really running hard and made for, and crossed, the watercourse. I rode straight for the tiger trap and, as I approached it, I began to wish I had not built it as it looked extremely formidable. I need not have worried as Shamara took it in her stride and I was away with my flying harriers. Only a few other horses followed me and the rest of the huge field were all over Saxtead as they tried to find a way round. The plan had gone very wrong but for the best of reasons and I was pleased with how well the hounds were going. They swung round and recrossed the watercourse, causing me to jump the tiger trap again, but soon after this they lost the line. While they were checked I saw that most of the ninety horses had found a way round and were now stranded again on the wrong side of the trap.

However, the rest of the day went well and we found a good hare on Trust Farm which ran via Dog Lane past Wood Farm, Worlingworth and across to Worlingworth Rectory, turned right-handed to Tannington Hall, through my front meadow and we lost the line at Chestnut Farm. At this point I decided to blow for home and put horses and hounds away in my stables. Bernard then took the hounds back to the kennels and I had a quick drink before hacking the borrowed horse back to Cransford. Maureen Becher kindly revived me with brandy and mince pies. My dear wife was waiting there to pick me up and on the way home we called at Church Farm for more mince pies and brandy and we ended the evening with dinner at the Calvers.

Sue Gooderham had a bad fall at Clopton on 29th December and needed to be carried back to the meet but fortunately soon recovered. We held the Hunt Ball on New Year's Eve and again it was at Orwell Park, Nacton, with 310 people attending. An excellent hunt dinner was held at Framlingham Crown on 10th January after the meet at Stradbroke. Thirty-eight of us sat down to dinner and the atmosphere was incredibly good with twelve people either singing or reciting, Flynn and Brian Bird, Rupert Montagu, Maurice Scott, John Parker, Ann Hawes, Sue Gooderham, Geoffrey Hennessy, Ben Fletcher and Jimmy Shand, as well as Sheila and me. On 8th January the committee voted to raise the guarantee by £400 to £3,000. At Thorndon on 24th January Jack Edwards promised to show a hare on her seat which he did and we were off at once but overall the day was moderate. The country was just a sea of wheat and in my diary I wrote: *'Dreadful day, impossible to hunt in this country.'* This remark was in direct contrast to an entry two days later at Coddenham, when I wrote: *'Very good day, Reg Cousins farm is a joy to ride over, always kept in perfect order and grass tracks everywhere.'*

The meet at Cretingham Bell on 28th January was one I shall never forget as again I was privileged to watch an astonishing performance by a hunted hare. Hounds were well behind her as she crossed the top of Friday Street and ran the meadows parallel to the river. She took her time before crossing Friday Street again and leisurely began to cross a plough below me. I sat listening to my hounds but keeping an eye on the hare and hoped to see her perform a classic double but she pulled off a completely different trick. I saw her stop, turn, and kick back, and another hare rolled out of a seat and ran away, our original hare nestling down in the vacant seat. She remained there with astonishing courage and confidence while hounds hunted the line up to where she crouched, then raced away on the fresh line. I had read about hares doing this but had not actually seen it before and I was so overjoyed that I said I would buy champagne when we got back to the Bell, but luckily for my pocket it was closed.

Hugh Clay opened up some new country for us at Theberton and we met at the Lion but strong winds ruined the day. Bernard usually asked if he could stay at the kennels on Mondays when we were hunting three days a week and so he was not there for the Tunstall meet on 11th February and Geoffrey Ingram-Smith and Sue Gooderham whipped-in to me. We had only begun to draw when news was brought to me that Nelson Wright had had a bad fall. For a while we thought it might be fatal and we waited for half an hour but then more news was brought that he was moving and then the ambulance arrived and took him to hospital. He recovered but was never quite the same again.

The Rendham meet on 7th February was virtually taken over as the birthday party of a newcomer, Barry Flaxman, a friend of Roy Dashwood from Norwich. He was a milkman and on hunting days he did his round even earlier than usual in order to be able to hunt, which I thought was highly commendable. The behaviour of these two men was usually acceptable when on their own, but together they encouraged each other in outrageous behaviour. Both men were very generous and Barry had given the very expensive luxury item of a television set as first prize for the draw at the Nacton Hunt Ball. At this meet he insisted that everyone drank port-and-brandies

and he provided suitable food and this extended to everyone at the meet. Roy Dashwood read out a long and very amusing poem of Barry's mis-doings when out with the Dunston and presented him with a wreath of flowers, woven around a lavatory brush. The hunting was excellent and the hounds were going really well when we came to Mr Bullock's farm, which was predominantly grass, with well-kept hedges. Mr Bullock was supportive of hunting and loved to see hounds on his land but, on this occasion, had asked me to avoid his farm as much as possible as he had a lot of cows heavy in calf. Hounds ran onto his grass but I did not worry, as I knew the hare was running in such a way that she would soon turn away from this farm. I stopped to watch the hounds hunt round back onto land where we could follow. 'Dash' and 'Flash', as they were known, carried on and jumped onto the grass, making a gap in the hedge as they went. I was, naturally, furious and as soon as I could get near them, I sent them home. The next morning as I was collecting the wages from the bank, I met another farmer called Jack Tate who was a neighbour of Mr Bullock. He had hunted with me in the past and I was completely taken aback when he greeted me with a frosty expression on his face and told me that he did not want to see the Easton Harriers on his land ever again. He would not elaborate on the reason and left still very indignant but I went to see him that evening and heard the whole story. On their way home Dash and Flash had passed through Mr Tate's farmyard, arguing with each other whose fault it was that I had sent them home. Mrs Tate, watching from the stable door of the house, was so appalled by their filthy language that she complained bitterly to her husband. I explained to Mr Tate that they were visitors and I had sent them home for bad behaviour, I was forgiven and the ban on the Easton Harriers was withdrawn.

On 14th February, after hunting at Bedfield Crown, I gave a talk on hunting at my home and about fifty or so attended. Two days later a couple of faces from the past were out as Fred Ling, who had been amateur whip to Captain Bernard, drove old Ernie Nunn around to follow us from the meet at Knodishall. We had a cracking good day and I was delighted that Ernie was watching the hounds work so well as he died nine days later.

On 21st February, Mrs Gingell brought her Cambridgeshire Harriers to Brandeston. The meet was moved from the pub, the Queen's Head, to Brook Farm because of Mrs Austin's funeral as Brandeston church is quite close to the pub. My opinion of the visiting hounds was that they 'hunted with a good drive but did not try at checks, always waiting for her to cast them, much higher note in their cry.' The day's fun was marred when the whipper-in's horse cut itself badly on the coronet but fortunately, the amateur whipper-in was a veterinary surgeon and had all medical equipment with him so dealt with the problem and received a kick in the head for his trouble. Five days later I took my hounds into the Cambridgeshire country and met at the Master's house. Hugh and Betty Gingell lived at Horningsea Manor

The field at the Invitation Meet in the Cambridgeshire country 26 Feb 1974, including Debbie Saffell

Photograph kindly loaned by John Finch

where Betty had her harriers kennelled at the bottom of the garden. Jack Steel drove my lorry and I went by car, taking Sue Gooderham and Ernie Calver with me. We had a good day and I was very pleased at how well my hounds went. At one time, Betty Gingell viewed the hunted hare drop down and run a ditch bottom, going under a bridge as it went. She showed me where she had seen it and I was delighted that when the hounds hunted up to us they dropped into the ditch bottom without hesitation and took the line right under the bridge and across some fields. For some reason unknown to me, scent always appears to be bad in ditch bottoms and hounds frequently lose it there, so when they hunted it without even pausing I was swollen with pride and pleasure, although Betty made no comment and neither did I. After hunting, some of the horses were sent home while the others were cleaned, fed, and watered, and we enjoyed a supper of paté, ham and tongue, pudding and cheese, with copious amounts of wine, beer and spirits. After a few songs, those with horses still outside returned home but those of us with cars moved into the drawing room and stayed a little longer.

On Thursday 28th February I had a busy day as I collected Sheila from Gatwick Airport, went to Ernie Nunn's funeral, and welcomed the Plumbes for their annual visit. Wetheringsett White Horse was the meet on the following day and we found a black hare but lost the line after only a few fields. I really wanted to find her again and I watched my hounds cast themselves in two circles and then I spotted her in her seat. The hounds were half way round their third circle

when she jumped up and gave us a good run over Mr Alston's grass but we had to give her best in the end. Bernard was riding Annabel, a young mare that I had bred, and towards the end of this hunt he had a bad fall which prevented him from hunting for the rest of the season. We had a good crowd at our Point-to-Point at Higham on Saturday 2nd March and we watched Keith Spindler win the Members' Race after Graham Croll had a crashing fall. After meeting at Framlingham Hare and Hounds on Monday 4th March we hunted towards Parham and on our return the landlord, Jimmy Finbow, had an 'advance' birthday cake waiting for me. Sue Gooderham was whipping-in to me on Rhythm, another of my home-bred mares, and had a fall on very rough ground but that did not stop her riding her again two days' later, whipping-in again, at Debenham Cherry Tree. The scent was very good, especially for March, and we had a good day, stopping at Pettaugh Bull for half-time drinks. I blew for home at three o'clock as we had a fancy-dress ball at Framlingham Crown that evening. Sheila looked very fetching as a hula-hula girl in a grass skirt, and I went as Bo Peep in a long blonde wig and a lovely dress, with a sweet little evening bag on a gold chain and a crook covered in ribbons and bows. A few of us decided to meet at the Laxfield Low House before going to the ball and when Dot Read, the landlady, brought the drinks, I let my long, blonde hair swing over my face. When she brought the second round of drinks she suddenly recognised me and almost dropped the tray of drinks. After hastily putting down the tray, she dissolved into uncontrollable laughter and refused to carry any more trays until after we had gone.

On Friday 8th March, my birthday, I had a private day's hunting at Southolt Plough and invited twenty people to join me at half past ten for a hunt breakfast of cold beef and ham. At the end of the day we had a really good run, almost to Stradbroke, and I decided to leave horses and hounds at John Capon's farm and telephoned for the hound van and boxes. I went back to the meet by car and ate some birthday cake but there was not the right atmosphere for a party. I had so often noticed that whenever I had planned to have a good day, it seldom worked out that way. I had picked my twenty guests, it was a private day so we could move off whenever we wanted, and yet there was never any real atmosphere. Everyone seemed to be waiting for it to happen so consequently it did not. Some of us went to dinner at Scole Inn but the quiet, sensible mood prevailed.

The next morning we met 'to finish the season', to use the old-fashioned phrase, at Hoxne Swan. A large mounted field braved the high winds and sleet and somehow we managed to have a fairly good day, which made us more than ready by three o'clock for the excellent tea provided by the landlord. The *après chasse* party went on until after four o'clock when we had to force ourselves to go home in order to hurry back for the End of Season Dinner. The dining room at the Hoxne Swan has the perfect atmosphere for a hunt dinner and we all enjoyed first-class food in good company, so felt it was a fitting end to the season.

I made the following comments in my diary after this final day's entry: '*A very poor scenting season, too mild and too much sunshine, terrible amount of wheat almost everywhere, cry of the pack has improved quite a bit. Very little trouble from farmers owing to keeping off all the wheat, which included me, which makes it almost impossible to hunt hounds.*' Looking back on the season, I could gather some comfort from the thought that although the scent had been poor for most of the time, the 9½ couple of young entry had entered very well. They had come from four litters, two of which were sired by Rockwood Pickwick[65] and Rockwood Landlord[63] and two by our own Hercules[65] who was of pure Easton blood and whose bloodlines went back to the beginning of the Stud Book in 1891.

On 20th February the committee met to discuss amongst other things, the proposal by the Eastern Counties Otterhounds to share the Easton Kennels. After much discussion, it was thought there was insufficient accommodation so this proposal was not adopted. At the same meeting, the Committee voted to increase the guarantee by £500 to £3,500 for the coming season, 1974–75. Although this was a step in the right direction, expenses were well above this and I was still having to put a great deal of my own money into the Mastership in order to run the Easton as I though it ought to be. In my speech at the AGM on 10th July 1974, amongst other things, I requested that it be recorded in the minutes that Stanley Tompkins had won his bet of £5 by attending every meet of the season.

1974–5

The previous season I had bred three litters, two sired by Hercules[65] and one by the Dunston stallion hound Salisbury[71], and the three bitches had produced 11 couple of puppies. As I did not go away on a hunting jolly this year, we were able to start walking them out on couples as soon as hunting ended.

The summer was to be crammed with drama and troubles, and the first trouble was with Dashwood. During the previous season Roy Dashwood and Barry Flaxman had become a real problem to me. They absolutely loved being with the Easton Harriers, especially the meets where the camaraderie, drinks and laughter just suited their tastes. The Easton field was very cosmopolitan and it should have been easy to absorb these two men without a problem but no matter how long the Easton remained in the pub, or however much drink was consumed, once we left the bar the party was over, hunting was taken very seriously, and gentlemanly behaviour prevailed. Dash and Flash were unable to make this necessary adjustment. In the field they were often noisy, they used offensive language and generally did not conduct themselves as they ought. An example of their behaviour was that, not being ready when hounds moved off, they might canter through the crowd of foot followers, up the middle of the road, until they caught up with the rest of us. An incident at Southolt Plough was the final straw and after this episode I reluctantly decided that the Easton could take no more. Most of the members were like-minded and their feelings were expressed in an emergency committee meeting which was called on 10th July. The entire minutes read

Pip Grainger, Gay Bridgeford, Maurice Scott, Gill Bowden, Jeffrey Bowden, Mary Garton, Sarah Edmondson, Tom Walne, Rosie Spragg, Brian Bird, Pandora Money

Photograph kindly loaned by John Finch

as follows: '*After hearing opinions from members Mrs Gooderham proposed and Mrs Saffell seconded, that Messrs Dashwood and Flaxman be asked not to subscribe next season. Carried without dissent, the meeting then closed.*'

Dashwood took great exception when he received the letter to this effect and instructed his solicitor to take legal action against the Easton on the grounds that he was unfairly banned on grounds of class distinction as he had started life as a barrow boy. Nothing could have been further from the truth. There was not the slightest hint of any snobbery in the Easton, in fact it was just the opposite, and absolutely everyone was given as genuine and enthusiastic a welcome as Dashwood had had when he first arrived. These unpleasant accusations from Dashwood called for another committee meeting on 24th October, with Captain Bernard in the chair: '*After considerable general discussion, J Parker advised that Mr Dashwood was unlikely to succeed in legal action and H. Kingston-Smith considered that all legal action should be avoided on financial grounds. A motion was put by the Chairman and seconded by G. Croll that the Hunt's solicitors be instructed that the committee had carefully reviewed Mr Dashwood's case and will not alter their decision. The meeting then closed.*'

More letters were received from Dashwood's solicitor and another committee meeting was called for 5th November with the Hunt's own solicitor, Mr Kerr, in attendance: '*Mr Kerr advised against running any risks of legal proceedings in view of high costs and it was decided to admit Mr Dashwood after an apology and an undertaking not to take part in hunt activities.*'

This unpleasant business eventually fizzled out but we had to endure some more visits until he eventually realised that he would not be forgiven and would not be welcomed back into the fold. Some years later when I was hunting with the Quorn, I saw Dashwood amongst the field. I was privileged to be riding with the Honorary Secretary so ventured to ask how he found Dashwood and explained how I had needed to ask him not to subscribe.

'Oh', he said, 'We don't mind. We take absolutely anyone here as long as they pay their subscription.'

I said that I found it difficult to believe that a leopard could change its spots. He grinned and looked sideways at me, and said, 'Well, last season he did get rather out of hand so I suggested that he might like to pay for the Earthstoppers' Dinner.'

The troubles of this summer were not yet over and this year's Peterborough Hound Show was destined to have a dramatic effect on the Easton Harriers as I had cause to dismiss my kennel huntsman in public. The number of packs showing had been getting smaller and smaller year by year and the problem was discussed at the Masters of Harriers and Beagles Association meetings in London. At the committee meeting, despite the presence of Mrs Gingell on the same committee, I said that the reason behind the declining numbers was that the Cambridgeshire Harriers won almost every class and this had disheartened other packs from attending. I proposed that an extra class be included for both dogs and bitches and this should be for packs that had not won two or more classes the previous year which would prevent the Cambridgeshire and one other pack from showing and gave the rest of us a level playing field. This proposal was discussed and adopted and became known as the 'Restricted Class'. I had the pleasure of donating a silver cup to this class which was called the Easton Harriers Perpetual Challenge Cup. Mr Michael Murrell from Earl Soham had won this cup outright many years before by winning the Member's Race on three consecutive years in the Point-to-Point and had kindly asked me if the Easton Harriers would like it back. I had, of course, really hoped to be able to win one of the restricted classes but it was not to be although we did have some prizes. Saunter was second in the unentered dog class, Taper was third in the restricted dog class, Safety second in the unentered bitch class, Dewlap second in the restricted bitch class, and finally Saffron and Satchel were second in the bitch couples. This was one of our better efforts as I did not breed to show. I was well pleased with our day and Bernard was delighted with five rosettes on his arm.

The East of England Show had decided to hold a mass parade of around ten packs of hounds in the grand ring which was to culminate in mixing all the hounds together in the middle of the ring. Masters, huntsmen and whippers-in were summoned to a meeting in a marquee to be given instructions of what was expected of us but Bernard was very reluctant. He did not help at all and my patience ran out when we were waiting in the collecting ring and a helicopter came in to land nearby. I threatened that if he did not do his job he would be looking for another one but he still did not help as I took hounds into the ring, made their lap, mixed them up, and then sorted them all out again, and so I carried out the threat. I told Bernard that I had meant what I had said and would not be requiring his services after that season, and followed up this verbal dismissal with a letter of confirmation the following morning. As the members often forget that the hunt staff are employed by the Master and not by the hunt, this started the usual unrest among the members who felt that they should have been consulted and that the dismissal was unfair as Bernard was a good man but Bernard left my service at the end of April 1975.

All was not gloom and doom. During the summer of 1974 plans were tentatively being made for another exchange visit, a phrase I think I invented for the French/English exchanges. I had become very friendly with Newton and Kate Bacon in Lancashire and Newton, who was Master of the Holcombe Harriers, had asked me to judge his puppy show. While I was with him, I broached the subject of an exchange visit and he thought it was a very good idea, asking me how it all worked and was very interested to hear how well the French visit had gone. The possibility of an exchange visit with the Holcombe was very enthusiastically received by many Easton members and plans were drawn to invite the Holcombe down to Suffolk in late November.

We were very late starting as our first early morning was on 12th October at seven o'clock. Thierry Clerc was once more over from France and watched us on this first morning before taking Caution, Salver, Pilgrim, Pickle, and Heather back with him to hunt in France. We had a total of nine early mornings, only two of which were in sugar beet. Conditions were usually wet and scent reasonably good. On Saturday 26th the hunter trials were held at Levington but while the start of some seasons were spoiled by being too dry, the start of this season was spoiled by being too wet.

We had to cancel the Opening Meet on 31st October as it was too wet and although we were able to hunt on 7th November at Worlingworth Swan there was none of the usual fun as Dashwood was there with a friend. We had one quick drink and moved off slightly before time and at the end of the day, I went straight home after boxing up my horse, as did most of the other members as Dashwood and his friend were already in the pub and no one wished to join them. I ought to have cancelled Laxfield on 14th but did not and we had a day of gale winds and thunderstorms. The rain fell so heavily that the ploughed fields shone like lakes in the intermittent sun. We hunted at Henley two days later but again it was far too wet, although we did have one brilliant hunt of over an hour, very slowly, and caught our hare. The Debach meet on 18th was cancelled but we hunted on 21st at Hoxne although, due to the conditions underfoot and overhead, we only stayed out for an hour and were soaked to the skin.

One of the Hoxne farmers had, as usual, written to say that he did not want us and although a visit from me usually put things right, this year I did not try owing to the extremely wet conditions. We met this farmer, not a happy sort of person, as we hacked back along Cross Street. He looked even more miserable than usual and, in reply to my cheery greeting, he just looked up to me and said, 'You ought to be bloody ashamed of yourself riding about on other folks' land as wet as it is.'

I said, 'Oh, don't be like that. Come into the pub and I'll buy you a drink.'

It was not long before he joined us and I could buy him the promised drink. I tipped the wink to the members and his glass was never empty. The pub was packed full of members and locals, who soon realised what the plan was. The atmosphere was simply the best and a great party broke out. We were in the pub for about three and a half hours and the star of the show was Maurice Scott who had us in stitches with his chicken impersonations and a tale about a Black Minorca. Maurice was wearing a really old fashioned black coat with a long and full skirt and his finale was to go up and down the room, crouched down on his heels, with his hands in his pockets, making the cries of a distressed chicken while at the same time flapping his 'wings'. Our dour farmer decided to join in and tried to follow Maurice, but not quite so successfully. Eventually we all went home and when I was in the bath I remembered that I had asked the farmer to join us at our hunt dinner at Hoxne Swan that evening. Before telling the Swan, I thought it would be best if I found out if he was actually coming, so I looked up his telephone number in the directory and was wondering how I would word my enquiry when the farmer's wife answered the phone.

'I'm sorry to bother you,' I said, 'but I saw your husband earlier and invited you both to the hunt dinner tonight at the Swan and I wondered if it was convenient for you.'

'Oh dear, Mr Harvey, that was very kind of you but something terrible has happened. Someone found poor Victor sitting on the pavement, not at all well, and brought him home, so I am sorry but we won't be able to come.'

Her reaction to my telephone call could have been very different had she known all the facts.

Arrangements for the visit of the Holcombe Harriers had gone ahead. Although it would have been possible for them to bring their hounds down to Suffolk, Newton and I decided it would be much easier if it were an exchange visit of members only. I much preferred to host the Holcombe first and then to go to Lancashire later, and Newton agreed with this request. After hours spent on the telephone we matched host and guest as well as we possibly could. Fifteen members of the Holcombe came down to Suffolk on Wednesday 27th November, complete with their horses, to meet their hosts at Saxtead Volunteer. The hosts were the Crolls, Birds, Scotts, Hawes, Gooderhams, Calvers, and Saffells, as well as Sheila and myself. I was afraid they would miss the turn to the Volunteer so I put a large sign on Saxtead Green to mark where they needed to turn off the A1120. They came in good time and, in fact, one of the Holcombe members, Paul Quinn, was sitting outside the pub when I arrived. The Dennington Hall estate was always good for visitors and we were always made so welcome by the Rous family so the first meet was at the Dennington Queen, and after a really good meet we moved off to draw at Jackson's Farm. The hunting was indifferent at first with hounds changing hares every few fields but later in the day the hunting improved, and I was able to show our visitors the Easton at their best with a real classic hare hunt, taking in Castle Farm, Low Farm, and part of Laxfield House. Some of this hunt had been across some old-fashioned country with a few real bullfinches and our guests' faces showed clearly where the brambles and thorns had left their trademark. In all we had three good hunts and I felt we had done well in front of the critical eye of the Holcombe's professional huntsman, Alex Sneddon, even though we were unable to catch a hare. Sadly, just as I was blowing for home, Alex's horse dropped dead under him. This was his best horse and he was really upset. Not surprisingly, the *après chasse* party was flat as no one felt like partifying. Bill Wilson, who did not ride to hounds but had a lot to do with the social side of the hunt, had volunteered to organise the evening's entertainment, a dinner dance at the Brudenell Hotel at Aldeburgh, complete with a cabaret, but the evening was doomed from the start. As well as the death of the horse, half of the party of forty-four were an hour late which ruined a very mediocre dinner and the cabaret was absolutely awful. Altogether, this evening was a definite flop and I looked forward to better things on the morrow when coursing at Tannington had been arranged at half past one.

Although we had fixed this late time to allow the visitors a lie-in and plenty of time to do their horses, there were only two guests and hosts present by half past one so we started the coursing without them. There were plenty of good strong hares and the coursing was excellent. Gradually the latecomers arrived and everyone thoroughly enjoyed themselves although it was hard work walking over the sticky clay. There were some very tired souls and Brian Bird, with his pick-up truck, was a very welcome sight. Brian ferried people back to the Hall where Sheila had an enormous coursing tea spread out in the dining room. I had set up a barrel of Adnams bitter and had bought three dozen half-pint mugs and altogether the tea proved great fun. Nothing had officially been arranged for the evening as it was thought best for the guests to have a relaxing evening with their respective hosts.

Saturday's meet was at Clopton Crown and, although there were no classic hunts, hounds ran hard all day. The party in the pub afterwards was first-class with plenty of laughter and singing and the final night's entertainment was, inevitably, a dinner at Framlingham Crown. They did not usually welcome private dinners on a Saturday night but, because we were such good customers, they made an exception. All fifteen guests and their hosts, plus six others, sat down at nine o'clock and left the table at half past midnight. The atmosphere was superb and we definitely finished the visit on a very high note. There were non-stop jokes, singing, and stories from the last mouthful of pudding until the end when I had great difficulty in stopping them, but I had promised the management of the hotel that we would not be too late. The evening and, indeed the visit, finished with 'Auld lang syne'.

Good hunting continued, but the meets at Framlingham Hare & Hounds and Stradbroke Ivy House were spoiled by the presence of the unwelcome Dashwood. I arrived at the meet on Saturday 21st December at Dennington with a feather pinned to my lapel. This caused considerable interest at first and great amusement later, when it found to be a feather from the boa of a stripper the night before. Michael Becher had given a stag party during which a stripper, as part of her performance, had sat on my lap and pinned on a feather. A £5 wager had been laid that I would not dare to appear at the meet next morning with it pinned to my hunt coat. During the same party, another bet was offered that hunting men could not shoot alongside regular shooters. I said this was not a fair bet and that the shooting men should also come hunting alongside the hunting men. This was taken up and resolved to be settled with the shooting first, then the hunting at Badingham White Horse on 20th January.

The Christmas Eve meet was just unbelievable. There were so many people at the Badingham White Horse that some could not even get inside to buy a drink until we had moved off. General Miller had died the previous night but Mrs Miller had remembered his wishes and sent down a bottle of port so we drank for the first time, not to his health, but to his memory. There were seventy-six mounted and the cap came to £85 but it was not a particularly good day with only one decent hunt at the end. The hare was found at the Brick Kiln and ran past Laxfield House almost to Brundish Lodge then swung right-handed past Mills Farm to the Manor and we lost her at Wood Farm, Badingham. This had been a fairly slow hunt with the most beautiful hound work and set me up on a high for Christmas.

The usual good crowd met us on Boxing Day and there were seventy-five mounted. I had spent some hours putting up jumps and gateways on the Cedars and Church Farm and took the field for a jolly round them all to begin the day. I cantered off, calling to my hounds, and just rode round the jolly with no attempt to draw. Bernard followed, pushing on the older hounds that hated this sort of thing. After the jolly we hunted properly and we ended the day with our hare being fresh found and hounds hunting on again, catching her and richly deserving their reward after their brilliant hound work. The Children's Meet was as usual at Helmingham Hall but his lordship was away from home so the meet was at the Smithy. Sixty-two children came but only Terence Saffell and Geoffrey Ingram-Smith to help me with them and soon after moving off Terence's horse lost a shoe so that left only Geoffrey in sole charge of the children. There was an awful lot of wheat and the children and Geoffrey became separated from us so Bernard and I returned alone to the meet with hounds where I found my daughter Bridget fast asleep in the cab, having boxed-up her cob.

The Hunt Ball was held on New Year's Eve and was as great a success as ever with a waiting list for tickets. During the ball I mentioned that I usually arrived first at the meet the morning after the ball, so Michael Becher immediately waged a £5 bet that this would not happen the next morning and I foolishly accepted the challenge. The New Year's Day meet was at Cretingham Bell at half past twelve as the meet is traditionally an hour later after the ball but when I arrived at eleven o'clock I found I had lost my bet. Michael Becher had been ahead of me and had left a note to that effect before going home. I always made a great point of stressing the old tradition that it is a

point of honour to hunt the morning after the ball. The meet was larger than ever, almost up to Boxing Day numbers, with eighty-one people mounted and the cap came to £94. The first hunt was slow but continuous and we encompassed most of Otley before returning to Cretingham. Many people thought this was a foxhunt and they might have been right as the cry did sound deeper but not deep enough for me to be sure. I blew for home at four o'clock and a party was soon in full swing in both bars. I ended my diary entry that night with: *'Excellent ball last night and as good a day's hunting as anyone could wish for.'*

Following the meet at Horham Rectory on 4th January, the hunting was very fast and towards the end of the day we ran from Valley Farm to Reading Green and back to Battlesea Hall. The distance travelled was not excessive but because of the speed and the amount of wheat we were separated from hounds and at one time we just did not know where they were. I absolutely hate it when I lose hounds. I found some of them and rode back to the meet with 6½ couple, leaving Bernard to find the others. Later he arrived with some more but we were still two couple light. The last one to be picked up had been hit by a car in Stradbroke but, fortunately, not seriously hurt. Losing hounds had ruined a good day and even two large glasses of malt whisky from Mrs Shand-Kydd failed to lift my spirits.

I had advertised for a new kennel huntsman and decided to combine interviewing five of the applicants with a day with the New Forest Buckhounds where two of them worked. I booked in at the Compton Arms Hotel at Stoney Cross and made arrangements to hire horses and hunt with the Buckhounds the next day. I left home at seven in the morning with Bridget and Stanley Tompkins and called first at the Oakley Foxhounds to interview a young man called Caddish, then at the Sandhurst Foxhounds kennels, followed by another man who was out of hunt service, before going on to the hotel, and seeing the two Buckhounds men during the evening. I had a fair day's hunting with the Buckhounds but decided at the last moment to stay one more day and hunt with the Hursley Foxhounds. Bernard hunted hounds at Debach in my absence.

In the evening of Wednesday 8th January, I gave a lecture on the etiquette and traditions of hunting and thirty-five attended. I was without professional help for the meet at Stradbroke the next morning and Sue Gooderham and Geoffrey turned hounds to me.

Miss Marriott, who lived at Wilby House, disliked hunting intensely and I usually went to some trouble to make sure that she was not disturbed by hounds when we were nearby. At some time in the past a six foot fence of chain link netting had been erected round the edge of the grounds but this had become rusty and had a few holes near the bottom which the hares used regularly to invade her vegetable garden. When hounds were in the area, the hunted hare would very often make for these holes and gain access to the garden. I usually sent a whipper-in on ahead to patrol the perimeter to stop hounds before they entered the grounds but on this occasion, 8th January 1974, the system failed and the whole pack were in the garden. I rode to the front gate to find Miss Marriott in a great state of aggravation ordering me to get the hounds out at once. I asked her to open the gate so I could come in and fetch them but she refused and at that moment everything went quiet and I thought that the hounds must have killed their hare. I was wrong. They had only checked and when they fresh found the hounds coursed the hare round the house right in front of Miss Marriott. I shall never forget the scene. Hounds were only a few yards behind the hare and as they tore round the corner of the house their feet kicked the bedding plants out of the ground. Miss Marriott was already livid with rage when hare and hounds came round the corner of the house for the second time, causing similar mayhem. I eventually got all the hounds out and now, looking back, it all seems very amusing but it was anything but funny at the time. The episode was discussed fully as we ate the steak and kidney pudding that Mary Calver had prepared for our hunting tea.

The meet at Thorndon Black Horse on 16th January was partly spoiled by the appearance of Dashwood and company but this soon paled into insignificance when Captain Bernard and his friend Frank Staples appeared. They had both hired horses from Tim Toller and I was delighted to see the Captain in the field again. Before I moved off I noticed that a patch of brussel sprouts had been very carefully wired round. Bert, the landlord, stood in the doorway of the pub so I pointed to the wire netting and asked him if he was having troubles from hares or rabbits.

'Neither,' he replied. 'I put that round to keep your dogs off them. Last year they pissed all over my sprouts and I couldn't fancy them after that and threw them all away.'

An excellent day's hunting was enjoyed by us all with one run through some rough bullfinches. We stopped for half-time at the Beaconsfield Arms when I looked at the assembled field, it reminded me of the old days as our faces and ears were torn and bleeding. This was

as good a day as we had had for some seasons and we returned to the meet with the adrenaline flowing. As it was Frank Staple's birthday, a party was soon in full swing and even Dashwood's presence could not dampen our spirits. Another brilliant day followed on Saturday at Coddenham and on the Sunday I interviewed another hunt servant at the kennels.

On Monday 20th January we had our special day to settle the bet made at Cransford on the night of the stag party that a shooting man could not do a whole day's hunting. Jim Bell was the only shooting man to take up the challenge and had been to Moss Bros in London to hire all the right clothes, boots, and so forth. Badingham White Horse was full of sportsmen, as the idea of the bet had generated a lot of fun and excitement amongst the shooting fraternity. Unfortunately, it was one of the poorest day's hunting I can ever remember with absolutely no scent at all so we were back at the meet at half past one but nevertheless it was a very good exercise to mix the shooters and the hunters together as, in my opinion, we did not mix enough which at times could lead to some conflict. We certainly did mix on this occasion, for three hours to be exact. We left the pub at half past four and Stanley Tompkins and Raymond Le Gry came home with me for a proper hunting tea.

Sheila and I left England on January 23rd for a few days hunting in France. On the first day, I rode a Russian horse that could really buck. As soon as I was on it bucked like a rodeo horse with all four feet off the ground at the same time. When it was time to move off Claudine Meignon asked in her sweet voice, 'Tony, how is your sitting?'

'Not very good' I replied, and she smiled and said, 'Ooh la lah.'

This hunt was long and difficult and, when the buck was killed, some hounds were found to be missing. I went back with Jean Bocquillon in the evening to blow for them. It was magical to hear and see Jean blowing his trompe in a moonlit forest, a memory I will always cherish. We returned home on Wednesday 29th and measured the distance of 337 miles from Baron to Tannington, excluding the Channel.

I had, of course, left Bernard to hunt hounds whilst I was away and he must have been disappointed when Thursday was cancelled due to wet, but he did manage to have a day on Saturday 25th at Ashbocking. I cancelled the following Thursday at Eye, as again it was too wet, but three good days followed, all with good scent and good weather. This made conditions right for the Point-to-Point on 8th February when Clarissa Webb won the Members' Race on Fast

Talker, a horse belonging to Graham Croll. One of the Holcombe visitors, Paul Quinn, had brought a horse all the way from Lancashire to run in the Open race and in the evening he joined us for a hunt dinner at Hoxne Swan.

At last the time came for our return visit to the Holcombe Harriers on Wednesday 12th February. Seventeen members of the Easton headed up north to Lancashire: Terence and Marion Saffell, Stanley and Kathleen Tompkins and their daughter Rita, John Finch, Maurice and Sue Scott, Jill Sillars, Robert and Ann Hawes, Brian and Flynn Bird, George and Sue Gooderham and Sheila and I. I was both surprised and delighted when everyone, whether in a horsebox or a car, arrived on time at four o'clock at the home of Mr Leo Stringman, which was conveniently only one mile from the M6. We were given a wonderful reception, a genuine welcome endorsed with generous drinks and a huge buffet tea. After an hour or so, some horses were transferred into our hosts' boxes before all guests departed with their respective hosts. Sheila and I went home with Kate and Newton Bacon for a delicious dinner, made memorable by wonderful Austrian wines as Kate was an Austrian.

The next morning Alex Sneddon, the professional huntsman, was waiting with his hounds at the Balcarres Arms

Newton Bacon with JAH

at Haigh, near Wigan. A very exciting day's hunting followed with the Easton members out of control for most of the time as the horses were very excited at galloping over grass and jumping fences instead of ditches. I was in disgrace twice in five minutes, first by committing the serious sin of crossing a meadow where we were not welcome, and then compounding the problem by breaking the post and rails on the way out. A lively tea in the pub completed the day's hunting and later we all met for dinner at a restaurant belonging to Tom Bracewell, one of the Holcombe members. Some of those who had come to Suffolk joined together into a choir and sang a song they had composed about their visit, to the tune of *The Yellow Rose of Texas*. Various people sang and it was all very enjoyable but the real star of the evening was Alex Sneddon, who sang two beautiful songs. Spontaneous dancing ended the festivities and, eventually and somewhat reluctantly, our hosts took us home.

Most of the Easton members, including myself, had never seen a properly organised coursing meeting and we were delighted to be taken to the final of the Waterloo Cup on Friday morning. The Waterloo Cup is the coursing equivalent to the Cup Final in football, and it was a privilege to see the finest dogs in the world coursing in pairs. After the coursing we went to Paul Quinn's house for refreshments and looked at his wonderful art collection before going on to see the famous Red Rum in his stable. There was no official get-together on Friday night and everyone did his or her own thing.

The Coach House at Smithills, near Bolton, was the venue for Saturday's meet when the weather was cold and clear and rather windy but proved to hold a good scent. I was invited to ride up with Alex Sneddon and particularly enjoyed this as the Holcombe hunt both fox and hare and I was given ample opportunity to watch them do both. A fox was quickly found in some laurel bushes but soon went to ground in a drain. Next we had a really good hunt on a hare which took us across real moorland with stonewalls and bogs. The bogs took their toll of Easton followers, including myself, and some were in real difficulties, but luckily all the horses managed eventually to extract themselves with no injuries. The walls were just the right height to jump and everyone was thoroughly enjoying themselves when, suddenly, they came to the edge and could see the whole of Bolton spread out before us. To us strangers it was quite a shock to be out in the middle of a wild moor, miles from civilisation, and then suddenly to come face to face with a town. Later on I caught sight of Sheila and Kate Bacon walking in the distance, so rode across to speak to them. Luckily, this placed me in the right spot to have the pleasure of holloaing a Holcombe fox away but hounds did not settle to it and soon changed onto a hare.

We returned to the meet at five o'clock for tea and to hear stories from Maurice Scott who was particularly exhilarated as he was the only one to have ridden across the moor without succumbing to the bogs. I was sad to leave Kate and Newton on Sunday morning; they had been wonderful hosts and both Newton and I were pleased at how well everything had gone, but we were not too flat as Stanley and I were driving on up to Triangle in Yorkshire to stay with Colin and Tizza and had another week's sport to look forward to. I became unwell on this trip and had to go straight to bed on arrival at Triangle and subsequently missed the Monday's hunt. On Tuesday I hunted with the Rufford Forest Harriers, a pack I had helped to start a few years earlier by giving them a draft of good hounds. After hunting I went into the kennels to see Tarnish, the last remaining hound from my draft. On Wednesday we hunted with the Wensleydale Harriers on foot and on Thursday we had a private day with the Windermere Harriers, with their famous Master and huntsman, Albert Benson. There was no hunting on Friday so I visited the Rockwood Kennels to try to find another stallion hound as Pickwick had been so successful but I was unlucky because all those I liked were too closely related to Pickwick.

Saturday was a never-to-be-forgotten day when the Rockwood Harriers met at Hazelhead Hall. This was one of the finest lawn meets I have ever been to and the hunting to follow was of the same standard. This was the first time I had seen John Loy hunting his hounds and he was every bit as good as I expected him to be. Late in the day, I persuaded him to draw once more but at a quarter past five he rode up to me and shook my hand and said that he really must go home. Just as he was doing this, another hare jumped up, hounds were gone, and this hare kept us busy until six o'clock. By this time there were only three horses left, John Loy, his whipper-in, and myself, and we were jumping the high stone walls in the dark by the time we finally finished. Shamara was very sore the next day as she had hit the first high wall. It had brought her to her knees but after that she treated walls with greater respect. We bandaged her up for the journey home on Sunday. Bernard had hunted the Easton in my absence, at Rendham, Brandeston, Grundisburgh, Eye, and Kelsale.

On Tuesday 25th February we met by invitation of the Cambridgeshire Harriers at Horningsea Manor, the home of their Master, Betty Gingell. Scent was rather poor but we managed to have two good hunts, both very slow but showing houndwork at its best so I was very pleased. During one of these hunts, Geoffrey Ingram-Smith's horse accidentally trod on Bella and broke a bone in her foot. The Cambridgeshire amateur whip, who was a veterinary surgeon, laid her across the front of his saddle and rode back to the meet with her and, by the time we had finished hunting, she was in a plaster of Paris cast and fully recovered to hunt the next season. After looking round Betty's show hunters, we went into the house for a wonderful meal and afterwards her brother-in-law, Luke Sykes, gave us a demonstration of all the calls on a coaching horn.

Christian and Antonelle Langdale came over from France and stayed with us before going to the meet at Wetheringsett White Horse on 27th February. The sun was so hot and scent so poor that we could do absolutely nothing. The hounds just followed me around, panting and taking every opportunity to jump into any handy pond. I decided to stop at half past one because it was so hopeless, and said to everyone that I would hunt again later in the day when the sun had gone down. We waited until half past three, unboxed horses and hounds again, and tried once more but scent was still hopelessly poor. I felt sorry for the loyal people who had waited to hunt again so I took them on a jolly, across country, to Rishangles Lodge. I blew my horn loud and clear with the desired result and after a stiff drink from Jack Edwards, I jollied back to the meet. I was very disappointed as it was just the worst possible type of day to experience when we had French visitors.

The Cambridgeshire Harriers paid a return visit to Kenton Crown on 4th March. They hunted very well and we covered a lot of country around Monk Soham and Southolt but I noted, as I had done before, that their cry was rather high pitched. After tea in the pub the Cambridgeshire visitors came on to my home to change before going to dinner at Framlingham Crown.

My birthday meet came on the right day, 8th March, at Bedfield Crown. Colin Plumbe had come down by car especially, so Sue Gooderham kindly lent him a horse. The meet was great fun with the pub packed with people. Colin made a presentation of four silver coasters, one for each year he had hunted, mounted, with the Easton. These coasters had the hunt button engraved on them and Colin continued to present another one each year for many years. We enjoyed four good runs, each one spoiled by running into groups of fresh hares, sometimes six or eight together, a typical March hazard. We returned to the meet at half past three where a spontaneous party erupted. I was pleased to see my neighbour, Mr Havers, who told me afterwards just how much he had enjoyed the songs. Also there was Arthur Cornish, a great local character who often came to the meets and would sing a song or two. When it was time to go, Arthur was far too tight to ride his bicycle home. I had just found a volunteer to take him home by car when he started to fuss about leaving his bicycle, so someone laughingly suggested that the Master should ride it home for him. Not to be beaten, I jumped on and rode it the one and half miles back to Widow's Nest in Worlingworth, receiving many strange looks when people saw me approaching in my green coat and hunting cap. When I finally arrived home I found that Sheila had arranged a surprise dinner party and seventeen guests were soon due to arrive. The dinner was as good as ever and afterwards the carpet was rolled back, records were played, and we danced into the early hours.

We finished the season with a fabulous day from Framlingham Station on Monday 10th March. Maurice Scott was at the meet and, before moving off, I told him to go home and put a bottle of whisky on his gate post because we would run straight to his farm. This was said as a joke but when we drew, the first hare took us to Brunswick Farm where we changed hares and the second one ran directly to Maurice's Brook Farm and hounds hunted in full cry right round Maurice's meadow, passing close to the farm buildings. What I had said in jest had actually happened and the run was so fast that Maurice, although in his car, was only just pulling into his farmyard when the hounds ran by. There were only two other horses up with us when this hunt ended at Rectory Farm, Kettleburgh. Hounds had not stopped running since the first hare

had been found. Two more little hunts followed with both hares lost in thick bushes before we found our final hare of the season and she turned out to be a real good one. She was found at Lindy Lea and ran almost to Earl Soham church, then swung left-handed past the village and ran parallel to the Brandeston road and was finally lost at Rose Farm. This had been a very quick burst with hardly a check and was a most exciting run on which to finish the season. I was delighted when, unexpectedly, Maurice Scott asked us in for drinks at Brook Farm. Horses and hounds were put into loose boxes whilst the boxes and trailers were fetched from the meet. Maurice and Sue did the day full justice and after cups of tea, champagne flowed and the season ended on a real high point. The good company, the generosity of Sue and Maurice, and the memory of the two long and fast hunts, all combined to make this the best end of season day I had ever experienced.

The final words in my diary for this season read: '*A very good scenting season, quite the best I can remember, lots and lots of very good runs but our hares nearly always lost in thick places, bramble bushes, etc. The wettest season I have ever known. Forty-eight days' hunting, five cancelled for wet, Bernard Needham leaving, Jim Wickham engaged for next season*'.

CHAPTER 6

WITH JIM WICKHAM 1975–80

On 1st May 1975 Bernard and Isobel Needham moved out of the round house at the kennels and Jim and Hilda Wickham moved in. Jim came from the Essex and Suffolk Foxhounds and at first I had felt he was rather too young and inexperienced to take sole control of the hounds but had then changed my mind and engaged him as kennel huntsman, little thinking that it would lead to such a long and happy partnership. Jim's temperament and outlook on life just suited the atmosphere of the Easton Harriers and when hunting started, he quickly learned about hare hunting, loved its venery and, as far as I know, did not hanker after foxhounds.

The annual walking out of the puppies on couples was not a problem at all as we only had two couple of puppies, the survivors of a dreadful new virus in hunt kennels which at first we called 'puppy fading'. I had bred the usual number of bitches the year before but we were just unable to rear the whelps. Bernard and Mrs Needham had done all they could but they just faded away at three days old. It was absolutely heartbreaking and we had only managed to rear two couple of bitches from one litter. Other hunts were also experiencing this trouble and the veterinary surgeons seemed to know very little about the virus. It was later identified as Parvovirus and it was a nuisance to us for many years. By the next year the bitches had developed an immunity and passed it to their puppies in their milk. We thought our troubles were over but once the puppies were weaned they lost their resistance and died between six and eight weeks. We overcame the problem by sending the bitches out to farms to whelp and in this way we were able to rear whelps until they were old enough to vaccinate.

Jim and I walked out six mornings a week and he quickly learned the names of the hounds. By June I felt confident enough to leave him to walk out without me while I went up to Yorkshire to judge the Rockwood Harriers Puppy Show. It would have been encouraging for Jim to win a few rosettes at his first Peterborough Hound Show but our success was limited to winning the Restricted Class with Saunter[74]. I drafted Saffrel, Satchel, and Rarity to the Clifton Foot Harriers as they were rather small and took them with us to Peterborough to deliver to the Clifton Foot Master there. I was honoured to be asked to judge the Harrier Classes at Rydal Hound Show in the Lake District on 9th August. After the show Newton and

Kate Bacon took us to dinner at Bowness and insisted that we had Windermere Char. Newton explained that it was a pre-historic fish that lives in the deepest parts of Lake Windermere and only a few are allowed to be caught each year. It was absolutely delicious and was a culinary experience that I shall always remember.

The first early morning was at Tannington on 15th September. We hunted in the sugar beet three mornings a week for two weeks, then started in the open. A total of eight early morning hunts were held at all the usual meets but one variation from the norm was the plan to hunt under the Hunter's Moon. The field was very select with just Stanley Tompkins and Maurice Scott in addition to myself and my new kennel huntsman. Unfortunately, clouds spoiled the effect of the moon but we all enjoyed ourselves nevertheless. The 2½ couple had been carefully selected for the depth and individuality of their cry so that I would be able to identify them in the dark. It was such a windless night that when Maurice Scott and I were standing in Dark Lane during a long check we distinctly heard three different church clocks striking nine o'clock. We surmised the three churches to be Dennington, Stradbroke, and Laxfield.

It was with a sad and heavy heart that I started this season's hunting, as I knew that I could not afford to continue. To make matters worse, Jim Wickham really suited me and we thought alike on most matters so I felt I would be letting him down if I resigned. The most depressing part for me was that I loved my hounds and my hunting but it did not seem possible to find a solution to the problem. The amount of money that I had to spend over and above the guarantee was far more than I could afford and there could be no compromise. I only knew of one way to be Master: to do my absolute best for the Easton, always putting high standards before financial considerations. I could not see any prospect of the hunt raising its income enough to raise my guarantee to a level that would enable me to continue. Many of the senior members were aware that a serious problem existed and the committee decided on 25th October (1975) to make a single payment of £750 to me by borrowing this sum from the Point-to-Point Fund. I was very grateful for this gesture of support but the £750 was only a small part of the difference between the actual costs and the guarantee of £3,500.

The Opening Meet on Thursday 30th October was well-supported with about sixty horses which were kept busy all day with numerous little hunts resulting in hounds running for most of the day. The opening meet dance at By-the-Crossways was as much fun as ever, with the Captain on top form. Fifty-seven people were mounted for the Charsfield Horseshoes meet on Saturday 1st November. I was pleased to see so many people out but knew that the main reason for them being there was not to watch my expertise in the field, or

Opening Meet 30 Oct 1975

Photograph kindly loaned by John Finch

the venery of my beloved harriers, but the hospitality they could expect after hunting. Julie and Geoffrey Hennessy held open house at Pear Tree Farm every year after the Charsfield meet. Their hunting teas were so splendid and the atmosphere so special, that many people would hire horses and pay a full cap in order to be able to join in the tea. The social side of the Easton Harriers had always been an integral part of the Hunt's character, as much a part of its history as the bloodlines of the hounds.

Hunting at Charsfield on this day was slow to start but, after drawing for an hour, a hare was found which gave us a very exciting hunt of just over an hour. The last part of this hunt was along the banks of the River Deben, from Letheringham church, behind Kettleburgh Chequers into the woodland of the alder carr. All along the river edge, the scent was so good that every hound was giving tongue and the acoustics were perfect and the cry was such that it caused every single hair on my neck to stand up. In the alder carr, hounds had a serious check and then started to speak across the footbridge. Each hound crossed the bridge in single file and then ran on across Maurice Scott's marshes. I gave my horse to someone and followed on foot but they lost the line near the Blacksmith's Shop in Brandeston, so I walked back with hounds. This wonderful hunt was just the perfect build-up for the tea to follow, which was just as good as always.

The meet at Worlingworth Swan was spoiled by the presence of Dashwood and the hunting was very moderate but the meet at Laxfield Royal Oak on 13th March proved to be a special day with some excellent hunts, the hounds catching a total of two brace of

well-hunted hares by the end of the day. One fast and straight hunt took us from behind Dennington Bell to behind Laxfield White Horse. The last hunt was a joy to watch and a joy to ride. Hounds hunted two and a half circles around Laxfield House and caught their hare. I blew for home at a quarter past four after a day of hare hunting at its best. Good scenting and good days continued with another excellent day from Otley White Hart on 22nd November. Jim and I had our work cut out to keep hounds in sight and had to jump barbed wired fences to do it. The field was badly left behind and by the time they caught up their horses were very blown and this necessitated a half time stop at Framsden Greyhound.

The death of Hugh Clay caused us to wear black armbands when the Dunston came for an invitation meet at Dennington Bell and the customary joint dinner was cancelled in respect. Hugh had been Honorary Secretary for many years and then Vice-Chairman. His funeral took place on Friday 28th November, with many hunting people present.

Jim Meads, the world-famous hunting photographer, came to the meet at Stradbroke Ivy House on 4th December to take action photographs for *The Shooting Times*. Holding his camera, he ran all day and was usually up with hounds but there was no good hunting because hounds were rather flighty as they had not been hunted for nearly two weeks because of the Dunston visit and a day cancelled for fog, and I took hounds home in the middle of the day because the field did some damage on Mr Morton's wheat. On Friday 5th December Tombal Paul came over from France to collect a draft of hounds for his Master, Christian Adeline, whose pack, the Rallye Alesia, hunted hare. I drafted Taper, who would only hunt for half a day, Heather, who was too fast, Saladin, who was mute, and lastly Safety, Sandon, Saracen, Saunter, and Saxon, who had not yet entered even though they were nearly four months into their second season. These last 2½ couple were all from one litter and had been sired by Dunston Salisbury[71], a hound I did not use again, needless to say. Christian

Adeline was happy to take them even though I made sure he knew of their faults.

On the same day as these hounds left I wrote to the Honorary Secretary, Terence Saffell, to resign from the Mastership. This was partly due to the nightmare of the endless winter wheat but mainly to the crippling amount of money I had to put into the hunt.

George Ralli was the new owner of Rookery Farm, Cretingham, and I was introduced to him at the Ashfield Place meet on 11th December. I was delighted to find that he was a sportsman as we had always had so much fun with the previous owner, Dennis Wilson. It was a brilliant scenting day and, very unusually, three times hares swam the River Deben into Brandeston country. One sharp run took us from Earl Soham Mill Hill, over the lovely grass and fly fences at Cretingham Lodge and on past Brandeston village where they finally caught their hare on Rose Farm. I presented a pad to Jill Graham who was delighted at having jumped her first fly fences, and to Jill Sillars, who was, regrettably, leaving Broadwater Park and moving away from Easton country.

The Waveney Harriers met at Brundish Lodge which was right on the border of our two countries but had not asked my permission so I felt obliged to hunt with them to ensure that they only hunted in their own country. At the meet I told them that I was there to make sure they hacked into their own country before drawing and that they had broken the rules of hunting but they looked so amazed that I was convinced they were unaware of the existence of a rule book. Doing my duty by the Easton cost me dearly as I cut my horse badly which meant it was off work for a long time.

Boxing Day Meet 1975

Photograph kindly loaned by Mrs Linda Davy

Good luck was on our side at Debenham Red Lion on 18th December. Mr Turner of Mickfield Hall had banned all hunting for many years owing to misdemeanours by the Norwich Staghounds. He telephoned me to say that he had enjoyed himself so much at the Hunt Cocktail Party during the previous summer that we were welcome to hunt his land. This was extremely fortunate as, during the day, hounds took a line right across his farm, and passed very close to his house. Saturday 20th was a very fast day at Dennington Queen and only Sandra Reeve and young Sophie Money were with me at the end. Christmas Eve was a great success with the usual wonderful atmosphere at the Badingham White Horse, with good hunting to follow. All those still out said their horses had done enough so I blew for home at a quarter past three. Boxing Day was also well supported with the police estimating the crowd at well over a thousand and there were approximately 80 mounted, which included my two elder daughters, Bridget and Judith. Bridget and I had spent two days putting up some jumps so I could take the field round on a jolly before hunting properly.

The New Year Day's meet was at Cretingham Bell and when I arrived at eleven o'clock there was such a crowd that I could find nowhere to park. There was an unbelievable crowd on foot and 120 mounted. I had a good laugh at the meet when Michael Becher played a trick on a courting couple. The girl was continually searching for her boyfriend's hand and entwining her fingers through his. The boyfriend moved his hand away and Michael substituted his in its place. Sure enough, the girl's hand came searching and began to entwine fingers, then she suddenly gave a start. Michael's hand was missing a finger.

The first hunt was fast and far-ranging and I had difficulty in keeping hounds in sight. They ran a circuit of Otley and I caught up only when they checked at Hill Farm, Monewden. This hunt had given the 120 riders a good run and the horses were stretched out for over a mile. Scent was good and we were busy all day but a couple of misdemeanours occurred. Ten children rode through Mr Lindeman's garden and I, along with five others, rode across a stubble which unbeknown to us had been direct drilled with winter wheat. As usual I went to see both farmers to apologise as soon as possible and the sins were, more or less, forgiven. There was a tremendous party in the pub afterwards and I sang in both rooms, old-fashioned country songs in the public bar to please Walter Chapman and his father, and hunting songs in the other room. The cap came to a record amount of £200.

The British Field Sports Society had announced that it wished to raise a Fighting Fund to finance counter-measures against the propaganda of the anti-hunting lobby, and hoped every hunt would make special efforts to raise money to contribute to it. I gave the matter some thought and decided to hold two Sporting Days, one to involve horses at £10 a head, and a foot day at £7 a head. I thought it would be more fun if these days were a mystery and the only information given about the first day was that it would be limited to the first twenty-five applications, that they must arrive at Tannington Hall, with their horses, for an eight o'clock breakfast, that the sport would last approximately fourteen hours, and that there must be 'no questions asked'. The second day would start at nine o'clock and there would be no breakfast but, like the first day, the sport would last fourteen hours and everything must be left to me.

The full complement of twenty-five duly arrived punctually on Tuesday 13th January for breakfast and Sheila produced scrambled egg, sausage, bacon and coffee for us without a hitch. Afterwards we retired to the bar that had been set up in the entrance hall under the management of Ben Fletcher. While we were all merry-making at the bar, the front doorbell rang, and I opened it to find my Rector, Bill Donnan, standing there with some Synod papers for me to study.

'Whatever's going on, Tony?' he asked. 'You don't usually hunt on a Tuesday, or as early as this!'

I explained that it was a special fund-raising effort and asked him to join us at the bar for a glass of port. This he did and, after a little while, he said, 'What a lovely atmosphere there is, everybody is so happy and jovial. Is a meet always like this?'

I replied that it was usually like this but that it was now time we were off. As we were about to leave the bar, the Rector laughed and pointed to the large, old rocking horse in the hall and said that he thought he would follow on it. I immediately asked him whether he would be sporting enough to sit on the rocking horse at the meet and have his photograph taken with the hounds. He agreed, and Sheila quickly fitted him up with her bowler hat and whip. Ernie Calver and I carried the rocking-horse across the yard and positioned it just in front of the stable clock. I mounted my horse and held the hounds up around the rocking-horse and the Rector climbed aboard and the photographs were taken. I wrote in my diary that I thought he was the best sportsman there. When we met again in the church vestry the following Sunday I said, 'The photographs came out very well. I have one for you and have sent one to your Bishop'. His face

was a picture of surprise and horror until he realised I was only joking.

The first hare led us to the back of the Hall where we were joined by Flash, my rough-coated lurcher, who proceeded to course the hare when she was fresh found. I was highly embarrassed but it delighted the field to see their Master responsible for this gross breach of the rules and etiquette of hunting. The next hunt was extremely good and when we caught our hare I gave pads to Sue Money, Sarah Edmundson, Pat Webster, and John Finch, and the pate to Stanley Tompkins. I blew for home a little after midday and we all returned to the Hall. Five people had arranged for their horses to go home and it gave me great pleasure to accommodate the remaining twenty horses in my stables. Ben was kept busy for half an hour at his bar until Sheila gave the order to sit down when she calmly produced a three course lunch of leek soup, meat and potato pie, and chocolate crunch. As lunch was ending I announced that the afternoon sport was to be coursing and the dog owners began to arrive and came in to give Ben some trade at his bar.

We walked in a line across the wheat fields to put up the hares and each time one was found we stood still to watch the coursing. A total of six strong hares were found, all of which beat the dogs after very exciting runs. Light was fading at four o'clock so it was back to Ben at his bar to buy the dog owners a beer and thank them for coming. We all sat down to a proper hunting tea of boiled eggs, toast, and a cup of tea. Sue Scott was helping Sheila with the catering and she and Maurice had donated dozens of brown eggs from their old-fashioned Wellsummer and Maran hens. As I went round the table carefully putting exactly a teaspoon of whisky in the cups of tea, an essential part of a proper hunting tea but never more than a teaspoon full in each cup, I thought how lovely it all looked, the happy, healthy faces as they cut their toast into 'soldiers' and dripped yolk on their chins. An unexpected surprise was that, while we were out coursing, a team of volunteers had come in to clean the horses for their owners. Hilda Wickham had taken charge of this operation and had the help of Rita Emeny, Hazel Judge, Judith Garford and two others. When tea was over I announced that all the horses had been cleaned and that the owners were to take them home and be back at the Hall by seven o'clock for the evening's sport.

There had been much speculation as to what the evening sport would be and the odds had come down heavily on the likelihood that it would be cock-fighting in the dining room but we remained more or less within the law with a little night hunting on foot. Jim Wickham arrived at a quarter to seven with 3½ couple of hounds and we had almost two hours of hunting but the hares were not very kind to us and ran in very large circles. Although we were following a fair way behind, there was no chance of losing them as their cry was wonderful and seemed amplified by the still night air. We returned to Ben and his bar at nine o'clock and an instantaneous party broke out with singing and dancing over the broomstick. I cannot remember who played the accordion but it was a great party which ended at half past ten with everyone tired, but very happy.

The following day, Wednesday, was the foot day and, as breakfast was not included, the meeting time was nine o'clock. With no restriction on numbers there were thirty-eight people present and the schedule was similar but instead of hunting in the morning we had some hawking instead. I had invited two professional falconers from the airbases at Bentwaters and Woodbridge, together with two amateurs, and they brought three goshawks and a falcon. The first flight was at Tannington Place where they took three moorhens and then we went to Braiseworth Hall where two more moorhens and a pheasant were taken. The wind had become too strong so it was almost impossible to fly the birds but we had a little more sport as Dusty Smith had brought his ferrets which flushed out a few rabbits and the two that ran downwind were taken. The wind was too strong to try for wild duck at the Hall so the hawks were put away by their respective owners. The wind had been bitterly cold and Ben did a roaring trade in whisky before lunch. I had persuaded Sheila that it did not matter if the lunch menu was repeated so she again produced leek soup and meat and potato pie but this time there was a choice of trifle or apple crumble for pudding. After lunch we coursed again on a different part of the farm and this time there were more hares and we battled against the strong wind to watch twelve or more courses before returning to Ben and his bar. Sheila and Sue Scott served a substantial tea which this time included sausage rolls, malt bread, scones, and mince-

pies, all freshly baked by Sheila which were absolutely delicious and everyone ate heartily.

The wind continued to be strong and I had doubts if we would be able to hunt with the 'Twilight Harriers' as they had become known. Luckily the wind had lessened when Jim arrived at a quarter past six with 3½ couples so we were just able to hunt. Hounds went away downwind with the first hare and it was difficult to hear but, when they turned upwind, the cry was glorious. Scent often improves at the end of the day, especially when it is going to freeze or snow is on its way. The moon was especially bright, usually a sign that it is going to freeze, and scent was so good that hares started to take hounds seriously and run in larger circles. This was not ideal and at one time only George Gooderham was with hounds, but luckily the hare turned back towards us, so we were reunited. The clouds blew away revealing a full moon, which had been taken into account when fixing this date, and I saw the unforgettable sight of all 3½ couple running in single file on the horizon, every hound clearly silhouetted against the moon, and every one giving tongue, the cry blowing back to us. This was a sight that very few people ever see and it caused me to quiver with excitement and pleasure. Soon after this I decided to stop. Most of the followers had been given a piece of string with instructions to catch up any hound they could, once they heard me blow for home. These instructions were not because the hounds were disobedient, but because of the amount of hares on the move at this time of night. Sober, Bella, Herod, Saintly, Blizzard, Banish, and Bangle were put in the hound van and all thirty-eight followers, plus Jimmy and I, were relieved to escape the wind and made straight for Ben and his welcome bar. We put on some records of French hunting horns to set the tone for yet another great evening. Despite having served over 150 home-cooked meals in two days, Sheila

Hounds in the dining room at Tannington Hall.
(back) Russell Mays, Sue Gooderham, Tony St Quentin, Ben; (ctr) Flyn Bird, Lenny Misson, Heather Prescott, Hazel Judge, Helen Misson; (front) Stan Grimsby, George Godderham, Ernie Calver, Bill Prescott, Rosie Spragg, Sheila Harvey   Photograph kindly loaned by John Finch

started off the singing and, when a record of accordion music was played, Len Mison and Ernie Calver danced over the broomstick. More people sang, soon the atmosphere hit that extraordinary Easton peak, and

I asked Sheila for permission to bring in the hounds. She was dubious at first but then agreed and Jim and I brought them into the dining room. Seeing them lying in front of the large, open fire created such an ambience, I hoped the evening would never end.

I was so elated that I recklessly baited Sheila by suggesting within her hearing that, as I still had some of the foxes' urine left over, we could lay a drag up the front stairs, along the landing, and down the back stairs, and have the hounds hunting round and round the house while we stood there drinking. I suppose it must be a sad reflection of my character that my wife actually believed I meant it. For a few seconds Sheila looked incredulous, before she realised it was all in jest. Another idea was rather less foolish. At about eleven-thirty there were only twelve of us left and I thought it would be fun to have a photograph of us all on the stairs with hounds up the centre. It had been a memorable pair of Sporting Days during which Sheila had skilfully produced over 150 meals at very little cost and £500 was raised for the Fighting Fund. For over a year this figure was unbeaten by any other hunt in Great Britain and it had all been the greatest fun. It would not have been possible without Sheila and her efforts were acknowledged later in the year when the British Field Sports Society presented her with a Certificate of Merit.

The next morning it was hunting as usual when hounds met at Kenton Crown on Thursday 15th January (1976). The meet was especially good as most people were still in high spirits from Tuesday's Sporting Day but the hunting was very poor as the ground was so dry that it hurt hounds' feet and they could only hobble over the ploughs and scent was nil. The only fun of the day was when Clarissa Webb somehow became wedged headfirst in a ditch and all we could see were her long legs waving in the air.

At Coddenham on 17th January I found out that it was Geoffrey Ingram-Smith's fiftieth birthday and, as we began to draw, I handed him the horn and said, 'Go on, hunt the hounds. You're only fifty once'. At a check he blew for hounds, they came to him and hit off the line. Geoffrey turned to me and said, 'Doesn't it give you a lovely feeling when you get it right?'

Hounds on the stairs at Tannington Hall. (back) Ernie Calver, Ben, Hazel Judge, Tony St Quentin; (ctr) Will Edmundson, Bill Prescott, Sue Gooderham, Maurice Scott; (front) Lenny Misson, Tony Harvey, Flyn Bird, Rosie Spragg, Russell Mays

Photograph kindly loaned by John Finch

Following my letter of resignation of 5th December a committee meeting was called for 30th December at which they decided to advertise for a Master offering a guarantee of £4,000 but the Chairman, Captain Bernard, was asked to approach me and offer me £5,000 if I would continue in office. I explained to him that, although it would break my heart to give up the hounds, the increase just was not enough as my personal input would still be beyond my means and I just could not afford to continue. On 22nd January, when hounds met at Thorndon Black Horse and Jim was hunting hounds because I had injured my back, the Chairman took me to one side to tell me that he was empowered to offer me £6,000. I said that I would consider the offer.

The Ashbocking Nelson meet on 24th January was very eventful as my horse Connors fell into a ditch on his back and, as hounds were running, I jumped onto Hilda Wickham's pony and finished the run. Hilda later returned Connors to me and retrieved her pony, only to lose it again shortly afterwards when her husband's horse, Copper, went lame and she walked it back to the meet. The little pony had had an exciting day, first carrying the Master and huntsman and then the kennel huntsman. We were giving a large buffet party the same night and during the evening I was pressed for an answer to the offer of £6,000 so I agreed to take on the hounds again and a suitable announcement was made there and then.

Both meets in the following week were cancelled for snow and frost but I decided it was just possible to go on foot at Southolt Plough on the following Thursday. Only eight people came and we did not stay out for very long. Moreover, for the first time ever at Southolt Plough there were no jollifications in the pub afterwards but this may have been due to the fact there was a hunt dinner that night at Framlingham Crown. The Waveney Point-to-Point was on Saturday 7th February and usually we either had an early meet or did not meet at all on a day when a neighbouring pack was holding its Point-to-Point, but the Waveney asked us to hunt as normal because they, in turn, wished to hunt on our Point-to-Point day. The following Tuesday we met by invitation of the Dunston at Winfarthing Fighting Cocks and there was a mounted field of twenty-two Easton members and eighteen Dunston members. The last hunt of the day was the best and after a fast and straight run we lost our hare on Burston Green. The Crown looked too tempting to pass but, sadly, there was no one at home. Twenty people from each hunt sat down to dinner at the Crossways Restaurant at Scole that evening and it was as much fun as usual.

A great day awaited us at Brandeston on St Valentine's Day, a hunting day after my own heart, and those of us who were there will never forget it. Maurice and Sue Scott held open house for a hunt breakfast at nine o'clock. This was a breakfast straight out of the pages of Surtees, with cold beef and ham, bread straight from the baker's oven, baked potatoes, pickles and chutneys. Thirty of us were welcomed with either glasses of claret or Adnams old ale, mulled in the traditional way with a red-hot poker. Ten-year-old Victor Scott was in charge of the mulling and had six pokers in the fire which he systematically plunged into the mugs of ale. After breakfast we made our way to the actual meet at the Queen's Head where there was quite a crowd waiting for us. The scent was very good and we had a superb day, enjoying the Scotts' hospitality once more before going home.

We had another extraordinary day two days later from Debenham Cherry Tree as scent was again 'very, very good'. Hounds flew, the hares had no time to double, and we covered a lot of country. One run from Winston took us through Boundary Farm, past Framsden Mill, and then crossed Jockey's Lane, through Valley Farm to the Bird Farm at Ashfield. The pace was so fast that we needed to take gates and fly fences in our stride as we crossed the grass at Framsden Hall, nearly reaching High House Farm before swinging left-handed to Mr Fox at Moat Farm, where she was caught. Another good run took us from Winston Green, down over the low road where we had to jump the watercourse or lose hounds. This watercourse is very wide and deep and it was only out of fear of losing my hounds that I attempted it on a tired horse. Luckily both Geoffrey Ingram-Smith and I made it safely over. This hare was caught at Wetheringsett and, as there was only the two of us with hounds and not another horse in sight, we hacked back to the meet. Meanwhile, Safeguard had gone off on a separate line with Jim Wickham supposedly trying to stop him. How hard he tried is open to speculation but Safeguard caught his hare

single handed and Jim gave the hare to an old man on a bicycle.

'Cor, thank you sir,' the old man said. 'There's enough meat on her to feed me and my dawg'.

Back at the meet I declared that this had been the best day's hunting I could remember in twenty years of hunting and said that we must not let this wonderful day end at the meet. We all agreed to meet at the Hare and Hounds, Framlingham, for a singsong, which went with a real swing as the adrenaline was still pumping. We finished the day with an impromptu champagne supper at Brook Farm and finished up the cold ham from the Breakfast. 'What splendid people these Scotts are' I wrote in my diary.

Three days later we were at Rendham White Horse and had another first class day with really good hunts. After the best one, I gave pads to one of the Calver twins (I could not tell them apart), Emma Capon, Clarissa Webb, and a lady visitor from the Essex and Suffolk Foxhounds. A fantastic tea awaited us back at the pub, put on by the new landlady. Again I quote the last part of my diary entry for this day: *'These last three days have been like nothing anyone could imagine as far as hare hunting is concerned, just lovely hound work with one hunt after another – I also heard several new voices, very distinctive, Lancer for one, Careful, and Cameron.'* The hounds mentioned all went on to become real stars in later seasons.

There was some fair hunting from Easton White Horse on 23rd February but the highlight was when one hare decided to run through the Farm Park and the hounds hunted steadily through the sheep and goats, not a single one offering to riot although temptation was all around. I felt very proud of my hounds and wished I had a film of the scene, or that there had been another huntsman there to witness it. Tony St Quinton and Jill Graham shared my car when the Easton met by invitation of the Cambridgeshire Harriers at Horningsea Manor on 4th February. The meet was held in the garden and the sun was so hot that we could hardly bear to have our coats on. Too many hares, as well as the heat, prevented any chance of real hunting and hounds were putting up fresh hares every few minutes. We returned to the meet quite early and went in for tea in the drawing room where we had some unexpected entertainment. During last year's visit, Maurice Scott had performed his egg trick which consisted of putting a half-pint mug, partly filled with water, on the table, placing a square tin lid carefully on top of the mug and an egg balanced on the outer case of a matchbox stood on its edge in the centre of the tin lid. When all these were carefully centred,

Maurice would hold a mallet and proceed to hold a mock auction until it would have been time to bang down the gavel. At this moment he would strike the tin lid which flies across the room, and the egg should drop into the mug and bob about in the water. I have seen Maurice successfully accomplish this many times and never seen a failure. We had barely taken a sip of tea when the Cambridgeshire members asked me if I thought that Maurice would do that wonderful trick again. I replied that he probably would later on in the evening but they would not listen to me and crowded round Maurice, begging him to do it there and then. The Gingells' manservant Francis, always very dapper in his white jacket with covered buttons, was summoned and asked to provide the necessary elements for the trick. I again implored them to wait until later to see the trick, as I knew that Maurice preferred to do it when he was relaxed after a couple of drinks but they took no notice of my request and called upon Maurice to perform. He took much longer than usual in setting it all up but, when he finally hit the tray, it was not hard enough and the egg lay broken on the carpet. Maurice tried again but the second egg lay broken beside the first.

Francis was hovering nervously in the doorway when Tony St Quinton said to Hugh, 'Oh dear, Mr Gingell, I do hope your carpet is insured.'

'Insured be damned,' he replied. 'This is fun! Francis, bring a whole tray of eggs!'

After tea I went to the tack room where there was a large photograph of George Race and read the inscription out loud to all the Easton visitors. George Race had died at ninety-two years in a pony and cart while following his Biggleswade Harriers, ending a Mastership of eighty-six years. We were offered a bedroom in which to change before dinner and Hugh came in with a bottle of whisky, glasses and a jug of water, saying, 'I'm sure you gentlemen would like a little drop while you are changing.' Dinner was superb, followed by a great singing session and it was well after ten o'clock when we reluctantly left the table and made our way home.

Two days later we were at Wetheringsett White Horse. I knew that Sheila, Flynn Bird, and Sue Gooderham had gone to the Wetheringsett Manor Hotel for lunch so when hounds lost the line just behind the hotel, I rode up and blew my horn until the girls brought us out a drink. The sun was so hot that I gave up trying to hunt and boxed up at three o'clock saying I would hunt again later. After partifying for nearly two hours we hunted again with only Ernie Calver and his twin girls, Sally and Susan,

Maurice Scott, Geoffrey Ingram-Smith, Jim and of course, myself. Those who stayed were rewarded with a classic hunt; the hare ran a large circle back to the field where she had been found but I had to stop hounds as it was almost dark. When we returned for the second time the landlady, Audrey, had tea spread out for us and insisted in buying us a round of drinks. This was so unexpectedly kind and generous that I was prompted to send her a bouquet of flowers the following day, a gesture she never forgot.

The Point-to-Point was held in rather foggy conditions on Saturday 23rd February and Debbie Saffell, Sally Hennessy, and Graham Croll rode in the Members' Race. The Point-to-Point dinner was held at the Cretingham Bell and Maurice Scott worried the waitresses when he stood up, held the wine list open, and very seriously recited his version of Little Bo Peep. The girls hurried away and came back with the landlord who, seeing who it was, just grinned and walked away. Graham Croll ordered a steak but before it came, he was asleep, exhausted from riding in the race. I called the waitress and asked her to bring a cushion instead of the steak. Again the landlord was summoned to sanction this and when the cushion arrived I put it where the steak should have been, gently pushed Graham down, and he slept happily all through the meal.

On 4th March we met for the first time ever at Yaxley Cherry Tree and had a fairly good day, which ended with a darts match against the Essex and Suffolk Foxhounds at the Lindsey White Rose. A large crowd met us for the meet at Knodishall Butcher's Arms on 6th March and a busy day followed with an unexpected good scent. My birthday meet two days later was at Southolt Plough where I received many cards and presents. When we eventually moved off, it was snowing and very cold but we managed to have a fairly good day with half-time at the Worlingworth Swan. Jack Steel prudently came and took the horses home and we were soon indulging in a great party with plenty of singing and some new songs. I eventually arrived home at seven o'clock and, after a quick bath, went to Framlingham Crown for a hunt dinner. This was Tony St Quinton's first hunt dinner and he stole the show with two excellent songs that he had written himself. We left the table at one o'clock in the morning ending a birthday of fourteen hours of non-stop fun and camaraderie.

Two days later hounds met at Stradbroke White Hart but the best part of the day, after only moderate hunting, was Mary Calver's famous steak and kidney pudding for tea. I could not stay long at the tea because Colin and Tizza Plumbe were arriving for their annual visit which encompassed the hunt ball, this year held at Melton Grange Hotel on Thursday 11th March where there was a waiting list after the maximum of 220 tickets had been sold. As it was obligatory to hunt the morning after the ball we met, unusually, on a Friday at Framlingham Station Hotel but at the usual later time of half past twelve to allow everyone extra time to recover. There was so much wheat that it was impossible to hunt properly so we rode twice round the hunter trial course at Broadwater Park before stopping in front of the house to enjoy two bottles of champagne, kindly provided by Colin and Tizza Plumbe to 'wet the baby's head'. Their daughter, Alice, had been born on 6th December and was just three months' old. The next morning at Bedfield Crown there were fifty-two horses which surprised me because there had been over thirty the previous day. The hunting was unbelievably good given that it was very late in the season and we had a superb day covering a lot of country. Shirley Smith stopped for the first time to sample the *après chasse* party and was enthralled by the singing and thoroughly enjoyed herself.

This was the last day of the season proper but we had a little more fun to come as on 17th March we had a joint meet with the Sproughton Foot Beagles, as far as I know the first time this had happened in the Easton's history. The Sproughton brought 8½ couple of beagles and I took 6 couple of little bitches. The novelty of a joint-meet caused much interest, a large crowd attended the meet at Saxtead Volunteer, and *The East Anglian Daily Times* sent a reporter and a photographer. When it was time to move off I was deeply embarrassed by the behaviour of my hounds because when the beagles came towards me, my six couple of bitches just fled. One couple took refuge in the ladies lavatory, some were jumping up at the doors of the hound van trying to get back inside, while others crawled under vehicles and one even bolted into the public bar. There was no pacifying them so I told the beagles to go and draw and I followed at a

distance. Once a hare was found my harriers joined in and all was harmonious for the rest of the day.

The evening took a slightly different format from usual and instead of a formal dinner, I arranged with the Framlingham Crown to have a hunt supper of soup, cold meats, and pudding for £1.50 per head. This was excellent value for money and I was only able to get this special rate as the management knew that they could expect very good 'wet' sales. The atmosphere in the dining room was just indescribable with renderings from both hunts. Tony St Quinton was in great form again and some beaglers later assured me that I sang about twenty songs in total. No one left the dining room until after two o'clock in the morning. This marvellous dinner marked the end of the season but I had some more sport when I took all three of my daughters and followed Charles Corner and his Eastern Counties Otterhounds from a meet at Gleveringham Fishponds on 3rd April. The otterhounds were, by this time, hunting coypu and we stayed long enough to see a brace caught before returning to watch the Grand National on television.

This had been a good but very difficult season, owing to a perfect autumn which allowed the maximum amount of winter wheat to be drilled. We had hunted on sixty-one days including the joint meet with the Beagles with only four days lost due to weather.

The joint meet with the Sproughton Foot March 1976

Photograph kindly loaned by John Finch

1976–7

We had 13½ couple of puppies to walk out which was a great improvement on the two couple of the previous spring. Sending the bitches out to whelp on farms had beaten the virus as the puppies stayed healthy for long enough to receive their vaccinations. I had used one Dunston stallion hound, Sapper[72], and the other four litters were by Herod[71], who had a good voice, who was absolutely dependable in his work, and whose bloodlines could be traced back to the original Easton. During the spring M. Gorard Lemarchand took a draft of hounds for the pack he had recently started, the Rallye Les Bleus. I could not help feeling rather proud that Frenchmen continually came over to England for my drafts and I think it was for two reasons, first that I always explained their faults, and secondly that their working quality was still of the highest even though they were drafts. In this draft, Patriot was getting rather slow and Layman had a terrible stern but both of these hounds were first-class and would be a great asset to a new pack. Safeguard and Sanction would lose interest and not try when scent was difficult, and Beauty was guilty of babbling on more than one occasion. Peterborough Hound Show was as enjoyable as ever but with very little success for the Easton as we only managed one rosette for second place in the bitches couples class with Debra[73] and Picture[73].

The season had an unconventional start as Graham Croll had asked his son, Nicky, what he would most like to do on his birthday and he had said that it would be to go hunting. His birthday was 31st August so the request was difficult for two reasons, first that it was too early in the season and, secondly, that it clashed with Barsham Fair. All my family looked forward to Barsham Fair as we went in gypsy caravans and stayed for a long weekend, including the Bank Holiday Monday. To accommodate young Nicky's wishes, I travelled home very early just in time to hunt 3½ couple on foot at nine o'clock in the morning with a select field of the birthday boy and his father, as well as Jim Wickham and myself. The hunting was sadly very poor as there were huge muck-spreaders busily doing their job which was not conducive to good scenting. There were no hares in the sugar beet so the morning was, unfortunately, not successful. I was very tired having had very little sleep for three days so we only stayed out for one hour.

The first early morning was at six o'clock on Tuesday 7th September at Tannington and was singularly unsuccessful as the hounds were flighty and the scent was nil. We did not go out on 10th September because of gales but in total we hunted fourteen early mornings with all the young hounds entering except Fanfare who kept by my side. October was a month of heavy rain so that, for the first time ever, I was forced to cancel an October meet for wet. It had been a most unusual year and I made the following notes in my diary on 28th October: *'Most extraordinary year – very dry last winter – terrible drought in summer – grass brown and dead for months – rain in October then great growth of everything – tree leaves became green again – chestnut trees came into bloom again – selfsown corn very thick, almost everywhere – selfsown fields of barley with long ears at the end of October, one at Cransford*

worth combining – mushrooms everywhere, including where they had never been seen before and they lasted for six weeks. Had four months rain in October – grass grew 18" high since October 1st from parched earth. Could see definite lines between each days drilling of wheat.'

At the AGM on 4th September 1976 the subscription levels were raised to £20 for under-16s, £50 for 16–21, £80 for farmers, £120 for farmer's family, and £150 for subscriber's family, while caps were £3 for children, £5 for the 16–21 group, £8 for adults on Mondays and Saturdays, £10 on Thursdays, New Year's Day and Boxing Day, and field money for subscribers at £1.50 for Mondays and Saturdays and £2 on Thursdays, and £1 for children. Because of raging inflation, Jim Wickham's wages had risen from £25 to £39.35 which, after deductions left him with £33 clear, plus all the kennel perks. These consisted of sales of skins, bones, offal, together with free electricity and two tons of coal with free accommodation. Only five years earlier Bernard had been earning £15 a week clear. Heather Hamm, my girl groom, now lived in a caravan in the stable yard and earned £15 but had very few deductions, while the grooms in 1971 had had £5 a week but 'all found', i.e. they lived in the house.

Thursdays were more expensive than the other days because most people preferred to come on a Thursday if they could so we tried to persuade members to hunt on other days as much as possible. The Thursday country was the best and, more importantly, the camaraderie was at its highest, moving off times were much more flexible, and double the fun. The regular Thursday field were the characters of the hunt and exuded that special Easton spirit to regulars and visitors alike. Locals also sensed this special camaraderie and took a day's holiday so as not to miss the meet. 'I told him last week I wor'nt agoin' to work on Thursday 'cos the hounds were turning off'. Farmers and employees were often at the meets together, the only difference being that the farmers usually went home after we moved off whereas their men would stay and make a day of it. Lastly, on most Thursday evenings there would be an impromptu dinner which would be arranged there and then amongst those in the pub afterwards, often at Framlingham Crown but not always.

The Opening Meet was on Framlingham Market Hill on Thursday 28th October and the police had kept a large area clear for us. The hunting was nothing special and left us looking forward to the dance at Captain Bernard's home, which was the usual outstanding success. I found myself in serious trouble at Charsfield on 30th October as several times during the day the large mounted field crossed a large stubble field, grown up high with self-sown corn. Unbeknown to me, this stubble was under-sown with a special mixture of grass seeds to make high-class hay for Newmarket. With the land so terribly wet, we had made a shocking mess of it and Mr Western was extremely upset. I went to see him the next day and when we walked on the field it was terrible to see the hoofprints all over the field, each one several inches deep and filled with water. What could I say? I could only apologise and say how sorry I was and that I would have gone to any lengths to prevent it, if only I had known. He acknowledged that I could not possibly have seen the under-sown grass under all the self-sown corn and said that as I had such a good reputation for caring and not doing any damage, he would accept my apology. He invited me into his kitchen and put a full bottle of Teacher's whisky on the table and we chatted for a while. After an hour or so, he said: 'Do you know, you are a most extraordinary man. You came here yesterday with your hunt and completely ruined a valuable crop, then sit at my table and we chat like old friends and just look at that whisky bottle – it's empty!'

'It is an ill wind that blows no one any good' and Jim Wickham must have been delighted when, at Worlingworth on 4th November, I felt so unwell that I handed him the horn and hacked home. Laxfield on 11th November was especially good fun as it was Graham Croll's birthday and he was going really well over the gates and hedges at Laxfield House on his Point-to-Pointer, Fast Talker. A dinner in his honour was held at Framlingham Crown

Jim Wickham

and the chef made a cake with 'Happy Thruster' written on it. Graham was a great 'thruster' and would ride at almost any fence.

Following our exchange visits with the Picardie Valois and the Holcombe, we had another with the Rockwood Harriers. Their members travelled down from Yorkshire on Wednesday 17th November and met up with their hosts at Saxtead Volunteer at five o'clock. The Master, John Loy, and his wife, Marjorie, stayed with Sheila and myself, the Plumbes with Ernie and

Mary Calver, Mr Lawton with Terence and Marion Saffell, John Legates with Maurice and Sue Scott, and Adrian Garside with Brian and Flynn Bird. We all met up for a singing session at the Hare and Hounds in Framlingham which was a warm-up for the meet at Debenham Red Lion on Thursday, 18th November. The atmosphere at the meet was so good that Colin Plumbe spontaneously broke into song with *John Peel* and I followed with a song I had recently written, *A toast to hare hunters*. I was delighted to find that the scent was fairly good and even more pleased to be able to show the Yorkshire visitors the Easton at its best when hounds hunted a complete circle, fresh-finding their hare on the field where she was found, then circling in a different direction back to where she was found. We failed to catch our hare but this had been a classic 'figure of eight' hare hunt, which pleased John Loy as much as it did me.

There was a party for fifty people at my home that night which went with a swing and we finished washing-up at half past two in the morning. The next morning I had arranged a day of Saluki coursing. Twenty-two dogs came and it was interesting to watch how their coursing varied from lurchers and greyhounds. They were much slower on the run up to the hare but showed tremendous stamina and stayed just behind their hare endlessly and hardly ever turned it. It was a properly organised match with a professional slipper and judge. Twenty-four hares were needed to complete the card but we failed to find the last hare, so the final was not run to provide a clear winner. Sheila provided an excellent lunch of salt beef and this was served in the Worlingworth Swan. The final meet for the Rockwood visitors was Clopton Crown on 20th November. I had at last been able to persuade Mr Bye of Catts Hill to allow us to hunt his land but things went sadly wrong as the first hare decided to run round the house and hounds did some damage in the flowerbeds and then, to compound the problem, a member carelessly rode down a wheat field right in front of Mr Bye's two sons.

On Tuesday 22nd November I went on a cruise for two weeks and left Jim to hunt hounds at Swilland, Stradbroke, Hoxne, and Otley, with Geoffrey Ingram-

Smith turning hounds to him. Paul Rackham, Master of the Suffolk Foxhounds, very kindly wrote to tell me that he had been out at Hoxne and had had a very good day but at Otley the outstanding bitch Heather was killed when kicked in the head by a horse. On a more positive and pleasant note I was pleased to hear that Lady Tollemache had joined the field.

Good scenting continued. We had a good day at the Children's Meet at Helmingham Hall and hunted across to the water tower at Crowfield. I was a little way behind hounds when I saw them check and begin to cast themselves, then suddenly put their heads up, and race away without speaking. I could not understand what was happening but as I rode a little nearer I could hear the reason. The Essex and Suffolk Foxhounds were running in Gosbeck Wood and my harriers were going to their cry. The joint pack ran to Valley Farm, Coddenham where, with a little difficulty, we were able to separate the two packs and I hacked back to Helmingham.

The new landlord of Badingham White Horse had been extremely rude to Sheila during the summer, so the Christmas Eve meet was held at Laxfield Royal Oak. The pub was next to the churchyard and a funeral was being held on the same day so we un-boxed well away from the church but still managed to have a good Christmas atmosphere, and we did not forget to drink to the General's memory. It was one of the finest scenting days a huntsman could ever experience and hounds could hunt a line an hour old. The hares did not have time to double, so the hunting was fast and continuous with one run taking us beyond Peasenhall. Prettylass was missing at the end of the day and I waited for a while at the pub for a while in case she turned up but then had to leave. During dinner that evening, the Laxfield police telephoned to say that she had come back to the meet and that a lady had taken her into her house and was very happy to keep her until morning. The next morning the policeman telephoned again to say that, after Prettylass had had a good sleep in front of the fire, she began to howl for her friends so, not wanting to bother me on Christmas Eve, he had collected her and locked her up in his garage at the police station but when he had tried to feed her that morning she had escaped and he had lost her. A little while later Judith, Bridget and I were leading the hunters up the drive to stretch their legs when who should turn in at the top of the drive but Prettylass. The old bitch had come five miles home to me. It felt like a real Christmas story and was unusual in that lost hounds

usually either remain at the meet or go back to the kennels.

The Boxing Day meet on Monday 27th December was as well supported as usual but was to prove an unfortunate day for me. I had put in a lot of work in making a good jolly around World's End Farm, Church Farm, and Dennington Place, and took the field for a gallop, all on grass, which included the twenty-three jumps that I had built. Later on I had a fall on the flat and was concussed and taken by ambulance to the hospital. Sheila rode with me in the ambulance and Ernie Calver brought a car behind to bring her home. I had dislocated the vertebrae in my neck and it has a kink in it to this day. I was out of hospital and could supervise the putting up of jumps for the New Year's Day jolly and on the actual day Sheila drove me around so I could watch the fun. A period of bad weather followed with three meets being cancelled and we should have begun our return visit to the Rockwood Harriers on Wednesday 19th January but this was postponed although Sheila drove me up to Yorkshire and we stayed with the Master, John Loy. John had asked to use Herod as a stallion hound so we took him up with us but went via the Meynell Kennels where I bought a mare called Bridget from the Master. I followed the Rockwood on foot as best I could on the Thursday. In the evening, we went to the Rockwood Hunt Ball with me in my green tails, sporting a surgical collar and I did manage a few gentle dances.

I did not ride again until 19th February but was not bored as there was a new initiative from the British Field Sports Society. This time it was a Membership Drive to encourage as many people as possible to become members. I was as keen to support this as I had been for the Fighting Fund and gave the matter a lot of thought. The first plan was to hold coursing meetings with a stipulation that everyone who wanted to run his dog must first join the BFSS. Maurice Scott was the local secretary for the Society and I met him for lunch at the Cretingham Bell to discuss these matters. The second idea was to involve members of the Easton in a recruiting programme and we decided to call a meeting at my home on Wednesday 2nd February. I set up a firkin of Adnams bitter together with cider and sherry and all the members came to hear a very good lecture on 'First-aid In The Field' given by our Easton member Dr. Will Edmundson followed by a speech about the membership drive and its importance from Maurice Scott. I was known amongst my members as a 'benevolent dictator' and I lived up to the dictator part when I made my speech and told them that I expected every Easton member to join the BFSS and to pay their subscription by Bankers Order. A cash subscription to Maurice Scott was not good enough. I went on to promise a private day's hunting to any Easton member who could get two or more new Bankers Order members and promised a very special reward, although no details were given, if any could get as many as five new members.

The next morning Sheila drove me to the meet at Yaxley where I saw Captain Bernard being driven by his sister, Lady Cynthia. I was shocked to see how thin and ill he looked. I followed for a while but then we went for lunch in Eye and missed seeing the spectacular ducking of Geoffrey Ingram-Smith in the watercourse at Gordon Grover's farm. There was a beautiful sunny day for the Point-to-Point on 5th February and it was chiefly memorable for the fact that Debbie Saffell won the Member's Race, having ridden the whole course alone as Graham Croll, the only other entry, had fallen at the first fence. Coursing people met up at the Worlingworth Swan on Wednesday 16th February to sign their BFSS membership forms before going on to Hoo Hall to course. When the coursing was finished we adjourned to Brandeston Queen for lunch where 'Bungay Roger' sang before producing a cooked hare's leg out of his pocket and eating it. The afternoon was spent with George Ralli at Rookery Farm where there was an abundance of hares, and twenty-nine new members were signed up. When the Dunston met by invitation at Eye White Lion I did not follow as I spent the day in the pub getting farmers to sign BFSS membership forms but we enjoyed the usual joint dinner at the Crossways at Scole with twenty from each hunt sitting down.

When I decided to try to hunt hounds again at Knodishall on 19th February I wore the surgical collar especially tight and Sue Gooderham kindly lent me her good, quiet Robin. Mrs Gingell and her Cambridgeshire Harriers were entertained at a lawn meet at Dennington Hall on Tuesday 22nd February and in the evening Sheila cooked a lovely supper at our home when eight visitors and thirty-six members of the Easton sat down to steak and kidney pie followed by blackberry and apple crumble or coffee caramel. After supper the singing started and Tony St Quinton again stole the show with the songs he had written. Maurice and Sue Scott gave another hunt breakfast on Saturday 26th February with beef and ham and fresh bread and baked potatoes for thirty-five people. The atmosphere at the breakfast was so good that singing started and it was quite difficult for me to persuade everyone to move up to the Queen for

the actual meet. Clifford Arbon, a famous local singer, sang a few comical songs at the meet as it was his birthday. There was one really good hunt in the shape of a large 'U'. Found on West Hill, she ran to Earl Soham, up towards Saxtead and back to Rose Farm, Brandeston. She was fresh-found here and she then ran exactly the same route but in the reverse direction back to West Hill. She was fresh-found for the second time and started back on the same route again but was eventually lost in a thick place. This had been a most unusual hunt of an hour and ten minutes with good slow hound work and a great cry.

The news of Captain Bernard's death on 28th February rather dampened the atmosphere at the special meet on 1st March at Southolt Plough for the Easton members who had recruited two or more new members for the BFSS. The hunting was very good and we all had great fun but there was one very unnerving tribute to the passing of the grand old man. One hare took us to Worlingworth station on a line which was exactly the same as one he often recalled from his days as Master when Elise Gooch and I were the only ones out.[1] It is very eerie and strange how often hares and foxes will do this sort of thing and many books have been written about these mysterious coincidences. I wrote in my diary: *'Captain Bernard died last night, one of the last of English natural gentlemen – never to be replaced. A tremendous loss to the country, and especially the Easton Harriers. He had always been such a good friend and adviser to me and set an example that I have always tried to follow; in church life, in hunting and in public service.'* The Hunt Ball was again at Melton Grange. We invited George and Mary Paul, Paul and Sheila Rackham, Tim Finch, and Peter and Jill Sillars to dinner at Tannington before going on to the ball, partly because they were my neighbouring Masters but partly because I wanted to see some red evening coats at our ball. The hunting at Bedfield the next morning was moderate as the ground had become capped, i.e. it had become hard and dry on top, and held no scent. We had planned to hold two more Sporting Days at Tannington Hall on Monday 7th and Tuesday 8th March to raise money for hunt funds and the Monday would have been a foot day but this was cancelled owing to the funeral of Captain Bernard. Tuesday, which was my birthday, was the mounted day and twenty-two people arrived for breakfast at

[1] There was a standing joke about the size of the ditches at the Southolt meet so, in the days of very small numbers hunting as in the 1950s, it is not surprising that there were only four horses out on this day, the Master and Ernie Nunn, and Elise, then Gooch now Quilter, and myself.

eight o'clock, bringing with them cards and presents. Tony St Quinton brought one which I was to open at once. It was a box of Phyllosan tablets, which were advertised as 'Fortifying The Over Forties', sent to me by his wife Anne as it was my fortieth birthday. We had a busy morning's hunting, covering a lot of country and hacked back to lunch through the Bedfield lanes, stopping at my grandmother's house where Charlie Goodsman took a lovely photograph of her talking to me over her garden gate, just one of three hundred that he took that day. We put the horses and hounds away in the stables and, after lunch, Bob Hicks arrived with his goshawk. It was my intention for him to fly at wild duck off the moat but this was not to be as the bird flew to the top of an oak tree and refused to come down.

I nonchalantly said to the assembly, 'Oh don't worry, we'll all go hunting again' and when we came round the corner of the house, Jim Chesson and Ivor Constance were waiting with the Waveney Harriers. Everyone was so surprised as even Jim Wickham did not know they were coming. We hunted in a different direction towards Dennington and had a fair afternoon. Jim and Ivor joined us for a proper hunting tea at half past four, then most members took their horses home and returned at half past seven to watch two films

Granny Rodwell

from the BFSS. One was called *The Piper of Nacton* and the other was about foxhunting. At nine-thirty Jim Wickham was waiting with 3½ couple and we went hunting under the moon, returning at around eleven o'clock. My birthday party then started in earnest and went on until four o'clock in the morning. William Gilbertson-Hart, known to all the Easton as 'Wild William', asked for a bed as he was in no state to drive home and had also declared that he would definitely come coursing with me in the morning. I took him a mug of tea at half past nine and found his brown boots, breeches, and coat still with the rose in the buttonhole, all strewn on the floor and I had some difficulty in waking him. He promised to dress and come down to breakfast but he did not appear. I was anxious not to be late for the coursing so went upstairs to fetch him. A decidedly tame 'Wild William' was sitting in front of the dressing table with the stock in his hand looking very unhappy.

'Come on,' I said. 'You'll make me late.'

'It's this stock, old boy,' he explained. 'I haven't brought my Moss Bros instructions with me.'

I tied it for him and managed to get him down to breakfast but when we arrived at Winston Hall for the coursing 'Tame William' was still half asleep, so I gave him a dog to lead and we set off across the field. He looked so incongruous in his brown boots and breeches and coat still sporting the red rose.

The last official day of the season was at Coddenham on 12th March where I presented Heather Prescott with a buttonhole, as it was her birthday. The scent was nil but there were enough fresh hares to keep us on the move and we had an amusing day.

A big coursing meeting had been arranged on the Dennington Hall Estate on 15th March for the BFSS membership drive. Maurice Scott could not be there to take charge and as I was still not completely recovered from the Boxing Day fall, I asked Major Rous if I could ride Shamara to cross the fields quickly, otherwise I could not have kept control. There were approximately a hundred dogs and a large crowd of spectators who all met up at the Worlingworth Swan as I did not disclose the coursing ground until the last minute. Everyone followed me to the Dennington Bell and we started from there. We coursed all morning and then had a lunch break at the Bell before moving to a different part of the estate for the afternoon sport. Gerald Ashley-Cooper, Regional Secretary of the BFSS, was with us so I asked him to write thank you letters to Major Rous and John Nesling, whose land we had coursed. I had difficulty in controlling such a crowd and would have stood no chance at all had I not been mounted. I sent them all home very happy at four o'clock and hacked Shamara back to Tannington to be ready to greet Reg Wright, who was driving down with his North Warwickshire Bloodhounds.

The special day at Southolt Plough for Easton members who had recruited two or more new BFSS members was not as exclusive as I thought it would be as every one of my members had done so, and they had really taken the cause to heart as no fewer than thirty-two had managed to recruit five new BFSS members. I had promised them something very special and so the bloodhounds would be meeting at Bedfield Crown on the following day, Wednesday 16th March. While Reg and I were having a cup of tea I thought it

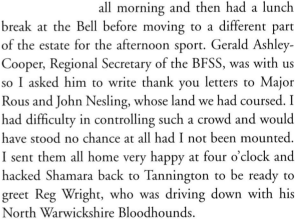

would be fun to 'hunt' Sheila and she readily agreed so, having left an article of clothing for the hounds to sniff, Sheila set off and ran round the garden and the paddocks back to the house. Hounds were laid on, hunted her line exactly, and licked her thoroughly at the end.

The day began with a hunt breakfast at the meet for the twenty members of the thirty-two who had managed, unbelievably, to recruit *ten* new Bankers Order members. This was to recognise their special efforts and Sheila again came up trumps and served a splendid breakfast of homemade bread, salt beef, and baked potatoes. The others joined us at ten o'clock and an hour later we started to hunt with the bloodhounds. Maurice and I had ridden the course the previous Sunday with the three boys who had volunteered to be the runners. Each one had to memorise his respective route and been instructed not to change his socks for a week. Strangely, there were no objections to this request. All the lines had been carefully chosen so that the mounted field could keep on the lanes as it was too late in the season to be riding across country but the runners could be on one side or another in the wheat field. Victor Scott ran from Bedfield church to Saxtead where there was a check at the Volunteer, while Shane Smith ran to Maurice Scott's farm at Brandeston. Then Maurice dispensed hospitality while Craig Girling ran from Brandeston to Earl Soham where there was a check at the Victoria. Shane Smith's second run was through the marshes behind Earl Soham chapel and the meadows at Earl Soham Lodge and across to Soham Town corner and Craig Girling ran the last lap back to Bedfield church. We returned to the pub at half past three where Jack Steel was waiting to drive my horses home. We felt it had all gone off very well and had been the greatest fun. Everyone was more than ready to crowd into the Crown for the lovely sausage rolls that Sue Scott had brought. The *après chasse* party lasted for nearly two hours but we were forced to go home as there was a dinner that evening at Cretingham Bell.

I was valeting my coat when I heard a lorry outside and went out to find Wild William behind the wheel.

'This is my transport today, old boy. Do you mind if I come in and wait until dinner time?' He was driving a Thames Trader lorry which had a huge bulldozer blade in the back. When it was time to go to Cretingham to dinner, Wild William said he did not know the way, so I volunteered to ride with him while Sheila drove Reg in the car and Wild William tried to keep up. He was approaching one corner so fast I knew it would be disaster, so I yelled at him and he slammed on his brakes. The bulldozer blade, which he had failed to tie down in any way, crashed into the back of the cab.

I shouted something else and he said 'Oh, I haven't been called that for years'.

We did eventually arrive safely at the Bell. After dinner, before the festivities, I made a speech and thanked Reg for bringing his hounds and complimented him on their excellence. I next thanked all the members for their splendid efforts and announced that, of all the hunts in the country, the Easton Harriers had signed up the most new BFSS members with just over 300 Bankers Order members. I was rather emotional as I made this announcement as I was thinking what a splendid lot of members I had who had done this. Only Maurice Scott and myself knew that the next best hunt had recruited only forty new members. All together, including those members gained in the many coursing meetings, the Easton had signed up 640 new members. During the coming months there were many moments when I felt proud to the point of embarrassment when I received congratulations on the efforts of my little harrier pack.

The next morning hounds, or at least a few of them, were out for the last time on 17th March for another joint meet with the Sproughton Foot Beagles at Framlingham Hare and Hounds. The landlord, Jimmy Finbow, made us very welcome but my harriers were again terrified when it was time to mix the hounds. Again, some crawled under vehicles while others fled into the pub where it proved difficult to evacuate them, not because there was any extra drinking which could have been the case but because the hounds were not to be found. The last couple were eventually found hiding in Jimmy's private sitting room. As last year, they hunted well together once a hare was found and they ran too well for me to be able to see very much. Queenie had a superb tea waiting for us on our return and later four beaglers came home with me to change before returning to Framlingham for the joint dinner at the Crown Hotel. I had negotiated a special deal with the manager and we enjoyed a soup, cold meats, pudding, and a half bottle of wine at £3.00 per head. For the after-dinner entertainment, I quote from my diary: *'Excellent singing and jokes from both sides – the beaglers really excelled themselves this year – Tony St Quinton was excellent also – Sheila managed somehow to get me out at about 1.00am.'*

1977–78

Jim Wickham was now beginning his third season with me. We had eight couple of puppies to break and as usual we started walking out on couples as soon as hunting was finished. I had concentrated on breeding for work, using mostly Easton stallion hounds, but in 1976 had reached a point when new blood was needed and went to the extreme of using all outside stallion hounds. The puppies we were walking out in the spring of 1977 had come from three litters, one sired by Dunston Barclay[70] and the other two by Cambridgeshire Chaplin[73]. Mrs Gingell, the Master of the Cambridgeshire Harriers, rarely spoke about the working qualities of her hounds but on two occasions I had heard her speak of Chaplin's outstanding voice and from this I knew not only that he had a good voice but also that he must actually have hunted otherwise he would not have been speaking. I had used him on these thin grounds but I was not disappointed and as an added benefit he brought some of the Cambridgeshire good looks.

Jim paraded hounds at the Suffolk and Framlingham Shows but I did not ride as my neck was still very painful from the Boxing Day fall. Peterborough Hound Show was held on Thursday 21st July and although I wrote in my diary that we won three rosettes according to the official book it was only one. We took Harriet to Peterborough as she was being drafted to the Clifton Foot and was taken back to Somerset by the Master John Boyd. We also had the company of two Frenchmen who spent the night with us at Tannington and left for home the next morning with some hounds, Jean Pierre Moreau taking Villager and Yves Guibert taking Rallywood to their respective hunts in France. Jim and I had a sad day on 9th August as we had to put down old Bangle and Banish, granddaughters of the famous Tangle. They had done ten seasons and were two of the finest bitches any huntsman could wish for.

Open Day – judging the hounds, Colin & Tizza Plumbe watching

On 10th July we held an Open Day at the kennels. This could not be called a Puppy Show in the normal way because there were no puppy walkers since all the puppies had been reared at the kennels but it was an opportunity for Jim to show off his domain and to create some audience participation we sold envelopes containing the names of the puppies and prizes were awarded in the usual way, but not the silver spoons. Miss Bala Paul and Tim Fogden, Joint Masters of the Sproughton Foot, judged the puppies and Tim and his kennel huntsmen, Jock, judged the terriers. For extra fun we held a sweepstake on every hound in the kennel which were judged in the grass yard by Kevin Mowles, a friend of Jim's from the Essex and Suffolk. There were also competitions to guess the height of a hound, and the weight of a couple. The support for these Open Days was very good with around 250 people attending, made up of members and supporters. It was very unusual for a hunt dinner to be held out of season but I held one at Framlingham Crown on Monday 18th July. Those attending had no idea that it was for a special reason as I wanted to award some hunt buttons. After dinner I made a short speech regarding the honour of receiving such a button and all that it stood for and then awarded it to Brian Bird, Louis Borrett, Gordon Grover, Bill James, Rupert Montagu, Lady Quilter, Clarissa Webb, Caroline Saffell, Maurice Scott, and John Hinde. Also present were the existing button holders, Terence and Marion Saffell, Ernie Calver, Stanley Tompkins and Geoffrey Ingram-Smith, but unfortunately Pat Webster, Rosie Mackman, Nona Shand, Rozzie Haag and Judith Hale, to whom I had wanted to present a button, were unable to attend. On 4th October Jill Graham was elected as Honorary Secretary and was a very worthy successor to John Capon who had held the same office for many seasons. Their responsibility was to arrange the meets and it is far easier to do this job if the secretary is an agricultural person. John Capon was a well-known and respected farmer and Jill was from a long-established farming family and was married to an agricultural contractor. Both were ideally suited to being meet secretaries. To complete the roll call of personnel, Hilda Wickham was doing two horses at the kennels and Heather Hamm the others at Tannington Hall, with the help of Christine Gladwell.

The Easton were fortunate in being able to call on the services of an excellent photographer in Charlie

Goodsman, son-in-law of our long standing member Nona Shand. We had had the idea of using his skills to construct a slide show which would show the whole of the hunting year, the bitches whelping on the farms, skinning the fallen stock and feeding hounds, inoculating the puppies, and every other aspect, however small, of life at the kennels which members and others do not usually appreciate. All summer he had been taking photographs and he already had over 700 by the time hunting started. Naturally he was ready and waiting at six o'clock for our first early morning on 29th September at Tannington. We had waited until the end of September to begin hunting as it was terribly dry and the ground rock hard but the early mornings were uneventful with hares quite difficult to find. Sheila often followed on foot with her lurcher, Kizzy, on a lead and one day she spotted a

Jill Graham

Photograph kindly loaned by herself

hare on its seat and we had a run with it. The first good morning was on Saturday 8th October when we met at half past six. Fifteen people were out and Charlie took amazing photographs because there was mist lying in dense bands between three feet and six feet above the ground so that the photographs showed people's heads and shoulders and their horses' legs with nothing in between. The photographs of Jim and I with hounds showed all the hounds and our feet and spurs and horses legs with just our heads and shoulders showing. They looked very weird. This was one of the best mornings I ever remember. Hounds were continuously speaking on drags, i.e. overnight scent, and they did not stop hunting for three hours with the most glorious cry throughout but even this did not encourage Waggoner to leave me and run with the pack. I was very disappointed as he had been out all the previous season and I had hoped that he would enter now he was a year older. Church Farm was as usual used to good effect for rabbit breaking, with Jaffa, Actress, Wanderer, and Careful all needing a little lesson about succumbing to temptation. Jim hunted hounds for the next two meets while I was away in Wales at the Welsh Cob Sales, and again on 22nd October when I was away at the Westhall

Cider Festival to watch the apples being crushed with horsepower.

Hunting was very poor at the Opening Meet on 27th October as scent was non-existent and as nearly the whole of the draw was drilled with wheat I was relieved when I could blow for home. For the first time in many years there was no Opening Meet Dance because of the death of Captain Bernard but we had a hunt dinner instead and my daughter Judith came as it was her fourteenth birthday. As usual the Hennessy hospitality attracted a large mounted field at Charsfield and the cap totalled £120. Again scent was nil but I managed a few jollies through the orchards and a very happy throng converged on Pear Tree Farm full of anticipation of the delights to come. I missed hunting at Worlingworth Swan because, just as I was leaving, Paul Elliott telephoned to say that all my unbroken Cleveland Bay crosses were out on the road at Bedfield and I had to go to catch them up, but I saw many of the field later on as I had arranged a hunt dinner to plan the details of a forthcoming visit to the Rockwood Harriers in Yorkshire. The dinner was limited to those people going on the trip and those present were Mary and Ernie Calver, Sue and Maurice Scott, Mary Garton, Elise Quilter, Tom and Sandy Walne, Marion and Terence Saffell, John Finch, Sheila and me.

We all left Suffolk on Wednesday 9th November to meet our Rockwood hosts at the Rose & Crown at Ingbirchworth. The weather was terrible and the wind howled through the keyhole in the pub door so the two roaring log fires were very welcoming. Our hosts gave us such a genuine and sincere greeting that we knew at once that we were in for a good time. Thursday's meet was at Three Acres, Hoydhouse, where Lord Savile was waiting to greet us which made us feel especially welcome as we were to be on his estate most of the day. The first two hours were spent drawing blank but then a hare was found and we had a good run over stiffish country. There were some formidable walls and post and rails but Tom and Sandy and Terence Saffell went really well and I recorded 'were a credit to the Easton.' Marion Saffell had a fall but was not hurt and Mary Garton's mount took great exception to a goat and bucked her off but the day ended with a good party at Adrian Garside's home where the Easton members reminisced and went through their personal excitement and thrills of riding over this type of country, so different from the ditches and plough or wheat of Suffolk. We visited the kennels the following morning and I took the opportunity to look at Clifton Foot Pirate and study his pedigree. He had been drafted to the Rockwood as he was too big for the Clifton and as he had Easton Precious on one side of his pedigree I decided to bring him back to Easton as he might prove to be a good outcross. The afternoon's entertainment was a shopping spree for the ladies and a tour round 'Tetley's' for the men, not a tea factory, as had to be explained to a disgruntled Ernie Calver, but the brewery, this tour having been arranged by Bob McCreadie who was a director of the brewery as well as Joint Master of the Rockwood. Before we went home, he showed us round the stables and the shire horses. Maurice Scott and I thought they had rather too much 'daylight' under them and looked rather like Clydesdales but we kept our opinions to ourselves. There was no official get-together on Friday night and Sheila and I enjoyed a fabulous dinner with John and Marjorie Loy, whose guests included the manager of Lord Savile's estate and two hunting farmers and their wives. It was a lovely evening spent in convivial company.

On Saturday we met at Carr Hill House for a lawn meet generously hosted by Nigel Sykes. Sadly, it was a day of terrible winds and hailstorms but John Loy invited me to ride up with him as he hunted hounds so I managed to keep reasonably warm. The scent was very good in spite of the wind and we had to ride hard at times to keep hounds in sight. The weather worsened and at around two o'clock we were forced to return to the meet. John and I were very relieved to get into hot baths before going on to dinner at the Wagon & Horses at Langsett but John must have caught a chill in the harsh conditions and was not well enough to attend the dinner. His Joint Master, Bob McCreadie, took charge and after dinner gave out Tetley presents to all of us visitors, cigarette lighters for the men and shopping bags and aprons for the ladies. The ladies' presents must have been of excellent quality as Sheila was still wearing her Tetley apron many years later. Following the presentation of the gifts, Bob honoured me by presenting me with the Rockwood Hunt button. The whole evening was a great success with plenty of songs and was a real high note on which to end the visit.

During our absence Jim Wickham had hunted hounds at Laxfield and Debach and we were soon back into our own activities as on Friday 26th November about ten were out under a full moon for a moonlight meet at Tannington Hall. We had an unforgettable hunt encompassing Fenton's Farm and Red House Farm, Dennington, before returning to where she was found, with the cry of the 2½ couple sounding almost eerie in the night air. A quick beer at Brundish Crown preceded a light supper at the Hall.

Earlier in the season a party of us from the Easton had gone to hunt in the Essex and Suffolk country on the occasion of a visit by the Hambledon Foxhounds. Geoffrey Ingram Smith had arranged this trip and it started with a hunt breakfast at his home before we moved on to the Saracen's Head at Newton Green near Sudbury. During the day Geoffrey introduced me to Prince Timu Mogul and invited him to join us after hunting for a substantial hunt tea which he had arranged with the management of the pub. The tea was fantastic and served in front of a huge log fire in a beamed room. The camaraderie was the best when Geoffrey asked me to sing a *A toast to hare hunters*. The Prince enjoyed the song and immediately ordered a bottle of champagne which prompted another song, whereupon he ordered a second bottle. This dangerous course of action led to numerous songs and equally numerous bottles of champagne. When it was time to pay for the tea and champagne the Prince's valet came up to the bar as if to pay his share but we waved him away saying that we did not expect him to pay for anything. What we did not realise was that the Prince never handled money and had sent his man up to pay for the champagne he had ordered. Our mistake was an expensive one as our shares were £17.50 each, or about half a week's wages for a farm worker. On 1st December the Prince visited us at Hoxne Grapes. Those of us who had been at Newton Green welcomed him and he asked me to organise a round of drinks as he did not know who ought to be included so I ordered one for every farmer, supporter, and member who was in the bar and they all drank to his health. It was a marvellous meet with a great atmosphere.

We found our first hare on Vic Last's land. Scent was very good and hounds just flew and ran over the River Dove into the Waveney country. The Prince was just behind me when we came to the river and I rode to a place where I knew I could cross, jumped from the bank into the river, rode down it for about fifty yards, and then scrambled out on the far bank. The Prince followed me and nearly fell off jumping into the river but once we were out I looked back again and he had a grin from ear to ear which said everything. We galloped on and came up to our hounds between Gate House Farm and Syleham and, as they were at check, I took the opportunity to pick them up and hack back into Easton country. During another sharp run, the Prince fell and disappeared from the field. I thought he had hurt himself and returned to the meet but about thirty minutes later he was with us again. It transpired that he was too proud to ride with a muddy coat so he had ridden off and, seeing a house and stables, had ridden into the yard. Hearing hooves in the yard the lady of the house came out. Luckily it was Virginia Bush, who sometimes hunted with me, as he said, 'My good lady, would you be so good as to brush me down?'

Without turning a hair, Virginia fetched a clothes brush and carried out his bidding. Just as the Prince was leaving, Virginia's husband came home to see a black man riding out of his yard, but the Prince just said, 'Oh do you live here? Your wife has just been very kind to me,' and rode away to find us again. After hunting the Prince told me just how much he enjoyed hunting in England because it was much less dangerous than his own country, where the natives shot at the nobility.

The landlord put on a lovely tea at the meet but I only stayed for about thirty minutes after hunting. After all the amusement of the Prince's visit I would normally have been elated and would have led the songs and merriment but on this occasion I just needed to disappear and do some serious thinking. I was very depressed about the conditions for hunting in the Easton country. Autumn after autumn favourable conditions had meant that around 90% of the draw was sown with winter wheat. The only fields not drilled were those left to grow sugar beet the following spring. I could see no prospect of it getting any better and, to make matters worse, fields were getting larger and larger as ditches disappeared under the bulldozer and huge expanses of wheat barred the way of the mounted field. I was torn between two obligations, one to the farmers and one to the members. A complete trust had been built up between me, as Master, and the farmers, and they had learned over the years that my word was my bond and that no damage would be done. More importantly, their individual wishes would be observed and I really knew who owned each field. My second obligation was to show good sport to my members which was becoming more and more incompatible with that to the farmers. After many years I had produced, through

breeding and selection, a pack of hounds that would virtually hunt themselves and from the edge of some vast expanse of wheat I could watch them, perhaps a quarter of a mile away, swinging round all together at a check like a flock of birds. Their excellence made my frustration and depression more acute as it constantly emphasized how impossible it was to have a large mounted field in such an intensively farmed country. I ought to have been pleased that the mounted fields were getting larger and larger but with a field of, say, sixty horses the trust between the farmers and myself was split in sixty different ways as anyone of them could do damage for which I would get the blame. I just could not have my mounted followers where I would have liked them to be and the rideable headlands and cartways were disappearing under the bulldozer.

That evening Jill Graham, the new secretary for meets, telephoned to say that she had received a letter from Lord Tollemache to say that he did not want us on the estate on 22nd December because of shooting. Both Lord and Lady Tollemache come from great hunting families and their support for a local hunt was seen as an example to other landowners. The letter asking us to keep off the estate was just the last straw and I sat down and wrote to Terence Saffell to resign my Mastership and to Jim to inform him that I had done so. Two days later at Stradbroke Ivy House, it was obvious that neither had received my letters. This left me with the unenviable job of having to tell them in person although a good day's hunting did lift my spirits and we all had lots of fun. On Thursday 15th December we had invited the Waveney to meet at Dennington Hall for a lawn meet but there was a ludicrous misunderstanding as they did not bring their hounds. After a half an hour or so at the meet, Lord Somerleyton suddenly said, 'Tony, I hope you've brought your hounds.' I thought they were pulling my leg but after a while they convinced me that they really did not have their hounds so Jim went back to Easton and brought out all the bitches. They had been fed and their stomachs were so full they all looked pregnant but they managed not only to run but also to really excel themselves, hunting carefully and seldom over-running, and their cry was outstanding. There was good, classic hunting all day and I was so proud and pleased. This was easily the best day this season.

On Saturday 17th December the hunting was as good as it could possibly be and included four classic circles bringing the line back to the field where she was found and just for good measure a very large figure of eight. The cry was simply unbelievable. I would not have thought it possible for such a volume of cry to come from harriers hunting hare. Jim had brought all the dogs, 16½ couple, and I would think this was the loudest cry I had ever heard from the Easton. It was clearly very inspiring as when they hunted past Low Farm, Worlingworth, one of Terry Cox's little daughters was leaning out of an upstairs window shouting, 'Git'im, git'im!' Most of the well-hunted hares were lost in thick bushes and, from a field of 73 horses at the start, there was not a single one left with us when Jim and I hacked back through the Bedfield lanes. We were both exhilarated as the whole day had been just pure magic and that cry would live in our hearts and minds for weeks to come.

I had visited Lord Tollemache after receipt of his letter and, explaining just how perfect his estate was for a Children's Meet, had managed to persuade him without too much difficulty to allow us to hunt on part of his estate. The meet at Helmingham Hall was on 22nd December and seventy-three children attended, as usual enjoying clattering over the drawbridge into the courtyard. We had one good run across Pettaugh but eventually got into trouble from Mr Styles who said he had not been notified we were coming. The Christmas Eve meet was at Laxfield and again there were over 70 mounted. The wind was too strong for good hunting but nevertheless we stayed out until after four o'clock. The Boxing Day crowd on Saxtead Green was even larger than usual with the police estimating it at around 1,200 people and the cars parked on the road stretching back almost to Framlingham, and a field of seventy-seven mounted. When I moved off I spotted my first kindergarten teacher, Miss Brownsword, and stopped to take off my hat and shake hands with her, which both pleased and embarrassed her at the same time. Anticipating a large mounted field and with so much winter wheat, I had spent three days preparing a course for a very long jolly. I started off through the meadows at the Cedars and, after making maximum use of Church Farm, went through Dennington Place and World's End Farm, then the grass lanes leading to Bedfield Crown. This was a jolly of about six miles and both horses and riders were pleased to stop at the Crown for nearly fifteen minutes. The field had no idea that they had only ridden half of the jolly and I set off again, over Hungers Green, through the meadows at Primrose Farm, up a cart track to Grove Farm, across the road and through the meadows at Holland's, passing over Bedfield Green and through the meadows at White House Farm before finally coming to an end and drawing for a hare at Low Farm. The hounds hated

these jollies and although Jim had left the old ones at home, he had to constantly push the stragglers on. The field had jollied for about ten miles, almost all on grass with over thirty jumps. Many told me later that for the next few days they were so stiff they could hardly walk. Towards the end of the day we had a very good hunt and caught our hare near the Gay Barn, and I presented pads to Michael Buckley and his sister, Clare. The following day I took the customary bottle of whisky, to Mr Last, Mr Wolton and the Bircham brothers as a thank you for their co-operation in allowing me to build the jolly.

We had a very jolly meet on Saturday 31st December at Stradbroke White Hart. One of the people there was an American, Dan, who had married one of the Cooper girls from Manor Farm, Framlingham, and usually spent Christmas with her family although we had missed him from the Christmas Eve meet this year. He revelled in the special atmosphere, and after hearing of the General's death had offered to buy cases of port to ensure that the tradition continued. He explained that he had been forced this year to stay in America for important business reasons but he had been completely unable to concentrate on the business in hand because he kept looking at his watch and imagining the scene: all the boxes arriving, the pub full of people, someone singing a hunting song; the tray of port handed round, the Master calling for silence and proposing the General's health. He concluded by saying that he might just as well have come to England for he was unable to keep his mind on his business, but was with us for every second of the day. After such an enjoyable encounter, the day turned out to be disappointing. Scent was non-existent, Jason, one of the best young doghounds I ever saw for his age, was killed in a fox snare at Gate House Farm, and to cap the misery the day did not follow the usual tradition as Mary Calver was unable to provide her famous steak and kidney tea.

A huge crowd was waiting for us at Cretingham Bell for the New Years Day meet on 2nd January. There were no fewer than 114 horses and the cap totalled £350. I had been busy taking down the jumps from Boxing Day and re-erecting for the New Year Day's jolly which involved an awful lot of work and time but was the only way that I could give the mounted field a good time as well as keeping out of trouble. A mounted field of 114 in an intensively farmed area is a Master's nightmare as many of those out would not be used to hunting so they would not be versed in farmer relations or, possibly, in proper control of horses unused to the excitement. The jolly was along the low meadows at The Rookery, up and over to Sparkes's Farm and through the lovely meadows at Cretingham Lodge, where we had a little 'check'. I went out onto the main road and near the bottom of Mill Hill turned into the Mill House paddock, along Earl Soham Rookery meadows, across to Boundary Farm, then I walked up the road and had one last jolly round the meadows at Grove Farm, crossing the river at Mr Western's Bridge Farm. After proper hunting a party to beat all parties started in the Bell on our return. Jack Steel had arrived to take the horses home so I was free to enjoy myself. The party did not end at the Bell as at some point we all moved to the kennels and resumed the party there. John de Vaux and Peter Judge were on top form and stayed the night with Mary and Ernie Calver. It was half past

Boys' Sporting Day

Photograph kindly loaned by Mr and Mrs Maurice Scott

one in the morning when I finally arrived home but that did not stop me being up bright and early for the Boy's Sporting Day.

This was the inspiration of Maurice Scott's son Victor who, hearing from his father how much fun the sporting days had been, had asked if it would be possible to have one for boys. Maurice was very keen and he and I planned it, along with the expertise and co-operation of Sheila and Sue. Thirty boys, who were sons of members or connected in some way to the Easton, were invited and duly arrived at half past nine to listen to a lecture by John Hinde about coursing. While John was given his talk there was a terrible hailstorm with thunder and lightening and gale force winds which was part of a nationwide storm which did a great deal of damage. The worst of it had passed by the time the lecture was over and we were able to course even though the wind was still so strong that the smallest of the boys found it difficult to walk. We managed to see four courses, two of which were particularly good. Lunch consisted of mugs of homemade soup and sandwiches, and I had stocked up with seven gallons of bitter which was made into shandy. After lunch it was time to go ferreting and we enjoyed an excellent afternoon with twelve rabbits caught before returning to the Hall for bangers and beans and more shandy. After tea it was

time for target shooting in the stables where there is a very wide passage running through. The doors at the far end were securely locked, then a sheet of plywood fixed to it and the targets pinned to the plywood. The top doors of the stables were closed to prevent the horses' heads being in the line of fire. The boys were divided into three classes, according to their age and the actual shooting was done under the close supervision of Maurice. When all the classes were completed it was back into the Hall for hot punch and mince pies until the parents arrived at nine o'clock to take the boys home. Apart from the gales, this had been very successful and the two boys who had enjoyed it the most were called Tony Harvey and Maurice Scott. The day raised £60 which was donated to the charity Riding for the Disabled and the local paper, *The East Anglian Daily Times*, was at Brandeston Queen on 15th March to photograph Sheila presenting the cheque to Miss Ginger Paul.

Good scenting conditions continued with some very good days, notable for the outstanding cry of the hounds. The Hunt Ball was held on Friday 13th January at Melton Grange Hotel and although the evening got off to a good start when Sheila and I were invited to a party at the Hennessys beforehand it proved to be an unlucky date after all as one of the members had an angry scene with his wife and went off home leaving his two guests stranded at the ball. Luckily we were able to offer them a lift home but the incident had soured the atmosphere. Ernie Calver broke with tradition and failed to appear at the meet next morning at the Coddenham Duke but scent was good and we had a brilliant day which blew away all the cobwebs from the night before. On returning to the meet Sue Gooderham's soup was like a miracle; I don't know if I have ever enjoyed a mug of soup as I did this. As we were enjoying it, a rather pale-looking Ernie Calver appeared.

'Well, Master,' he said. 'I've come to the meet.'

'It doesn't count to come at the end,' I retorted. 'Your fine is to buy a round of drinks for everyone!'

Applications for the Mastership had been received from Jeffrey Bowden and Keith Spindler but, at a

Committee Meeting on Friday 3rd February, I agreed to take on hounds again for another season. The guarantee was increased again to £8,000 but the main reason for my continuing was the run of good days which had lifted my spirits and made me feel that I just could not walk away from these wonderful hounds.

A very cold period followed with fixtures cancelled for frost and snow. We just managed to hunt at Thorndon on 26th January but with sleet and strong winds. A meet always seems especially good if there are farmers present and this year, at Thorndon, we had Jack Hammond and David and John Edwards and their wives, which gave a real feeling of welcome. During the day, in spite of the strong winds, hounds worked out three doubles in quick succession. I noticed that a small group of people on the road were taking a particular interest in the proceedings. I guessed by their gestures to each other that they understood what they were looking at and recognised at least two out of the three doubles. This prompted me to go over to speak to them and found out that, by an extraordinary coincidence, they hunted in Pennsylvania with Tony Garvin to whom I had exported some of the Easton Harriers some years earlier. The *après chasse* party had that special spirit that the Thorndon ones seemed to generate and it was made all the better as John and David Edwards joined us but we were forced to leave at a reasonable time as there was a hunt dinner at Framlingham Crown. During this party John Edwards expressed regret at not having a horse to join us all in the hunting field. Ernie Calver immediately offered his Rupert and a bargain was made for Wetheringsett the following week. Conditions were so bad at Knodishall on 28th January, with sleet and strong winds, that I dare not hunt and should have returned home with hounds but there was such a large mounted field that we decided to go for a ride. I took them along tracks to the Plough & Sail at Snape where we had a quick 'nip', then Sue Gooderham took charge and we enjoyed a warming gallop in the forest before returning to the pub where sandwiches were ready to be handed to us on our horses. We returned to the meet having at least exercised ourselves and our horses.

On Tuesday 31st January we made our way into the Cambridgeshire Harriers country to meet at Horningsea Manor. Jack Steel took my lorry with the horses while a party of us went to a hunt breakfast at Five Winds, Bromeswell, the home of Geoffrey Ingram-Smith. As we sat at the table, Geoffrey confessed to having bought all the ingredients for the breakfast but had not asked his wife, Monica, until that morning. We all arrived punctually at the meet at half past eleven could not move off until one o'clock as there was too much 'bone' in the ground. There had been a hard frost and the sleet storms did not help at all. When we eventually moved off the hunting was moderate, although we showed enough sport to stay out until half past three. While we had been hunting, Jack and David Steel had driven the lorry on up to Oakham to pick up a hunter that I was to have on trial, and they were back waiting for us when we returned to the meet. The evening was as good as usual with a splendid dinner and plenty of singing. The Cambridgeshire always wanted me to sing the song that I had written about the last meet at Tannington Horseshoes, but it was Mary Garton who stole the show with her recitation, beautifully read, about Masters of Hounds. We left the Gingells just after ten o'clock but it was so foggy that, by the time I dropped off Tony St Quinton, Mary Garton and Jill Graham, it was well after midnight when I reached home. My friend Paul Rackham, who was Master of the Suffolk Foxhounds, invited the members of the Easton Harriers to have a day with his hounds at Thornham Horseshoes on 2nd February. Several coverts were drawn blank until a very pretty fox was found: it was a deep red with an unusual amount of white on it. I had a good view of this fox as Paul had invited me to ride up with his huntsman, Tom Batterbee. The scent was almost non-existent but I still thoroughly enjoyed myself, just listening to Tom's horn and voice. In later years I heard a good number of huntsmen in the field, but seldom heard one with such a voice and horn as Tom.

The news that John Edwards was going to ride to hounds had caused considerable interest and there were an unusual number of farmers at Wetheringsett White Horse on 7th February. He was to ride Ernie Calver's sensible and steady Rupert and I lent Shamara to Ernie. John jumped every obstacle as it came and at the end of the day he jumped a large ditch just behind me, very successfully. With so many farmers out it was no surprise to me that the *après chasse* party was one of the best and a stranger sang some sea shanties, which made a refreshing change. The next five days hunting were cancelled through frost and snow and one of these was an invitation meet in Dunston country but twenty from each hunt still met for dinner at The Crossways in Scole. At the conclusion of the snowy period we had a day on foot from Easton White Horse. We moved off with 33½ couple and the cry, as they took a line along the river edge, was beautiful to hear.

I was pleased to see one double worked out properly which I would not have thought possible with this number of hounds. On Tuesday 21st February there was a joint film show between the Easton and the Sproughton Foot in Debenham Community Centre and, in spite of it being terribly foggy, there was a good turn-out of around 250 people.

Paul Rackham invited me to bring my harriers and hunt in the Suffolk country and the meet was arranged for Tuesday 21st February at Westhorpe Lodge. I was delighted as I was able to show the foxhunters some slow, but perfect, hare hunting, with hounds working out two doubles before catching their hare. Scent improved and the last hunt was a good run to Mr Black's farm which resulted in a long hack back and it was nearly five o'clock when we reached the meet. In the evening we had a joint dinner in the Crossways Restaurant in Scole and I quote my diary entry: *'Excellent meal, atmosphere and company – non stop jokes, songs and recitations all evening – I tried to stop at midnight but no one wanted to go – John Fazackerly told a host of jokes.'*

I would love to erase Saturday 25th February from my life but, since I cannot, I shall confess my sins. When I arrived at the meet at Glemham Crown I was still not sober from the night before and stupidly had a couple of whiskies before moving off. Quite soon I realised I could not carry on and gave the horn to Jim but I knew there would be a problem because if I went home, the hounds would come with me regardless. I stayed in the field until they found and began to run and then I walked back to the meet and put my horse away and had a long sleep in the cab. I was so ashamed of this disgraceful behaviour that I decided I would not touch any spirits for the rest of the season.

A few days later it was Herbert Breese's Diamond Meet at Saxtead Volunteer on Tuesday 28th February. The Plumbes made sure they were in Suffolk for it, and also Joseph Hampshire from the Rockwood who had become great friends with Tom and Sandy Walne who had stayed with him on our visit there. Most of the old members turned out to support Herbert but there was no party as such at the meet due to a mix up. I found out that a mistake had been made between the kennels and my stables and I did not have a horse at the meet so I slipped out to make arrangements to rectify the problem but the pub just emptied because everyone thought I was about to move off. Little did we expect that it would be a really outstanding day. Hounds hit off a drag as soon as we started to draw, worked up to their hare and

put her off the seat, and then caught her after a good hunt. The second hare gave us a fantastic run. She was found just behind the meet and ran parallel to the Framlingham road to New Town, swung right-handed and crossed the road at D'Urbans Farm to Red House Farm, then to Kettleburgh church and crossed the Easton road to the river edge. I thought she had swum the river but hounds kept this side and hit off the line through the marshes and roughs, passing through the meadows at Home Farm, crossing a road again and through Maurice Scott's big meadow and across to Kettleburgh Lodge where she was lost in a thick place. This hunt had been continuous with hardly a check and the horses that were still up with hounds were in need of a blow. Later in the day, after stopping at Kettleburgh Chequers for half-time, we were ready to enjoy another good run. As we left the Chequers Ernie Calver viewed a hare on the skyline. We laid hounds on to the line, well behind her, and they took it past Hill Farm towards Framlingham before actually coming up to her. They put her off her seat and she ran to Victoria Hill, right-handed over Lampard Brook to Easton Park, where they checked for the first time. Jane Pitcher had viewed her going into some rough at Martley Hall but she had not stopped in the rough and hounds took the line on past the Stud Farm, only to lose the line completely near a stinking slurry pit. Everyone said they had had enough so, as we were so close to the kennels, Jim and I let Sandy and Tizza lead our horses back to the meet while we walked back to the kennels with hounds. I am not sure if we did actually walk as I think we were floating along on a cloud of ecstasy.

I had great difficulty in getting Herbert to agree to come to the special Diamond Dinner at Framlingham Crown. Normally, he ate very little so I stressed to the management of the Crown that he must have tiny portions and it all went to plan. He held pride of place at the table surrounded by all his old hunting friends: Vera Pulham, Judith Bull, Barbara Buller, Irene Freeman, Mr & Mrs Fred Ling, John Moyle, and his brother, Alfred. There was, of course, a good singing session, with Herbert joining in with obvious enjoyment. I made a short speech congratulating him for having been a member for sixty years and presented him with a half-gallon bottle of whisky. Herbert responded with a short but very emotional speech.

The next day we held a private day's hunting at Hoo Hall at three o'clock for little Alice Plumbe. We went on foot and I took 10½ couple, some of which I wanted to watch closely. I found that Warrior and

Jangle spoke well, but Gaylass was mute. We caught our hare and I presented Alice with a pad which still hangs in her home. In the evening we gave a private dinner party in honour of the Plumbes' visit and the main topic of conversation was the sport we had enjoyed from the Diamond Meet. Thursday's hunting from Eye was fast and furious with long runs which took us well out of our notified draw and covered most of Occold and Southolt. The Calvers gave a dinner party for the Plumbes which was a perfect end to this fabulous day and the third dinner party in a row for us all. Our Point-to-Point was on Saturday 4th March and the entries in the Members' Race were so poor that I had to enter one of my hunters. Caroline Saffell rode Dante for me but the old horse gave her an awful ride, pecking badly at every fence and a lesser jockey would have been tipped off at the first fence. In spite of Caroline riding him so well, he fell after one and a half rounds but luckily did not injure his jockey.

The Saffells gave a lawn meet on 6th March and, as we were short of country, they kindly suggested that anyone who wanted to could ride round their hunter trial course before starting to hunt. My 'birthday' meet was at Southolt three days later and Elise Quilter kindly gave me a silver hare as a birthday present but I had to make the sad decision that this was to be the last day for Herod. He had done seven seasons and just could not run up anymore. After a moderate day's hunting at Rendham, Sheila and I went to dinner with the officers at RAF Bentwaters to make arrangements for an Easter Monday dance in the Officers' Club. A very good day was had at Debenham but the field did a lot of damage in some wheat. The next day, I spent hours raking it by hand to fill in all the hoof marks so that they did not fill with water and kill the wheat that was left. The damage was about a mile long and my back ached by the time I had finished.

The scent was very good for the meet at Brandeston Queen on 15th March but often spoilt by the high wind. I presented pads to Heather Prescott and Mary Garton after one particularly good hunt. One final day's sport remained, the joint meet with the Sproughton Foot Beagles at the Hare and Hounds at Framlingham. The first hare decided to enter people's gardens, then the playing field, so we got hounds away as quickly as possible and the next hare took us to Cransford. It was not a good day's hunting but a lot of fun was had by all. Sixty people packed the dining room at Framlingham Crown for the joint dinner and the après dinner entertainment proved better than ever. The beaglers were on top form with Tim

Fogden stealing the show with a clever song about a London hunt. It was such fun that I could not tear myself away until half past one, despite knowing that I had in front of me a four o'clock start and a twelve hour journey in a Thames Trader lorry. I was taking two horses down to the West Country for a hunting holiday with Terence Saffell based at Chard.

There had been fifty days' hunting with eight days lost due to frost and snow which meant that I had hunted hounds a total of 539 times. This had been an extremely good scenting season with lots of brilliant days, some of which had been fast and continuous, when it was a case of sitting down and riding hard across country, while others had been classical, with great displays of pure venery.

1978–79

In the breeding of this season's entry I had remained in kennel and the 10½ couple were all sired by Easton stallion hounds. I used Lancer[73] on one bitch, as he had such an incredibly good voice, Sampler[74] and Carpenter[73] had sired a litter each, and old Herod[71] had proved that, even at his age, he was still fertile and had sired a litter of five puppies. We had high hopes for this year's Peterborough Hound Show as we had a particularly beautiful unentered bitch called Garland but she was only second in the unentered bitch class although we also had third prize in the best couple of doghounds. As was becoming customary, we took some draft hounds to deliver and handed over Action, Acorn, Berkeley, and Wary to Jean Pierre Moreau for his Equipage des Janvris. Although I always supported Peterborough I was definitely not a 'show' man but I thought it would be fun to try to beat Betty Gingell's all conquering Cambridgeshire Harriers. Garland had been second to the Cambridgeshire at Peterborough but I thought her light colour might give her the edge at the Honiton Hound Show in Devon as the West Country Harriers are all lemon and white like Garland. So I made arrangements to take some hounds down there and to kennel them with Peter Over who had put up horses for Terence Saffell and I a few months earlier. We took Lawyer and Beatrice as well as Garland and Jim brought them down in a little trailer behind his car, while I took my daughter Judith and her friend Candy Ireson. The show was held on 3rd August. Lawyer let us down by being very shy, the brood bitch class was very exciting and Beatrice narrowly missed being third, but Garland won her class and beat the Cambridgeshire which was the lowly objective. I brought the hounds home in their trailer and gave the girls the responsibility of looking out for police cars but they fell asleep, I was stopped, and the police really threw the book at me. I was driving a trailer without a triangle on the back, exceeding the speed limit for towing a trailer, using the outside lane while towing, and exceeding the ordinary speed limit! I had beaten Betty Gingell but that red rosette cost me dearly.

Another excitement during the summer was the fuss over Tom Walne's complaint to Weatherbys, the governing body of racing, that an unqualified horse had been run by Keith Spindler in the Members Race of our Point-to-Point. Before a horse can run in a Point-to-Point it must have a certificate proving that it has been 'regularly and fairly hunted' which was usually interpreted as the horse having been out hunting a minimum of eight times. The Master of the Hunt is responsible for issuing these certificates and has to sign it to say that the horse is properly qualified but because I was not always sure of the horses' names I relied on the honesty of the owners when I issued them. In this instance I had been tricked by Keith Spindler who had properly qualified one horse but when applying for the certificate gave me the name of another horse which he had just bought. Wetherbys took Tom's complaint very seriously and there was the most dreadful fuss. We all had to attend a tribunal in London and were called in one at a time to give our account of what had happened. The panel of stewards took a rather high-handed, overbearing, attitude towards me, and I became more than a little annoyed.

'Well, gentlemen,' I said, 'I have come here at great inconvenience and must point out to you that this is not a court of law and I can walk out if I wish. To you Point-to-Point racing is important but to me it is just a nuisance and a waste of a hunting day. A good cheese and wine party makes more money for the hunt than the races and I would not have a Point-to-Point if it were not for the fact that a lot of my farmers love a day's racing and I can welcome them in the Master's hospitality tent.'

This very blunt statement altered their attitude considerably and I then explained how the mistake had occurred and assured them that I would try to prevent it from ever happening again. Whatever the official outcome, it did not stop us from holding a Point-to-Point the following year.

We had a change of plan for the horses this season and kept them all at the kennels under Hilda Wickham's charge, with Sally Dunlop and Christine Gladwell as grooms. We started hunting on 19th September at Tannington in the sugar beet and had out all 31½ couple of hounds. We were joined by Robert Rous with his wife, Theresa, Charles Corner, Mary Garton, and Ernie Calver and my youngest daughter, Charlotte, who followed on her bicycle. She pointed out to me that at one time the sun and the moon were shining at the same time.

This season I broke my golden rule about having no one out for the first few mornings, and bitterly regretted it. On one of the early days two members tried to help whip-in but only succeeded in scaring two puppies so much that they hid in the sugar beet which this year had huge leaves. Method and Saucy were missing at the end of the morning and, although I went back to the beet on foot, I could not find them. Method came to the stable yard at half past nine but I still could not find Saucy. The men who were harvesting the sugar beet reported seeing her on three different occasions but, in spite of going out each time, I could not see her. I fetched a few hounds from the kennels and walked around with them, hoping that their presence would give her the necessary reassurance to come out of hiding. She was seen so often by the farm workers that I knew she was still in the sugar beet and I hunted in the beet the next day (Thursday 28th), as normal, feeling confident that she would join the other hounds, but she did not. Jim, Geoffrey Ingram-Smith and I were all riding in the beet and we drew it thoroughly in all ways, but none of us could see a trace of her. I just could not imagine that the other hounds would not find her. I eventually gave up and went home. As soon as we had left, she was seen again. It was maddeningly frustrating and I was at my wits end to know what next to try. The following day I spent hours riding up and down in the sugar beet field with a few hounds but there was still no sight of her. On Saturday morning we hunted properly in the sugar beet for two hours, with all the hounds but still not a trace of her. By now she had been in this field for four days but finally, while I was having breakfast after hunting, I had an idea to trap her. Jim brought over some very smelly flesh and we made a trap with a pig weighing machine so that she would have to enter the pig weigher to get at the flesh which, once touched, would release a weight and the door would slam shut. She was, of course, very hungry and soon came to the smell of the flesh and was caught. I would not have thought it possible to lose a hound for five days in a field of beet but it just emphasises how, essentially, a hound is a pack animal and how lost and scared they feel when alone.

The early mornings continued but I decided to hold one that was really out of the ordinary. I thought it would be fun to have a special day when only horses which had been driven to the meet in a cart would be allowed to hunt. I took the hounds in a float pulled by my daughter's cob Henry from which I later hunted hounds. Jim drove another of my driving cobs called Ruby and Geoffrey Ingram-Smith had Punch who was a heavy type with lots of feather on his legs and normally pulled my gypsy caravan. This idea created a lot of interest and there was a fair crowd at Bedfield Crown to see us off. Twelve horses and ponies followed hounds and Mother Nature was kind to us as scent was very poor so we were just able to manage on our 'make-do' hunters. There was a tremendous party in the crowd in the Crown afterwards with Ted Chaplin bringing his cob into the pub, whereupon Maurice Scott proceeded to auction it, getting the price up to at least three times what it was worth. He had no difficulty in getting bidders as everyone knew that it was only in fun. After the auction, the cob was tied to the gaming machine until it showed signs of leaving its calling card and was hurried out.

The Ride & Drive Meet – Geoffrey Ingram-Smith on Punch

It was very foggy at the Great Lodge on 14th October so I put the field all around a wood, rather like cub hunting, and the hounds rattled a few hares round and round in the wood for an hour or so until it was clear enough to hunt in the open. The first hare found in the open brought out a curious aspect of hound behaviour. This hare was black and had a humped back and hounds hunted it with a very deep cry and a real hatred, in sharp contrast to their usual joy in following a sweet scent. I was home only just in time to follow the beagles who were meeting at the Hall at one o'clock. Sheila had been ill for a few days but rose from a sick bed at half past six to bake for the beagle tea.

When I got home from church the following morning Graham Redfern was waiting with his eagle to fly at hares. It was a male golden eagle and had a wing span of over six feet. It was so heavy on his wrist that he needed a special stick to support his arm. He flew it at a number of hares but, as the bird would only fly downwind, it required us to do a lot of walking to find enough hares willing to oblige. It was fascinating to see the number of birds that appeared to mob the eagle. In less than thirty minutes there were about a hundred birds circling above us making as much noise as they could and, when the eagle actually flew, the rooks and some of the others dive-bombed it.

JAH and Charles Corner at the Ride & Drive Meet

The Opening Meet was held, as usual, on Framlingham Market Hill outside the Crown Hotel where, the night before, I had been guest speaker at the NFU dinner. *The East Anglian Daily Times* was there in force as the newspaper was writing a special article about hunting. The draw was completely free of wheat and there was a good serving scent which meant that we could enjoy some long slow hunts with first class venery. Lady Cynthia, Captain Bernard's sister, gave her permission for the Opening Meet Dance to be held again at By the Crossways and everyone was so pleased to be there again. It was the perfect end to a good day's hunting.

We had another first on 21st November when we had a joint meet with the Dunston in their country at Burston Crown. My hounds were very hesitant at first about mixing and Cameron dropped his stern and went straight back into the lorry but soon all was well and we moved off with the Dunston huntsman,

Ralph Baines, hunting the joint pack. There had always been some friendly rivalry between Ralph and myself and I was pleased to see that it was more often the Easton hounds who were first to hit off the line after a check. The hunting was very exciting with some grass, post and rails, and hedges and we caught a brace of hares. I presented Sue Gooderham with a pad and took it home to mount it for her as a thank you present for lending me her Robin on which I had enjoyed a fabulous ride. There was a joint dinner at The Crossways at Scole but this was spoiled as Dashwood and Spindler had invited themselves into the Dunston party. This upset the table arrangements and some of the Easton guests had to eat on another table. There was none of the usual atmosphere and almost everyone went home quite soon after dinner.

A large mounted field and foot followers met us at Otley on 25th November but almost every field was drilled with wheat. I did the best I could but it was only a moderate day. It was cheered by a wonderful tea put on by Russell and Vera Mayes but I could not even enjoy that as Sheila telephoned to say that my Cleveland Bay stallion was loose and running around in Dennington. Mrs Rous helped me to find him and he was finally caught at Dennington Place. I was then away for a while taking Sheila on a holiday of her choice and left Jim to hunt hounds but the Hoxne and Stradbroke meets were cancelled for frost and snow so he only managed to hunt hounds once and that was at Southolt on 7th December. A party of us hired a coach to go to the Dunston Hunt Ball and there were four of us in green tailcoats as Maurice Scott and Brian Bird had had theirs made soon after receiving their hunt buttons. An extremely good day at Clopton the next morning, Saturday 9th December, cleared our heads and I was pleased it was such a good day as Louis Borrett was out with his niece from Paris. I was then away for a while on a hunting holiday and again left Jim to hunt hounds from two lawn meets, at Newton Hall, Swilland, and at Ashfield Place where they enjoyed a good day.

The Children's Meet at Helmingham was cancelled due to frost and snow but we were able to hunt on

Sue Money arriving at the Ride & Drive Meet

Saturday 23rd December at Brundish Crown. We had, for many years, been barred from some farms in Brundish owned by a German, Mr Faulkener, because of damage done during Captain Bernard's mastership but the farms had changed hands and the new owners, the Read family (a father and two sons), had said we were welcome. I tried very hard to catch a hare as I wanted to present the pate to Tony St Quinton in his home parish but was unsuccessful. There were the usual amount of extra people hunting due to the Christmas holidays and considerable damage was done to the Read family's wheat. I could have cried when I saw it. For fourteen years we were not welcome on these farms and now with all this damage it looked as if we would be barred again. I was out before daybreak with my rake and spent some hours raking in the hoof prints and making it look a little better before I went to see the Reads to explain what had happened. All was well as they were a very friendly and easy-going family.

The Boxing Day crowd was not as large as usual as Ipswich Town Football Club were playing Norwich City at home. We unboxed as usual at Church Farm where we were highly amused when Geoffrey Ingram-Smith tried to kiss Ethel, Herbert Breese's long-serving housemaid. We had another long jolly, very similar to the year before, and started to hunt properly at about half past one. The scent was very good and we had some long runs, one of which took us past Wood Farm where Mrs Nesling had viewed her across the road towards Chandos Farm but this line was lost at Oak Tree Farm. We hunted into the dark and it was after five o'clock when we boxed up. We were one hound light which my daughter Judith had correctly identified as Destiny, but Charles Corner telephoned to say that he had her shut in at Bedfield.

Frost and snow stopped us at Laxfield on 30th December but I decided to go on foot for New Year's Day at Cretingham. I moved off with every hound in kennel, 31½ couple, and had relied on a good covering of snow to protect hounds' feet, but this had blown off in some places. There were far too many lines and hounds were running in full cry in all directions which delighted the large number of foot followers. Charles Corner and his son Richard had agreed to whip-in to me and after an hour or so they managed to stop all the hounds and we walked back to the meet to find that Hilda had taken the lorry back to the kennels. I stood with hounds outside the Bell while someone drove Jim to the kennels to collect the lorry so we could box up hounds. The only day of mounted hunting between 30th December and 20th January was our invitation to meet by the Waveney Harriers on 17th January at Chestnut Farm, St Cross, when Jim hunted hounds as I was taking Bridget for an interview at Leicester University. I was able to join the Waveney for the joint-dinner at Harleston Swan at eight o'clock with twenty people from each hunt and the meal was very good, as was the atmosphere and the après dinner party went with a swing. The next evening I gave a talk about hunting in a private room at the Crown & Anchor in Framlingham. This was only open to members' families and there were about thirty-five present. There was a unanimous request for another talk specifically on hound work and this was fixed for Monday 29th January.

We hunted on foot at Glemham Crown on 20th January which gave me a good appetite for a surprise birthday dinner party I had arranged for Sheila. I had managed to get five of her cruising friends to come and stay and persuaded Brian Bird to take her out to lunch and get back late enough for me to have them all installed in the drawing room when she returned. It all went perfectly. Mrs Hart, our daily help, cooked a delicious dinner and Tony and Anne St Quinton joined us at short notice when someone failed to arrive. The next morning, which was Sheila's actual birthday, there was another surprise, this time a lunch cooked and smuggled into the Hall by Sue Scott with other ladies bringing canapés.

We hunted every hound again, on foot, from the kennels on Saturday 27th and there was a fair scent so I passed the horn to Charles Corner, a great veneur and ex-Master of Otterhounds, as he was much fitter than me and could keep up with hounds. The evening of the talk on venery was terrible with driving snow but still twenty-five people turned up

Hunting on foot in the snow

at the Crown & Anchor. The Point-to-Point on 3rd February was cancelled owing to ice and snow but we did manage to hunt two days later at Ashbocking Nelson where we had a very busy day. During the day I noticed that Dewlap had become deaf. This was a very sad discovery as she was an excellent bitch. She was missing at the end of the day and not found again until the next morning and, of course, could not hunt ever again because she could not hear the horn or, more importantly, the other hounds.

Colin and Tizza Plumbe had arrived for their annual visit and Colin came with me to hunt with the Mid Essex Beagles on Wednesday 7th February. This put us in the right frame of mind for an Easton hunt dinner that night at Framlingham Crown and, although the meal was awful, the atmosphere was good and after dinner I presented Colin with the Easton Hunt button. We hunted next day at Debenham Red Lion and were joined by some of the Suffolk Foxhound members, including their Master, Paul Rackham. The scent was very poor and I could show no sport to either the Plumbes or the Suffolk visitors. That evening we had a small concentrated discussion about venery at Town Farm, Wilby. Those present were Tizza and Colin Plumbe, Sue and Maurice Scott, Rupert Montagu, Mary Garton, myself and our hosts, Mary and Ernie Calver. This started at eight o'clock and ended after midnight. On Saturday 10th February the Easton met for the first time ever at the Blaxhall Ship and a reasonably good day followed but I handed the horn over to Jim for the last hour and left early as I was hosting the most important dinner party of my life.

I had been concerned for some time that the dignity of our Hunt Ball was diminishing, especially in the number of green evening coats. After the death of Captain Bernard, there were only two men who had Easton evening coats, Ernie Calver and myself, and this did not suit my ideas of a real Hunt Ball, with everything done to the highest possible standards. We had visited other Hunt Balls where there were paper tablecloths and paper napkins and so forth and, to my mind, these affairs were a dance, not a ball. The ladies set the tone of a hunt ball with their lovely dresses and hairstyles and the rest of the ball should complement them and the efforts they have made. Consequently I felt there should be a respectable number of green evening coats and only those who had been awarded the Hunt Button were entitled to wear one of these. To some extent it was my fault that the number of green coats had dwindled nearly to nothing as I had presented very few hunt buttons while I had been Master because I had been a little too strict about awarding this honour but I had rectified this at the hunt dinner in July 1977 when I had presented hunt buttons to fifteen members, of whom eight were men. In the ensuing months I had let it be known that I would like some members to consider having an evening coat made and the response was beyond my wildest hopes. Seven men, including some of those who had already held the button, had had them made and I wanted to thank them in some way that would give them an opportunity to wear their green coats. It was discussed for months and we came up with a plan to have a 'white tie dinner' with nine courses. The idea of nine courses was so that each man in turn could separately propose a toast. I had an extension made for our dining room table so it would seat eighteen people comfortably and I was prepared to pay for caterers to come in so that Sheila could relax and enjoy herself but she would not hear of it. She told me very firmly that she wanted to do it and gave great thought to the menu to ensure that it could all be properly managed on the night. I took the menu to my wine merchants, Berry Bros & Rudd in St James' Street, and, after complimenting me on the menu, they recommended appropriate wines for each course. Those invited were Geoffrey and Monica Ingram-Smith, Brian and Flynn Bird, Ernie and Mary Calver, Terence and Marion Saffell, Stanley and Kathleen Tompkins, Louis and Barbara Borrett, Maurice and Sue Scott, Rupert Montagu, Rosie Spragg, and, of course, ourselves as hosts. The Borretts, the Tompkins, and Rupert Montagu had all asked for beds so these five stayed the night.

On the night the table looked magnificent, adorned with grand menus, beautiful flower arrangements, and silver candelabra and coasters. As the guests arrived they were served with Black Lanson Champagne, and the ladies looked quite stunning in their beautiful dresses which set off the new coats to perfection. Bridget had volunteered to be the wine waiter and took the job very seriously, while Mrs Hart held sway in the kitchen with the assistance of her granddaughter Sadie and my daughter Judith as waitresses.

The Cambridgeshire should have visited us on 13th February but were snowed in, although there was no snow with us so we hunted with our own hounds at Yaxley and had a good day which included one hunt with a classical figure of eight during which I had a fall and spat out some teeth into the ditch. In the evening it was planned to hold a joint dinner at Tannington and this still went ahead. In spite of it being only three days after the 'white tie dinner', Sheila cooked for a large number of people. The hunt was trying to raise funds for a new hunt van so, although we gave the dinner, we charged all Easton members £5 each towards the new van. Seven of the Cambridgeshire made the effort to come and the après-dinner party was as good as ever with Heather Prescott starring with her new song. Thursday 22nd February should have been our invitation meet in the Suffolk Foxhounds country but it was cancelled for snow although, again, the joint dinner still went ahead and twenty from each hunt joined together at The Crossways at Scole. The foxhound members had made a great effort and provided the majority of the after-dinner entertainment. We hunted on foot at Laxfield and were joined by about a dozen Essex and Suffolk members. Jim brought every available hound and we had some sport with one good hunt ending with the hare being caught, although I must admit that I was not up with them. The foxhunters gave us a few songs afterwards and it was all very jolly. That evening I was privileged to be included in George Gooderham's 'Woodcock Dinner' which was just as perfect an evening as any man could wish for, with the most superb wines.

On Wednesday 28th February we held the joint meet with the Sproughton Foot Beagles at the Hare and Hounds in Framlingham. The scent was just right for foot following and we caught the first hare after one and a quarter hours having completed a classical figure of eight. The second hare decided to give the College boys a treat and ran close under the classroom windows and round the playing field and across to the swimming pool. There was no dinner on this occasion and, although the tea was splendid, I did not stay for long as I wanted to go to the hospital to see my grandmother. At Rendham on 5th March I saw the most amazing thing: two hares both running quite fast collided head on and stunned each other. One recovered quickly and ran on but hounds killed the other before it recovered. The Scotts gave another hunt breakfast on my birthday, 8th March, and we moved up to the Brandeston Queen for the actual meet. One hare found on Rose Farm, crossed the road at the Gun Club, swam the river and ran on through Monewden. When we eventually caught up, I could see the hare, very tired, only a field or so in front of hounds but she took refuge in an overgrown pit and we had to give her best. Crowfield Rose on 15th March was a heartbreaking day for me as Merryman was killed by a car in exactly the same place as Jason had been in an earlier season. He was only in his first season and was already a real star, blue mottled in colour and with a voice like a bloodhound. I had no heart in the hunting after that and just wanted to go home but at the end of the day we were a couple of hounds light. Lawful returned to the meet and the new Herod was found in the Round Wood in a snare but fortunately it had pulled tight round his ears instead of strangling him. The only bright spot of this miserable day was that I noticed that Peter Bailey had his spurs on upside down so fined him the traditional bottle of champagne. Peter did better than that and came back with two bottles as he had enjoyed a good win at the racetrack.

My eldest daughter looked very elegant with her hair piled on the top of her head when she attended her first Hunt Ball, partnered by Ernie Calver's son Richard. This was held again at Melton Grange on 16th March and we dined with the Hennessys on the way. It was an unusual ball for me because, of the 220 people there, I knew all but one table, partly because of the number of farmers who were there. The afternoon meet was at Bedfield Crown and I have never seen such a crowd at a small pub; those inside were jammed like sardines and there were hundreds outside. It was the best end of season day I have ever experienced, with good scent and hounds ran hard all day. I blew for home at four o'clock as my horse was just about finished and Jim had tired out two horses.

It had been a difficult season with no scent and dry conditions to begin with then, as the scent improved, snow and frost had stopped us and many days were spoiled by high winds in the latter part. Hounds had hunted a total of fifty-one times with ten days lost to frost and snow.

1979–80

We had fewer than the usual number of puppies to walk out, just five couple in all from three litters, one sired by Clifton Foot Pirate[72], one by our own Actor[77], and a third by the Suffolk Foxhound Stratford to try to introduce a little blue mottling into the Easton. Stratford was a perfectly blue-mottled dog and had a very good voice so I thought it would be fun to

experiment in a small way but I only kept a couple of bitches from this litter, Quest and Quiver, and these were entered in the appendix section of the Stud Book.

We naturally had high hopes that Garland would do well at Peterborough Hound Show and entered her in the Restricted Bitch class with hopes of winning it but she only achieved third place which was the only Easton rosette of the day.

There were fifteen early morning meets, including the 'Ride and Drive' meet which was again held at Bedfield Crown but was not so well supported as the previous year. I had a visit from Michael and Brigid Roffe-Sylvester of the Taunton Vale Harriers for a few days hunting but was unable to show them any decent sport. At the last early morning at Badingham Bowling Green, it was a great pleasure to see the Reverend Hartley out again on his bicycle with his field glasses. He had been my parish clergyman when I had lived at Badingham but was now the Rural Dean. He used to follow quite often on his bicycle and really understood hunting and frequently wove it into his sermons.

The Opening Meet was on exactly the right day, Thursday 1st November, and after one particularly good hunt I presented pads to Ernie Calver and 'Wild William' Gilbertson-Hart. I did not blow for home until after four and was then pressed by 'Wild William' to call at the Hare and Hounds for a half of bitter on the way home. When I did arrive home, Sheila had a real hunting tea ready for me which was most appreciated.

The Hennessy hospitality attracted over eighty mounted followers for the meet at Charsfield. The hunting was brilliant and the field were able to enjoy a trouble free ride as there were plenty of stubbles, as well as the famous Youngman orchards. Everyone congregated at Pear Tree Farm and the wine flowed freely as we enjoyed a marvellous beef stew followed by a huge cheese board. Andrew Meeson, who was an occasional visitor, had bought a set of buttons with a fox on them and received a lot of teasing from his friend, Ernie Calver, who introduced him to everyone as 'the Master of the Hyde Park Foxhounds'. To finish the day, six of us went to Fritton Nags Head to sing to Daisy, the landlady, as it was her eightieth birthday. Sheila and I then had a holiday in Singapore, staying with my sister Sarah and her husband Michael Buckley. Jim was delighted as, as usual, he was left to hunt hounds but the prospect of our flight was very worrying to some of our older friends. Jack Steel, who drove us to Ipswich Station on the first leg of our journey, was very tearful when we parted as he was convinced that he would never see us again, and another old friend was Arthur Cornish of Worlingworth. Sheila often sent some food to him and, on this occasion, when she delivered it, he rode with her to the meet at Stradbroke. I said I would give him a lift home and on the way he told me how anxious he had been and just how much he had missed me. I was very touched at his concern and listened how he described how he had felt like 'throshing the embers out of the fire' as he thought of us in the air. The hunting at Stradbroke on that day was difficult as Aujesky's disease had broken out in some pig herds.

On 1st December there was only a small field of twenty-five horses at Hoxne Grapes but they were to have the most fantastic day as we only just managed to keep hounds in sight and had to blow for home quite early as all the horses were finished. There would undoubtedly, have been a good party in the pub but the jukebox killed all thoughts of that. We had an unexpected visitor at Southolt Plough on 6th December as Bob Brunyee, an officer from the cruise ship with whom Sheila and I had become quite friendly, turned up. He played the accordion and, although he had not brought his with him, I sang some sea songs in his honour and another sailor who was there, a rough old sailor who returned home at Christmas time to pluck turkeys, was brought to tears and sat with his handkerchief in his hand.

At Clopton on 8th December there was not a single field that was not drilled with wheat and I took it as a tremendous compliment that not one farmer had written to say we were not welcome. There could be no better demonstration than that day of the trust that could be built up between a Master of Hounds and the farmers. I told Julie Hennessy to collect

Probably unboxing at Church Farm, John Suckling on foot

only half-caps as we would only be able to do so little but the day turned out to be one of the most fantastic hare-hunting days of my whole life. The first hare ran in convenient ways so we were able to use tracks and lanes to watch hounds hare-hunting at its absolute best with our hare being fresh-found three times and eventually caught after a hunt of over forty minutes

with hounds unaided in any way. The rest of the day was equally brilliant and the following day I bought an Ordnance Survey Map and marked each hunt with full details of the runs, the fresh finds, and so forth. We had another brilliant day on Thursday 13th at Laxfield with long runs, one of which ended when the hare swam a moat but the hounds were not inclined to follow suit. The Children's Meet was at Debach in the most terrible conditions with gale winds, sleet and rain and the best part of the day was the tea put on by Celia and James Miller.

Monday 7th December was a sad day for the Easton. We had lost one of our greatest characters and Herbert Breese was buried in the little church at Saxtead, so close to his home. The church was full to over-flowing and the parson gave an excellent address and even found a passage about pheasant shooting from the bible.

Bridget was home from St Andrew's University and brought some student friends with her to the meet at Stradbroke on 20th December. None of them had ever seen hunting previously but showed great interest. The meet was very quiet at Dennington Queen on 22nd December but we certainly made up for it on our return. Geoffrey Ingram-Smith played carols on his accordion and soon had the whole pub singing. Ernie Kersey was there in his Father Christmas outfit and the atmosphere in the old, beamed room, was just perfect. There was one and a half hours of non-stop singing, either communal or solo; fifteen songs were sung solo and young Pandora Money starred with her song about a pit disaster which reduced several people to tears. The Christmas Eve meet was at Brundish Crown and by this time I had become good friends with the Read family and was welcome to go anywhere on their land. Young Nicholas Read had his first day's hunting on his pony and fell off several times. Ernie Calver was supposed to be looking after him and after one fall shouted to him to hurry up and stand up. The little boy turned as much as he could and replied, 'How can I get up when the pony's standing on my coat!' The hunting was very good and continuous but somehow the field were lost for most of the day which was a great shame as there were lots of strangers who had paid a cap.

Although we no longer had a host in Herbert Breese, we carried on the tradition of unboxing at Church Farm on Boxing Day and hacked to Saxtead Green to find the largest mounted field the Easton had ever seen, 115 horses. I had not planned a jolly this year and, as I looked at this huge field, I wondered if I would be able to cope with so many. I had planned a stop at the Hall for half-time and Sheila was ready and waiting with masses of mince pies and sausage rolls and gallons of hot punch. This created a welcome diversion and we had some decent hunting to end the day. Jim injured his eye which prevented him hunting at Stonham on 29th December and an added difficulty were the silver hares there which we did not want hounds to hunt. Two were clearly seen by hounds and needed some effective whipping-in by Geoffrey Ingram-Smith to stop them. New Year's Day at Cretingham was unfortunately cancelled due to frost but we took hounds and paraded on foot. The crowd was as large as ever at the meet with over 150 people outside with drinks in their hands. The meet two days later was also cancelled but we did manage to hunt from the Hare and Hounds on 5th January where Jimmy Finbow made us as welcome as ever. This was the first time that we had drawn the same country for a second time in the same season.

We had some trouble at Rendham on 10th January when the excitement of hounds running caused two ponies to jump out of their paddock. They galloped all the way to Wickham Market before they stopped and their owner, Mrs Cushions, was rather upset but she eventually accepted my apologies. There were many fresh faces amongst the field of about seventy horses at the Coddenham meet on 12th January and they were not to be disappointed as the scent was good and we covered a lot of country. Young Susan Clark was out on my daughter's cob Henry, and she wanted to see her uncle, Reg Cousins, so when we came near to his Valley Farm, Wickham Market, I blew the horn and Reg came out and dispensed very generous hospitality so we were all rather pleased that we had called on 'Uncle Reg'. It was a special day for me on Thursday 17th January at Debenham Cherry Tree as it was the 700th time I had carried the horn and as it was also Geoffrey Ingram-Smith's birthday we had two reasons to celebrate at a special dinner at Snape Plough & Sail that evening.

Two Sporting Days had been arranged to raise funds to tarmac the yard at the kennels. The first was on Tuesday 22nd January and 25 people had paid £15 each for a day to hunt with each kind of hare-hound. They started at seven-thirty hunting with the Easton and had a really excellent 'day' as the first hare ran from Worlingworth, round Bedfield and Saxtead before returning to where it was found. The pace was fantastic and the horses were really 'cooked' when hounds finally lost the line. At least four people rode up to me and said they knew where she was sitting between two electric poles but I thought she deserved mercy and left her in peace. Breakfast followed at the Hall and then it was the turn of the De Burgh Basset Hounds but scent had disappeared and they struggled to hunt at all so we returned for the lunch of corn beef hash and chocolate soufflé. After lunch John and Sarah Austin were ready with their Norfolk Beagles and we were privileged to see some beautiful hare-hunting. John Austin is the only man I have ever seen who could stop a pack of beagles off a fresh hare with just his voice. It was both a great pleasure and an education to watch such a man hunt hounds and it made me feel quite envious to see his expertise. He was persuaded to stop a little after four o'clock and we returned for a proper hunting tea. Hilda Wickham and her girls had cleaned all the horses and they were taken home but everyone was back by seven o'clock.

After our hare-hunting extravaganza we needed a real change for the evening and there had been some wild guesses but none were correct. Taking our inspiration from the Boys' Day we set up a target shooting range in the front hall of my home with the targets on a sheet of plywood over my office door. There were two classes, one for men and one for the ladies, and it was almost compulsory to shoot. If any Health & Safety Inspector had strayed in they would have fainted with horror as Len Mison was running his bar at the other end of the hall and the inspector would have been even more unhappy had he known how cheap the drinks were, at just 20p for a whisky. The shooting competition held everyone around the bar as they could drink and watch at the same time and this built up a great feeling of camaraderie and the two hours before dinner just flew by. Supper was served at nine o'clock and Sheila produced an incredibly good game pie with baked apples stuffed with almonds, to follow. Inevitably, there was a great singing session and the first people began to leave just before midnight and the last at two o'clock in the morning. This had been an excellent day and a unique one for us all as no one had previously hunted with three breeds of hounds in one day. The great Easton Harriers spirit had been at its best and Sheila had served 120 meals, ably helped by Sue Scott and Mary Calver.

The second Sporting Day, on Wednesday 23rd January, was a 'foot' day and started at nine o'clock. Graham Redfern brought his golden eagle and flew it at Brundish in the field behind the old Blacksmith's Shop. The first flight was at partridge and was unsuccessful but luckily the bird returned to Graham almost at once. Graham kept up a most interesting commentary in what he was doing, and why, which all of us enjoyed as there was not one amongst us who had any idea about falconry and it was an education for us all to hear the terms used and have things explained. For instance, we had no idea that for the week preceding a day in the field the bird was carefully weighed each day as a rough guide to determine how hungry it is. If it is not hungry it will not bother to fly and if it is too hungry it will eat what it catches and not fly again. He also explained that an eagle is very relaxed about its hunting as in the wild, sitting on a mountain ledge, it can see prey below all day long and it is not until it becomes hungry that it bothers to try to catch anything, and even then the quarry must be running down wind. The last flight was at hare and was successful. It was marvellous to

right to left: **Judy Brewster, Terence Saffell, Bridget Harvey, Isla Prescott, Henry Miller, Tim Last, Ernie Calver, Will Edmondson, Tony St Quentin, Colin Plumb**

watch the hare running as fast as she could and the great eagle seeming to fly so effortlessly, the wings just giving slow rhythmic beats, yet gaining on the hare. The eagle, although not having eaten any of the hare, was not inclined to fly after the kill so we had a slight change of plan. Taffy Elliot had arrived early from Wickford with five dogs for the afternoon coursing so he ran his dogs and showed us great sport. This filled in the morning until it was time for lunch.

Len Mison did a roaring trade at his bar before we sat down to a meat and potato pie followed by crème caramel. There was inevitably coursing for the afternoon's sport, first at Wilby Manor and then at Tongates and everyone enjoyed themselves immensely and had worked up a thirst and an appetite by the time we returned to the Hall. We again sampled the delights of Len's bar before Sheila served her famous 'brandy cake' for tea and then there was target shooting again until at eight o'clock a supper of a delicious salt pork and vegetables, followed by apple pie and custard, was served. Mostly the après entertainment is spontaneous, sometimes it needs a little prompting to get it going, but on this night people were content to sit and talk about the day's sport and most of the conversation was centred round Graham Redfern and his golden eagle. Thanks to Sheila's great efforts we had raised £480 for the fund to tarmac the yard at the kennels and thoroughly enjoyed ourselves at the same time.

At Thorndon on 24th January we had visitors from the Suffolk Foxhounds, the Waveney, and the Dunston Harriers and although I was hoping to be able to show them exceptionally good sport we were unable to find a hare. Hounds were drawing most oddly. Instead of spreading out and drawing properly, they formed little groups and walked about the fields in single file, noses to the ground but not speaking. I rode across the ploughs looking to see if I could find any slot marks as I wondered if a herd of deer had passed by some hours before but this was not the case. This odd behaviour completely baffled Jim and I and we drew for an hour or so, then moved to a different area. Hounds then started to draw normally and a hare was soon found and we were away. The hunting was as good as I had hoped and I was relieved that the visitors could see my hounds hunting as they should. Visitors who understand hunting are always impressed by two things in a pack of hounds, first how well they draw and secondly, and most important, how they cast themselves without any help. Time and time again on this day they would check and swing round altogether in a small circle always behind from where they had checked and then another larger circle. During these first two circles hounds were tightly packed together and looked like a flock of birds wheeling round in the sky. When they hit off the line again they turned with such eagerness that some lost their balance and fell over. This is called being 'tied to the line' but it does not often mean to this incredible degree. I have never met a huntsman who could recall hounds turning so sharply that they lost their footing.

As we hacked back to the meet Jim and I were well pleased with hounds' performance in the latter part of the day but were still perplexed about their early odd behaviour. When we got back to the meet, all was revealed. The first draw had been coursed by men with lurchers earlier in the day and this explained not only why there were no hares but also why there had been little groups of hounds going in single file. The coursed hares had turned and twisted during their course and left lines all over the fields which, by the time we drew, had become faint but just enough for the hounds to follow if they walked slowly and concentrated but not strong enough to speak to. Local people in the pub informed me of the coursing and left us in no doubt about what they thought of the men who had deliberately coursed on the morning of our visit. Not a case of field sports pulling together.

Five days later we were at Horningsea Manor for our annual meet by invitation of the Cambridgeshire Harriers but I was not impressed with my performance and the diary entry was brief, and I quote: *'Miserable day, spent with little scent and a lot of interference from the host as to where to draw etc – hounds rather flashy – excellent party in the evening, did not leave until after 10.00pm. Riding with me were: Mary Garton, Jill Graham and Mary Calver and we called at Beyton Bear on the way home.'* Jim hunted hounds on 31st January and 2nd February as Sheila and I went to St Andrews University to visit Bridget.

Although I love the ladies dearly, it is possible that I could have been accused of being a classic male chauvinist pig when I organised a 'Gentlemen's Day' on Tuesday 5th February to raise money for the 'Tarring Fund'. This was to be limited to ten men at £10 each and Terence Saffell, Bill James, Jeffrey Bowden, Maurice Scott, Gordon Grover, John Capon, Geoffrey Ingram-Smith, Ernie Calver, Louis Borrett, and Will Edmundson joined Jim and I at the Willoughby Arms at Parham at eleven o'clock to move off as and when we felt like it. The feeling of masculine camaraderie was heightened by the delightful old surroundings and the whole scene could have come from the pages of Surtees. The old landlord and his tiny wife did their best to keep up with demand but their methods were rather slow. As he served a drink she would ask him what it was and write it on a card with the price alongside. The landlady was not much higher than the bar but could just manage to write on it.

In my mind's eye I can see her now, licking her pencil and looking up into her husband's face as she slowly said, 'Now what was that dear? Oh, a whisky. Was there anything in that, dear? Oh, some lemonade.'

If there were six whiskies and lemonades each one was laboriously written down and the total added up equally carefully and methodically with much pencil-licking at the end of each round. For twelve hard drinking men bent on having a good time, this slowness was exasperating but, at the same time, very funny and we could laugh at ourselves. There were even longer delays when another bottle of whisky was needed. The landlord would slowly climb the spiral staircase and return even more slowly with the whisky. He could only bend one knee enough to come down so it was one slow step at a time. Those of us who were eagerly waiting down below would see first his ankles, then his calves, then the bottom of the whisky bottle as he carried it at arms' length. Eventually it arrived and he would start to carefully pour into the measure as there were, of course, no such new-fangled things as optics. These journeys upstairs were fairly frequent but it never occurred to him to bring two at a time. Likewise, although each round was identical, each drink had to be written down again. All this created an euphoric atmosphere and the adrenaline was pumping even before we left the pub. Eddie Kerridge, the road officer, perfected the scene by singing *Phil the Fluter's Ball* which was a surprise to us all as we were unaware that he could sing.

We moved off and drew towards Marlesford Hall after crossing the river behind Hacheston Blacksmith's Shop. There is no doubt that a small field is ideal for hare hunting and 3½ hours of near perfect venery followed. Each man was intently watching the venery and there was no 'coffee housing' to lift hounds' heads. There was much wisdom and experience in Beckford's advice to the young man starting a pack of harriers to invite no more than six of his friends to join him. Of course, there was some liquid refreshments in the Willoughby before going home but we did not stay very long as we were all looking forward to the next part of the day. Each of us took our wives to the Cretingham Bell for dinner in the evening and, as each lady arrived, she was given a buttonhole which had been kindly made by Sue Scott. I was disappointed when the meal proved to be 'moderate' as this was intended to be the great finale of the day and it rather spoiled the atmosphere so the evening was quiet with none of the usual Easton spirit.

Members of the Easton Harriers were invited to join the Suffolk field at Thornham Horseshoes on 7th February. The hunting was moderate with the foxhounds continually rioting on hares but the dinner was very good and twenty from each hunt assembled at the Crossways at Scole. The foxhunters had a fund of good new songs.

Scent remained good for the next few days, culminating in an exceptional day at Cretingham Bell on 16th February. There were lots of children out so I thought I would give them a jolly through the lovely valley at Rookery Farm. I had only just started when a hare jumped up and ran the length of the valley. The acoustics in this valley are unbelievable and the cry seemed as though it had been magnified artificially. The line turned left-handed up to Framsden Hall and ran on hard over Birds Lane and across into Otley. I was riding as hard as I could but hounds were almost out of sight and earshot when, luckily, they turned and I was able to get on terms with them again. At this moment they split and I stayed with the ones still on the hunted hare. They re-crossed Birds Lane and the hare was lost behind the farm buildings at Valley Farm, Framsden. This had been fast and furious and the field were strewn out for about a mile. Jim arrived with the others that he had stopped and we had two more little hunts which conveniently allowed us half-time at the Greyhound. The next hare was found at Shrubbery Farm at Cretingham which ran through Framsden Hall, crossed the river and ran over part of Uplands and then turned left-handed through Ashfield Place to the river near the crossroads at Ashfield Swan. I cast them across the main road and they hit it off again and screamed along the low meadows towards Debenham, then lost the line completely near a hollow log. I cast all around very thoroughly but to no avail and I was convinced that the hare was in the hollow log so I asked for a volunteer child to crawl through. Rachel Graham offered and I shall never forget her little face when it popped up at the other end and she said, 'It's not in here, Master.' We gave the hare best and it seemed a good point to blow for home as the horses and ponies were very tired so we hacked very slowly back to the Bell.

Jim hunted hounds two days later as I was in London for a Masters of Harriers and Beagles Association meeting where I successfully spoke very strongly against a proposition to save money by printing the studbooks in paperback form. I also proposed that all Joint Masters should be members of the Association and not just the senior Master. Due to 'popular demand' hounds met next morning for a second Gentlemen's Day, this time at Kettleburgh Chequers. This time those present were Dick Johnson, Idwal Humphrey, David Steel, Ernie Baker, Mike Bloomfield, Peter Bailey, Nick Freeman, Mark Wayne, Maurice Scott, and of course Jim and myself. The meet was the greatest fun imaginable and with no ladies to censor us it was quite late when we moved off. There were lots of songs and jokes with Idwal Humphrey clearly the star with some very good numbers. Somehow betting started as to whether hounds would follow me into the bar and when the total bet amounted to £35, which would of course go to the 'Tarring Fund', I asked the landlord and the landlady for permission to try. They were highly amused and agreed but stupidly I took no account of how long the hounds had been waiting in the van. I brought them straight into the bar and they proceeded to relieve themselves all over the room. I though it was wise to move off immediately, having first offered a hasty apology to the landlady as I went out, but the proceeds of the day, including the bet, meant that the 'Tarring Fund' had reached its target of £1,200.

The hunting was fairly good with extra fun caused by men changing on to each others horses. They was some beautiful music when hounds ran along the banks of the Deben from just behind the kennels to Valley Farm at Wickham Market. The cry brought Fred Ling from out of his house and he was delighted and very surprised to see us as the meet had been at Easton the day before. I explained that it was a special Gentlemen's Day and he said that there was no such thing during his day which was when he had been amateur whip for many years during the 1950s. I took hounds back to the kennels directly from Valley Farm and obtained a lift to the meet where I was delighted to find the landlady had completely forgiven me and treated the whole episode as a huge joke. The dinner on this occasion took place at Snape Plough & Sail, the ladies were again presented with a buttonhole, and the Gooderhams put on a delicious set dinner of soup, paté, fish, and lamb, followed by a pudding, and a very generous amount of wine for £6 per head which was excellent value. The après dinner entertainment was first class and we had an impromptu cabaret when Peter Bailey stood on a chair to sing but started to laugh and could not stop. This proved to be infectious and in no time the whole table was laughing at nothing at all.

At Wetheringsett two days later I was in trouble for moving off on time. There was such a crowd at the meet and the pub was so full that it was not possible to get a drink so I thought I might as well go hunting. Sue Gooderham had not had time to finish taking the cap and became so angry that she took herself off home without even unloading her horse. At Brandeston on 23rd February scent was good and the hares had gathered as they tend to do at this time of year. This was a bad combination as hounds split in six different ways, each group running hard with the good scent. The best part of the day was the party at Stella Mitchell's cottage afterwards. The hunting was moderate at Framlingham Station on 28th and, unfortunately, a member's horse kicked the hound Rachel. Jim took her off to the vet and Sarah Edmundson mounted his horse and finished the day. We finished at the Gun Club at Kettleburgh so I hacked back to the kennels with hounds instead of returning to the meet then hurried home as we were holding another 'white tie dinner'.

Non-hunting men married to hunting ladies are not entitled to wear hunting evening dress coats as, of course, they do not hold the hunt button but they could wear the correct attire for a ball, namely a white tie and a black tailcoat. Knowing how I wanted to raise the dignity of the hunt ball a number of men had black tails made or had acquired them. In order to thank them a dinner was held along the same lines as the previous green tailcoat dinner. Those present were Will and Sarah Edmundson, John and Sara Capon, Mike and Pat Webster, John and Jill Graham, John and Fiona De Vaux, Ian and Sheila McKay, Anthony and Elise Quilter, and Bill and Heather Prescott. The Prescotts were so terribly late that we sat down to dinner without them and when they did appear they had their legs pulled as John De Vaux had driven 140 miles to be there and was on time. The menu was Salmon mousse served with a Chablis, Soup and Sherry, Sole (cooked by my daughter Judith) served with a Loire, followed by Sorbet, then Jugged Hare with a Burgundy, followed by plain Green Salad, Fruit Tartlets and Sauterne, Devils on Horseback with the remains of the Burgundy, Stilton and Brie with a Claret before finally the port decanter made its rounds.

Two days' later on 1st March there was a record crowd for the Point-to-Point. Stanley Tompkins ran two horses in the Members' Race which were ridden by the sisters Caroline and Debbie Saffell. It was a very exciting race and they came over the last fence side by side but, inexplicably, one of the horse's legs broke as it landed and this tragedy marred the whole day.

The Saffell's Lawn Meet at Rookery Farm was on 6th March but once again the draw was completely drilled with wheat. I sent the field twice round the hunter trial course and then tried to hunt and had the fastest hunt I have ever seen. Hounds were running so fast that they 'flattened out' and were noticeably much lower than usual. At a check I ran across the

wheat on foot and cast them and they ran on and caught their hare. It had been such an extraordinary hunt that I presented the trophies to the whole of the Saffell family, the pate and all four pads. There was an excellent tea at Rookery Farm afterwards but I did not stay long as I had so much to do preparing for the ball which, this year, was going to be at my home.

As I left home that morning sixteen ladies and a lorry load of flowers arrived to decorate the house and marquee. The main marquee was for sitting out and for breakfast and there were three others, one for the caterers, one for the bar, and one for the discothèque. The dining room in the Hall was used for the main ballroom. This was to be a real, old-fashioned ball where the hosts dined their parties at home then came on to the ball whenever they chose. The invitation was for half past nine but it was half past ten or later when most people arrived. Ron Findon's band was so good that the floor was packed all evening. The ladies' lovely dresses complemented nine Easton green tailcoats and perhaps twelve or so red ones from the Dunston and foxhound neighbours and many black coats but the most distinguished of all was Charles Corner in his blue otter hunt coat. Any number of shops and many hours had been spent by the ladies, including Sheila, in choosing dresses, and the results were fantastic. All looked fabulous and were much sought after on the dance floor.

The 'breakfast', served from half past midnight until three o'clock, was provided by Noreen Pritchard-Carr, who was thought to be East Anglia's top caterer. She was so revered that most people who used her services were terrified of her and let her do just as she wanted but I plucked up courage and said that I would like kidneys to be served. She drew herself up to her full height, gave me a withering look and said: 'Oh, you want me to do kidneys do you? You know that I have catered for all the best families in East Anglia (and proceeded to list about ten of them) and they have always been perfectly satisfied with my breakfasts but I suppose, Mr Harvey, if you really would like kidneys, then I could just do them for you.' The kidneys were delicious and highly praised by many people. Douglas Weedon ran the Zodiac discotheque very successfully until I made him stop at five o'clock and I just managed to get everybody out of the house by six o'clock. It had been a fantastic ball and every bit as good as I had hoped.

The next morning was a combination of my birthday meet and the après ball meet and was held at Tannington Hall at half past twelve using the same bar. The hunting was first class and hounds ran hard all day. Mrs Crisp and Ivor Constance were out from the Waveney and I presented them with trophies after one extremely good run. There were not many people left when I blew for home at half past four and hacked back towards the Hall where there was a good crowd round the bar waiting to help me celebrate my birthday. These celebrations were cut short as another ball was starting at half past seven. This was called the 'Neckwrapper Ball' and was for the pony and cart enthusiasts. There was a tremendous atmosphere and, although very different from the night before, it was equally enjoyable. Colin and Tizza Plumbe had arranged their annual visit to coincide with the balls and they enjoyed both nights, this latter one ending a little earlier at three o'clock.

Colin and Tizza unboxed at the kennels and we all hacked up to Wickham Market White Hart on Monday 10th March for what was to prove an awful day. We were wet through before we arrived at the meet, it was freezing cold, and our second hare ran over the A12 which had recently been converted to dual carriageway at Ufford. I could not get to hounds who had

JAH with Hounds

crossed, then checked and were beginning to come back. I shall always be grateful to the lorry driver who not only stopped his lorry so it blocked both lanes, but also stood on the other carriageway and stopped the traffic until hounds were all safely back. In all there were four very near misses and it was dreadful to witness. After that I went home, although it was only two o'clock. It was party time again that night as my brother and I thought we would use the marquee once more to give a party for all the farm workers and their wives which ended at half past two.

On Wednesday 12th I had a highly unusual task as the new landlord of Crowfield Rose had said that he did not want us to meet there. I went to see him and called at the pub one lunchtime to find quite a few locals there that I knew, one of whom was Dick Last. He had recently written a terrible letter to the Easton, addressed to the meet Secretary Jill Graham, saying that the Easton were 'more cruel than Hitler and the Nazis who sent people to the gas chambers'. Dick had never been the most cheerful of men but had always let us hunt on his farm and I wondered what the cause

was for his change of heart. In the pub I thought I knew the reason as he had a new woman with him. The locals were firmly on my side and when I left the pub three hours later the landlord said that not only were we welcome, that he would apply for an extension and Dick Last and I were on far better terms and he even said that perhaps he should not have written the letter. She looked furious.

Three days later we did meet at the Crowfield Rose for the last meet of the season. There was a good crowd at the meet so I think the landlord would have been pleased but the hunting was very poor as there were far too many hares. If nothing else, it blew away the cobwebs for those of us who had been at the Waveney Hunt Ball the night before. In my diary I made the following notes: *'More wheat than ever before, 85-90% in most places. A very open and mild season – only two days lost for frosts, sadly one of these was New Year's Day. Best scenting season I have ever known. The field had behaved very well, although a fair amount of wheat damage done but on the whole, had been very good. Spent between 75–85 hours raking in wheat where people had not kept to edge, doesn't do much good but it looks better.'*

Some of the latter remarks need qualifying as they appear to contradict each other. When I say that 'the field behaved very well' it is important to take into account the size of the field. These were often sixty or more horses out and up to one hundred and fifteen on Boxing Day. With so many horses out, there are bound to be some who sidle up a field and make a mess, although the rider is doing his best. The 75–85 hours spent raking was done to prevent my present superb relations with the farmers being spoiled. I would go to any length to prevent this happening and the main reason for the raking was to prevent the hoof prints filling up with water. It was a back-aching job and would at times take three hours or so the next day. I must emphasize though, that I was very particular about the wheat, and hoof marks fifteen inches from the edge were not acceptable to me.

Rachel Graham investigating the tree trunk – see page 143

Drawn by Jason Gathorne-Hardy

CHAPTER 7

SEASONS 1980–85

We had a large entry of puppies to break, 16½ couple from four large litters, three of which were sired by Easton stallion hounds and one by Dunston Carver[77] but I only had a few weeks to get to know and break them as we started walking them out later than usual this year, in the first week of April. When the Easton season had finished I had gone away for a hunting holiday in the West Country and I was leaving home in mid May to spend seven weeks on the road with two horses and a gypsy caravan. I was planning to drive the 300 miles to Appleby Horse Fair and back again and was being sponsored to raise money for Driving for the Disabled. I was fortunate in having the company of Tom Walne driving his own horse in a second caravan. Tom was a very enthusiastic member of the Easton Harriers and often helped to whip in and he was being sponsored to raise money for the Thomas Wolsey School for disabled children in Ipswich. This year's Peterborough Hound Show started off with some excitement when the Easton won a rosette in the first three class es, as Bailiff[80] came third in the unentered dog class and Tapster[79] was third in the entered dog and later won the restricted class which meant that the Easton had won the Easton Harriers Perpetual Challenge Cup.

It was good news to read that a new pack of harriers were starting in Staffordshire and, as they were asking for hounds, during that summer I sent them a draft of good, reliable hounds of various ages that would be a sound nucleus on which to base a new pack. This pack was called the Staffordshire Moorland Harriers and I became very friendly with the Master and huntsman, Eric Elliott. He was so pleased with the draft of hounds I had given him that he invited me to judge his first hound show. I was invited to stay with him and his wife, Marcia, who had kindly arranged a dinner for my first night but it was to be a most embarrassing dinner for me. There are only three things that I cannot eat, owing to an allergy, nuts, spinach and blackcurrants. The first course was eggs Florentine, i.e. spinach, the main course was trout cooked with almonds, and when the pudding came I could really have cried as it was a meringue basket filled with blackcurrants spilling over the edges and lovingly entwined round the handle. Marcia must have spent so much time creating this beautiful dinner, and especially the magnificent pudding, but

each time I sadly refused each course, she managed to stay cheerful and provide an alternative.

At the end of the summer we went into voluntary quarantine as we thought we had the dreaded Parvovirus in the kennels again, and this delayed the start of hunting, but our fears were unfounded and we actually started hunting on 24th September. We had four successful mornings at Tannington, all in sugar beet and meeting at 6.30am. I left Jim to hunt them for the next two mornings at Church Farm, Saxtead, and Cretingham Bell, as I had been invited to appear at the Horse of the Year Show at Wembley with my horse and caravan on account of the trip to Appleby. Each night there was to be a special parade called 'London Pride' featuring all the prizewinners of the Show classes and others. It was great fun to be part of the great Wembley circus and I paraded in the stadium at four o'clock and nine o'clock each day for the whole week, along with, among many others, Moggy Hennessy on her show horse. So as not to break with my tradition of eating goose on Michaelmas Day, Mary Calver kindly cooked one and brought it down to Wembley but I only just managed to eat it on the right day as it was a quarter to midnight when I took my first mouthful of goose sandwich. While I was away there was some trouble after the Cretingham meet with Mr Lindeman's wheat but I was able to settle this by making a donation to the Monewden Scanner Appeal. The last early morning hunt was at Badingham Bowling Green and it was a sad day for both Jim and me. Three couple of old hounds were having their last day as Jim would have to put them down before the season proper began. Hounds cannot just 'retire' and, as they get older, inevitably they get slower. The problem with this is that these good old hounds were trusted by the rest of the pack as these younger hounds had heard these voices all their hunting days and they had never been wrong. As a result, if hounds checked after a fast hunt, the old hounds would be two fields behind but still speaking so the rest of the pack would run back to them, thus losing time.

The Opening Meet was on 30th October and Tom and Sandy Walne were ready with a violet buttonhole for everyone, an old Easton tradition for the Opening Meet. There was a large crowd on the Market Hill at Framlingham to meet us and the police had kindly reserved a space for us. The hunting was poor at first as it was sunny and quite hot but later it turned cool, scent improved, and we had two very good runs which thinned out the large mounted field and there were only three left when I blew for home at three o'clock. I had missed the voices of the trusted old hounds who would have been prominent during the first hour of poor scent but would have been left fields behind when the rest ran well. The Opening Meet Dance was held at my home but Sheila was able to relax for once as Pat Goldsmith did the catering and the Easton White Horse ran the bar. One hundred and five people came and the dance floor was full all evening.

At Stonham Ten Bells on 8th November I was to be in dire trouble and have great pleasure all at the same time. The meet was always a difficult one because of avoiding the white, or silver, hares on Mr Tydeman's Broughton Hall but this year it was even more difficult because Mr Williamson had telephoned to say that he also had a white hare and did not want it hunted. These two farms formed a substantial part of the day's draw and I had been wondering how to keep out of trouble. I had briefed the two whippers-in and another person to always be in a position to stop hounds in whichever direction should they be on a white hare but I need not have worried as we did not see a white hare all day. An ordinary brown hare was found which ran to Coddenham passing through several woods. Hounds were absolutely flying and I found myself crossing country that I did not know existed. It was very distinctive because of the old-fashioned farming, the ploughing was stetch work and about four inches deep just as it had been done when I could first remember. I knew that I was out of my draw and could see some ladies looking agitated but could not stop to explain as I would have lost my hounds. When the field caught up with me I was on Reg Cousins' farm at Coddenham and they told me that the ladies were very upset and angry. When I got back to the meet it was almost dark but I had to try to find the unknown farm which I discovered was called Dial Farm. Eventually I found the entrance and drove across meadows, opening and shutting gates as I went, and finally came to the farm. It was really dark and when I knocked on the stable door of the house, and the top half opened to reveal a real old-fashioned kitchen with an oil lamp burning on the table. I introduced myself and said that I had come to apologise and explain what had happened. The two ladies standing silhouetted against the flickering lamplight expressed their displeasure in such a charming, Victorian, way that it was almost

a pleasure to be scolded. Their anger was subsiding when I noticed a lantern approaching in the darkness. It was another lady carrying two pails of milk with a yoke across her shoulders. When the first two told her who I was, I received another tirade about how upset the cows were but they soon calmed down again when I asked them about their farming. The ladies were four sisters, of whom one drove the tractor, one milked the cows, another looked after the chickens, and the fourth kept house. They explained that the last time they had had a major disturbance was when an aeroplane flew very low over the farm during the War. We parted on very good terms and I came away with a pound of butter and a large piece of home-made cheese; the memory of the taste of that cheese makes my taste buds tingle as I write. The farm and the ladies' life-style was an absolute time-warp from before the First World War and the farm had remained isolated from the outside world as it was surrounded by large woods. I felt extremely privileged to have met these four ladies and to have seen a glimpse of their world into which I would have loved to disappear, especially if I could have exchanged their Fordson Major tractor for a pair of Suffolk Horses.

At the AGM was held on 12th November the caps were increased to £10 and the field money doubled from £1.50 to £3.

Earlier that day the Waveney had met by invitation at Brundish Lodge at half past eleven and I was put in a potentially embarrassing position as the Master, Mrs Crisp, asked me to ride with her amateur huntsman, Ivor Constance, and give him some hints about hunting hounds. We had been hunting for about an hour when Ivor said, 'Please feel free to say whatever you want because I've got a lot to learn.'

This made things a little easier for me and, as there were some hounds running mute well ahead of the others, I said to him, 'Well, for a start, you need to shoot those ones at the front as soon as you get home.'

"Good God, I daren't do that! She (i.e. Mrs Crisp) thinks they are the best hounds and wants to breed from them.'

I had not fully appreciated how much freedom I enjoyed as 'Master and huntsman' and, to the same degree, how much others were handicapped. Ivor did very well with the material he was given, having hounds in good control and hunting them well and quietly, but the hounds were really rather poor as, as well as the two couple running mute in front, there was another couple of old hounds speaking behind, and most of the rest had not entered properly because they had no example to copy. The Cambridgeshire Harriers visited us on 22nd November at Dennington Hall and again I was not very impressed as they hunted with very little drive or cry once the hare was out of sight and at least half the pack were running mute. We had a dinner for 25, which included eight Cambridgeshire visitors, at my home, and Sheila produced an excellent dinner of tomato soup followed by salt beef, and we did not get up from the table until one o'clock. Visitors were coming thick and fast as the

JAH, Jim, and Geoffrey Ingram-Smith

Suffolk Foxhounds met, by invitation, at Debenham Lion on 27th November and again I quote from my diary: '*Found at Ulveston Hall and hunted him in a large circle slowly to beyond Michael Last's and back into the straw barn where he was found. Tom Batterbee hunted them extremely well – fox running ditches for most of the time. Drew Aspall Wood and had a fast run to Bedingfield Hall where he was fresh-found in some sweet corn and run to ground in a small covert at Redlingfield Hall where he was dug out and accounted for. An excellent hunt with a 3½ mile point and hounds cast only once. We had run past Southolt church and across Rookery Farm much to the anger of Mr Abbott. The owner of Redlingfield Hall, James Risk, provided home-made cider for us all. Dinner at Scole Crossways, twenty from each hunt – Suffolk people a little late for dinner as it was after six o'clock when we left the meet – good dinner with plenty of singing etc ended at 2.00am.*'

It was bitterly cold and snowing on Saturday 29th November when Sue Money dispensed hospitality at Debach Airfield, the meet usually described as Debach 'Post'. Hunting was fair and we finished with a good run, catching our hare very near the meet, but we were frozen and the tea at James and Celia Miller's home was especially welcome. The day was very wet and cold but the scent was good and the hunting fast and furious, covering a lot of country. I just made it back to the meet in time to change my clothes in the lavatory and hurry across the road to entertain the Over Sixties Club with local Suffolk songs for three hours or so from three o'clock.

There was a large field out at the Otley White Hart meet on 6th December but only I was privileged to witness a most extraordinary sight. It was snowing fast but scent was good and it was difficult to keep with hounds. At one time I had lost them and then thought that I came up with them casting themselves in a field. The snow was sticking to my eyelashes and it was difficult to see clearly but when I rubbed the snow away I found I was not looking at my hounds but at a field full of hares. They were playing and running in little circles which was why I mistook them for hounds. I rode to the lea of a hedge and once out of the driving snow could clearly see this amazing sight. I made a rough count and thought that there were over a hundred hares in this ten acre field. Why they had all decided to assemble there I had no idea but it was an extraordinary spectacle that I had never seen before or since. Vera and Russel Mayes put on a splendid tea which revived and thawed us out and that first cup of tea was a real lifesaver.

Three brilliant days followed with a classic figure of eight hunted at Hoxne during which the line passed through a builders' yard twisting between heaps of bricks. Hounds stuck to her line but were distracted by the dogs barking at a nearby boarding kennel. I cast them and they ran on to catch their hare. That evening we returned to the meet for dinner with my friends, the St Quintons, as it had been far too good a day to end at the meet. At Ashfield, hounds seemed glued to the lines and caught three brace, all well-hunted. We had a mixed day at Southolt on 18th December as one hound was kicked at the meet and taken to the vet by Sheila and another was hit during the day by the blacksmith, Arthur Howell, on his rounds but we had some good runs, the best of which was from Suddon Hall at Kenton through a field of sprouts, past Kenton church to beyond the cider works at Aspall. The country from Swilland on 22nd December was, as usual, unrideable because of the amount of wheat so the field had a ride round the Saffells' hunter trial course before we started and then another round the Newton Hall course at the end of the day. The Saffells really spoiled us for tea with a roast turkey and all the trimmings during which Rozzie Theobald's little girl curled up and went to sleep on a pouffe like a kitten. Considerable damage had been done to wheat because a large proportion of the field were out for the first time so, as it was a moonlight night, I spent two and a half hours raking out the marks that night and another hour or so at dawn.

My daughters played a trick on me at Christmas Eve at Brundish. Hunting was not brilliant so I was able to have Judith up with me for a while, then she disappeared for a while and when 'she' reappeared I had a shock as, in fact, it was Bridget. Judith had been going home early so she and Bridget had changed clothes in the Ladies at the pub and Bridget had jumped on Mickey and ridden back to the field. When we returned to the meet I heard that, while we had been hunting, one of the great local characters, Percy Abbott, had been found dead in his cottage at Brundish. I had learned some of my songs from him years earlier.

There were a little fewer in the crowd at Boxing Day but they were very generous and a record cap was taken of around £500. Many people said that the jolly was the best ever and certainly Mark Wayne's horse was enjoying it as it became so wound up that it ran away. When Mark realised that it was, in fact, running away and that he was completely out of control, he did a very brave thing; he jumped off. He dislocated his arm but nevertheless it had taken a lot of courage to jump off at that speed. Some good hunting followed and the last hare brought us into my front meadow and the line was lost halfway down the drive. I could not just ride away so blew my horn for a drink and had a glass of the wine that I had already decanted for the dinner party that night. It was by now quite dark and as we hacked back to Saxtead the white patches on the hounds really stood out and the effect was quite moving. New Year's Day brought the usual large crowd with 81 mounted and they enjoyed a good jolly, all on grass, but the hunting that followed was almost nonexistent as the hard land was crusty and dry and there was no scent. The Children's Meet at Crowfield Rose on 3rd January was ruined as the Essex and Suffolk Foxhounds had been in the area and all the farmers were up in arms as they had not ridden with the same consideration as the Easton.

Two days later we held a second Boys Day at the Dennington Bell. I could not hunt hounds as I had injured my knee so Jim Wickham hunted them with Paul Reed whipping-in. Maurice Scott and Bill James were mounted so that they could do their best to control the boys and set a good example. The boys rode a variety of ponies, many of which were borrowed for the occasion. The young gentlemen were Victor Scott, Stuart and Craig Girling, Matthew Bird,

William Clough, Daniel Rimmer, Patrick and Guy Edmundson, Angus Herron, Johnnie Gooderham, Guy Quilter, Edward and Henry Miller, and Richard and Michael Baker. My knee still prevented me from riding at Bedfield, so Jim hunted hounds and I followed in the car with Gordon Corner as chauffeur. A Wellington boot gave my swollen knee enough room to ride and, although I was uncomfortable, I was able to hunt at Laxfield Royal Oak on 10th January. The hunting was good and Brian Bird gave an excellent party in the pub afterwards. The singing was particularly good with young Pandora Money stealing the show with two delightful songs. Mark Wayne was not hunting because of his dislocated shoulder but he, and his brother Nigel, joined us afterwards. I suddenly noticed that Mark was standing there with one Wellington boot on exactly like me. He had quietly slipped out to his car where he had a pair of Wellies. It was a good joke and I said a few appropriate words. At the height of the party, Sheila came into the pub and called me to one side to tell me to tell me that Mark and Nigel's mother had died. They were both still in the pub and I had to break the news to them but, almost at once and in unison, they said to keep the news to themselves, as their mother would have hated to spoil a good party. Sheila drove them to the family home at Palgrave and I went home as soon as I could and was driven over to Palgrave. We stayed with Mark and Nigel and their father, Clive, until eleven-thirty then made our way home. Mrs Wayne's funeral came on a hunting day so Jim hunted hounds so that we could attend. My head stockman, Kenny Warne, lent his black mare to Bob Soar to pull the hearse, which I knew would have pleased Mrs Wayne.

I missed the next three days due to my continuing knee problem but did manage to hunt on the Gentlemen's Day in aid of hunt funds at the Willoughby Arms, Parham, on 27th January. It was very foggy and we were in the pub from eleven o'clock until one o'clock when I thought it had cleared enough but once I was into the draw I realised it was still too thick. As we were all on our horses I felt I ought to take the field for a ride so, trying to remember the geography of the country, I rode along the edge of the fields, turning left or right as I thought, and felt very pleased with myself when out of the fog loomed Marlesford Bell, which had been my destination. We had a couple of drinks there and then re-traced our steps to the meet where we had a little too much to drink and, although we took our wives to dinner at Cretingham Bell as planned, we were not quite at our best and it was rather a quiet and subdued evening.

The day from Thorndon on Thursday 29th January was the most frustrating sort of day possible, a combination of excellent scent and too many hares. Hounds split into three groups, with each group screaming along and impossible to stop. I managed to stop one at Eye Park, Jim stopped another at Wetheringsett Manor Hotel, while the third was running hard through Lampitts Farm which was supposed to be closed to us because of Aujesky's disease. This was possibly the best scent I ever experienced but was no more than a nightmare of a day because of the number of hares. It was nobody's fault, least of all the hounds, but nevertheless, very frustrating. Two days later at Knodishall, it was just the opposite with pure hare hunting at its best. Brian Bird witnessed the whole of a classic figure of eight hunt and I presented him with the pate.

At Eye White Lion on Monday 2nd February I thought I was going to hunt with no field but, at the last minute, Bibi Smith arrived driving her cob in a cart and exchanged the harness for a saddle. Then her mother, Mimi Smith appeared and much later still, the Saffells and Elise Quilter. I moved off with my exclusive field of five and was soon in trouble as Gloria French's Shetland ponies escaped from their meadow and joined us. It was amusing to see Geoffrey Ingram-Smith retrieving two at a time, one under each arm. One great hunt dominated the day with three complete circles, fresh-finding her twice on the field where she was originally found. I think we might well have caught this hare but I lost concentration when Jim had a spectacular fall with his horse falling into the furrow, throwing him clear but right into the ditch itself. In the pub afterwards the Saffell family, who had just returned from hunting in Ireland, introduced us to a Punch based on port which was the hunting drink of the Irish pack they had recently hunted with.

Hounds met at Winston Hall on the 5th February for the first time since the Duke of Hamilton's days. The first hare took us over Winston Green into an abundance of hares, where the hounds split. Each time I managed to stop a few hounds, I shut them in a farm shed and fetched a few more, and so on, until they were all together. I hacked back to Winston Hall and drew again and enjoyed two hours of the best hare-hunting anyone could possibly wish to see with hounds even pushing through thick bushes. I was very pleased as we had a field of forty-seven which included many visitors, some of whom were from the Essex and Suffolk Foxhounds who had promised to come at a darts match held the previous evening at

Henley Cross Keys. There was only John Capon and Ernie Calver left with us when I blew for home and we joined the others at Winston Hall for a splendid high tea of jacket potatoes and beef stew, Stilton cheese and apple pies. The atmosphere was so good that singing broke out while people were still eating and the large number of visitors thoroughly enjoyed themselves.

The next day's hunting was at Blaxhall and I was told afterwards that a lady from Tunstall Old Rectory was very upset about hounds having got into her garden. I went to see her early the next morning and met her as she was walking out of her gate. I apologised for coming so early and explained that I was doing so before church. She told me she was just walking to church and this broke the ice and all was forgiven.

The second Gentlemen's Day, again for hunt funds, was held on 10th February at Kettleburgh Chequers, in bitterly cold weather and snow storms. We had all the usual fun at the meet but when we tried to hunt visibility was poor. We were rewarded with one good run to Hoo, then through Charsfield, finishing just behind the kennels where I decided to blow for home. On hearing the horn, every hound in the kennel started to sing and it was glorious to listen to them as I hacked back along the river bank taking the hounds I was hunting back to the kennels. Our respective ladies were dined at the Snape Plough & Sail where again we enjoyed a delicious dinner.

Colin Plumbe presented me with another silver coaster at the Framlingham Hare and Hounds on Saturday 14th February while down for his annual visit. It was quite frosty, with a fair amount of snow and I almost cancelled as all the other East Anglian packs did, but I was glad I went because we had a good day, even if it was rather risky. The day ended with a lovely dinner party at the St Quintons.

It was not only the weather that was causing us problems as we were also restricted by stock diseases. The meet at Kelsale on 16th February was cancelled because three farms had the pig disease TGE (Transmissible Gastroenteritis) and three days later we could only hunt half the draw at Wetheringsett because of Aujesky's disease. In this restricted area I managed to get into trouble from a gang of rabbit catchers but, at the end of the day, I went back and walked across the fields to see them and made my peace. When I returned to the meet the party was in full swing, 'a real Wetheringsett do.' John Finch had planned to give us a lawn meet at Feoffee Farm, Ashbocking, but unfortunately this had to be cancelled due to TGE and worse was to come as, when Jim was hunting hounds at Brundish Crown because I was away, Labourer was killed by a car. He was an excellent hound and we had planned to use him as a stallion hound that year.

I only hunted half a day at Easton White Horse then handed the horn to Jim as there was so much work to do preparing for the hunt ball which was again to be held at my home. A tremendous amount of work went into the preparations but on the night it looked superb; the house and marquee were filled with flowers and the early morning starts at half past four all seemed worthwhile, as did the late nights sorting out five pail fulls of snowdrops. We took our houseguests to Framlingham Crown for dinner and were back punctually at half past nine for the start of the ball. An hour later it was in full swing and the 320 guests divided themselves between the disco and the main band. Both dance floors were kept full until breakfast was served, which again included kidneys. The band stopped at three o'clock and the discothèque at five o'clock and the last twenty-five people converged on the kitchen where we consumed four bottles of champagne and it was nearly seven o'clock when I went to bed.

The après Ball meet was at Tannington Hall at half past twelve with a good turnout, which included Nigel Wayne still in his dinner jacket from the night before. The hunting was superb and one hunt exceptional. Hounds had been speaking on a drag for about ten minutes and I could see Ernie Calver on the lane holding his hat in the air. I quietly nudged the hounds in his direction and they hit off the line and started to run in earnest. They ran to Fenton's Farm, through World's End and across to Chandos Farm, Worlingworth, where they fresh-found her and hunted back to Wood Farm, Tannington and, with the slightest of checks, ran on again to World's End to Tannington Lodge where she was fresh-found for the second time. She ran on to Dennington Place, crossing the main A1120 towards Framlingham Hall. During the whole of this wonderful hunt, the hounds were completely unaided, and in fact, I was never close enough to do so had I wished to. Tom Walne and Ernie Calver had viewed her, very tired, crossing the last field but we lost the line and this very game hare richly deserved to be left to run another day.

There were not many of us left at the end of this hunt but, once back at the meet, we quickly joined the others at the bar in the marquee. This had received a face-lift and now had the dance floor from the disco and the bandstand from the ballroom ready for the Neckwrapper Ball in a few hours' time. It all looked just as I had hoped, especially all the flower arrangements which had been placed around the edge

of the bandstand. Nigel Wayne, who was not a hunting man but had attended the meet still wearing his dinner jacket from the night before, had followed hounds for a while with his girlfriend in his car but had become bored and decided to go into Framlingham. His car was the longest, widest, sports car I had ever seen and even on this very wet day he kept the hood down so both he and his girlfriend were soaked through. Traffic in Framlingham brought them to a stop and Nigel noticed a lady looking at them in amazement. Quick as a flash, he asked her if she could direct them to the Hunt Ball.

'Well, yes I can,' she said, 'It's at Tannington Hall but I'm sure it was last night.'

Nigel just turned to his girlfriend and said, 'We've got the wrong night, old girl.'

They left the poor lady unable to believe what she had seen but Nigel was back at the bar at the Hall when those of us who finished the day came in and he immediately bought us a round of drinks. The camaraderie was out of this world, all tiredness had been replaced by the adrenaline from the fantastic day's hunting.

Nigel turned to Ernie Calver and said, 'I wish I could ride to hounds and wear those clothes and be thought a sportsman.'

'Well,' said Ernie, 'You can wear the clothes at any rate,' and they proceeded to strip and change clothes, much to the amusement to all present, especially as Nigel was about fifteen inches taller than Ernie and his trousers were far too long for Ernie.

Two rounds of drinks later they decided to have a 'hunt' and the two of them set off round the marquee at a canter, Ernie still in Nigel's dinner jacket and trousers, and Nigel in Ernie's breeches and hunt coat. When they came to the bandstand, with the flowers all round the edge, they thought they ought to jump this 'hedge' but as he jumped Ernie tripped over the extra length of trousers and wreaked havoc with the flowers. There were about fifty of us watching this performance which heightened the already good atmosphere. Ernie, although one of the Easton's best-loved characters, was well-known for his forgetfulness when it was his turn to buy a round. After the 'hunt' and his most unfortunate fall, Nigel bought a large round of drinks and asked Ernie if he would like a double. Ernie replied in his usual way, 'Thank you, my dear cousin, thank you.'

'Don't thank me,' Nigel replied as he removed the wallet from Ernie's jacket. 'It's your money I'm buying it with.'

He then proceeded to pay for the whole round with Ernie's money. It was one of the best jokes that I ever saw with the Easton and we laughed about it for many years afterwards.

I just had time to change into my horseshoe-button suit before the Neckwrapper Ball guests began to arrive. It was a great night and I had a bet with my wife that she couldn't get Joe Parravani to dance. He was over seventy and had never been on the dance floor but Sheila won her bet and Joe enjoyed his first ever dance. His wife just could not believe it. This party, like the hunt ball the night before, ended in the kitchen at half past six. The next day was my birthday and I had arranged for my friends to meet me at the Dennington Bell. This party was very well attended, perhaps too well attended and went on rather a long time and ended up with breakfasts of eggs and bacon at Tannington Hall at two o'clock in the morning. The next morning, Monday 9th March, hounds met at Pettistree Greyhound where the hunting was just good enough to blow away the cobwebs from the weekend and freshen me up for yet another party as my brother and I had again decided to have a party for all the farm men and their wives and children in the marquee which again went off very well. This had been a birthday weekend to gladden my heart jam-packed with fun and action, lovely girls to dance with three nights running, good food with plenty of laughter and not forgetting the odd dram or two.

Scent was very good for the Southolt meet on 12th March. Ernie Calver, always ready for a little fun, offered his horse to Fred Edwards, a farmer from Wingfield. Fred and his brother Jack had hunted before the War but Fred had not been on a horse for many years. He did not take much persuading as the Edwards family are always ready for a dare and he stayed out for two hours but said he was very sore and stiff. We had two visitors from the Dunston Harriers, Robert Crawford and Tim Finch, who had not brought their horses but were following on foot. The combination of the farmers and their wives and the Dunston visitors, assured us of a good singing session in the pub afterwards.

The last meet of the season was at Cretingham Bell on 14th March. I had intended to keep mostly to the roads as the land was being harrowed and drilled but the last hare of the season had different ideas. We found just behind the meet and she ran through four gardens, then some buildings, then more gardens before setting off for Framsden Hall. Here she turned and passed by Foxes Farm bearing right and running behind Helmingham School, crossing the road on a dangerous "Z" bend and I just managed to get to their heads and stop them at North Park Farm before they went onto the Helmingham Estate where we did not have permission to go. The whole of this hunt had been at galloping speed and very few horses finished this run. Amongst those who did were Christine Crisp and Ivor Constance from the Waveney which did not surprise me as both of them were usually very well mounted. I hacked back to the meet thinking how pleasant it was to finish the season on a high note.

1981–82

Once again we were late in starting to break the puppies because I had gone away for a hunting holiday in Cornwall at the end of our own season and did not return until 5th April. We had 11½ couple of puppies from five litters, three sired by our own Labourer[78] and two litters which were a quarter foxhound, sired by one of the blue-mottled foxhound crosses, although I kept only two couple of the best-marked ones and gave the others away. We had a little success at Peterborough Hound Show with a third prize in the stallion hound class, with Tapster, a second in the restricted class with Garland, and another third with Wary in the under 19' class. The season started with the first early morning on 29th September but after only two more we had to miss ten days owing to Parvovirus flaring up in kennel. The first advertised early morning was at Thickthorn Farm, Horham, on 24th October and there were sixty-one people mounted and many others on foot.

There were fifty-five mounted for the Opening Meet on Thursday 29th October and a good crowd on the Market Hill. We had three really good hunts and caught our hare each time but the last one was special because hounds never saw their hare until it was killed as I had laid them onto the line and there were no fresh finds. I did not enjoy the Worlingworth Swan meet as I was very angry with a certain member from Laxfield who had stolen my girl groom and the hunting did not improve my temper as the hares kept going in and out of ditches and running the ditch bottoms. I went straight home after boxing up my horse. Why hares should decide to run the ditch bottoms soon after being found is somewhat of a mystery and no logical overall reason has ever been found. Often it may be that the hare is injured and feels it cannot run fast enough but in today's example there were three hares that did so, one after the other, and it is unlikely that they were all injured. When a hare has run the brows of the ditch and the scent is just right, it will move and hover over the middle of the ditch and I have often seen hounds speaking on both sides of the ditch, each group with their noses pointing inwards where the scent is hovering. With a ditch-running hare I have seen the scent rise enough to allow the hounds to hunt in the same way.

At Henley Cross Keys on 19th November, I put Hilda Wickham to a major test of loyalty by asking her to do a very unenviable thing for the good of the hunt. I had become acquainted with a businessman who had recently bought a business in Framlingham. When he found out that I was Master of the local hounds, he told me how he had hunted regularly in Kent and never ever went home before hounds but I suspected that this fellow did not know much about hunting at all as he used the right expressions in entirely the wrong context. He said that he could get some of the Point-to-Point races sponsored

Hilda Wickham

and, as this was important for the Easton, I decided that I could listen to almost any amount of his flannel to get some sponsorship. I let it be known that he was likely to get sponsors and the members drew him into their company as they did all newcomers to the area. The outcome was that he said he would like to come hunting and one of the members offered to lend him a horse for the Henley meet. I had serious doubts of whether this fellow had ever been on a horse so I suggested that he might like to ride out on exercise for a few mornings. I told Hilda to expect him to telephone and asked if she would personally escort him out on exercise, and warned her to be prepared for the worst. The evening of his first outing Hilda telephoned me to say that he was hopeless and definitely had not been on a horse before. The old hunter had plodded around the exercise route with resigned boredom, he was just managing to keep in the saddle, and all was well until he needed the lavatory. He got off at Kettleburgh Chequers and used the facilities and then could not get back on. He was quite portly so when he had his foot in the stirrup iron Hilda put her shoulder under his bottom and heaved. This might have succeeded but his boot slipped out of the iron and Hilda collapsed and ended up with him sitting in her lap. The grooms who

were exercising the other hunt horses rode up to see Hilda sitting on the road holding two horses with our potential benefactor in her lap. Following Hilda's report of this fiasco I made a point of bumping into the intrepid rider in Framlingham the next day and inviting him for a drink so I could ask him how he had got on.

'Oh very well,' he replied. 'It was really lovely to be on a horse again.'

I asked him if he would like to hunt at Henley Cross Keys and he said that he would but asked that I awarded him the hunt button first as he would not like to be seen in the hunting field in plain buttons. I sidestepped the request. On the day of the Henley meet he arrived very smartly attired in all the correct clothes and I moved off very gently and walked all the way to the draw. Hares are usually scarce at Henley so I expected to be some time in finding. I drew for over an hour and then had a sharp little burst and all thoughts of his welfare were forgotten as I tried to keep with my hounds. When hounds lost the line, I hacked back and met a group of riders with our newcomer firmly penned in the centre looking rather pale. Hilda broke away from the group and rode up to me looking more grim-faced and serious than I had ever seen her. She begged me to give permission for her to take him back to the meet as she was so scared that he would injure himself. While we had had our little run he had just dropped the reins and held on to the front of the saddle and she had had to overtake him and ram the horse into a hedge to stop him. I was highly amused and asked if Hilda if there had been any other problems but these were limited to a pee stop and luckily John Capon was there to lift him on again. As soon as I walked into the pub after hunting he bought me a half of bitter and before I had taken more than a few sips he asked me if he could have a green coat.

He did not hunt again as far as I can remember but he did sponsor a race himself and persuaded other firms to do the same. He arranged for me to go to London and meet the publicity promoter from a champagne firm. I was well received and tasted four different champagnes before an excellent lunch with still more champagne as a result of which I fell asleep on the return train, failed to change trains at Manningtree, and found myself at Thorpe-Le-Soken, a God-forsaken spot on the edge of the world in furthest Essex. There was no staff at the station which was lit by a single light bulb and without a torch I had the greatest difficulty in finding a telephone. I eventually succeeded and obtained a taxi to take me to Ipswich Station. It was all worth it in the end as the company came up trumps and sponsored two races.

Hounds met at Wetheringsett on 26ᵗʰ and, after drawing for a while, Ernie Baker saw a hare on her seat and cracked his whip to start her. I laid hounds on the line and the scent was at first rather poor but in the second field it became stronger and we had a fairly good hunt although at the end we had to give her best. This was a busy day and it was after four o'clock when we returned to the meet, but we did not stay long as there was a darts match at Kettleburgh Chequers, the Hunt *versus* the Farmers. This was a really good evening with good food and great camaraderie. A 'Farmhouse Fayre' was held at Dial Farm, Earl Soham, where our hosts, Will and Sarah Edmundson, made us very welcome and the whole event was very successful. When it was over I took to Sheila, Val Pickersgill, Mary Calver and Flynn Bird to lunch at the Volunteer.

Some beautiful hunting followed the meet at the Dennington Bell. It was over half an hour before we found a hare which gave us a circular hunt and hounds would have lost the line had Brian Bird not put me right and I cast them back onto the line. The whole of this day's hunting was text book stuff, hounds could have been covered by the proverbial blanket, and there were double circles and figures of eight, all day. The only part that was not out of the textbook was the fact that we did not catch a hare, losing them all in bramble bushes. I ended my diary entry with: *'I could have stayed out until midnight – a lovely days venerie.'*

We met at Otley on 5th December. Sue Scott viewed a hare away and I laid hounds on the line and we had a fast hunt to just short of Cretingham Bell. She dropped down into the valley and crossed the river to Rookery Farm and ran along the valley before re-crossing the river up to Framsden Hall where the line was lost in some pheasant cover where I dared not linger. As always happened when hounds ran along this valley, the sound of their cry was amplified and I was in ecstasy, feeling as though my skin was all goosepimples and every hair was standing up. Vera and Russell Mayes gave us a splendid tea, which was a fitting end for such a grand day, although we did not

know that we would not hunt mounted again until 21ˢᵗ January because of snow. We hunted on foot on Christmas Eve at Dennington Bell and took 24 couple of hounds but only stayed out for about an hour as the snow was so deep.

On Boxing Day we paraded hounds on foot to a crowd of about a third the usual size which I thought was extremely good in the circumstances. Jack Steel, knowing that we had houseguests, was very worried that I would come home from the meet the 'worse for wear' and tried to persuade me not to go into the pub. I did not heed his advice and went into the pub where there were about a hundred people all wanting to buy me a drink, but I went very steadily. We sang hunting songs and local songs and it was all great fun but it was getting dark when we left to go to drink to my grandmother's memory. This was a tradition very similar to that of drinking to the memory of General Miller on Christmas Eve as, after her death, Mary Calver had said that she would always be at her cottage on Boxing Day with homemade sloe wine to drink to her, in memory of the many times we had managed to stop there on Boxing Day and she would hand out to us through her window glasses of her homemade wine. Just as we were leaving, Peter Bailey appeared at my elbow so I asked him if he wanted to come as well. He asked where we were going so I said 'Tannington Street to drink to my grandmother's memory.' He had not listened properly, did not realise that Tannington 'Street' was where my grandmother's cottage had stood, and did not know where to go, so he drove into the courtyard at Tannington Hall where Jack Steel was waiting in a state of great anxiety.

He rushed up to Peter and said 'Where is he? Where is he? Is he drunk?'

'No,' said Peter. 'He's gone to have a drink in the Street. Can you tell me where this street is?'

'What the devil are they doing drinking in the street?'

'They've gone to have a drink with his Granny'.

'There! I knew it, I knew it!' cried Jack. 'I begged him not to go into the pub, and now he must be blind drunk. His granny's been dead for two years!'

When Peter eventually arrived in the Street and told us this story we laughed so much that I think we spilt most of our sloe wine. How my dear old grandmother would have loved that story. I went back to the Hall and was just about to settle down to a snooze when the Wayne family and Charles Corner drove into the courtyard full of Boxing Day spirit and we settled down around the kitchen table. Five bottles of champagne later, they disappeared and I sat down to dinner to which I did full justice, as I was absolutely ravenous.

We hunted on foot again at Hoxne Swan but only eight members moved off with me, although they included Ivor Davis who was very interested and asked many questions about hunting hounds. On our return we found another twenty or so members who had deliberately arrived too late to join the walking part of the hunt. A larger field of around 25 moved off with us on foot from Framlingham Hare and Hounds on Wednesday 30th December. Hounds ran too fast for most of us and only the Edmundson and Rimmer boys kept up with hounds. When I caught up hounds were in the Mere and the boys told me where hounds had 'thrown up' i.e. stopped speaking. I cast them into some small bushes and Hero grabbed hold of a coypu but he let it go and hounds took off after it, jumping into the swollen river and needing assistance to get out. We walked back through the Mere and Castle grounds to enjoy one of Queenie's splendid teas in the Hare and Hounds. With no horses to take home, an extended singing session followed tea. When I left the meet I drove through an awful flood at Kettleburgh on my way to see Julie Hennessy who had said she would resign from the committee. Good committee members are few and far between and I managed to persuade her to reconsider but on my return the flood was even deeper, water came in the cab and the tidal wave in front covered the headlights. That evening Tony St Quinton and I waded out waist deep into floods at Bruisyard to rescue some horses which had been trapped by the rising floodwaters.

We met on foot again on New Year's Day and the hares were very kind to us and ran in relays back and forth in front of us. A great singing session broke out in the Bell afterwards and it was so good that we all agreed to meet later on at the Hare and Hounds for another singing evening where I recorded that over thirty songs were sung. The Children's Meet was also on foot at Crowfield but it was not so much fun without their ponies and only twenty-five children followed. Ivor Davis hosted a hunt dinner at his Grapevine restaurant in Framlingham on 7th January which was given so I could award some hunt buttons. On these occasions the guest list was made up entirely of those who either already had the button or would be presented with it that evening so no-one's feelings were hurt. We had soup, pork, and a dessert trolley, coffee and a half bottle of claret at £6 per head, which was very reasonable and I awarded buttons to Pat Webster, Judith Hale, Jill Graham, John Finch, Jeffrey Bowden and my daughter Bridget. Also present were

the Scotts, Bill James, Calvers, Saffells, and ourselves. Everyone did very well to get to the dinner as the weather was still appalling and it had been the coldest day for a hundred years

Mounted hunting resumed on the 21st January at Sweffling and scent was good, as it was again at Coddenham two days later. The hunting was rather indifferent, but that evening a film show at Brandeston Village Hall was very well attended with over a hundred people present who included Ralph Coates whose daughter, Marion, had won the hearts of the nation on her famous show-jumper Stroller. The ciné film was of our journey with the gypsy wagons to Appleby Fair. This evening made a change from our usual social events and raised £150 for hunt funds after deducting hire of the hall.

I was pleased and heartened that eighteen Easton members made the effort to go to the Cambridgeshire invitation meet at Horningsea Manor on 26th January. The first few hares ran where we were not allowed to go and then one obliged and we had a reasonable hunt. At a serious check Debbie Saffell rode up and told me she had viewed her into some rough so I cast them there and the crash of music was delightful, almost deafening. I was in pure ecstasy, my heart was swelling with pride, and I was especially pleased that it had happened when Betty Gingell was close by. The evening was as much fun as ever. As the men were changing in one of the bedrooms, Hugh Gingell brought in a bottle of whisky as usual and flicked on the television. It was a programme about the West Country and included stag hunting but this was the best film I have ever seen for clearly showing the amount of time the quarry is ahead of hounds. It was after half past ten when we finally left the wonderful Gingell hospitality, but that did not prevent us calling at Beyton Bear as usual on the way home.

A fast and furious day followed the Hoxne meet on 28th January when Malcolm Crowther rode a new horse called Bayman for me. It was a hard test but he said that the horse had gone very well. One hunt finished at Eye where the field all said they had had enough but I thought it was a shame to waste this good scent and drew once more. This hare took us right back to Hoxne and entered the park and hounds hunted past the ruins of the old summerhouse and vegetable gardens and lost the line where the Oakley Park Harriers' kennels had once stood. The next evening Sheila gave a supper party for hunt funds and I made up a quiz of 125 hunting questions. Eighty people were expected and I had told everyone who had a hunt button to form a team of four and to be its captain. We had half the questions then stopped for a supper of homemade tomato soup, meat pie with mashed potatoes and mushy peas, and chocolate crunch, and then had the second half of the questions before the teams exchanged papers for marking while I read out the answers. I was very pleased with the result as the winning team had a score of 108, the second team 106, and the third 103, while most teams had between 85 and 95 which showed how knowledgeable the Easton field were at time. After the quiz, Terence Saffell presented Sheila with a dozen red roses from the men and an elaborate bowl of flowers from the ladies and gave a vote of thanks for this night and all her numerous other efforts.

Stradbroke Hempsheaf on Saturday 30th was an exceptional day. The first hare was found on Horham airfield and ran past Thickthorn Farm, crossing the River Dove up to Rookery Farm, Wilby, and on across Duncan Morton's farm to Town Farm where she turned and crossed Mr Woollatt's land, where we were not welcome. The pace was too fast to stop and offer any apology as the hounds raced on over Stanway Green down to Valley Farm at Worlingworth, where she turned right and followed the River Dove where I had to use my wirecutters to get into George Barker's meadows. Hounds then swung up hill through Kersley Hall and then turned again and raced parallel to Cole Street. Here there was a serious check and I was able to stop hounds. It seemed a great shame to stop them but there was no choice as if I had not done so I would have lost them. This hunt had been continuous with hardly a moment's check and all at galloping speed. The horses were well and truly spent and stretched back for a mile or so. Most people dismounted and stood by their steaming horses. This remarkable hunt appeared to have been with the same hare. While it is almost impossible to believe that a hare could stand up before hounds at that speed for so long, if they did change hares it was not noticeable as they never stopped running. A very pretty hunt finished the day, one of slow, pure venery that was only seen by Jim and myself as all the other horses had returned to the meet. This day had shown two completely different

Paul Yeldham and Duncan Morton

styles of hunting a hare, the first with the scent so good that the hare could not double at all and hardly dared even to turn, and the second with the hare ten minutes ahead and able to make all her doubles and twists. The wirecutters in their case were attached to my saddle for every day's hunting, hanging on the other side from the horn case, but were only used one in four or five seasons.

The meet at Rendham White Horse on 1st February was well supported and the scent was good with hounds running out of the draw twice. During the day hounds took a line into Bruisyard Big Wood which was full of red deer but they hunted the line well into the wood, ignoring the many deer lines. Later on this happened again and I told the field they could come into the wood and there were a few sightings of deer. Jim stayed outside and holloaed our hare away and both Jim and I were delighted that hounds had not succumbed to the temptation of hunting deer. During the day I saw a total of twelve dead hares in various places and the state of decomposition suggested that they had died in the long period of snow. Tony St Quinton and I went back at night with wood and tools and mended the Forestry Commission gates that had been broken at Bruisyard Big Wood.

In her capacity as Chairman, Marion Saffell had told members that she expected everyone to raise a minimum of £50 each to offset the amount of money lost during the six weeks when we could not hunt because of snow and we had the greatest fun while everyone was using their ingenuity to raise their quota. We wanted people to raise the money rather than simply give it as this would have been difficult for some of the less wealthy members. Heather Prescott realised her target by giving a hunt breakfast at Blaxhall on 4th February and charging each person £2.50. After the breakfast it was difficult to find a hare but Mark Partridge viewed one away, I laid hounds on the line, and they took it into the Forestry Commission woodland where the cry was magnified and I was riding along lost in the ecstatic memory of hearing the glorious cry of French hounds hunting in the French forests. A group of deer spoiled this hunt by running in front of hounds on the line and hounds stopped hunting. These deer were fallow as opposed to the red deer we had seen three days earlier in Bruisyard Wood. That evening I gave a talk in the form of a question and answer session at the Grapevine restaurant in Framlingham which twenty-six people attended.

Our Point-to-Point races were held on 6th February and it just could not have been a better morning to draw the crowds as it was mild and still. Ivor Davis had raised over £1,000 in sponsorship and he had arranged banners to thank the sponsors. The hunt always sent a free car pass to every farmer over whose land we hunted and I was interested in how many actually used it so I asked

Maria Wickham and JAH at Helmingham Hall

the gatekeepers to collect the farmers' passes and it was over 300 of the 800 sent out. Malcolm Crowther rode my new horse Bayman in the Members' Race but he refused at the open ditch. I cannot remember who won the race but Ian Mckay was second and he had ample opportunity to celebrate as the Supporters Club were holding a party at his home, Kettleburgh Old Rectory, that night.

On Monday, 8th February, the meet was at Dennington Queen and it was to be another fast day with runs to beyond Framlingham and back to Badingham and when hounds lost the line the horses were really cooked. The last run was the fastest and brought me back to Dennington church, hounds were gaining on their hare but I saw her enter a cottage garden so stopped hounds and went back to the meet. When I had boxed up horses and hounds I had to ask someone to take me back in the car to find the mounted field as the horses were so tired they simply could not keep up.

The BFSS Area Secretary, Chris Wells, and his wife joined us for the lawn meet at Winston Hall on Thursday 11th February. We were rather late in moving off then had one fairly good hunt but then got amongst too many hares and that ruined the next hour although another good hunt concluded the day. Bill James entertained us to a right royal feast on our return in the lovely unspoiled Victorian atmosphere of Winston Hall: stew and baked potatoes with home

produced farmhouse butter, apple pie with lashings of fresh cream from the Jersey house-cow, and cheese and celery with decanters of port to finish the feast. In true Victorian manner, each singer stood in front of the mirror over the fireplace in turn and Chris Wells said he had never stopped at a meet so late but that he had never enjoyed himself so much.

An Old Time Music Hall Evening was held in Brandeston Village Hall on Friday 12th February. Many of the Easton members, including myself, performed on the stage either singly or in groups. Sue and Maurice Scott and Leila Turner masterminded it and many hours of rehearsal had been spent on certain pieces. The performers were too numerous to mention individually but our own hunting 'doctor in boots', Will Edmundson, did a very good turn as an Arab Sheikh and it gave me an idea. When his performance was over and the clapping easing up I went onto the stage and, standing beside him, I bet him £50, for hunt funds, that he dare not take his surgery next morning wearing his Arab costume. Ivor Davis stood up in the audience and said he would match my bet, then others also offered to bet him, and the wager soon totalled a staggering £250. The poor man was not really left much choice; he could be unsporting and thereby lose the hunt £250 or surprise his patients the next morning. Unfortunately, my mother was his first patient the next morning and took a dim view of her doctor's attire. I got a serious telling off when next I saw her. 'I understand that it was your stupid idea for the doctor to take surgery as an Arab. It could easily have given someone a heart attack!' All the bets were honoured and the good doctor was not drummed out of the Framlingham practice.

Three really good days followed, good classical hunting with many fresh finds and figures of eight. The last of these was at Cretingham and after we had hunted the last hare for about fifty minutes I spoke to an old man standing by his bicycle who said he had seen 'old Sally' cross the road and 'her feet were as big as tennis balls'. This was caused by very sticky earth and I could not bear to think of her being hunted with such an unfair disadvantage so I stopped hounds and we hacked back to the meet. Jim later told me that he had also seen her with balls of mud on her feet and I cannot remember this ever happening on another occasion. The day at Wetheringsett White Horse on 25th February brought together an interesting variety of people as John Graham and Eric Furness from Derbyshire were there, along with Rozzie Theobold and her seven-year-old daughter who was enjoying her fifth season, and Hilda Diplock celebrated her eightieth birthday in the pub afterwards, complete with a cake, pot plant, and a card from all from the Easton Harriers.

Unusually, hounds met on a Wednesday on 3rd March so as not to clash with the stallion show at Newmarket, and Jim hunted hounds. Colin Plumbe was down for his annual visit so I did not go to the stallion show but held a bye day from the kennels, taking all the young hounds, plus two couple of old ones. There were only five of us out: Jim and I, Maurice Scott, Ernie Calver, and Colin, and after half an hour I handed the horn to Colin and he hunted them and caught his hare quite near Len Mison's bungalow. This prompted thoughts of half time drinks but blowing the horn had no effect so Ernie and Colin rode round flicking thongs of their whips on the windowpanes. This eventually woke up Helen, Len's wife, who was in a deep sleep because she was a nurse and on night duty. Instead of being cross at the vulgar awakening, she poured us a tumbler of whisky each. While I sipped my drink I noticed that Ernie Calver kept casting longing glances at the horn, so I offered it to him. When we had finished our whiskies and wished Helen sweet dreams, Ernie went off to draw. A hare was soon found and Colin let out a wild Lakeland holloa, which scared the hounds and stopped them dead in their tracks. They, along with all East Anglia, had never heard such a yell. There was a hunt dinner that night at the Grapevine in Framlingham with a great atmosphere, good food, excellent wine, and plenty of songs; it was after one o'clock when we rose from our tables.

The mounted field of sixty-two enjoyed a curious day following the meet at the Saxtead Volunteer on 6th March. Each hunt was quite short, about ten minutes or so, and was always spoiled by fresh hares, but the curious part was that each time the fresh hare intervened she ran on in the same direction. After six or seven changes we were just outside Debenham, five miles away as hounds ran. I have never seen the like before or since. Some huntsmen might have been tempted to pretend that it was all one hunt but it was in fact just a relay race.

My birthday meet was at Laxfield Royal Oak on the 8th March. The members gave me a bottle of vintage port, Grahams '63, and a huge ripe Stilton cheese, Hilda Diplock and her friend, Marion, gave me a bottle of Scotch and my daughter, Bridget, presented me with two bottles of Saint Rothschild claret. Having carefully packed away my presents in the cab of the lorry we moved off to yet another curious day. There was a reasonable scent even though I expected there would be none as the land was so dry that when the hare ran there was a little cloud of dust behind her and when hounds hunted along the line they raised a real cloud of dust.

I took it as a great compliment that seventy-five people turned out on a Monday night for my birthday hunt dinner, which was only four days after the last one at the Grapevine restaurant. This restaurant had replaced our old favourite Framlingham Crown as the standard of the Crown had declined once it was taken over by a national chain and the Grapevine belonged to Ivor Davis who was a great supporter of the hunt. For some reason I was not in the mood to sing. Tony St Quinton did his best to kick if off with an excellent new song but no one followed suit and we just sat and chatted, most unusual for 8th March. A beneficial chain of events was started on 11th March when Stanley Tompkins' lorry became stuck at Occold as Mrs Hall from Church Farm fetched a tractor and pulled it out, Stanley then brought her to the meet, she enjoyed herself greatly and, eventually, this led to me getting permission to open up a large area of grass behind Church Farm. Henley on 13th March, provided us with a classic hunt with two fresh finds then went on to catch our hare but later things did not go quite so well as we got among too many hares, a problem that often occurs in March because they tend to congregate at that time, and then hounds killed one at a lady's feet and naturally she was rather upset. The day ended with a sharp run to beyond Gosbeck. There were not many out at Pettistree Greyhound on March 15th but the small field included Christine Crisp, Master of the Waveney, and her son. The first hunt was outstanding which always pleased me in front of a visiting Master but sadly the rest of the day was very poor. Nevertheless, we were not destined to go home in low spirits as Stanley Tompkins had asked the landlord, David, to provide us with lamb chops on our return and fifteen of us consumed thirty chops with masses of salad and fresh bread and this impromptu meal sparked off a terrific party. I arrived home at seven o'clock to find a very worried and cross wife who, not unreasonably, said that I ought to have telephoned her.

There was a large crowd at Worlingworth Swan on 18th March. Despite being so late in the season, scent was good but we had an excellent illustration of the way Mother Nature takes care as hounds found three does in kindle but could not hunt them at all once they were out of sight as pregnant does hold no scent at all. The next hare was a jack and we had a great run nearly to Brandeston but during this run Ernie Calver's old horse Rupert came down in Hollow Lane and both Ernie and Rupert were badly shaken and could not carry on.

To make maximum use of all the new green tailcoats I thought it would be fun to have a small 'End of Season' Ball limited to members and two of their friends. This was held in the 'function room', a converted barn, at Brome Grange and 99 people sat down to a six-course dinner with dancing between most of the courses. This was a first-class evening and everything I had hoped it to be and we danced into the early hours. Sheila and I, Mark Wayne and the Hennessys had all booked chalets and the party continued in one of these afterwards. I particularly remember drinking still champagne in Mark Wayne's chalet with the manager, Frank White. It was five o'clock when I finally went to bed. I breakfasted next morning at Brome Grange with the Hennessys then hurried home to change into my hunting clothes for the meet at Brundish Crown at half past twelve to finish the season. During the day I jumped into a disused garden at Downs Farm and my horse went down on its knees. Somehow I stayed on board but Jim followed me and was not so lucky. His horse came right down and struck him on the side of his head but I did not realise he was badly hurt so we carried on hunting until Hilda rode up to me and asked me to order Jim back to the meet as he was concussed. In the pub afterwards, it was decided that we ought to finish the season with a dinner so this was arranged on the spur of the moment for the Grapevine, about twenty-five people attended, and the season finished on a truly high note.

1982–83

We showed hounds as usual at the Peterborough Hound Show and had no success with the dog hounds but a little with the bitches as Garland[78] was third in the restricted bitches and Bargain[80] was second in the brood bitch class and later she was awarded Reserve Champion. I took a large draft of hounds to Peterborough to hand over to Anthony Barker, Master of the Windermere Harriers. This was part of a policy I had generated owing to the extreme trouble we were having with Parvovirus at the Easton Kennels. My master plan was to have some hounds carrying all the main Easton bloodlines in the Windermere kennels so that, in the event of the virus doing its worst, I would have a reserve of the old bloodlines in safety. Every hound was out for the first early morning as there were no bitches in season, but this amounted to only 25½ couple owing to the large draft having gone to the Windermere. The young hounds entered quite soon but they only had ten early mornings.

John Watson, hunting correspondent for the *Country Life* magazine, had been in contact to say that he would like to write up our Opening Meet. He duly arrived on Wednesday afternoon in time for a visit to the kennels and he seemed to be quite impressed by the hounds, especially by their level height and similarity of type. It was desperately important that we gain permission from Sir Alan Wigan to ride on the headlands of his rape as it divided the draw into halves and John Watson enthusiastically entered into the cause of working on him which, in the end, was successful. I mounted John on Ben, a very steady horse, easy to ride and very safe over the blindest of ditches. We unboxed on the Cransford road as usual and hacked into Framlingham calling at the Hare and Hounds where Sandy Hewitt was waiting with violets for everyone's buttonhole. John was most interested in this tradition but I could tell him nothing of its origins. Jim Meads, the world-famous photographer, was present and took photographs of the sixty-five beautifully turned out horses as they stood on the Market Hill in the large area cordoned off by the police for our benefit. The hunting was only average, which was a disappointment, but there was one amusing incident as a hare ran through Jim Meads' legs while he was taking a picture. I blew for home at a quarter to four and then John and I had a real hunting tea in the drawing room at home while he made copious notes for his article before going to the Opening Meet Dance at Glevering Hall. The supper was good but we did not stay long as John was tired so we returned home at half past ten.

As usual, the second meet of the season was at Charsfield and, as usual, the legendary Hennessy hospitality afterwards was extended to double the number who were out mounted. The following Wednesday, Sheila and I went up to stay with Tom Bracewell, Master of the Holcombe Harriers, in order to arrange events for the intended visit of the

Easton members. On 9ᵗʰ November I travelled up to Staffordshire and stabled my horses at the Staffordshire Moorland Kennels before staying the night with the Master, Eric Elliott, and then going on the next day to hunt with the High Peak Harriers at Sparklow. The huntsman, Paul Goddard, had drawn me a map and I arrived in very good time The High Peak country was pure heaven with firm grass and stone walls for as far as the eye could see. When most of the field went back to the meet for second horses I left and collected my other horse and groom and journeyed on up to the Holcombe. The Easton members had met their hosts at the Charnock Richard Services on the M6. Carol and Ernie Baker, Gay Bridgford, and Kathy Driver were to stay in a holiday cottage in Tom Bracewell's yard, Sheila and I were staying with the Bracewells, and the other Easton members who travelled up were Sarah Edmundson, Elise Quilter, Judy Brewster, Ernie and Mary Calver, Tish and John Finch, Elaine and Nick Fensom, Richard Lee, and Rupert Montagu. Brian and Flynn Bird and their son, Matthew, were surprise visitors.

Our first meet with the Holcombe Harriers was on Thursday 11ᵗʰ November at Deerplay. I rode Demelza and was very proud of my members who were beautiful turned out, especially Judy Brewster. High winds prevented any good hunting but the Easton brigade loved galloping across the moor, jumping stone walls and some low gates. It is a Holcombe custom that when 'Home' is blown, all men remove their hats so we, of course, did likewise. That night the visitors each dined with their respective guests. Newton Bacon, ex-Master of the Holcombe, had asked Anthony Barker to bring his Windermere Harriers and hunt on Friday but he had been very reluctant as he had an important meet the next day, the annual joint meet with the Blackcombe Beagles but as soon as he found out it was for me and the Easton Harriers, he agreed at once. We met him and his daughter Heather, who was to hunt hounds, at the Plough Inn at Selside. We never should have moved off as the wind was approaching gale strength but we managed to see some hunting then they went away on a fox and we saw no more of them. Anthony ordered us all back to the pub as we could not help him or Heather in their troubles. I felt terribly guilty as I was the cause of all this chaos and telephoned during the evening but he was still seven couple light, having taken only six and a half home with him. Back in Lancashire, our hosts Tom and Sheila Bracewell went to a Country Landowners dinner so we took their daughter, Lisa, out to dinner

at the Black Horse. Lisa had cooked delicious meals for us on Wednesday and Thursday evenings.

Saturday morning saw us at Ribblesdale Farm, Hesketh Bank and the weather had done a complete turn round and it was sunny, mild, and still. Alex Sneddon, the huntsman, drew open moor land but the scent was very poor. I rode with Alex until my upset stomach sent me back to the meet although I continued to follow in a car with Flynn Bird. I was unable to leave the meet until Kathy Driver and David returned as I had brought their horses and they did not return until after half past four but I eventually arrived back at Tom and Sheila's home, I was delighted to find Kate and Newton Bacon there. We spent a most enjoyable hour before going to a Leisure Centre for a typical Lancashire evening with hotpot, followed by apple pie and cream. I replied to a toast to the horse by singing *The Battered Brigade* which was about the knocks and scars of a bold hunter. The Easton members made their way home the next morning but I stayed and had a Sunday morning hunt with the Pennine Foxhounds and then moved horses and groom to Clifton near Penrith for a further hunting jolly, managing to hunt with ten different packs in as many days. In my absence Jim Wickham hunted hounds at Laxfield, Debach, Henley Cross Keys, and Clopton Crown.

The Cambridgeshire Harriers visited us on 2ⁿᵈ December for a lawn meet at Dennington Hall at the kind invitation of Robert Rous, but I was shocked to see how badly hounds had gone downhill. They hunted with almost no cry and they were very riotous, especially on rabbits. Jim Wickham tried to stop some with some skilled whip work but they dodged him, passing under his horse in their determination. Their own amateur whip, Richard Mead, needed to dismount to whip them off pheasants which were in a release pen but not before they had killed six or seven. Later on it took four whippers-in to drive hounds off some wheat back to Mrs Gingell, the Master and huntsman, with the four of them in a line abreast behind hounds. It was very sad to see these beautiful hounds in this state. Fifteen Cambridgeshire visitors came to tea at Tannington Hall with eleven of them stopping for supper. Dandy Corner worked hard helping Sheila to prepare the supper for sixty people. We had Sheila's special 'up market' shepherds pie, with carrots cooked in brown sugar, followed by apple pie and a cheese board. It was quite late when the party broke up. It was unfortunate that there was such a marked contrast between this day and our day at Otley on 4ᵗʰ December which provided fast hunting with convenient tracks so we were able to ride abreast of hounds and could watch them work. We covered a huge amount of country with a tremendous cry ringing in our ears as we galloped well out of our draw to Pettaugh, just short of the Bull. Two brace were accounted for, one brace of which had no time to turn as the scent was so good. During one of these fast hunts, Nick Fensom rode up alongside me and shouted, 'Now what price the Cambridgeshire?'

The next two days were cancelled for floods, then another for frost, but the meet at Hoxne Swan on 22nd December was a memorable one. We had a quick burst during which my horse, Falcon, lost his footing and crashed down on a track. Jim Wickham was close behind us but literally rose to the occasion and neatly cleared both Falcon and me, galloping on to keep with his hounds. It is a curious fact as to how often we had an outstanding day on Christmas Eve and so it was this year for the meet at Dennington Bell. The first hare took us to just short of my home and back towards Dennington, through Fenton's Farm to Saxtead, turning back behind Church Farm where Tom Walne saw them safely over the main road. They then ran on to Framlingham Hall turning back to Dennington where Jim and I managed to stop them. This great hunt was very fast and the only person

Tom Walne

with us at the end was Tom Walne who had, yet again, missed a good run as he put hounds' safety beyond his own pleasure. Every Master should have a Tom Walne. There was not a horse even in sight as we slowly hacked back to the meet in the dusk but they gradually came up with us in ones and twos. I rated this day very highly.

There was a huge crowd at Saxtead on Boxing Day with just over eighty mounted. I had put up jumps as usual for the 'jolly' and everyone except hounds enjoyed the fast ride with all the jumping. Proper hunting followed the jolly with three good long hunts which thinned out the field until there were only ten or so left. New Year's Day at Cretingham had the usual enormous crowd and I had a 'jolly' prepared for the mounted field which started along the valley at Rookery Farm and crossed the river, up to Framsden Hall turning back across the Rookery again to Cretingham Lodge, Earl Soham Rookery

and along the valley and finished up at Red House Farm Brandeston. This jolly lasted for two hours, all on grass with thirty-two jumps. It had necessitated a lot of work as the jumps had to be taken down from Boxing Day and re-erected of course all collected again the next day and stored away for next year. The real hunting was very poor, as there were too many hares with consequently no good runs.

The Children's Meet was again held at Crowfield Rose and had a very good turn out of children and enough adults, which made a pleasant change. The Helmingham Estate is perfect for a children's meet and so was the hunting with lots of short runs, ideal for small children and those on leading reins. The meet on 8th January was at Stradbroke Ivy House and, after some indifferent hunting on Horham airfield, a hare was found at Valley Farm. This ran via Park Farm and then crossed the road to Depperhaugh into Waveney country. I was then in unknown country but the run ended at Syleham School and Jim and I were grinning from ear to ear and our horses were covered in white lather. It was not the distance but the speed that made this run so memorable. We had used both whip and spur to urge our galloping horses ever faster just to keep hounds in sight and riding over strange country had added an extra zest. One hound, old Lawful, was missing after this quick burst and we had to wait for him to catch up so I said to Jim that I knew a better place to wait than this old school and we rode to Wingfield Green and blew my horn outside Ted Chaplin's cottage. Ted needed no asking and appeared with a bottle of Teachers whisky and some glasses. Between sips I blew my horn and Lawful came up with that dejected look old hounds have when they have been left behind.

The Waveney invited us for a lawn meet at Red House Farm, Wissett, on Wednesday 12th January. It was not exactly a lawn meet as it was held in a garage where a large number of muscovy ducks had spent a considerable time and the extra special polishing I had given my boots seemed rather a waste of time. Sherry was being served but Colonel Mike Tomkin, our host, smiled and said, 'I bet you would rather have something a little stronger' and brought me a stiff whisky. We unboxed and assembled in a meadow where I was told to draw some grassland first. This had lovely trimmed hedges over which the field were invited to jump whether or not hounds were running. The first hunt was almost a classical circle but two fresh hares jumped up towards the end which rather spoiled the hunt. Scent improved all the time. Hounds were so biddable that I only needed to blow once and they would fly to me as they had the previous time we had been invited by the Waveney when Bernard and I had called this their 'party manners'. When they were hunting they ran in a tightly compacted group and their cry was superb. The day ended with a fast hunt with my horse tiring under me and I was worried about losing hounds but I just managed to stop them at Corner Farm, Rumburgh, at half past three. As we hacked back to the meet Ivor Constance complimented me on how well hounds had hunted together as a pack and on the volume of cry. Mike Tomkin provided a much-needed beer. I thanked him and floated off home in a state of ecstasy.

Scent was very good and a first class day was had at Glemham on 15th January with Dougie Ruth going great guns on his Appleby, a cob he had bought at the horse fair. Twenty songs were sung after hunting. I had been to the NFU dance the night before and I ended my diary entry with: '*a great twenty four hours - just how life should be spent*'. Another great day followed at Brundish on 20th January, slightly marred when hounds again managed to get into Miss Marriott's garden and compounded their sin of entry by killing one of her bantams. I was in trouble again two days later at Yaxley when a horse jumped out of a paddock and galloped to Stonham Parva. A couple gathering firewood stopped Jim to say that a horse with a green jacket had galloped past out of control. Jim was desperately worried as my grey mare Demelza had taken off with every other rider except me and he assumed that the horse with the green jacket was Demelza and me. Then he saw both Terence Saffell and me and knew we were both safe and the horse with a green jacket proved to be the loose horse which was wearing a New Zealand rug.

Thorndon Black Horse on the 27th January was a fun-packed day. The meet was really very special and had a wonderfully old-fashioned atmosphere, the scent was excellent and hounds pushed their hares so hard that we were continually running out of our draw. In the pub after hunting there was an hour or so of singing then the members drifted away until there were only four of us left when two smart businessmen in pinstripe suits walked in. Joyce, the landlady, had been teasing me saying that I had not sung because

Geoffrey Ingram-Smith was not there with his accordion so I sang a song. The businessmen bought me a double whisky and asked for another song, a dangerous chain of events. Nine songs and eighteen whiskies later, I said I must go home as I had a dinner party to go to. I arrived home just after seven and bathed and changed calling at Stradbroke Ivy House then on to dinner with Chris and Rupert Montagu. The dinner was superb and the main course was their own Dexter beef. My diary entry for the day gives detailed accounts of the hunting and the fact that we ran into the middle of a shoot and ends up with: '*A great day – good hunting – hounds and the company of the best – a day like we used to have fifteen years ago – hurrah*'. I am not sure why I thought that life had been better fifteen years earlier. Looking back, I find it difficult to believe we used to consume that amount of whisky, but we did, almost inevitably without a hangover.

My brother Robert hired the shooting rights on the Wentworth Estate and when hounds met at Knodishall Butcher's Arms on 29th January I could hear his guns and he could hear my hounds running but, luckily, we managed to keep our respective sports apart. When hounds came to Blaxhall Ship on 5th February the pub was crowded to overflowing. Louis Borrett, who had a cottage nearby, had arranged with Jim, the landlord, for us all to have a stirrup cup prior to moving off. We had half-time at Walk Farm where the Prescotts dispensed hot punch and mince pies. Soon after this we found and had a classic hunt in a figure of eight, part of which was through the Prescott's farmyard and part on the common. It was very pretty to see hounds working amongst the gorse bushes, rather like hunting in another county. Louis Borrett had a splendid tea waiting for us in the pub after which there was a singing session. Louis really enjoyed himself and stayed to the bitter end, which was after five o'clock, this was a particular treat for him as, although his cottage was near by, his main home was in East Grinstead.

The next morning Chris Wells, the Regional Secretary of the BFSS, telephoned me to say that Gordon Craggs had complained to him and asked him to come over and inspect where I had cut his wire. I could not believe my ears as for the past two years he had invited me to cut some holes in the old rabbit fencing which was now falling down but was still dangerous to cross owing to the main strainer wires. Why had he not rung me?

Jim hunted hounds at Easton on 7th as I was away and he reported that he had had a good day and a deer had jumped right into the middle of hounds but they had been rock steady. The next six days were cancelled due to snow and ice and one of these was an invitation day in the Suffolk Foxhound country. The snow and frost had gone enough for us to meet at Debenham Cherry Tree on 19th February and hunting was fair. A young hound, Major, swam out into a pond and moved the hunted hare from some rushes, and then hounds hunted on and she was later caught. Stella Mitchell's horse came down on the road and was badly hurt. A trailer was brought and the horse taken to the Saffells for treatment. The clock was turned back two days later at Crundisburgh when I was delighted to see Judith Bull and Barbara Buller and Peggy Harrison together again, as well as Betty Kingston-Smith and Richard Wilson, both riding. Hilda Diplock was eighty-seven on 24th February when hounds met at Rendham. Mary Garton had made her a cake and we sang to her; she had hunted for eighty-three years. Her birthday provided the only fun of the day as most fields had been top-dressed with artificial manure and there was no scent at all. Jim was ill for the Brandeston meet on 26th February but we had one good hunt, the classical circle, with hounds running from scent to view until they caught her while she was still running, which was very unusual.

Lady Blanche Cobbold eventually forgave me for the sins of my predecessor, Captain Bernard, and invited us to meet at Glemham Hall on Monday 28th February. Lady Blanche had kept the hunt going during the war and without doubt the Easton would have gone out of existence had it not been for her Mastership. She had taken great umbrage at the decision to put down almost all the pack in September 1961 and, although I had tried very hard, it had taken me twenty years to get her to forgive and forget so I was terribly pleased that at last the rift had been healed and hounds were back again at Glemham Hall. This was the first time that hounds had met there since the War. Captain Marriott was there and asked for a photograph of him and Lady Blanche together, as they were both Masters of the Easton.

Lady Blanche Cobbold and Captain Marriott at Glemham Hall

The Southolt meet was very subdued and sad on 3rd March as I had received the news that my old friend and hunting companion, Stanley Tompkins, had died, but there was consolation in the knowledge that he had died exactly as he would have wished, during a good run across Exmoor. He was galloping alongside the huntsman, said, 'This is what I really call hunting,' and fell dead from his horse.

The Point-to-Point was held on 5th March in beautiful weather and the attendance was a record. In the Members' Race, Robbie Haag rode my George and Paul Yeldham rode his own horse and they went round neck and neck but sadly, Paul's horse fell at the one from last and George fell at the last. Meanwhile Sandy Hewitt was riding her cob in a race all of her own and came on at her own pace, receiving great applause as she passed the crowd, and we were all sure that this plucky lady would finish the course but unfortunately the cob ran out at the open ditch second time round. Jaguar had been the main sponsor for the races and their representative came to the Supporters Club cheese and wine party at Winston Hall that evening. When the party was over I asked Bill James, our host, if he would get the whisky bottle out so we could make a fuss of the sponsors. This he readily did and a good party was quickly in progress. Tom Walne offered to drive the sponsors back to their Ipswich hotel. Sandy Hewitt was not too tired after her race and sang some songs, as did Iris Kindred, Ernie Calver and myself. I rather over-did the whisky and became belligerent when Sheila wanted to go home, but we finally left at two-thirty, thanking Bill for his generosity.

I awoke next morning, frozen with cold, and thought I was in a churchyard as I could see two gravestones sticking up. My mind raced back to being awkward and telling Sheila that I would get home under my own steam. I first thought that I was in Winston churchyard, which was very close to Winston Hall where the party had been. Then I thought that it couldn't be Winston as the gravestones were far too close so it must be Debenham. 'Yes, that would be it. I started to walk home and stopped for a rest in Debenham churchyard'. Just then I moved a little and realised I was in the back of the Volvo and the 'gravestones' were in fact the front seats, silhouetted by the moonlight shining through the garage windows. I went upstairs and as I was so cold I grumbled at Sheila for leaving me. She simply answered, 'I had enough trouble getting you into the car. I certainly wasn't going to bother getting you out!' I was a little late for church at eight o'clock.

A Gentleman's Day at Wetheringsett White Horse was arranged which coincided with my birthday on Tuesday 8th March and seventeen men paid £12 pounds each which was going towards the BFSS Fighting Fund. We had one of the best pubs to meet at, the best of country to hunt, and this ought to have been a first class day but everything went wrong. Firstly a group of ladies had walked up from the village and were nagging at us to move off. It was ironic that the members had paid £12 each to be free of their responsibilities towards ladies only to have their day spoiled by other peoples' wives. The scent was unbelievably good and hounds were hunting beautifully when an awful accident occurred. A tree had blown down and the boughs shattered leaving one piece sticking out with a jagged edge about five feet from the ground. Ernie Calver was

Geoffrey Ingram-Smith

in front of me, riding along and intently watching hounds, leaving it all to his horse, and when they came to the fallen tree and his horse went round the end of it but, because Ernie was not looking where he was going, a jagged piece of bough went between the saddle and his leg. It pitched Ernie off and ripped open his breeches and made a deep cut along the inside of his thigh. Will Edmundson took charge of the leg while someone else galloped to Dairy Farm to telephone for an ambulance and Peter Freeman came with his Land Rover and took Ernie to the farm. Ernie was far more worried about going to hospital because he was wearing an old pair of Mary's tights than he was about the horrendous wound which ran from just above his knee to his crotch. He kept telling me to get on with my hounds and not worry about him but I stopped hounds and we all waited at Dairy Farm

until he went off in the ambulance. I telephoned to Ernie's house and his son, Richard, answered and said that his mother would come at once to the meet so I handed the horn to Jim and went back to the meet to wait for her. Jim showed them great sport and £193 was raised for the BFSS but, not surprisingly, there was none of the usual atmosphere. I went to see Ernie in hospital the next afternoon. Sandy Hewitt had already been with a basket of grapes, which she told Ernie 'had some corn in the bottom', and when Ernie moved the grapes he found a bottle of whisky.

Hounds met at Framlingham Station on Friday 11th March. This should have been the morning after the Hunt Ball but the ball had been cancelled because of a lack of support, possibly because the previous year's ball at Brome Grange had not had quite the usual excellent atmosphere. Too many hares spoiled the day and there were no quick runs. We met again the next day at Bedfield Crown, to finish the season. There was a good crowd at the meet and a large mounted field who enjoyed galloping across the wheat fields at Tannington as it was dry enough to ride on Harvey wheat. There was no classical hunting yet it was a fun day on which to end the season. Sheila put on an End of Season party at Tannington Hall for which we charged £12 per head towards the BFSS Fighting Fund. For supper we had salmon mousse, fish pie, and apple pie and coffee. Black velvet or bucks fizz was served freely all evening and the party ended at half past two.

We had hunted on fifty-one days with eight days cancelled for floods, snow and ice. This season was the last of an era as at the end of it Geoffrey Ingram-Smith retired as amateur whipper-in. He was a great ambassador for hunting and always got on very well with everybody. His tremendous enthusiasm and his accordion playing all helped to create the great atmosphere at this time. There is a saying that, when one door closes, another one opens but this is not necessarily true. When Geoffrey stopped hunting he left a gap that has never been filled and his name will always be linked with the best of fun during a special era of the Easton Harriers.

1983–84

At Peterborough Hound Show it was back to normal and the best we could do was a third in the restricted bitch class with Bargain. I had also planned to show hounds at the Lowther and Rydal Shows in the Lake District but this had to be cancelled because we were then struck by a serious outbreak of the Parvovirus and many of the puppies died. The decision to take hounds to the other shows had been a conspiracy between me and Hilda as she had warned me privately that Jim was in desperate need of a holiday but would not consider leaving his hounds. I had thoroughly agreed with her and had thought up this plan so that I could tell him to stay up in the Lake District between the two shows. Jim was very upset at losing so many puppies and was in need of a break more than ever so even though we could not show hounds I persuaded him to come with me to Rydal Show, for a three day break. The natural place for us both to stay was with the Barker family where the Windermere Harriers were kennelled and, although the Barkers were fully booked for bed and breakfast, Jim and I had a caravan each. Jim thoroughly enjoyed the Rydal Show with its special Lake District atmosphere and he and Anthony Barker became great friends, especially as we had taken a draft of hounds for the Windermere. We took Chaser, Alison, Grumpy, and Growler

Bernard Needham, Rob Haag and Gordon Grover

but I am not sure how we did so without the risk of spreading the dreaded virus.

The season started with Teresa Pomeroy and Lindsay Baker as grooms and Robert Haag as the new amateur whip with the horses stabled at the kennels. This season we decided to do all hound exercise from Tannington Hall instead of the kennels because the entered hounds always got excited and associated Tannington Hall with hunting and it would do them good to find out that this did not necessarily happen. We had planned to start hunting on 22nd September but my back was being troublesome so Jim took hounds on exercise instead with Robbie Haag and John Suckling. John often whipped in on foot for either the Waveney or Easton although on this occasion he was mounted. Hounds were allowed to stray onto some stubble which had been spread with

muck which contained the carcasses of some dead turkeys. Naturally, hounds had started to eat these before being sent back to the road and later on in kennel three hounds became ill. Crafter recovered but Tippler and Villager died. We made a proper start on 28th September and the early mornings were much the same at usual except that I spent a week away between 20th and 27th October on a hunting holiday. It was unusual for me to do this before the Opening Meet but the Plumbes, who were now living in the Clifton-on-Teme country, were shortly to move to Scotland and, with such an excellent base, it was too tempting to miss. As usual Jim enjoyed hunting hounds in my absence and I returned in time for three more early mornings before the Opening Meet on 27th October.

Fifty-nine people were mounted, including Dougie Ruth who paid his subscription in notes on the Market Hill. There was the usual good crowd and when we moved off I was pleased to see Peggy Harrison and Judith Bull waiting to watch us draw. I so enjoyed old members keeping in touch. The draw was very fully drilled so I had put some jumps in the gateways on my meadows at Bruisyard to amuse the field. I had also started to build a hunter trial course which included a stone faced bank and this was enjoyed by the braver of the field. Unfortunately my daughter Judith had a fall when another horse cut across in front of her and she was taken off to hospital with concussion. It was her twentieth birthday and the *East Anglian Daily Times* the next day had a large headline 'Master's daughter in birthday fall', but she was allowed home the next day. The hunting was very poor as Mr Peat did not want us in his wood as his pheasants were still in release pens. This left us with little country so I did not take much persuading to go to the Hare and Hounds afterwards. The Hare and Hounds had always been a favourite pub of the Easton Harriers and the landlord, Jimmy Finbow, was a tremendous character who always made us feel especially welcome. It was pitiful to see this great character on this day as his eyes had sunk into his head and he seemed confused but he still managed to do what he had always done and found a walnut whip for each of us to take home to our wives. The Supporters Club held another

Opening Meet Dance at Glevering Hall which was particularly good and had the old atmosphere like the best of the days at Captain Bernard's home.

The next day a big landowner telephoned to say that, even though he had inspected all his fields and could find no damage at all, would we keep off his land in future. I was really depressed about this; how could I ever win?

I was delighted with Robbie Haag's performance as amateur whip. I had thought that he would be first class and he did an excellent job at Charsfield on 29th October. My daughter Charlotte and her friend, Jeanette Cox, cycled to the meet, followed enthusiastically, and then cycled back to the kennels from where I gave them a lift home. At one point during the day I was in danger of losing hounds and to avoid doing so I carefully walked my horse along the edge of a lawn thinking it belonged to Richard Hunter who I thought would not mind. Unfortunately, it was not Richard's but belonged instead to Mr Young. He was naturally very upset but forgave me when I had been to see him and explained the circumstances. We had a good day at Worlingworth and a very unusual thing happened. Some hounds were hanging around with me while others were hunting their hare towards me but the hounds that were with me stood still and the hare ran into their mouths.

I organised a party to go to the Suffolk Foxhounds' Ball on 4th November and invited all the men who possessed Easton evening coats, booking a private room at the Angel Hotel, Bury St Edmunds, for dinner. Nine couples sat down to dinner where the main course was leg of lamb en croûte, which was wheeled in and carved at the table. Almost all the men had second helpings from a fresh leg of lamb. The atmosphere at the dinner was wonderful with the ladies looking fabulous in their beautiful gowns and it was quite difficult to find the resolve to get up and move. We walked across the square to the Ball in the Athenaeum and hung up our overcoats. No one was yet dancing but the band was playing and, having found our table and the ladies having put down their handbags, we just moved spontaneously onto the dance floor, nine couples twirling round the floor, green tails flying, the ladies all happy and smiling. I felt my heart would burst with pleasure and pride in the Easton Harriers. Gradually the other guests started to dance and I felt that the Easton had opened the Ball. It was one of the proudest moments of my Mastership and I shall never forget that feeling.

The following Tuesday, a hunt dinner was held at the Grapevine in Framlingham, where we enjoyed paté, game pie and pudding with a half bottle of wine for £7.30 per head. After dinner I presented hunt buttons to Ernie Baker, Mark Wayne, Robert Haag, Idwal Humphrey and Paul Yeldham. Laxfield on 10th November was a disastrous day because at the last moment two shooting syndicates asked us to keep away and we only saw two hares all day, both of which immediately ran to Richard Hickson's sugar beet where he had his pheasants, so had to be stopped. The second time this happened his house cow and two ponies jumped out. The cow was caught but the ponies galloped to Framlingham with Isla Prescott in hot pursuit.

At Debach on 12th November we enjoyed the first good scenting day for some time and it was heartening to hear the volume of music again. At the meet I was surprised to see my mother, sister, nephew and niece, but even more surprised to see Fred Ling, aged seventy-three, mounted on one of James Miller's ponies. We did not have much country because of shooting but were just able to hunt as Richard Taylor had said we could use his land despite the fact that he was shooting the following week. Janet Baxter gave a half-time break of mince pies and hot punch and, to round off the day, James and Celia Miller gave their usual tea of bangers and mash. Robert Rous was with us at Clopton on 19th November and I was pleased to be able to show him some good sport; most people went home after two hours, as their horses were exhausted.

The Cambridgeshire Harriers invited us to meet at Cottenham Race Course on 22nd November. There were twenty-four people from the Easton who included my guests David Steel and Chris Wells, who were riding my horses Rose and Charlie, and Eddie

David Steel and Hilda Wickham

Kerridge, our new Road Safety Officer who had replaced Ben Fletcher the previous season and who was riding my horse Ben. David Steel had offered to drive me to the meet in his car and on the way we hooted and waved as we overtook all the horseboxes, but then his car broke down and all the horseboxes overtook us. We managed to get a lift in Sue Gooderham's box and Hugh Gingell sent one of his men to tow the car to the meet. Once again when we were visiting, the hounds had their best party manners and were unbelievable biddable and, just for good measure, when the hunted hare went into thick bushes, they pushed in as eagerly as foxhounds and went on to catch their hare. It was extraordinary to watch them do this and Jim and I could hardly believe our eyes as they usually shy clear of brambles and thorns. Tea was served in a building on the course and many compliments were paid to me on how well the hounds had hunted and how they hunted together as a pack. Eighteen of us stayed for the evening which was as much fun as ever and we left at half past ten. Jim Wickham towed David's car home behind the lorry but the rope was far too short and David had a dreadful journey, and complained that Jim did not even stop once to check if everything was all right.

We did not hunt the following Thursday but we still dined in the evening when Dougie Ruth and John Keeble enjoyed their first hunt dinner. The next morning Maurice Scott and I attended a working lunch at Brent Pelham as guests of Captain Barclay where we discussed British Field Sports Society matters and listened to an excellent speaker. At Dennington Bell on 26th November I only completed half a day before handing the horn to Jim as my horse Charlie was travelling to Worcestershire the next day where I had planned a second hunting holiday with the Plumbes. Jim hunted hounds for the next two weeks and then at Cretingham Bell on 15th December he was complaining loudly that I had come back as this had spoilt his run of hunting hounds. This caused amusement all round and we moved off for some brilliant hunting.

My daughter Bridget was writing the history of the Easton Harriers and on Friday 16th December we had a lunch party at Tannington Hall for all the old members so she could plunder their memories of Captain

Rupert Montagu

Bernard's Mastership. Those present were Terence and Marion Saffell, Josie Lofts, Denis Holland, Jill Ganzoni, Judith Bull, Barbara Buller, Fred Ling, Mrs Longe and Alfred Breese. At Dennington Queen on 17th December I was delighted to see John Kellaway's son, Martin, and niece, out hunting. John owns the Great Lodge at Framlingham and always welcomes hounds. I telephoned him that night and he said that the youngsters had enjoyed themselves.

A first class day was had at Hoxne Swan on 22nd December. Some very ordinary little hunts started the day before Rupert Montagu, who was whipping-in on foot, told me where a special hare was sitting. This hare he had often coursed with his long dog so he knew her well and told me she was sitting in her form at South Green. We found her and she ran a huge circle during which she passed through the garden of the Flowerdew family at Denham. The Flowerdews hated hunting and Sod's Law caused the hounds to check and cast themselves around in their garden. When I caught up the Flowerdews had brooms in their hands and were pushing hounds away. It might have been comical but was not and Rupert said he would do his best to appease the situation as he knew them from coursing. The Flowerdews asked, 'Why can't Harvey gallop about on his own wheat?' but their brooms, luckily, pushed hounds back onto the line and they ran on across Tom Moore's farm and caught their hare one field from where she was found. This had been a great hunt and I presented pads to Guy Quilter, Maria Wickham, Linda Holywell, shortly to become Linda Bothway, and, of course, to Rupert Montagu. It gave me special pleasure to present this last pad as Rupert was a great sportsman, who whipped in on foot, was always in touch with hounds, and was an authority on venery.

I spent all of Friday putting up jumps for Boxing Day which meant that I had not made preparations for the Christmas Eve meet on Saturday, so on Saturday morning I was out an hour before it was light checking details of where to draw and opening the barbed wire in the valley below Moat Farm, Dennington. This was an annual chore as some years earlier I had obtained permission from John Nesling and David Paul to make places in their barbed wire that I could open and shut on hunting days. The whole valley was wired from Fosdyke's Bridge to Brundish church, a distance of over half a mile but I made nine openings and opened them all before each hunting day and closed them the day following. On this occasion I did it on the hunting morning and, as I neared Brundish church to open the last place, a fox jumped out of a willow tree just in front of me.

This Christmas Eve was another exceptional day. The meet was crowded and the Dennington Bell was packed full but we did not forget to drink to the General's memory. Lady Blanche Cobbold watched us unbox and move off and when she saw that the grooms had decorated my horse with Christmas baubles, she said, 'They would not have dared to do that to me in my day!' There was a field of sixty-seven mounted and hounds ran hard from the start. We were quite near Tannington Hall at just after one o'clock so I sent Maurice Scott on ahead to warn Sheila that we were coming and we all stopped for hot toddies which gave our horses a much needed rest. The next hunt was another continuous run with barely a check and soon after two o'clock there were only a few of us left, one of whom was my daughter Judith on her horse Mickey. I called her up to ride with me and she was thrilled to watch the hounds at close quarters. They were hunting with a good cry and so closely packed together that, at checks, they shouldered each other like rugby players in a scrum. It was almost dark and Judith and I walked our tired horses through the valley on our way back to the meet. There is always a special atmosphere when hunting on Christmas Eve and hacking home with my daughter and hounds seemed to enhance it even more. It left an indelible imprint in my memory.

Boxing Day was not as well supported as usual. The crowd was smaller and there were only forty-five horses. We had the usual jolly which ended at Bedfield Crown where two tame Belgian hares were running round the pub so I needed to keep a sharp eye on the hounds. The hunting that followed the jolly was brilliant and we covered a great deal of country and, as most people's horses were reduced to a walk, I blew for home at three o'clock. The next day, with the assistance of Tim Last from World's End Farm, I collected up all the jumps in the morning and then erected them again after lunch for New Year's Day. The Christmas spirit lingered for the day at Brundish Crown on 29th December. Ernie Calver started the day off by inviting us to call at his house for a glass of port before we went on to Jill Graham's home for a hunt breakfast. This was Jill's effort for another Chairman's Appeal and, during breakfast, Kathy

Driver was running a Baby Competition for the same cause. She had obtained photographs of many of the Easton leading characters and we all had to guess who they were. Both ladies exceeded their target of £40 each. We made our way to the meet where we found a large crowd had gathered and about fifty horses and I was presented with a drawing of the meet by the five-year-old granddaughter of Gwen Elliott, the landlady. Soon after I started to draw hounds hit off a drag and followed all the windings and twisting of the hare with a great cry and worked up to where she was on her seat, then she ran a large circle and hounds caught her behind the St Quintons' house at Brundish. Hounds were unaided throughout this run and had been closely monitored by the Corner family who were following on foot and had especially enjoyed the drag to begin with. The rest of the day was full of pure venery and was simply hare hunting at its best. I was in ecstasy and my enjoyment was enhanced because the Corner family were always in close contact with hounds. As they are all great veneurs I knew how much they would be enjoying the day themselves.

At a party the night before Tony St Quinton and Peter Bailey had firmly declared that they were going to follow hounds on foot but they had not appeared at the meet. At half past three Tony strolled into the pub wearing varnished yellow wooden clogs with flowers painted on the top, and Peter followed him wearing plus fours and highly polished shoes. I had never seen a pair of more unlikely hare-hunters in my life and there was a great deal of leg pulling. During the day I had seen Captain Morgan (*alias* Dougie Ruth) stop at the Dennington Bell while hounds were running, tie his horse to the rail and go into the pub. I declared that this sort of behaviour was not allowed when hounds were actually running, and deserved a stiff penalty so I fined him a round of drinks which delighted him.

A mixed day followed the meet at Laxfield, with no scent at first although it improved later. I burst through a thick place and lost my watch but luckily Catherine Corner, who was foot following, saw it and returned it to me. The modest day did not matter as most of us were looking forward to the New Year's Eve party at the home of Robert Bothway, where we celebrated his marriage to Linda the day before. I had asked Jim to hunt hounds from Stradbroke White Hart on Thursday 5th January as I could not spare the time due to the preparations for the Hunt Ball the following day and he gave them an excellent day although it started in an uncertain way as Terence Saffell, who was in charge, had forgotten his bridle but luckily he managed to borrow one from Duncan Morton. Hounds ran hard all and they finished in the dark.

After the disaster of the cancelled ball the year before, we had put a great deal of thought into a venue and eventually decided on Framlingham College and were lucky enough to get the permission of the Governors. Tickets were in high demand and were of two types, of £15 to include dinner and £8 to come after dinner. I had bowed to pressure from the lady members to have a ball which included dinner as they were finding it increasingly difficult to give dinner parties at home before coming on to the ball. The cheaper tickets proved very popular amongst the young and my elder two daughters gave a dinner party at home and charged their friends £5 each thereby raising £60 for the Chairman's Appeal. Having the ball at the school involved a great deal of hard work and I was there from nine o'clock on the Tuesday until four-thirty on the Friday, the day of the Ball. The 160 'after dinner' guests had their own tables in either one of the common rooms, or in a marquee, which had been erected in the Tuck Box Courtyard that opened into the main dance floor. The Bursar, Trevor Fanshaw, had put five men at my disposal so all the benches had been carried out of the dining room and replaced with chairs. Tony St Quinton, who had recently returned from Holland, kindly volunteered to collect the 100 three-branch candelabra from Tottenham and Ivor Davis provided the three hundred extra long candles that were needed. These provided the only light in the dining room which created a very special atmosphere. The Assembly Room opened off the dining room and this was completely cleared and used as the ballroom. Mary Calver was in charge of an army of ladies whose floral arrangements transformed the College into a real ball scene. We ran the bar ourselves with help from Ivor Davies who supplied us, and took advice from George Coleman and John Appleby who were both highly-respected landlords. Don Corcoran's party had, inadvertently, not been booked in correctly and, as the maximum number of tickets had been sold for dinner, Sheila offered to take our house party to dine at the Crown and I asked the Saffells and the Borretts if they would mind joining her. This arrangement kept the number of diners at the maximum of 240, including myself. Bill Nekrews, the Chef at the College, provided a splendid dinner of paté, fish, duck a l'orange, pudding, cheese, coffee and mints, all for £7 per head. Two hundred and thirty-nine portions of duck were served and one steak for Maurice Scott who does not like duck and was not allowed to forget this privilege for many years. The band was the Galvanos who proved to be excellent and the ballroom was full all evening with a profusion of black, green and red tailcoats and of course, the most important ingredient of all, the lovely full-length ball dresses. There was a disco in another room and, although this was well-supported, I was surprised to see how many of the youngsters were in the ballroom. Altogether, the ball was a huge success and our evening ended with champagne round our kitchen table with my daughters singing hunting songs.

The après ball meet was at Bedfield Crown at midday and this was well-supported with much jovial camaraderie but the hunting did not go well. My horse, Charlie, was cantering up the grass headland beside some wheat at Firs Farm, lost his footing and fell into the ditch with me landing well ahead of him and sitting in a foot of water. Hounds meanwhile had run to Bedingfield Hall and right into the middle of a shoot and disturbed the pheasants prior to the shoot. Two more horses fell into ditches and the tractors required to get them out caused a lot of damage to wheat. I went to see the farmer, Roy Creasey, who was rather upset but, nevertheless, gave me two large glasses of sherry and Mrs Creasey gave me a pot of heather for Sheila. After such a disappointing day, Mark Wayne decided to cheer us all up and, having agreed a corkage charge with the landlord, brought in a case of vintage champagne for us all. This very generous gesture lifted our spirits and when all had gone home the Corner family returned the hospitality by inviting Mark to join them for a supper of jugged hare during which, I am told, the champagne continued to flow.

Another excellent day was had from Glemham Crown on 12th January with the best run taking us from Glemham, round Cransford to Framlingham where she ran round the Pageant Field, then across to White House Farm to just short of Dennington where she was lost. John Appleby, who was the landlord of Saxtead Volunteer, had kindly offered to give twelve evening meals to raise money for the Chairman's Appeal and, after such an enjoyable day, it seemed a good idea to take advantage of the offer but I was not quite at my best having celebrated the good day rather too well. The meet at Yaxley Cherry Tree on 14th January ought to have been cancelled but it was not until we were out in the open that we realised how strong the winds were. I decided to stop almost immediately but, before Jim could get to their heads, hounds had found two hares and divided. I managed to stop my half and returned to the meet and boxed them up and then asked someone to drive me in the lorry to look for Jim. We met him coming down the main road with his half of the pack and, as he was almost at a place where he could turn off the road, we turned the lorry round and followed him. Just a few seconds after he had turned off the main road a wooden garage was whisked up into the air and flew towards Jim and the hounds but, luckily, it landed about five yards behind the last hounds and smashed into smithereens. I have never been so thankful to box up all my hounds as I was on that day.

A meeting was held on Tuesday 18th January at the Grapevine Restaurant to discuss two topics, chiefly the impending visit by our French friends, the Picardie Valois, but before that there was another problem to deal with as Ivor Davis had supplied the drinks for our bar at the Hunt Ball on a sale or return basis and we had badly over-estimated the consumption. Many cases were untouched but this left Ivor with a cash-flow problem so when all the members had arrived I explained the situation and asked them to buy as much as they could to help relieve the problem. Some people responded well and others not at all. In particular, two men who were thought of as pillars of the Easton Harriers stood outside the room, nervously peeping round the doorpost from time to time, and did not spend a penny with Ivor. This behaviour was both mean and unprincipled as that year Ivor had obtained approximately £2,000 in sponsorship for the Point-to-Point and had given a case of Famous Grouse as a raffle prize which had raised £550, as well as supplying the bar at discounted prices.

The French visit was discussed in detail and the next morning Sheila and Bridget flew from Stansted Airport to France to finalise the arrangements. The most important information required was the height and weight of each riding guest, their riding ability and how much English they spoke. The next three meets were cancelled for snow and frost, followed by another one due to excessive wet when it all melted. I tried a new idea when the last one was cancelled using the new communication system as while cancelling the hunting I also said that there would be a ride in the forest starting from Blaxhall Ship which was led by Isla Prescott. I did not ride as my daughter, Bridget, wanted to ride with her friend, Martin, who had come to stay in order to go to the Essex and Suffolk Ball the night before. There had been twenty in our party, John and Jill Graham, Mark Wayne and his girlfriend, George Gooderham and his sister, Johnny Gooderham and Isla Prescott, Mary and Ernie Calver, Sally Calver and Martin, Paul and Jacky Yeldham, Sheila and I and our daughters, Bridget and Judith, who were partnered by

William Good and Swin Rogers. As I had driven the lorry to Blaxhall I obtained a lift in a car with a lady called Judith and we went ahead and I had a round of drinks ready for everyone when the riders stopped at the Butley Oyster. While they were enjoying the stirrup cup Judith went round and took orders for a meal at the Ship on their return, which included fourteen steak and chips.

Diana Greenfield was very cross with me for meeting at the Blaxhall Ship on Thursday 3rd February as her home, Lime Tree Farm, is adjacent to the pub and her children could only hunt on Saturdays but this had been arranged to suit the French visitors. They had expressed a wish that they would not be required to jump so I had arranged the meets at Blaxhall and at Knodishall to coincide with their visit but it all came to nothing as the French changed the date of their visit at the last minute. The first part of this day was a nightmare as early potatoes were planted under polythene and even the hounds were forbidden to cross this as their toenails would puncture it. The last part of the day was spent at Wantisden and Butley where we could ride absolutely anywhere, but there were no hares. The next day I went to see Bill Kemball and asked him if he would consider leaving the hares when he shot to which he readily agreed as he had not realised they were so short. The only fun of the afternoon came when Ernie Calver approached Jim Wickham to offer him his flask. Ernie was just behind him when Jim cracked his whip which caused Ernie's horse to shy violently, leaving Ernie sitting on the ground with his flask still in his hand.

Two days later we were at Knodishall Butcher's Arms where the draw was mostly on the Blackheath Estate. Two days before the meet I had received a letter from the estate stating that, after consultation with the keepers and the farm manager, hunting was forbidden on the estate but I was suspicious of this as it was my brother Robert who hired the shooting there so I telephoned him and he said that of course he had not given these orders. He then telephoned the head keeper who confirmed that he had not been consulted on this matter and I drove to Blackheath and found Robin Coe, the farm manager, who stated very firmly that it was nothing to do with him and he also had not been consulted. It was therefore assumed that the estate secretary had taken it upon herself to concoct the letter, apparently because she was against hunting despite the fact that she worked on one of England's finest shooting estates. How much truth there is in the old Yorkshire saying, 'There's no'wt so queer as folk.'

The Chairman of the Windermere Harriers, Michael Bentley, paid us a visit when the hounds met at Easton White Horse on 7th February but he did not see the normal Easton Harriers as the conditions were so terribly wet that I decided to hand the horn to Jim and be my own Field Master as Terence Saffell was not able to come. The landlord of Cretingham Bell had matched John Appleby of the Saxtead Volunteer and had given twelve dinners for hunt funds which were taken up on 8th February and raised £90. In all twenty-two people were there and the ten extras paid the landlord for their meal. The guests included Bill James and Margaret Menzies who had just become engaged so I bought a bottle of champagne, said a few appropriate words, and gave an appropriate song, following which Mary Calver sang *A Foxhunting Husband* which lists all the disadvantages of marrying a hunting man, but it was Isla Prescott who stole the show with a song that her mother had written for her.

Geoffrey Ingram-Smith and Sue Money paid us a surprise visit at the Southolt Plough and Geoffrey played his accordion as he did in the old days. It was such a delight to see these two friends again and it brought back so many happy memories for most of us. The meet was highly amusing but the hunting was frustrating; scent was good but conditions were so wet that even I dare not ride on the land and was hunting hounds entirely from the roads. I was astonished when, following a very hard day on Saturday 11th February, there were forty-two mounted two days later at Pettistree Greyhound. Don Mann, owner of Rendham Grange Farm, allowed me to do some work to improve the hunting from Rendham White Horse. He and I spent almost all of Friday cutting two rides through a long narrow wood prior to the meet on Saturday 18th. These two rides proved very helpful and added to the sport that I could show to Donald's son, John, and his girlfriend, Jenny, and her father, Ben Denison. I was delighted that this turned out to be a good day for it was the first day for all three of them. There were two sharp runs and, during one of these, I became separated from my hounds. When I caught up, I found my daughter Judith happily jogging along behind them, grinning from ear to ear, and calling out, 'It's all right, Daddy. I'm with your hounds.' Altogether, it was an excellent day's hunting.

It was delightful to turn the clock back and meet again at Colston Hall, Badingham, on Tuesday 21st February. Colston Hall had been a famous meet for the Hamilton Harriers and then the Easton in the early years of the century, and was where the first moonlight hunt was held on 27th March 1871, but we had not met there within my memory. Geoffrey and Sonia Russell were very generous with their hospitality and made us very welcome. Sonia had spent her childhood at Colston Hall and used to hunt with the Easton but had given up. It must have been half-term as there were over forty children and very few adults. The hunting was good but, when I saw just how much damage the children were doing, I decided to make it a short day. This was not the only problem as Mr Cousins from Home Farm, Bruisyard, was reported to be shooting at hounds with his shotgun although this was rather incongruous as he also objected to his neighbour, David Barham, shooting.

The next afternoon we were due to meet our French guests for another exchange visit. Thirty-three members of the Picardie Valois were due to meet us at Framlingham Crown at four o'clock and most of them had arrived by ferry at Felixstowe. As on the previous visit, much thought had been given as to who should stay with whom and, after light refreshments and much hugging and kissing, the Easton hosts departed with their guests: Robert Bothway with Mr & Mme Demory; James and Celia Miller with M. Benoit Fandre; Terence and Marion Saffell with M. Albert Michon and Dr Lexonnel; George and Sue Gooderham with M. Michel Peters and M. Philipe Demory; John and Tish Finch with M. Marc Bitterlin; Ernie and Mary Calver with M. Jacques D'Orsetti and M. Ben Courtier; Richard and Libby Hickson with M. & Mme Dubreuil; Maurice and Sue Scott with M & Mme Gilibert; Mary and Paul Garton with M.Yzon Gasser; Jeffrey Bowden with M. & Mme Baledenite and M. & Mme Delaloyel; Will and Sarah Edmundson with M & Mme Le Royer; Michael and Pat Webster with M & Mme Ponce. Jean and Christine Bocquillon of course stayed with Sheila and me, as did two unexpected guests, M. & Mme Guibert, who were unhappy with their allotted hosts and refused to stay with them. Four guests had said that they would prefer to stay at Framlingham Crown and these were M. & Mme Moizard and Hubert D'Orsetti and his girl friend. As usual on the first night each host dined their guests at home.

I had chosen Saxtead Volunteer for the meet on the Thursday as I knew there would be a large crowd. The pub was full to bursting point and when it was time to mount up Sheila took charge with clipboard in hand to sort out the correct horse for each visitor. Eight horses had been hired from Newton Hall at £27 each per day. Tim Last rode a hireling and lent his own good horse to a Frenchman. Sandy Hewitt and Elise Quilter also lent their good horses. I lent Rose, Ben, Mickey, and Falcon, who was ridden by Michel Peters, the only person I would have allowed to ride him. Sixteen Frenchmen rode with Christine Bocquillon the only female visitor to ride. One farmer always gave the same precise instructions at this meet so, anticipating this, I had arranged to have his wishes typed out in French and handed a copy to every visitor who rode. This worked well and he was most impressed. The crowd of spectators on Saxtead Green resembled a small Boxing Day meet and before moving off the guests delighted the crowd by blowing several fanfares on their trompes. The sound of the trompes had an extraordinary effect on my horse, Demelza, who stood staring in the direction of the sound, shaking like a leaf with every muscle trembling with excitement from the hoof upwards. The visiting Master, Jean Bocquillon, did not ride but Sheila drove him round and piloted him so expertly that very often he was able to see the hunted hare pass by and then watch

JAH on Demelza

the hounds hunt it. On one occasion he was delighted to be able to put hounds right at a check and they ran on eventually to lose the line completely in the Edmundsons' garden at Dial Farm. I drew for the last time on Maurice Scott's farm at Kettleburgh and this hare gave us a fast hunt which ended in some bramble bushes, just behind the meet. As it was half past three, I thought this was the moment to blow for home. During this sharp run many of the horses were left well behind and they caught up in ones and twos during the next half hour.

The dinner at Framlingham Crown was not quite as I would have wished although the table looked most impressive with French and English flags and the menu printed with a meet scene and the Picardie Valois hunt button at the top. The courses were in French but they did not reach French standards. The melon was not ripe, the fish course was excellent but was followed by very underdone duck and what was supposed to be syllabub could best be best be described as blancmange in a glass, with a good cheese board to finish. Fortunately, this did not spoil the incredible atmosphere and there were many toasts proposed

from both visitors and hosts alike. At about half past one the party looked like finishing but the manager, Mr Harkness, invited us into the bar for a drink on the house and asked for more songs. This rejuvenated the party which finally ended at half past three.

The next morning one or two people from both sides of the Channel were a little sleepy for the coursing meeting at Tannington Hall at half past nine. There were fourteen dogs, mostly lurchers, which were run singly, and some first class coursing was enjoyed by all, especially the French. The coursing was very exciting and, on several of the courses, the hare was turned fifteen times or more, but none were caught. By half past twelve all fourteen dogs had run at least once and both dogs and humans were ready for a rest. As we walked back to the Hall for lunch we called at Brundish Crown where we all enjoyed a pint before joining Sheila for a lunch of home-made tomato soup, and hot salt beef put into baps. Ernie Calver and I carved the salt beef and John Capon dispensed either beer or cider from a table in the entrance hall. There was a choice of three entertainments for the afternoon, shopping, a tour of the farm by the agronomist, Ed Brown, or a visit to Sandon Saddlery and then onto the kennels. Jeffrey Bowden had generously offered to host a party at his home, Haughley House, on the Friday evening. He offered both French and English wines and was quite surprised and delighted when the French guests all chose the English wine. For supper we had potted shrimps followed by steak and kidney pie and a large variety of sumptuous puddings. After supper the trompe blowers, stood on the staircase and blew a series of fanfares and to finish, I asked them to blow our National Anthem. With difficulty I managed to draw the party to a close soon after eleven o'clock.

The next morning we went to the Suffolk Foxhounds meet at Long Melford Hall. There were sixteen French visitors mounted and twenty from the Easton and this swelled the mounted field to just over a hundred. Sadly hounds drew covert after covert blank and, although a fox was finally found after an hour or so, scent proved to be poor and hounds could do very little. The only pleasure of the day was hearing the voice and horn of the huntsman, Tom Batterbee. We were quite near the meet at half past three so we said goodnight to the Master, Paul Rackham, who said how sorry he was that he had not been able to show the visitors a better day. Tannington Hall was the venue for the last night's party and the guests began to arrive at eight o'clock. They were offered gin, whisky, or sherry and it was interesting that all the French drank sherry as they are never offered it in France. Sixty-eight people sat down to supper soon after nine o'clock, and had smoked mackerel followed by boeuf bourguignon. Jill Graham had helped Sheila with a delightful selection of puddings, Jill's two daughters, Lucy and Rachel, together with Jeanette and Carol Cox were the waitresses and Gordon Grover made an excellent wine waiter. After supper we all crammed into the drawing room to watch a video made by Charlotte Demory of the visit so far and this was hilarious. While we were watching the video, tables were dismantled and cleared from the morning room and music was played so dancing was soon in full swing. The dancing went on until about half past two and then Sheila suggested that the remaining guests retired to the drawing room where a few bottles of champagne ended this evening and the three days of fun. At four o'clock we decided it was time to go to bed.

We saw our guests off three hours later as they were catching the ferry from Felixstowe and then went back to bed for a couple of hours before tackling the job of putting the house back to normal. We were delighted when Robert and Linda Bothway appeared to help us, which was an extremely kind gesture considering that they lived well over twenty miles away. When all was finished we lunched at the Hoxne Swan and reminisced about how well everything had gone and what fun it all had been.

On the day that we had taken the French guests to the Suffolk Foxhounds, Jim had hunted the Easton at Kelsale Eight Bells and reported that he had an excellent day with very good scent, although only twelve people were out and there was a similarly small field, after all the hectic fun of the French visit, for Lady Blanche's lawn meet at Glemham Hall. Captain Marriott was at the meet and I thought how delightful it was to see the two of them together again as Captain Marriott had at times hunted hounds for Lady Blanche during her Mastership. The Captain was not well enough to get out of the car but remarked how well the hounds looked and how level the pack was. This was praise indeed from such a stern critic and I remembered his words twenty years earlier when he said that he doubted I would ever make a Master of Hounds. I appointed Robert Bothway to be the Field Master for the day and we enjoyed grand sport.

The Waveney Harriers came by invitation to Dennington Hall on 1st March but I did not hunt with them as I was taking Sheila to Parkeston Quay to catch the ferry to Holland as she was going to stay with the St Quintons who were living near The Hague at the time, and then went on to Cheltenham. Some time previously I had been robbed of all my driving harness and the police thought they had found it at Cheltenham but unfortunately it was not my harness. Colin, Tizza and Alice Plumbe arrived on Friday for their annual visit and hunted with us at Framlingham Station on Saturday (3rd March). The first part of the day was spent drawing blank, then we found and had a long and twisty hunt from the edge of Framlingham to West Hill at Brandeston, during which we passed two gangs of men rabbitting. Luckily, the rabbits had been 'hurdled' and hung on sticks high enough in the hedge so as not to be a temptation to hounds. After this run Ian McKay insisted that we called at his home, The Old Rectory at Kettleburgh, for mince pies and port. These were particularly welcome as the day was very rough with almost gale-force winds and heavy showers.

The meet on Monday 5th March was very exclusive with only John Finch, Richard Baker, Gay Bridgford, and two other ladies, one of whom was the landlady of the Golden Key. There were too many hares so we had no sport and experienced terrible trouble in keeping hounds together. I returned to the meet with only ten couple, someone led Jim's horse back to the meet while he went off with Harold Pitcher in his car and returned with three couple, and the remaining 1½ couple were later caught. It had been one of those days that make one realise how thin the line is between an excellent day and a fiasco, like this day. My birthday meet was at Thorndon Black Horse on 8th March and there was a large crowd at the meet which sang 'Happy Birthday' to me before we moved off but it was a disappointing day. The scent was quite good but the day was fraught with worry as there were open snares over a large part of the draw. Whenever Jim and I saw one we jumped off our horses and closed them up but at least one couple of hounds were snared although luckily rescued before they choked. This completely spoilt the day and I was relieved to be back at the meet with all my hounds.

Mr Harkness, manager of Framlingham Crown, was very upset that the meal for the French guests had not been up to scratch and offered me another dinner at only £5 per head to make up for the previous shortcomings. I settled on this kind offer for my birthday dinner and fifty-five people sat down to leek and potato soup, lamb, and apple pie, all perfectly cooked and presented. Sheila gave me a beautiful watercolour of Jasmine and Jangle, two of my favourite bitches, which had been painted by Elaine Fensom and still hangs in pride of place today. Sheila was, in turn, presented with a brooch by members of the hunt for all her sterling work during the French visit. Two of my unkind members, whose initials I suspected were MW and GB, paid for a kissagram girl to visit me at the dinner table which ought to have been very pleasing but the unkind devils had ordered a 'roly poly' girl and she was very 'roly poly'. It was a disgusting sight, one roll of fat lapping over the next like a female Michelin man. I did not know what to do with her when she reached me so decided to make the best of a bad job and stood up and sang an appropriate song. I put my arm across her back as I sang and it disappeared into a roll of fat. Everyone at the table thought this the best fun ever and thoroughly enjoyed seeing their Master in such an embarrassing situation.

The last meet of the season was at Bedfield Crown on 10th March. There was a reasonably good scent but, for some reason, there were many hares on the move which meant there were lines all over the draw with the usual problem of the pack dividing. John Keeble, who could not really ride properly, borrowed my Rose and, under Hilda Wickham's care, managed to keep out for two and a half hour and roundly declared that he would learn to ride and come out regularly next season although this was not fulfilled. David Steel from Bull's Hall borrowed my Ben and was amongst the seven mounted who finished the day, who also included my daughter Judith on Mickey and my groom Theresa on Charlie onto which I changed for the last run.

Following the official end of the season, a Gentlemen's Day was held at Debenham Cherry Tree on Monday 12th March. Paul Rackham had completed ten seasons as Master of the Suffolk Foxhounds and I invited him to be a guest but the centre of attraction at the meet was Bill James as this wily bachelor, who had escaped the net for many years, had finally been snared and was soon to be married to Margaret Menzies. James Miller had booked a kissagram and a delightful shapely little girl in scanty black underwear and fishnet stockings appeared and we persuaded Bill that he ought to practice for his wedding day and carry the girl over the threshold. His photograph was taken in this action along with others. When his bride-to-be hacked his horse down to the meet, she was persuaded to come into the pub and Bill took her up in his arms in her blue jeans and polo neck jumper and photographs were taken in the identical position as the kissagram. This fun start did not continue and the day's sport was moderate with far too many hares. I was embarrassed to think that Paul was witnessing this shambles with hounds all over the place but knew that he would understand. We took our respective ladies out to dinner to Cretingham Bell which was the finale of the season.

We had hunted on sixty-one days, losing only four days through bad weather. It had been a very good hunting season but the country was now 95% drilled with wheat and while we had in the past tried to avoid wheat fields altogether, now we were forced to ride very carefully round the edge of wheat fields and I hoped there would be no repercussions next season. I was quite relieved to have finished the season as the pressure of squeezing in work between three days a week hunting was beginning to tell and I was seriously thinking that next season would be my last. As usual, the problems boiled down to time and money. This season the committee had increased the guarantee by £2,000 with an additional £610 to allow for inflation but this still left a serious shortfall. One way to reduce the pressure would have been to hunt fewer days but, if I was going to be Master, I wanted to do the job properly and a great deal of the workload was the organisation of the many social events that were held.

Nevertheless my personal feelings and wishes to retire from the Mastership had to be put behind me as a great threat to the continued existence of the Easton Harriers had loomed. This threat was the youthful enthusiasm of James Barclay who had become Joint Master of the Essex and Suffolk Foxhounds and was trying to take over and hunt almost the whole of the Easton Harriers country. This dark cloud had hung over me and spoiled my enjoyment of this grand scenting season and it was extremely worrying. James Barclay was a force to be reckoned with as he was a member of the famous Barclay family who had been Masters of the Puckeridge Foxhounds for hundreds of years and carried considerable authority in the hunting world. The Easton Harriers had nearly the lost the country once before in the early days of my Mastership when the newly-formed Norfolk and Suffolk Foxhounds had attempted to take over all the Easton country. I knew that, if the Essex and Suffolk hunted our country, the wonderful relationship that I now enjoyed with the farmers would be ruined. There were only fifteen farms of over eight hundred in our country where the Easton were not allowed and this desirable situation had been built up from the position when I became Master when we were allowed on fewer than half the farms but it did not mean that all the farmers were pleased to see us. In many instances it was a case of tolerance as long as there was not the slightest damage done and I had spent back-breaking hours raking in hoofprints where there were marks only eighteen inches out into the wheat in order to maintain the fragile knife-edge balance between being told to keep off the farm or being allowed to go.

During my visits to the Essex and Suffolk in their own country I had seen a completely different approach to farmer relations and was appalled to see them cutting across the corners of wheatfields and often riding two abreast around the edges. This sort of attitude and thoughtless behaviour would have ruined in one season all the trust and goodwill that I had built up over twenty seasons. Some farmers would have differentiated between what the foxhounds did and what the Easton did but the vast majority would not and it would be simply a case of damage by 'a hunt' and a blanket ban would have ensued. It was easy to understand this attitude from the farmers if they were not at all interested in hunting but only tolerated us because of tradition and while there was no inconvenience and no damage was done. We had another advantage as, with such a large country of 400 square miles, the Easton only went to each meet once a year which helped tremendously with farmer relations as they knew that they would only see us once a year. I was convinced that at least half our farmers would ban hunting altogether if the foxhounds hunted the Easton country in addition to ourselves. I just could not bear the thought of my hounds having to be stopped continually on the edge of farms where we were not welcome. I had bred them carefully and hunted them carefully and encouraged them to stick to the line of the hunted hare. How upset and confused they would have been while hunting the correct line to have whips cracked in front of them to stop them.

I knew that if I did not stay to fight this battle it would be lost, first because I had been through the nightmare once before and secondly because I was on the committee of the Masters of Harriers and Beagles Association and as such could count on their full support. A new Master, without experience, would have stood no chance at all. I had a choice of either resigning the Mastership which was what I wanted to do but would see all that I worked for over twenty years destroyed, or continue as Master and fight the battle. I had always put the Easton first.

1984–85

As always, the first duty of the season was to break in the previous year's puppies. There had been four litters, all pure Easton with no outside blood, but there were only 6½ couple of puppies because of the continuing ravages of the Parvovirus which had killed many of the whelps of the previous spring. Peterborough Show brought some successes with Nelson being third in the unentered dog class, Bargain winning the restricted bitch class and Capital winning the restricted doghound class, thereby winning the Easton Harriers Challenge Cup. This pleased me enormously as my hounds had then won both classes that I initiated and, of course, hoped to win.

At a committee meeting on 30th April the guarantee was increased by the rate of inflation (4.5%) which represented £640 and brought the guarantee to £15,450 but another financial worry arose in the necessity of providing a cold store at the kennels. During the summer Colonel Allen, who lived quite close to the kennels, had mentioned to me on a number of occasions that the smell from the kennels was becoming offensive and he thought that it came mostly from the flesh during the hot summer weather. The Colonel had been a hunting man so was sympathetic to the problem and offered to donate £500 himself towards a cold room if such a thing was possible. The only practical solution to this problem was to convert the garage which was adjacent to the flesh house and could have a connecting door and it was obviously a highly desirable thing to do but hunt funds were very low and there was no money available. A solution came from a most unexpected source, namely, the BBC who approached the Easton to enquire if we would take part in a film to be shot outside Easton White Horse. Gordon Grover, Tim Last, Patrick Edmundson, and Tom Walne built in all the insulation, we obtained a second hand door from a scrap freezer lorry, and with the savings made by their efforts and Colonel Allen's £500 and the money from the BBC, the garage was converted into a cold room at no cost to the hunt. Later on Colonel Allen asked for another favour from the hunt as, when he had held a garden party, the puppies in the grass yard had heard strange voices and jumped up at tin sheets that formed the fence, so he asked if he could rent a strip of land to form a buffer zone along the length of his garden. This was negotiated and agreed and Tom

Walne erected a chain-link fence a few yards from the original although the strip of land was let on a formal basis to Colonel Allen at a peppercorn rent.

Filming with the BBC was, of course, very exciting. The plot was that a daughter of a grand country family had brought her unknown boyfriend down to the country for a weekend. On the Saturday the boyfriend was taken to the meet at the local hunt to see his host and hostess and the daughter hunt but, unbeknown to them, the boyfriend was an 'anti' and had plans to spoil the day's hunting by rubbing the hounds with aniseed at the meet, believing that hounds would then only follow him. The difficulty was to make sure that the hounds followed the actor when they should. The producer asked me if there was any way that we could ensure this and I told them that hounds would follow him anywhere if he had some biscuits mixed with chopped liver. At the first rehearsal the actor got among the hounds and let them sniff the liver, then he crouched down on his heels and proceeded to quietly back off taking

Members at the BBC canteen lorry

the hounds with him. All would have gone well except that he lost his balance and fell on his back, letting go of the biscuits as he fell. These spread all over his stomach and the hounds lined up on either side, gobbling up the biscuits, looking just as though they were feeding from a trough. The cameramen were laughing so much that I thought they would fall off their van. I had always hoped to see the incident on the television programme *It'll be all right on the night* but I never have, possibly because the cameramen were laughing so much it was not properly filmed. There were many rehearsals in the morning, and then we put the horses and hounds away, to enjoy a sumptuous lunch from the BBC catering bus. The afternoon ought to have gone smoothly but various things went wrong. An aircraft screamed low over us, a tractor and muck spreader roared through the village from time to time and finally, just when all seemed perfect, the scene was ruined when one of Jim Wickham's friends cycled away from the pub and shouted, 'What are you doing Jimmy? Today int' a huntin' day.' Finally, all was done to the satisfaction of

the producer and the hunt obtained that very useful cheque.

The early mornings started on 24th September to hunt in the sugar beet at Tannington as usual. Nettle and Priceless were very nervous and confused by the very high leaves on the beet and I had to do a lot of coaxing and calling but after a few mornings they became more brave and joined in with the other hounds. There were in total twenty-one early morning hunts as we were going four mornings a week, sometimes taking only doghounds and sometimes only bitches, and it was noticeable how lazy the doghounds were when drawing. The early mornings had been relatively uneventful except for the wettest day ever recorded in Suffolk, when on 6th October, three inches of rain fell.

The Opening Meet was held on Thursday 1st November on the Market Hill, Framlingham, with sixty-two people mounted. As usual, we unboxed at Cransford and hacked into Framlingham and made the customary call at the Hare and Hounds but were disappointed as it was not open. Dear old Jimmy Finbow, the landlord, had become so old that, for the first time ever, he had forgotten us. The best hunt of the day was on Framlingham Great Lodge where John Kellaway always made us so very welcome. The remainder of the day was spoilt by a large landowner at Badingham, who used the new and topical reason of hare conservation to ask us to keep off his property, regardless of the fact that this area was teeming with hares. The Opening Meet Dance was held at Glevering Hall and as Sheila refused to go, I went with Tony St Quinton and Penelope Reinarz, meeting up with Ronnie Kindred and others for pre-dance drinks at the Pettistree Greyhound. Two days later we were at Charsfield where, for a pleasant change, due to the Youngman's large orchards, there was plenty of rideable country and good sport was enjoyed by all, before going to Pear Tree Farm for our annual treat, the famous Hennessy hospitality. There were well over forty out at Worlingworth Swan on 8th November and all enjoyed a great day. I handed the horn to Jim at two-thirty as I had urgent work to attend to.

The next morning, Ronnie Kindred and I left the kennels at eight o'clock with drafts of hounds for the Holcombe Harriers and Staffordshire Moorland Harriers, meeting the respective huntsmen, Alex Sneddon and Paul Goddard, at a service station on the M6. On the following day Ronnie and I enjoyed a day with the Windermere Harriers near Shap Fell and the next day brought home a litter of whelps that Anthony Barker had bred for me at the Windermere Kennels. These were out of Cobweb, an Easton bitch drafted to the Windermere and sired by Rockwood Pirate. The litter consisted of three bitches and two dogs and we dropped them off with Margaret Elwood at Tuddenham, who had agreed to keep them until after their vaccinations. This litter was the fruit of my plan to avoid the danger of the Parvovirus by breeding Easton bloodlines I could trust at the Windermere kennels.

The next time I hunted hounds was from the Kings Head, Laxfield. The hunting was brilliant and hounds ran hard all day. During one great run we passed Lane Farm, Brundish, and noticed an unusual amount of activity although it was only later that we discovered this was because the owner, Mr Smith, had just shot himself. At the end of this run my horse Demelza was absolutely finished and I walked her back to Brundish Crown and waited until Theresa, my groom, could bring me Falcon to finish the day. The hunting was so exceptional, and I was so engrossed, that it was not until I finished in the dark that I realised that I had absolutely no one still out with me. I hacked back to the meet with hounds 'all on' and settled down to celebrate this incredible day. Some of the others were drinking James White's cider with a brandy chaser. Needless to say I joined them which proved to be a very bad idea as I needed someone to drive me home.

A party of us went to the Suffolk Foxhounds' Ball on Friday 16th November and I had to ask Jim to hunt hounds the following day as I was unwell but this was not because of an obvious consequence of the ball as I had drunk only water. Jim hunted hounds again at Wetheringsett White Horse on 29th November as I was in London, officiating at a tribunal in a dispute between North Bucks and the South Herts Beagles. It must have been a classic day as I received a very complimentary letter from John Austin, Master of the Norfolk Beagles, who was out and for whom I had the greatest respect as he was not only a great veneur but also a great hound man. He was the only man I ever saw who could stop his hounds off a fresh hare with only his voice and no whipper-in.

Hounds met at Stradbroke Ivy House on 1st December and after some local hunting a hare was found that gave us a really good run. Found on Horham Hall, she ran over Thickthorn Farm to Rookery Farm, Wilby, and on through Beggars Wood at Worlingworth Hall and across to Wilby Green, running close behind the Brundish Crown. There had not been a check up to this point but I handed the horn to Jim and told him to carry on as I needed to be home early. Hounds ran on to Brundish church and swung right-handed up to the Downs Farm where she was lost in some thick hedges. This run had been continuous, with only momentary checks, and as I walked my horse home to the Hall, I realised just how very tired he was. It was hard to hand over the horn in the middle of such a run but I needed to leave early because I was holding another green tailcoat dinner. Since the first celebration dinner on 10th February 1979 seven more gentlemen had had green evening coats made so fifteen people, including Sheila and me, sat down to a nine course dinner cooked by Sheila. Each man in turn proposed a toast to sport between courses. I said Grace and thanked the gentlemen for honouring both myself and the Easton Harriers by having their coats made. The courses were hare paté, soup, salmon, sorbet, lamb, green salad, pudding, savoury, and finally the cheeseboard, and those present were Sheila and Ian McKay, Marion and Terence Saffell, Margaret and Bill James, Agnes and Idwell Humphrey, Mark Wayne, Sarah and Will Edmundson, Caroline and Jeffrey Bowden. It was a most enjoyable evening and the food a great credit to Sheila's expertise.

The Cambridgeshire Harriers were invited to meet at Dennington Hall, home of the hospitable Rous family, on 6th December. We enjoyed a very good run and at the final check, where the line was lost, one hound spoke right up to the edge of a pond, so I think she had taken to water although I could not see her. The remainder of the day was spent with short runs, and hounds were hunting much better than for some years but were still rather light on cry. Sheila could not entertain the visitors so I asked Jeffrey and Caroline Bowden if they would entertain them at Haughley House which was conveniently situated on the visitors' homeward route. Caroline produced a delicious dinner and the atmosphere was excellent, with much laughter and friendly banter.

Jim Wickham will never forget the meet at Rookery Farm, Grundisburgh, on Thursday 13th December. Every hare found ran directly to houses and entered their gardens so Jim and Robert Haag spent all morning stopping hounds from entering the gardens until Jim had a terrible fall. He was riding his favourite mare Polly when she tripped in the furrow and somersaulted, landing with her quarters in Jim's lap which broke his pelvis in two places. The ambulance was sent for and he was carried on a stretcher across a very rough, ploughed field but the ambulance men were not used to crossing such rough land and gave Jim a rough ride, almost dropping him several times, so some of the Easton members relieved the stretcher bearers. When I went to see him at the hospital he was very miserable. He just could not bear to think of having to lie still for any period of time and he had the window wide open as he could not stand the heat in the ward. He was out of action for several months but as always the stalwarts of the hunt pulled together. In the field it was the efforts of Robert Haag for his outstanding skill in whipping-in, David Cook, who was a groom at the kennels but who had also helped to whip-in, and Tom Walne, who, as always, had shown great unselfishness and would miss a great deal of sport to ensure that he was at the right place at the right time.

JAH presenting a copy of "If St Peter has Hounds" to Lady Tollemache at Helmingham Hall

Hilda took on the duties of collecting the flesh and was greatly helped by Dr Edmundson's idea of raising £800 to buy an electric winch for the van to help her load the carcasses and other labour saving gadgets. The unstinting efforts of Elise Quilter and Sue Gooderham transported the horses from the kennels to the meets.

It was ironic that two days after Jim's accident we should have an outstanding day from Worlingworth Swan. The heading in my diary reads in large capitals '*WONDERFUL VENERIE PACKED DAY*' and I will quote the last entry: '*Last run most notable for pure venerie – she had done a classic full circle – all hounds running under the proverbial blanket – into Chandos Plantation including a lap of Wood Farm Garden in and out of farm buildings – she then crossed and re-crossed a ditch six times with hounds working out each piece exactly – she then ran the headland and dropped into the ditch running in the water, back under hounds hunting the headland above. Samson dropped into the ditch and spoke well in the running water and another*

couple joined him – she then did exactly the same thing again and, after a short check, was caught. I gave pads to: David Steel, who was out on Mickey, Robert Haag, Richard Baker and Edward Miller.*'

I rode back to the meet glowing with pleasure at the excellence of the hounds and thinking how I could describe the day to poor Jim in hospital.

Two more exceedingly good days followed on 22nd at Dennington Queen and 24th at Dennington Bell. I could not have a jolly on Boxing Day as, with Jim in hospital, it would have been impossible to keep hounds coming on with me but I need not have worried about entertaining the large Boxing Day field, as hounds ran practically non-stop all day. It was one of the days that I have noted as being '*The best day I think I have ever had with the Easton Harriers.*' I drew The Cedars and hit off a drag, hounds spoke on this for about five minutes, then I saw Charles Corner with his hat held high. I laid hounds on to the line and they ran to Tiptoe Hall, Soham Town Corner, and Windwhistle, where they dropped down into the valley and hunted through my brood mares into the marshes behind Earl Soham Chapel, then swung up past Earl Soham Lodge where they checked for the first time. This gave me an opportunity to speak to the owner, Bruce Hinton, who made us very welcome. Hounds soon sorted out the check and ran back to Soham Town Corner, down Bizzie's Hill and across to Tiptoe Hall. At this point there was only a handful of horses still with us. Hounds feathered on to Wood Farm, hunting very slowly and working out twenty-five to thirty zig-zags exactly. It was such a joy to watch. At Wood Farm they began to run on strongly, past Ashwell's Mill and Oak Hill, back to Bizzie's Hill where a check of five minutes or so allowed the horses to get their wind. When they had sorted out this check they ran on over Bedfield Green to Tiptoe Hall where she was 'given best'.

The horses were in desperate need of a break so we slowly hacked through the lanes to Bedfield Crown for half-time and, after a thirty minute break, I drew Shed's Farm where we found at once. She ran to World's End, Whitmores, Tannington Lodge, and

Woodlands, before turning back to run to Downs Farm and Fenton's, again doubling back to Downs Farm, past Dennington Lodge, crossing Severals Lane to Boxbush Lane, crossing the main A1120 road at the water tower, to turn to Framlingham Hall and Saxtead Bottoms, recrossing the main road to Dennington Place where there was a serious check. I cast hounds back and they hit off the line and crossed the main road for the third time and ran to the Great Lodge wood, where I managed to stop hounds as it was quite dark. I hacked across country to Dennington church Farm where we met the hound van and boxed up hounds. It was freezing hard as we hacked our tired horses back to the meet in the dark.

Freezing weather continued and, although we did manage to hunt on New Year's Eve at Cretingham where there was a large crowd and more people mounted than Boxing Day, we were unable to hunt again until 26th January, due to snow and hard frost with temperatures down to six degrees at times. The hunt ball was held again at Framlingham College on Friday 4th January. Tickets were £16 with dinner and £8 to come after dinner. A total of 207 people dined and 234 came after dinner and it was as much work as before but a great success. It was impossibly wet when the snow melted but I did hunt at Stradbroke on 26th January as the draw was towards Hoxne and this area is well served with tracks and bridleways and also has a disused airfield. We managed to keep in touch with hounds without going off the tracks and everyone was very pleased to be out again. A reasonably good day was had on 31st January at Laxfield Oak and was notable for a tree coming down across the road at Sunflower Hill. Eight men dismounted and managed to move it and Sue Scott later did an amusing drawing of me cracking my whip over their backs. Another amusing part of this day was that Major Mole, alias Tony St Quinton, managed to finish the day with no buttons left on his coat. We had a lovely sunny day for the Point-to-Point at Higham on 2nd February and a large crowd watched Robert Haag, Sally Hennessy, Jenny Baxter, Debbie Saffell, and Isla Prescott ride in the Members' Race, which was won by Isla, but four days later the meet was cancelled because the snow was back and it was still deep three weeks later but I decided to hunt on foot at Kettleburgh Chequers on 23rd February. There was quite a large field but after two hours hunting we were content to stop as it was exhausting work in the deep snow. In the pub afterwards someone remarked how well young Colin McKay and Philip Yeldham had leapt a ditch full of running water. Later, Philip was overhead saying to

Colin, that he was not afraid of water, unless it was in a bathroom. The same night another green tailcoat dinner was held at Tannington Hall on the same basis as the previous ones with each man proposing a sporting toast between the courses. I stood up from the table at half past two and fell over like a stone.

The snow prevented mounted hunting during the whole of February except for the Gentlemen's Day at Blaxhall Ship on Tuesday 26th. Each man paid £15 and the weather did a complete turn around as it was very mild with the sun shining warmly on the snow and we drew towards Butley. There was no serious hunting as hounds were often feathering along on old deer lines but the gentlemen had a good time as the draw was mostly of unploughed light land after carrots had been harvested and they were able to ride across the fields almost everywhere and could follow directly behind hounds. Unfortunately this got the horses rather wound up. I had difficulty in holding my horse Bucks Fizz and, at one point, Louis Borrett could not stop his horse and galloped across a road, narrowly missing a car. It was so warm that hounds got really hot and, when we came across a huge puddle in the middle of a field, I rode into it and they came in to refresh themselves. Richard Baker rode his horse into the centre and plunged into a hole with the water up to the top of his saddle but he managed to get out unscathed.

A hunt dinner was held at Cretingham Bell on the following evening and I had persuaded the landlord to donate the cost of twelve dinners to hunt funds if I filled his dining room. The cost of the dinner was £7.50, thus raising £90 for hunt funds. Forty people dined on steak and kidney pie, with a marvellous pastry crust, and with a good selection of starters and puddings it was a most enjoyable evening. It was accompanied, of course, with plenty of singing and after dinner I presented hunt buttons to the younger generation of members, Johnny Gooderham, Isla Prescott, Patrick Edmundson, Guy Quilter, and Richard Baker.

At Rendham White Horse on 28th February fate was very cruel to us. Even though many of the ditches were still level full of snow which would have made for treacherous riding, I decided to hunt because we had now missed a month's mounted hunting but we were prevented by a dense fog. I was driven around by car at midday, one o'clock and half past two but, although I was desperate to hunt and had a large mounted field waiting to go, I just dare not attempt it. As always, in adversity the Easton rose to the occasion and a good party was soon in progress in the pub.

Dougie Ruth had brought his parson to the meet and when I declared a 'sing, say or pay' session the man in the cloth took his place in the circle. To be involved in a 'sing, say or pay' one either has to sing a song, tell a tale or joke, or pay for a round of drinks for all involved. Seventeen people sat down in the circle and the fun began with Dougie Ruth being the only man to pay, the rest of us having performed, including our clerical friend who told a rather risqué joke. The second round came and, again, Dougie elected to pay which meant he had then paid for thirty-four drinks. During the third round, he told a good joke so did not have to pay. It was so typical of this generous and sporting man that, when I asked him afterwards why he had elected to pay for two rounds when he could have told a joke, he just laughed and said that someone had to pay for drinks as he did not want to see the party go flat. The parson was definitely the star of the party and told some very good jokes.

Luckily we were nearing the end of the season as the next day my head girl, Theresa Pomeroy, broke her collar bone while jumping my driving cob, a first cross hackney Welsh, who was very lively and could jump like a stag. We met at Occold Beaconsfield Arms on Saturday 2nd March and were at last able to hunt again but the long-awaited day was spoiled because at the meet I received a note asking us to keep off Church Farm. The whole of this farm was grass but it was enclosed into large paddocks by barbed wire fences and I had obtained permission to make proper places where the wire could be opened and shut. I spent four days there with a farm worker, tractor and trailer and, in total, we made twenty-two places to open, some in the boundary fence and the rest on one paddock to another. Before each day's hunting I would walk round and open all twenty-two barbed wired gates and the next day went back to shut them all. This tremendous amount of work gave so much pleasure to my members as the hares crossed and re-crossed this area several times in a day and everyone loved to ride on the grass. On this day we were asked to keep away as a syndicate was holding a day's ferreting there which I could not understand as I could not see what difference we would make to a day's ferreting as all the rabbits would already be in their burrows. However, I overcame my intense disappointment and managed to have one good run over the old-fashioned country at David Drummond's farm at Cranley. Bursting through these thick hedges made me feel very nostalgic as I remembered when all the Easton country was like that. As it was Tim Last's birthday a party was soon in full swing when we returned to the pub.

Tuesday 5th March was unique in the history of the Easton as, following some good natured chaffing from the girls, a Ladies' Day was held at Glemham Crown. I was very tempted to ask Betty Gingell to bring her Cambridgeshire Harriers as she had a female whipper-in and the whole day could have been exclusively ladies but I did not pursue it as, if I was not out, no one would know the notified draw and there could have been repercussions afterwards. I took 10½ couple of bitches to the meet and twelve ladies paid £15 each and had very good value as the scent was good and the bitches, of both species, just flew all day. At one point we had a run through the woods at Marlesford Hall which was full of aconites and snowdrops which seemed very appropriate for my 'fair' field and there was one very noticeable difference from the Gentlemen's Days. The meet was very quiet and after hunting they came into the pub but only stayed a few minutes. A few days later I was accosted by the landlord in Framlingham. 'Now look you here Tony,' he said. 'Don't you never do that to me again. I spent all day a'sittin in Lowestoft Court to get an extension just to sell you a pint and them wimmin twelve cups of coffee.' Another difference was that the husbands were not taken out to dinner that evening.

Two days later we were at Thorndon Black Horse. Colin Plumbe was down for his annual visit but had a miserable day's hunting. There were too many hares and hounds were constantly split. Romany was missing at the end and I spent all the next day from just after six in the morning until four o'clock looking for her, eventually finding her at Mendlesham which meant she had crossed the main A140 Ipswich to Norwich road. The best part of the day was in the pub afterwards with incredibly good singing. Colin was on top form, as was Ted Chaplin and another man called George. It must have been exceptionally good as Richard Hickson broke his own rule and came into the pub after hunting and stayed until well after closing time. It was decided to hold an impromptu sing-song at the Dennington Bell that night and it was another truly great party, with Richard Hickson leaving the pub well after closing time to go home and fetch a book, in order to read out a sporting poem. This was enjoyed by us all.

The next day was my birthday, 8th March, and I gave a party to all hunt members at Tannington Hall, during which a painting of me on Demelza with my hounds was to be unveiled. The artist, Rosemary Lodge, had come down from Burnsall in Yorkshire for the party and was heartily congratulated on her expertise by all present. I made a special thank you speech to Hilda Wickham for her outstanding efforts in coping with all the extra work involved during Jim's incapacity and at the end presented her with her hunt button. Robert Bothway then announced that I had been selected to be President of the Masters of Harriers and Beagles Association.

The meet the following morning was at Bedfield Crown which turned out to be the opposite of Thursday's disappointment. We found two travelling jacks and between them they led us over the seven parishes of Bedfield, Worlingworth, Horham, Wilby, Brundish, Saxtead and Tannington. Only Robert Bothway and Richard Hickson finished this day with me. Three days later we met again at Bedfield Crown for a Gentlemen's Day. I had a very special relationship with my neighbouring farmers, and on the principle of 'whipping the willing horse', I often hunted their land and they showed great tolerance of me and my hounds. There were only ten gentlemen and we were very late in moving off because Jack Steel was on top form and told one good joke after another. We only had one good run which took us to Windwhistle and, as we were so near Earl Soham, we decided to have half time at the Victoria. We stayed on our horses in the back yard and had three halves of bitter and a huge plateful of sandwiches and the atmosphere was so good that Paul Yeldham spontaneously broke into song,

Terence and Marion Saffell
Photograph kindly loaned by John Finch

followed by Maurice Scott reciting *Phil the Fluter's Ball*. This was not intended to be a serious day's hunting and it certainly was not, but we had lots of fun although I needed to keep myself within bounds as I was chairing the local Conservative AGM later in the evening.

The meet on Saturday 16th March at Wetheringsett White Horse was the end of an era, as the brewers had given notice to Audrey, the landlady, so this was to be her last meet. The next morning I arranged for a bouquet to be sent to her from Easton Harriers. The day's sport was very good with one memorable hunt of forty-five minutes. For me, this was very special as I only had four couple of hounds with me, three couple of which were in their first season. They were hunting so well that they appeared to be 'tied to the

line' and pushed each other around at checks and it was delightful to see these three couple of first season hounds hunting with such accuracy. At the end of the day, we were one hound light but Robert Haag and I managed to find Actor who was old and appeared to be deaf.

Monday 18th March was chosen for a lawn meet at Winston Hall as it would be appropriate to mark the first wedding anniversary of Bill and Margaret James. I had arranged for Julie Hennessy to bring flowers for the happy couple. Gordon Grover viewed a hare away which was noticeable for having very small ears and I laid hounds onto the line. The scent was very good and we had two and a half large circles of classical venery with this hare before fresh hares spoiled this hunt and caused hounds to go off in three different directions. Some of these hounds went as far as Stonham Aspall and others to Cretingham. Shepherds pie followed by apple pie with the usual lashings of fresh cream ended the day and soothed the aggravation of the divided pack.

The last day of the season was at Brundish Crown on 21st March. This was the fiftieth day of mounted hunting and there was a large field to enjoy a brilliant day. A hare found just outside Stradbroke ran over Wilby Hall, Grove Farm, Brundish, and Downs Farm, until the line was lost at Dennington Lodge. Very few horses ended this day but a good spread awaited us at the meet and everyone went home exhilarated and looking forward to the evening. The End of Season Ball was held at Brome Grange and 130 people sat down to a four course dinner, for which the manager had agreed with me a very modest £10 per head relying on good sales of alcohol to make his profit. I had invited neighbouring Masters to join us: Ivor Constance of the Waveney, Conrad Lockey of the Dunston, and James Barclay of the Essex and Suffolk. I had made a point of asking James Barclay because I was determined that the bitter boundary dispute and his attempt to take over our country, would not develop into a long-standing feud. The atmosphere was electric right from the start with inter-course dancing with black, green and red tailcoats whirling around. Tim Last was wearing his new green tailcoat for the first time and looked very dashing. I had booked a chalet and the evening ended with some of the die-hards having a nightcap with me.

We had enjoyed fifty days hunting with fourteen lost due to bad weather.

At the AGM I thanked all the people who had worked so hard to keep things going after Jim's accident, and also the cappers, chiefly Julie Hennessy, and the road officer, Eddie Kerridge, and emphasised how they never missed a meet. I stressed that there must be enough riders in the Members' Race otherwise we would not be able to hold a Point-to-Point as, with only two or three entering, the Jockey Club did not consider it a race and no hunt can hold a Point-to-Point without a Members' Race. Rupert Montagu had agreed to help me with the administration and, as such, became the Master's Secretary, a new office within the Hunt. No one could have done a better job than Rupert; he was both very efficient

Dougie Ruth, Master of the Kelsale Harriers, with Peter Bailey and JAH at The Dennington Bell

and also extremely diplomatic in keeping me up to scratch. I apologised for the cancellation of the French trip and informed the meeting that it had been re-scheduled for the 17th November next season. To beat the Parvovirus, three bitches had been sent away from the kennels to whelp and to rear their puppies until the vaccinations were effective. They were put into the tender care of Mary Calver, Sarah Edmundson, and Margaret James and their efforts proved extremely fruitful as twenty-three puppies were successfully reared. The inability to breed at the kennels, and the heartbreak of seeing the puppies die, had been a great worry to me and it was a great relief to know that this experiment proved successful.

My daughter Bridget had been working hard on the history of the Easton Harriers. As part of her extensive research, she had examined the stud book in detail from its formation until the present time. I was delighted to be able to report to the AGM that the pedigree of every hound in kennel could be traced back in an unbroken line to the hounds, then called the Hamilton Harriers, which had been one of the founder packs in the first Stud Book of 1891. Lastly I pointed out that the next season would be the seventy-fifth anniversary of the Easton being formed and also the hundred and twenty-fifth year since hounds first came to the village of Easton as the Duke of Hamilton's pack.

CHAPTER 8

THE LAST SEASONS 1985–89

1985–86

Jim was back in action again during the spring and we had managed to rear 11½ couple of puppies and were able to start breaking these once hunting had finished. Peterborough Hound Show was spectacularly unsuccessful with only Tapster[79] gaining a third in the stallion hound class. We held a barbecue and barn dance at Tannington Hall on 13th July to thank the farmers. The barn was lit up by powerful spotlights shining inside the seven gypsy caravans, which were all facing inwards around the edge of the barn. It was most effective and the whole event was a great success. There were around 400 people there and the barbecue was expertly cooked by American members of the Supporters Club. Easton Harriers members ran the bar and, although the prices were very low, the profits still offset most of the cost of the food. Many letters of appreciation followed this event, some of which I read out at the next committee meeting. Wages were creeping up and Jim Wickham now earned £94 a week, Theresa Pomeroy, head girl, £50, Maria Wood, experienced groom, £45, with Louise Flint and Karen Smith earning £27.50 on the Youth Training Scheme.

The season began on 17th September with hunting in the sugar beet at Tannington but with absolutely no scent for the first month it meant the young entry were learning very little. The first morning when hounds could hunt a little was 19th October but the dry conditions continued and the ground was far too hard to even consider letting hounds hunt anywhere other than in the sugar beet right up to the Opening Meet. We had a total of seventeen early mornings from Tannington Hall but the young entry were none the wiser. On the night of Monday 28th October, forty six people came to Tannington Hall to hunt on foot in the sugar beet under the Hunters' Moon. Sheila gave us all supper afterwards and £75 was raised for hunt funds.

The dry conditions gave me a real dilemma about the Opening Meet as the rock hard ground cut hounds' pads or, at worst, knocked a toe down. The Waveney Harriers had had their Opening Meet the Saturday before us and let hounds hunt in the open and lamed every hound. I had two alternatives, either to cancel the Opening Meet or to do the best I could and I chose the latter so the Opening Meet was held on Thursday 31st October on Framlingham Market

Hill. The manager of the Crown Hotel, Robert Stein, welcomed the fifty-eight mounted with a glass of hot wine punch served from a table on the pavement. The turnout of the fifty-eight was absolutely impeccable and I was very proud to see them mingling with the huge crowd of spectators. I had let it be known that we had intended to unbox on Saxtead Green instead of at Cransford and quite a few people joined us there to hack into Framlingham. I moved off from the Hill and turned into the Mere to ride under the awesome castle walls, passing on through Great Lodge and into some sugar beet at Dennington, which proved blank. I then moved on to draw more beet, which was also blank so eventually came to Tannington where we found a hare in the beet and had a small hunt. The next entertainment was to ride down the front drive of my home and let hounds refresh themselves in the moat while Sheila refreshed the followers with glasses of sherry. I finally made my way back to Saxtead through the Bedfield lanes. I had done the best I could and fortunately the field understood and tolerated the lack of sport.

A slight shower enabled me to attempt to hunt at Charsfield on Saturday 2nd November and the famous Hennessy hospitality made up for the lack of sport. Moggie Hennessy had her leg pulled unmercifully all day as someone had overheard her say, 'Well, I suppose I had better do my duty,' before going around to greet various men with a kiss. Another slight shower enabled us to try to hunt from Worlingworth Swan on 7th November. There was only one little run where the line crossed the River Dove opposite Honeypots Farm. It is the most formidable place and I did not attempt to jump it so we found another way round but when I reached hounds, Robbie Haag was with them so I knew he must have jumped the river. As far as I know, this is the only time the jump has been attempted, let alone achieved. There was a good tea waiting for us at the meet and as usual, the Easton made the best of a poor day with plenty of fun and laughter.

The poor scent lasted until it was time for us to go to France on Sunday 17th November. After two miserable months we were all full of anticipation of the fun to come. Most people decided to drive their own cars, crossing on the ten-thirty ferry from Dover and the camaraderie on the ferry clearly showed our high expectations of the fun to come. Those going to

France were Sheila and I, Anthony and Elise Quilter, John and Tish Finch, Jeffrey and Caroline Bowden, Sandy Hewitt, Tim Last, Idwal Humphrey with his daughter Sarah, Will and Sarah Edmundson, Maurice and Sue Scott, Mike and Pat Webster, Terence and Marion Saffell, Tony St Quinton, who came to make a film, and Rupert Montagu who came mainly to write up the trip. On Monday morning the Easton members and their hosts met at the Musée de la Venerie at Senlis. This provided a most exhilarating two hours. Our hosts, Jean and Christine Bocquillon, kindly provided a delicious lunch for everyone at their home, Ferme du Grand Logis at Baron, and then in the afternoon we went to the Musée Vivant du Cheval, the Museum of the Living Horse, at Chantilly, which was housed in the indescribably beautiful stables built by one of the Princes de Condé who, it is said, believed that in the next life he would return as a horse. After the museum we went for tea and whiskey with an Englishwoman, Wendy Millbank, and then we moved on to a sumptuous dinner held in the Tipperary Restaurant in Chantilly.

Our host pack, the Picardie Valois, had very kindly waited until our visit to hold their St Hubert Mass which is normally on the day of the Opening Meet. St Hubert is the patron saint of venery and his saint's day is on 1st November. The St Hubert Mass was held in the church of St Jean aux Bois and was extremely moving. The congregation was made up mostly of those wearing the colourful green French livery, with gold frogging on the pockets and lapels, and our own more restrained English coats. I read the lesson in English immediately after M. le Curee had delivered his in French. There was a hound held in front of the altar and the remainder of the pack should have greeted us when we came out of church but the lorry had broken down and they were not there. Jean Bocquillon, as Master, was very upset and fussed about what he could not help but I made the down-to-earth English suggestion of going to the pub until they arrived, a French girl standing nearby agreed, so off we all went into the café.

A good red deer had been harboured at Arzilliers so we all moved there before unboxing. We visitors were all mounted on hired French trotters, most of which would have been sent home from an English meet. They arrived on a great articulated lorry that held eighteen horses and the driver just turned them loose from the lorry, knowing that they would not go anywhere. The tack was unbelievable, like old dry sticks, and when I tried to tighten my girth I realised that it was already in the only remaining

independent hole as all the others had split right up to each other, forming two long slots. The morning was very cold with four degrees of frost and a light covering of snow, and scent was poor but after the roe was found we saw some beautiful and painstaking hunting by the magnificent French hounds. It was pure magic for me to see these hounds hunting on such a faint scent and yet, when red deer stags and hinds crossed the line, they ignored these strong fresh scents and persevered with the hunted roe. The roe was given best at Pierring near the site of the original kennels and I was very relieved at the decision as I was frozen. We had an opportunity to change our clothes at Antoinette Gilibert's house before going to the army mess at Compiègne for dinner. M. le Curee was present and made a witty speech at the expense of us English visitors. The seating plan was first-class with all English visitors either next to or opposite natives who spoke English. The atmosphere was great and Jean and I both spoke and then the singing started. The French especially enjoyed *Let's all go a hunting today*. All good parties must come to an end and we were in bed by midnight, well contented and very happy.

We hunted again the next day with Monique de Rothschild's Staghounds at Bray although I did not ride as I was feeling as if I had the start of influenza. The Easton members were horrified to see the same old screws being unloaded as they had hunted the day before. The temperature was still four degrees below and the scent was still poor. I followed with Jean Bocquillon by car and as I was shaking with cold we stopped at a charcoal burner's fire to warm ourselves. Soon afterwards I asked Jean if he would send a message to the Master that would she be kind enough to kill, as we were ready for the barbecue, but he replied that anyone who sent such a message to Monique de Rothschild would be very brave or very stupid. Tim Last had the worst luck possible as on the first day his horse had pulled and was unstoppable and on this day his saddle was so uncomfortable that he just could not continue and when he saw Jean and I, he jumped off and refused to ride any further. The horse was then taken from him and Tim rode with us in the car. Monique de Rothschild gave the stag best and took us all back to her kennels and hunting lodge where we were revived with champagne or whisky. When our spirits were lifted we left to go again to Antoinette Gilibert's home again to change before going on to Haute Fontaine for a most magical evening to end the visit. This magnificent house was a perfect place for our last party. Tim and Sandy were fortunate to be guests in this house and an excellent dinner was provided by Wendy Millbank. The atmosphere was electric and the evening ended with some songs from Tim Last, Sandy Hewitt, and myself, and an excellent recitation by Rupert Montagu.

I was very ill all the way home on Thursday and did not rise from my bed until the following Sunday lunch when I was required to carve a brace of pheasants but I could not concentrate at all. It was a very peculiar feeling. I was still not well enough to hunt hounds for our invitation meet with the Cambridgeshire at Cottenham racecourse on 26th November so Jim stepped in and had a really good day with a splendid start when someone capped a hare away and he laid hounds on the line with a crash of music. The Easton members apparently astonished the Cambridgeshire by performing over post and rails on the racecourse as the hunt crossed and re-crossed the course. I came up for the evening's celebrations, which were as good as ever. The next hunting day was cancelled for snow but I was well enough to hunt hounds on 30th November at Dennington Bell. Christine Bocquillon and her daughter Catherine were over from France and were staying with us. I was pleased to be able to show them a fair day with plenty of good venery, which they both enjoyed.

Appropriately, Friday 13th December was the date chosen for another meeting regarding the vexed question of the Essex and Suffolk wanting to hunt our country. Lord

Helmingham Hall – moving off up the drive

Somerleyton, as Chairman of the Masters of Harriers and Beagles Association, came to support me and I put my case strongly that most of my farmers would not welcome two mounted packs, especially one that was not as careful as us. When I said that the Essex and Suffolk had plenty of country of their own I was told they had lost a great deal to urban sprawl and new roads but I pointed out this was their problem. Remembering how I had seen them riding two abreast around wheat fields, I asked if all their country was open to them, and restated my belief that any attempt to hunt my country with two mounted packs would cause *both* packs to be barred in no more than two seasons. Lord Somerleyton backed me up to the hilt and said that it would be the same in his country

(he was ex-Master of the Waveney Harriers) and, in his opinion, no arable country could support two mounted packs. The vast gulf that existed between the two hunts' attitude to their farmers was illustrated when one of the Essex and Suffolk team turned to me and said, 'So Tony, you're saying that the main problem is that your farmers won't have two packs hunting over their farms. Well, we shall have to educate them shan't we?'

I was exasperated by this arrogant attitude but kept my cool and quietly pointed out that the Easton farmers owned their farms and had done for generations and that I thought it was he who would be educated. After this remark there seemed little point in continuing the meeting and it was agreed we would meet again later on.

Following this depressing meeting, an excellent day's hunting was had at Bedfield Crown on 14th December. Hounds ran hard all day and during one run Ian McKay cut his head very badly. There were over ninety children mounted for the Pony Club meet at Helmingham Hall on 21st December. The day got off to a very bad start. A local man hacked to the meet from Pettaugh with a child. The cattle grid at the main entrance had been boarded over but somehow he thought that he ought not to ride in via the main entrance so went round to the side entrance where the grid had not been boarded over and, without thinking, rode over it. That a horse ever attempted to cross it, I find difficult to believe. Somehow the child's pony got over but the man's horse fell through and was firmly wedged and it was at first thought that the horse would have to be shot. Lord Tollemache was furious and said that he thought it was the man who should be shot and not the horse. The whole scene reminded me of a passage in a Surtees book when Lord Scamperdale says, 'Sing out Jack, sing out. Do you think that just because I am a lord and can't swear or use coarse language that you may do as you like?' It was difficult for me to know what to do as I felt I could not move off and leave this situation behind me. Lord Tollemache had ordered gas cutting tools and a machine to force the bars apart so I asked Robert Bothway to lead the children in a gallop around the park to keep them happy for a while and after an hour or so the horse was freed relatively unharmed. The day's hunting was perfect for a children's meet, plenty of slow hound work with a few fast gallops, all on the estate which is so suitable for young children as there are plenty of cart ways and communicating gateways. The troubles of the day, however, were not over as Sandy Hewitt fell on some rough ground and broke her collarbone.

The Dennington Bell was the meet for Christmas Eve and a fine day's sport was had, packed with good venery and ending well into the dark with me sitting on my tired horse blowing for some hounds with the moon shining clearly above me. A good singing session ended this blissful day. Boxing Day was a disaster. It had rained heavily all over Christmas, the River Deben had overflowed its banks at the kennels, and the deluge continued during the week. I was wet through to my skin within ten minutes. The usual Boxing Day crowd was reduced to about twenty stalwarts and Marion Saffell and about twenty-five others were brave enough to give me moral support by appearing mounted. In spite of all the gale winds and torrential rain I did try to hunt but once out in the open fields I decided to give the weather best and was home by one o'clock.

We were unable to hunt at the next meet owing to the excessive wet but were able to go on New Year's Day at Cretingham Bell when Jim hunted hounds and reported a very good day. I was at Framlingham College overseeing the preparations for the hunt ball on Friday 3rd January. The ball was again a 'sell out' with a long waiting list despite an increase in the price of a ticket which were £20 including dinner and £10 for those arriving after dinner. Two hundred and forty people dined and two hundred and sixty came after dinner. The band in the main ballroom was the Galvanos and instead of the disco we had a group called the Peagreen Philharmonic Pullover Set who were excellent and kept their dance floor packed with all ages. The ball was voted the best ever and ended at about two o'clock. Nigel Wayne had taken rooms at the Crown Hotel and had insisted that we join him for a champagne breakfast before hunting. I went early to the College to start to clear up and then went down for the breakfast where the champagne flowed. Nigel amused himself by shooting the public as they passed the open window with party poppers. I excused myself from the party and returned to the College to continue clearing up and was joined by Will and Sarah Edmundson. I stayed as long as possible and then home to change quickly into my hunting clothes

and to arrive at the Stradbroke White Hart, slightly late, but very peculiar weather conditions caused me to cancel hunting. A light rain was immediately followed by frost and although there was no 'bone' in the fields, the roads were just like a skating rink and a horse could not have stood up. I went home again, changed out of my hunting clothes and hurried down to the College and continued to clear up. I was joined by Ernie Calver and John Capon and later by Hilda Wickham and Catherine Corner. It was on such occasions that my members would really break my heart as so few turned up to help with this mammoth task but the five of us worked through until six o'clock and returned again on Sunday morning until the work was done.

Monday 6th January at Laxfield Royal Oak provided a lesson to be learned about scent. At first it was practically nil and as the day went on it slowly improved until, by the end, it was very good and it had begun to freeze. Wet weather set in and I cancelled mounted hunting and went on foot. I was very disappointed when only five turned up but one of these was Mark Wayne who had been to a twenty-four hour party. An outstanding day followed on 16th January at Brundish Crown. The hunting was brilliant right from the start, hounds covering a lot of country. Towards the end of the day I decided to draw behind Wilby Hall and while hacking across the meadows, hounds hit off a line with such a crash of music as I had never heard before. She ran three large circles, often viewed by Gordon Grover and Bill Peart who was following in his van and a few other foot followers. Each time the information was that she was about ten minutes ahead of us. This hunt lasted for one hour and ten minutes and neither myself nor the hounds ever saw her, hounds were never helped or touched from beginning to end, and always cast themselves at checks and worked out all the doubles, of which there were plenty. At the end of this hunt hounds took a strong line up to a large patch of dense brambles in the middle of a meadow, puss having taken refuge in there and hounds surrounded the bush marking like foxhounds at an earth. Here she was given best and richly deserved to live to run another day. Jim and I were in ecstasy and as were riding back to the meet and Jim said he felt as if he were floating above his saddle.

Ian Cook, ex-landlord of the Dennington Bell, was out with us at Glemham Crown on 18th January, having bought a horse intending to hunt with us regularly.

The 75th Jubilee dinner was held at Framlingham College on 15th February 1986. This was, in fact, a double celebration as it was also almost 125 years ago since the beginning of the pack's recorded history as well as being 75 years since the establishment of the pack under the name 'The Easton Harriers'. I desperately wanted all the members who were hunting when I first started, to be present and with much persuasion I made them promise to attend. Some members I needed to visit twice and one even three times but finally they all agreed. Cars were arranged to collect each member and return them whenever they wanted to leave. In the end none of them wanted to leave until after eleven o'clock and it was a special pleasure for me to have them all there together on one table. Andrew Jennings, a great hare-hunter whom I knew well as we had served together

Tizza and Colin Plumb

on the Masters of Harriers and Beagles Association committee, had agreed to be our guest speaker. My daughter Bridget, having written the history of the Easton from the earliest days, had extensive knowledge about the Duke of Hamilton so I persuaded her to come back from St Andrew's to propose a toast to the Duke. The dinner went very well. Rupert Montagu had worked ceaselessly to ensure everything was perfect and the College catering staff, headed by Bill Nekrews, surpassed themselves. It was an evening to remember with nearly two hundred past and present members plus a few guests enjoying the atmosphere but it was over far too quickly.

Two more above average days were held, and then came a lull due to snow and frost so we did not hunt again until 8th March.

On 6th March I had to cancel our hunting at eight o'clock in the morning and, on impulse, decided to use the day to visit the Rufford Forest kennels as this private pack were being given up by Lady Anne Cavendish-Bentinck and she had offered some to me. I asked Sheila if she would like to come with me and we had always had a hankering to stay at the Old Bell at Barnby Moor, an old coaching inn, but we were to be greatly disappointed. The dinner was quite good but the room was tiny with hardly any furniture and the bathroom was even worse. When we arrived at the kennels we discovered that the Master of the Pendle Forest and Craven Harriers was already there

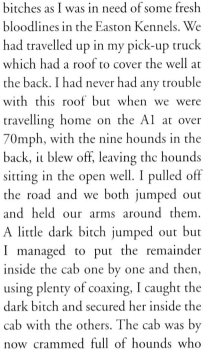

selecting the hounds he would like and that my friend John Loy of the Rockwood Harriers had been the day before and had taken 16½ couple of the best, so there was very little choice for me but I took 4½ couple of bitches as I was in need of some fresh bloodlines in the Easton Kennels. We had travelled up in my pick-up truck which had a roof to cover the well at the back. I had never had any trouble with this roof but when we were travelling home on the A1 at over 70mph, with the nine hounds in the back, it blew off, leaving the hounds sitting in the open well. I pulled off the road and we both jumped out and held our arms around them. A little dark bitch jumped out but I managed to put the remainder inside the cab one by one and then, using plenty of coaxing, I caught the dark bitch and secured her inside the cab with the others. The cab was by now crammed full of hounds who managed to put on the hazard lights, set the wipers going, and blow the horn almost continuously, but we then set off back along the road to retrieve the roof which was sitting in the fast lane. As we were carrying it back a police car stopped to ask if we were all right and Sheila, with her sweet smile, assured them that we were, blithely ignoring the heaving mass of hounds in the van cab and the flashing lights, wipers, and horn blaring. The roof was extremely heavy but somehow Sheila found the strength to lift her side high enough and we replaced it in its correct position before transferring the hounds to the back. Using red binder twine, the 'farmer's friend', we tied it down again and then completed our journey but it had all been a waste of time and effort as I did not like any of the hounds in their work so did not breed from them.

Hunting resumed on 8th March coinciding with my birthday and was the greatest fun with a grand day's hunting following a meet at Rendham White Horse. The birthday celebrations continued with the End of Season ball at Brome Grange which I had deliberately brought forward to fit in with my birthday. The dinner was not very good but the atmosphere made up for all shortcomings. The draw was excellent with thirty-two prizes including one ten-pound note. A magnum of champagne and a lovely painting by Sue Scott were felt to be far too good for draw prizes so we held an auction. The auctioneer was Maurice Scott and proved grand fun. At the end the Wayne family were bidding against each other to help raise funds and the champagne made £20 and the painting 500 guineas so it had proved a good idea. Tickets for the draw were £5 each and it shows the level of atmosphere as the draw raised £1,200 from only 150 people. As usual I had a chalet for the night, a perk from the management, and my birthday ended with a small party continuing in it, making a perfect birthday of seventeen hours of constant fun.

For a novel fundraising occasion, I decided to have a 'Couples Day', following the Gentlemens and Ladies Days and Marion and Terence Saffell kindly offered Rookery Farm, Grundisburgh, for a lawn meet. The other couples were: Mr & Mrs James, Mr and Mrs Hardwick, Mr & Mrs Theobald, Mr & Mrs Yeldham, and Mr & Mrs Scott, and each paid £15. The meet was excellent but the hunting very poor, redeemed by a delicious turkey and gammon lunch, served with excellent wines. We had the Gentlemen's Day on 18th March, meeting at Southolt Plough at eleven o'clock but it was hot and sunny so no one was in a hurry to move off and most had lunch before we finally moved off a little after two o'clock. By this time the heat was gone, the scent was very good, and we hunted into the dark. Framlingham Crown was the chosen venue for the dinner that night which turned out to be as good as usual and it continued into the small hours.

The Point-to-Point was held on 22nd March with terrible weather, strong winds and rain. Five ran in the Members' Race and Jim Hardwick, Jenny Baxter, and Harry Spencer all took a tumble, leaving Robert Bothway to win and Kevin Lee to come second. The season ended with a great day at Bedfield Crown. During the day, David Steel's unbroken colt jumped out of his meadow and hurt its shoulder, which did not prevent it from going to Kenton Crown before it could be caught. Only fourteen people turned up for the dinner that evening which was very disappointing, but those who did made up for it and we had great fun. There had been fifty days' hunting, plus two days in France, with thirteen lost to bad weather.

1986–87

The season started as usual with the breaking of last year's puppies and we had a good young entry this year, ten couple from three litters, two of which were all Easton and the third an out-cross sired by Dunston Ladbroke[80]. We gained three rosettes at Peterborough Hound Show, a second with Webster and a third with Nelson, both in the restricted dog class, and a first in the restricted bitch class with Welfare.

Since 1983 we had managed to inveigle Jim Wickham into taking a holiday by entering hounds at the Rydal Hound Show in the Lake District, and he really enjoyed these outings but this year I had been invited to judge the harrier classes at Rydal so instead I entered hounds in the Lowther Hound Show, which is also in the Lake District. During our time 'up north' Jim arranged that the Barker family would bring the Windermere Harriers down for a visit to Suffolk. This was fixed for 17th-24th September but, when the time came for the visit, conditions were far from ideal as it was very hot and the ground was like concrete. Anthony Barker, Master of the Windermere, and Sheila, his wife, stayed with Jim and Hilda at the kennels, with Diane, their youngest daughter, who hunted hounds and her friend Paul who whipped-in. How they all fitted into the round house, I am not sure, but with such a tight schedule, they hardly had time for sleeping. Jim was the only one mounted when the Windermere met at Tannington Hall on 18th September at five in the evening but it was very hot and the scent was nil. Paul elected to hunt hounds but little could be done in such terrible conditions. The six Lakeland visitors and ten from the Easton came into the Hall afterwards for soup and pork and onion dumpling, a speciality of my Sheila's, ending with apple pie. Because the visitors wanted to see the Easton hunt, I agreed, against my better judgement, to try to hunt them on the Monday, again at five in the evening. It was an education to watch hounds as none of them showed any enthusiasm for their first day's hunting, all they wanted to do was sit at the edge of the sugar beet. They showed no interest in drawing and were clearly telling me that I was mistaken and it was not yet time to begin the season. We had a quick supper of cold pork and baked potatoes before going down to the King's Head at Laxfield to show our visitors an old-fashioned Suffolk pub.

The Windermere hunted their nine couple again on the Tuesday at seven-thirty in the morning. Scent was a little better and we enjoyed a few short hunts with me driving my pick-up truck across the stubble with the Barker family in the back. After breakfast at the Hall I drove them all back to the kennels in a horse-drawn carriage before going on to Orford for a trip on the *Lady Florence*, which was owned and run by my retired amateur whip, Geoffrey Ingram-Smith. As we cruised up the Alde, Sue Money cooked a delicious hot lunch, which we ate at four o'clock. Our guests departed the following day and as Jim had worked wonders in persuading them to bring their hounds to Suffolk, a thing I had tried to do for years but never could, I was terribly disappointed that conditions had not been better for them. We had our first real early morning on 4th October. Although the conditions had not improved at all, the morning dews were heavy and I hoped for a little scent at dawn and was rewarded. All the young hounds left me and went with the older ones but we could do very little real hunting.

I always held my Michaelmas Goose Dinner on 11th October but this year it fell on a Saturday and Sheila refused to cook that night fearing that I would probably drink too much and not be at my best to read the lesson at the Harvest Festival the following morning. She suggested a wonderful compromise, a revival or reconstruction of the meal described in Surtees' *Hawbuck Grange* which was about a harrier pack called The Goose and Dumpling Hunt because they dined on goose and apple dumpling after each day's hunting. Hounds met at Tannington Hall on 11th October at eleven o'clock and only those men who had been personally invited by me could attend. [This was in accordance with the book] although as I sent an invitation to every male subscriber it was not very exclusive. I had sent 'At Home' cards with a photocopy of the relevant chapter on the Goose and Dumpling Hunt. I lent horses to Maurice Scott (Judy), Tony St Quinton (Punch), Michael Buckley (Rose), Mike Carter (Polly), and Robert Haag (Bucks Fizz) and the others present were Messrs Borrett, Calver, Yeldham, Cook, Saffell,

Sheila and Judith dressed for the Goose and Dumpling Hunt

Wayne, Edmundson, Bothway, Morton, two Bakers (Richard and Ernie), Montagu, Ruth, Walne, Capon, Hickson, Finch, and Hardwick. Unfortunately, the hunting was practically non-existent as the conditions were still rock hard.

When I decided to go home, I told Maurice Scott to take two others and ride ahead to Brundish Crown and order beer for everyone. Scotty was in real Surtees mood and strode into the Crown calling out, 'Innkeeper! Innkeeper! Fill me twenty-seven half pints of your finest ale.'

The poor man was terrified and refused to serve him, thinking he had a madman in the pub, and to make matters worse, the poor man was just standing in for the real landlord who was away, but luckily Will Edmundson walked in and, in very professional tones, said he was the local doctor and we really did

need twenty-seven half pints of ale. Finally, the beer was drawn and, refreshed with our drink, we made our way back to the Hall and put all the horses away. I had a nine-gallon barrel of Adnams bitter set up in the front hall and plenty of red wine and was looking forward to dispensing hospitality to my friends. As we walked across the courtyard to the house we were met by two females in old-fashioned long dresses and long hair. I did not recognise my daughter Judith at all, and only just managed to recognise my own wife. Unbeknown to me, they had read up on the Goose and Dumpling Hunt and were appearing as Mrs Thumper and her maid.

We enjoyed several glasses of bitter, and then Sheila brought through three of the geese. Ernie Calver, Ian Cook and I carved the geese, which were accompanied by hot red cabbage, mashed potato, peas and sprouts. All twenty-six of us ate heartily and, at an appropriate moment, I proposed the ancient toast, 'He who eats goose on Michaelmas day, shan't money lack, his debts to pay.' Many of us had second helpings of goose before enjoying the final course of apple dumpling and cream. During the meal, Robert Bothway stood up and proposed a toast to his hosts and, later on, young Richard Baker gave a splendid vote of thanks to Sheila, Judith, and I. The whole concept had been so successful with such a marvellous atmosphere that the event was talked about for many a year afterwards.

One of the best letters that we received afterwards was from Will Edmundson:

Funtime Farm
Dukes Ifham
Suffolkshire

Thursday Sixteenth October 1986

Tom Trumper Esq., MH

My dear Master,
It is with the most pleasant recollections that I reach for my quill to send to you my heartfelt gratitude and appreciation of the amusement and hospitality offered to myself and other sportsmen at Jollyrise Hall this Saturday past.
It was a matter of regret to have to leave my trusty mare in stables, but perhaps the business of hare hunting should not too long be dwelt upon as reports from mounted

hunters indicated no abundance of hares. Indeed hounds were said for their diversion to have had recourse to a short job on stoat!

Notwithstanding being mounted only upon shanks' Pony much interest was gained by engagement in conversation with a legal sportsman similarly disadvantaged. Imagine our delight, however, to observe our good friend Scott, accompanied by the versatile Captain Morgan and a sportsman who earns his bread in the City of London, taking a line somewhat different to that of hounds but leading straight and true to the Inn In the hamlet of Brundish. Imagine also the disbelief upon the face of the Landlord when our friend Scott gave the order "Innkeeper, draw twenty-seven half pints of good ale and serve them upon two trays – and I will treat the bar! (This latter being of little consequence there being therein but one good man taking respite from his daily toil). All, however, was revealed upon the arrival of the mounted throng who thence commenced to quench their thirst, and some amusement was to be had in the observation of Joe Stumps with tankard in one hand and whip in the other preventing hounds from alarming the assortment of fowls in the Inn yard.

And thus, hare hunting put aside for the day, the company repaired to Jollyrise Hall, the welcoming residence of our gallant Master.

Now it has been truly said that there are two things in this world that there is seldom any mistake about – the smell of a fox and the smell of roast goose, and as the happy sportsmen made their way from the stables to the Hall the smell of the latter was most encouragingly evident. Horses having been most comfortably accommodated in the ample stables adjacent to the Hall the sportsmen repaired within, there to find their Master's faithful Clerk in charge of a cask of good ale which was dispensed with alacrity and generosity. Thus the hospitality began but the company were soon summonsed to the parlour, there to be greeted by Mrs Trumper magnificently attired in a black silk gown with cherry ribbons to her cap looking most becoming and buxom. Furthermore she was attended by a nice fresh looking maid in a blue cotton gown with crisp corkscrew ringlets dangling down her merry healthy cheeks, and whose presence greatly added to the amusement of the company in general and one sportsman in particular!

Thus to the serious business of the day with the arrival at table of several well fattened and finely roasted geese, amply attended by stuffings, vegetables, sauces, gravy and the like, with abundant quantities of fine wines to accompany the fare.

Silence then was the order of the day, with the exception of a voice hallooing out "Wench" from the Master who required more stuffing. And thus the scene – until the dishes presented a most beggarly account of bones.

The floodgates of conversation now began to be loosened and toasts were drunk, not the least appropriate to the company than that of freedom from indebtedness for those who should eat a goose at the feast of St Michael.

The dumplings now came rolling in (the apple crop having been abundant this year), well filled with raisins and topped with sugar and a fine thick cream. Cheese followed and as glasses were recharged and charged again conversation flowed from the pleasures of hare hunting to the relative culinary merits of the penned or grass fed goose, and many another subject until the gentlemen discerned that time was passing and other duties demanded their attention.

Thus, dear Master, we took our leave of yourself and Mrs Trumper and the fair maid and of each other, each sportsman convinced that:-

    There's nothing can compare
    To hunting of the Hare

And thus I ask you again to accept my gratitude for as fine a day's amusement and entertainment as any sportsman could wish,

And remain,
Yours sincerely,
    Jogglebury Crowdey
    Stickmaker
And part time physician and surgeon

Two days later it was fun and games again in the form of the Ride and Drive Meet at Bedfield Crown when only horses that have been driven to the meet were allowed to hunt. The morning was not favourable as there was dense fog and this, combined with my telephone being out of order, left many people wondering if we would go or not. Hounds were taken to the meet in a four-wheeled pig van driven by Peter Crockford, driving a Suffolk Punch, the whole turnout being borrowed from Easton Farm Park, courtesy of the Kerr family. Peter followed hounds riding his Suffolk called Ben. My groom Tracy rode my Hackney cross mare, Bella, who became so excited that she reared and fell over backwards, luckily not breaking the tree in the saddle, or hurting Tracy, who was soon on board again. We had a large field as those who rode were Tom Walne, Sandy Hewitt, Karen Wainer, Carol Goddard, Susan Whinney, Sylvia Morris, Harriet Palmer, Jack Driver, Tessa Styles, Ann Graham Johnson, Christina Harrison, Mark Wayne, Ian Cook, Maria Davy, Paul Reed, Juniper West, Juliet Keating, Susan Townsend, John Parker, Carol Baker, Elizabeth Jones, Tracey Hammond, Dougie Ruth, Peter Crockford, Mary Garton, Tracy Feavyear, and, of course, Jim and myself. The actual hunting was very poor but no one cared as it was all such fun. We stayed out for one and a half hours and then back to the meet, where the 7½ couple of hounds needed to be lifted into the pig van because it was so high and there was no ramp. The party afterwards was electric with one of the smaller ponies being brought into the bar for good measure.

The next morning, 25½ couple met again at Tannington Hall for what should have been serious hunting but the dry conditions caused the scent to be absolutely nil. The only point of note was that Granville seemed a little 'careless with his tongue' and he would need to be watched for this babbling. The same conditions remained until Saturday 18th October when, with twenty-five people out and some good sport, Granville confirmed that he was indeed a babbler. Ernie Baker lamed his horse so he handed it over to his son Richard to take back to the meet and took Richard's horse so that he could continue to look after his daughter, Sarah, who was out for the first time. After boxing up the lame horse young Richard strode into my stable yard and asked of my groom, Tracy Feavyear, if she wanted anything exercised. On being given Rose he rode back to hounds, and took back his own horse from his father saying, 'Take this, it will be much better for you to look after my sister.'

I went on a hunting holiday so Jim hunted hounds for the next four early mornings but I was back in time for the Opening Meet on Thursday 30th October. Leaflets about the forthcoming *All Thanks to His Grace*, my daughter's history of the Easton, were handed out to the crowd by Rupert Montagu and other volunteers but it was a dreadful day. Conditions were terrible with almost gale-force winds which spoiled any chance of a hunt and the field behaved so badly on some wheat that I confined them to the roads for the remainder of the day. In my diary I wrote *'The worst opening meet that I can remember – last year we could not hunt but this year was worse - I spent the whole day wishing I had given up last season.'* As usual, though, the pendulum swung the other way and after the Charsfield meet, which traditionally followed the Opening Meet, I wrote *'Most rideable piece of country imaginable, all the orchards and lots of stubble as well - a good field out – Lady Cranbrook borrowed Rose for her granddaughter - good fun day, usual splendid hospitality at the Hennessys.'*

The Worlingworth Swan meet on Thursday 6th November was notable because James Barclay brought his huntsman and another huntsman from Somerset and they followed by car. The weather was very unkind with hot sun and very poor scent and the only hunt of the day was provided by the first hare which ran through the paddocks at Red House into the precincts of the Worlingworth Garage. It was a novel sight watching the hounds giving tongue in and out of the cars for sale and every hound speakings as they took the line between the two petrol pumps and over the road and almost impossible to believe that

they should have been able to follow a scent on that oily, petrol-soaked surface. They ran across to Bedfield Lodge, where they checked but I cast them and they ran on over Bull's Hall, past Wood Farm, Worlingworth, to Oak Farm, where it was handsomely caught. After this spectacular hunt, the rest of the day was virtually non-existent but there was a splendid tea waiting for us when we returned to the meet. The tea got off to a superb start when Mark Wayne telephoned from the Stock Exchange with instructions to 'treat the house' on his behalf. Later on his brother Nigel telephoned and, asking how many were left in the pub and being told that there were about eight, gave instructions for everyone to be treated to a treble each as he would not be outdone by his brother. Most had a double but no one accepted a treble. Somehow Mike Bryan managed to put his lorry in a ditch at Saxtead on the way home. I was telephoned to say they could not get the horses out of the box and that the police were there so Sheila drove me over in the Volvo, I got the horses out and persuaded the policeman that the most important thing was to get them off the road, as it was dark. He agreed so Mike and I led the two horses home, sitting on the boot of the car while Sheila drove. Normans of Cransford came and lifted out the lorry and the horses stayed with me overnight.

There were sixty-five out at Brundish Crown on 8th November and we had the great pleasure of hunting the most delightful country at Wilby Hall. Nelson had been left at home because he was suspected of running on without scent but Jaffa seemed to have developed the same fault, so I decided to leave both at home for a while. Jim and I could not understand why they had suddenly become 'jealous' after being so good. They would ignore the hound who was speaking and just go off across a field with no line, just trying to distract the leading hounds who did have the line. The much-anticipated hospitality of Ernie and Mary Calver took a different turn this year as we were served Coq-au-vin instead of the usual steak and kidney pie. On Sunday night I had a very serious talk at the kennels with Jim as he had been hinting that he wanted to retire. I invited him to stay and offered him a chance to hunt hounds but he still seemed determined to go. I also wanted to give up the Mastership and with Jim wishing to go, I was very depressed.

The meet at Debach Post on 15th November saw three generations out hunting: Fred Ling, who had whipped in for Captain Bernard, with his son and daughter-in-law, and his granddaughter. The following Wednesday (19th November) Marion and Terence Saffell, Ernie Calver, John Capon and Bill James, came for supper so I could ask them how I could retire without letting down the Easton Harriers. No conclusion was reached during supper and after they had all left I was very depressed because it seemed as though there was no one among the younger ones to take on the responsibility. I wrote 'I fear I can see the Harriers falling from their high position at the moment to almost disbanding if there is not someone to come forward'. I had always considered that the perfect option would be a joint Mastership between Robbie Haag and Jeffrey Bowden with Robbie hunting hounds. He and his family were well known and respected in the farming world and his ability with hounds, plus his knowledge of venery, would have ensured that he would make a first-class huntsman,

Maria Wickham, Field Master for the Children's Meet

while I knew that Jeffrey would be adamant about maintaining the high standard of the social side of the hunt. The combination of talents would have been ideal but, sadly, this did not materialise as Robbie said that he could not spare the time or the money and Jeffrey was not keen.

On 27th November we met again at Wetheringsett but, the pub having been sold by the brewery and the new owner having changed its name, it was now the Cat and Mouse and no longer the White Horse. When I asked him why, he said that he had been a salesman to pubs and that there were hundreds of White Horses but never a Cat and Mouse. He thought this would put the pub 'on the map' and so it did. I was delighted to see Dr Hutt at the meet which reminded me of the old days when he tied his hunter up outside his patient's gate as he hacked to and from the meets. A great day followed. The country was very rideable and after some good hunting, by far the best this season, hounds settled to a line and treated us to a classic hunt of two large circles in the London Hill area, fresh finding her four times, with hounds finally catching her in the sugar beet near London Hill. I was thrilled and wished that I had some visiting huntsmen to have witnessed this hunt.

On Friday 28th November the Supporters Club held a 'Mr and Mrs' evening along the same lines as the popular television programme in Earl Soham Village Hall. The idea was that one of the couple was put into a sound-proof box while the other was asked six questions. The one in the box then came out and was asked exactly the same questions and hopefully would give the same answers. Jim Wickham was question master with John Finch and Don Corcoran in pretty frocks with ample cleavage to be his glamorous hostesses. Sheila and I were the first on stage and got one question wrong out of six. The question was: 'If your husband was in a late night party in a pub, would he just stay out or would he telephone you to say he would be late?" Sheila said that I would telephone and I said that I probably would not, otherwise we got them all right. The whole evening was the greatest possible fun and the audience sat rocking with laughter, wiping the tears from their faces. Crawford Stopher ran the bar and Pat Goldsmith provided a hot pot supper and was helped by the ladies from the Supporters Club Committee.

Two days later it was too foggy to hunt at Dennington Queen but quite a few of us went to the meet anyway. Paul Yeldham and Penel Reinarz sang but somehow as the hounds were not there, the atmosphere did not feel right and the sing-song did not get going. Tony and Anne St Quinton had two Dutch friends there and we all had lunch together and left at about two o'clock. Mark Wayne and Penel had the bit between their teeth and did not want to stop the party so went on to Carley & Webb in Framlingham and bought lots of booze, insisting that Penel's little dog also be wrapped in brown paper and left for the Kennels, where I am told the party continued. A Farmhouse Fayre was held at Tannington Hall on 2nd December. Invitations had been sent to all farmers, together with a pre-publication rate flyer for the forthcoming book *All Thanks to His Grace*, and there was a good response as nearly two hundred people came. I purloined three pigs from Tannington Pigs Ltd which were butchered and ready for the deep freeze, Robert Bothway gave a lamb, Ernie Calver gave two chickens, and many other people arrived with vegetables and so forth.

Sheila had baked many fruit cakes and Christmas Puddings, and had made aprons, pickles, and much more, to sell. Carley & Webb held a wine tasting, as did Aspall Cider with their mulled cider proving a winner. Once people began to drink this mulled cider a party was soon in progress. Jim Mutton from Southolt gave a huge wing rib of beef which I raffled at £1 per ticket and this made £170. A ciné film of the Easton Harriers was shown in the drawing room and it took two showings for everybody to be able to see it. This rounded off the evening which raised £700 gross profit which, together with the £300 from the 'Mr & Mrs' Evening, meant that £1,000 had been raised in less than a week, all with the greatest fun.

The Cambridgeshire Harriers came down to visit us on Thursday 4th December meeting at Dennington Hall although the house was being renovated so the usual hospitality was dispensed this year from the garage. These invitation meets were always such happy affairs as by now, after so many years, we had many long-standing good friends in the Cambridgeshire. I had recently bought a new horse, Manhattan, and I decided to ride it to hounds for the first time but I had a rough ride with lots of desperate plunges that upset my back so I returned to the meet at half past one. Theresa Rous somehow managed to give sixty-four people a splendid tea before everyone dispersed. Some of the Cambridgeshire took their horses home and returned for dinner, while others put up their horses at Tannington Hall and changed there. Sixteen Cambridgeshire visitors sat in the drawing room and waited for the Easton members and the Rouses to arrive. For supper Sheila served home made tomato soup, her special 'up market' shepherd's pie, followed by blackberry and apple crumble, or chocolate soufflé. The party atmosphere was at its best and tales, jokes and songs came from both hunts. Betty Gingell absolutely loved this part of the dinner and no one seemed to want to go home, although they had sixty or more miles to travel. At half past eleven I thought I would signal the end of the party by singing *The place where the old horse died* which is usually guaranteed to kill any party spirit but this time it failed to work and the party continued. Most of the Easton members were still at the table at two o'clock and the Cambridgeshire visitors later told me that it was well after three o'clock when they climbed into their beds.

There were so many people at the Southolt Plough meet on 6th December that it was almost impossible to get inside the pub. Peter Johnson from Southolt Park, who always gave us the turn-off, was rather late

arriving at the meet. I naturally wanted to get him and Mrs Johnson a drink but had a real struggle to get to the bar. Peter believed in the old saying that having hounds on your land brought you good luck for the year and once told me that he had a very bad year in farming the year I had not brought my hounds because of the weeks lost to snow. A great day's hunting was enjoyed by all with two hunts lasting over forty minutes. At the end of the day I was debating whether to stop but decided to draw just once more and found and had a good hunt. She ran the perimeter of Derek Scott's Bedingfield Hall, crossing to Sycamore Farm, Kenton, and turned and made for Monk Soham church where she was lost. This hunt had been at a great pace and only Idwal Humphrey and his son were with me. It was a case of sitting down and riding across country as the hounds put themselves right at every check and were running again just before we got to them. So, for the three of us, it was non-stop. Arriving back at the meet at half past three, I quickly swallowed two half-pints, then home and left again at a quarter past four to drive to Banbury where I had arranged a two-day break that Sheila deserved more than me.

The best hunt of the season was at Stradbroke Ivy House on 11th December with hounds running like demons all day, and another almost as good from Bedfield Crown two days' later. There had been very heavy rain and the country was so wet that we really ought not to have hunted but Richard and Michael Nesling had given permission for the headlands of wheat to be ridden and what a difference that made. As usual when it is so wet, scent was first class and good runs were enjoyed with hounds going away to Southolt Green and, turning back, they changed hares. The second hare took us to the back of Earl Soham marshes. The horses had really done enough but we enjoyed a few twisting little hunts to finish the day.

Jim and Hilda had definitely decided to leave at the end of the season so I had placed an advertisement for a kennel huntsman and had narrowed down the list of applicants for the position. Mark Powell, from the East Kent Foxhounds, came on trial at Hoxne Grapes on 18th December and showed considerable talent and I was impressed at what I saw. I was glad to see that both Rupert Montagu, who was not only the Master's Secretary but also an expert whipper-in on foot, and John Suckling, who was really a Waveney man but also whipped-in with us on foot, were out as I would need their assistance with a lady at South Green. We had inadvertently disturbed her pets' picnic a few years earlier. She had two guinea pigs, four rabbits, three goats and some hens, two fluffy cats and a Pekinese dog and had set out a lovely picnic for them in the little paddock behind her house. Various little cloths were laid out on the grass for the respective pets and she had supplied their particular delicacies and settled down herself, when, through the middle of it all, ran the hunted hare. A few minutes later she was followed by 14½ couple of hounds running on a strong line. Absolute chaos ensued as the pets flew and ran in all directions and, not content with the pandemonium it had already caused, the damned hare made a small circle and crossed the paddock again. It sounds very funny but I was not laughing when the offended lady pointed a 12 bore shotgun into my face at a range of about fifteen feet. With never a thought for Jim, I gave Demelza a good jab with my spurs and fled, waiting for the shot to hit my back although luckily she did not fire it. Since that day I had always been particularly wary of straying on her property and on this day, with the help of Rupert and John who remained close to South Green, hounds were kept away from it.

The Children's Meet was held at Helmingham Hall on 22nd December and seventy-five children clattered over the drawbridge into the courtyard which was one of the highlights

Left to right: Kirsten Theobald, Gordon Grover, Jeffrey Bowden and Tom Walne

of their day. They had a lovely view of a fox which jumped up in the middle of a ploughed field and, although hounds attempted to hunt it, it soon went to ground. A lunch party was held at Tannington Hall on 23rd December to launch *All Thanks to His Grace*. This was the history of the Easton Harriers from the period from 1860 into my Mastership. About twenty-five older and retired members who had helped Bridget were present and Lord Somerleyton, who had written the Foreword, gave an address and complimented Bridget on her research and style of writing. We were pleased that 280 books were sold at the pre-publication discount and by 3rd February (1987) 425 of the 500 printed had been sold.

Christmas Eve was a good day but with no great runs. As we had to hack past Tannington Hall on the way back to the meet I wanted to slip away home

but hounds constantly broke away from Jim and came back to me, so I was obliged to hack back to the meet with them. Boxing Day at Saxtead Green was an outstanding day, especially for Jim, whose last Christmas Box collection was the best ever. There was such a crowd at Bedfield Crown for half time that I could not get through with hounds and had to stop on the edge of the crowd. Bedfield Crown used to apply for, and received, a licence for an extension to remain open after hours on the grounds that the Easton Harriers so often managed to have a half-time drink there on Boxing Day and I doubt very much if this has happened to any other hunt. Debenham Cherry Tree on Monday 29th December produced a terrible day on every count as it was terrible for hunting and then there was a disastrous accident. We had nearly all come out of the back drive of Winston Hall when a driver came along at a great speed and just missed my daughter Judith but hit Jeffrey Bowden's horse full square, scooping horse and rider up the bonnet, over the roof, and dropping them off at the back. By some miracle they were not killed but the horse needed many stitches and Jeffrey had a cracked skull and lost his sense of taste and smell. This was a disaster for such a gourmet as Jeffrey with a cellar full of fine wines.

I did not hunt hounds on New Year's Day as I was too busy preparing for the Hunt Ball so Jim hunted hounds and had only a moderate day as there were too many hares. I went along to see them on their return and found Jim in a very happy mood, the members having provided him with many festive drinks. The ball was held again at Framlingham College on Friday 2nd January (1987). There were some early problems, the worst of which was a flood in the marquee in the Tuck Box Courtyard. Horrie Plant, the foreman at the College, and I managed to get the water out and I sent down to the local DIY for wooden splines to support the roof to prevent it from happening again. Tickets were again £20 including dinner and £10 after dinner and 240 people sat down to dinner but there was such a demand for the dinner tickets that Sheila got together a party of 60 people who had the best interests of the Easton at heart, and dined them all at the Crown Hotel. The meal there was more expensive than that charged at the school but the hunt bore the difference. My daughter Judith took a party of eighteen to the Market Place restaurant and the Wheelwrights Restaurant was also booked full and I was pleased that the ball had brought so much business to Framlingham. In all, another 255 people joined the ball after dinner. The whole was a great success, due in no small measure to the long hours and hard work of my daughter Bridget and the expertise of Mary Calver and her band of helpers in festooning all the rooms with beautiful flowers which, I felt, were the best ever. Rupert Montagu did an excellent job with the wine bar, especially the girls he brought with him as waitresses. I received a lovely thank you letter from the Head Master, Laurie Rimmer, who said how much he had enjoyed the ball and that it was the best function he had ever attended at the College and the best organised.

The Wayne brothers gave another champagne breakfast in the Crown Hotel on Saturday morning. Following such a marvellous ball, this ought to have been the icing on the cake but was completely spoiled by reports of bad behaviour the night before. A prominent member had brought a party to the ball and had booked them all in at the Crown Hotel but they had overdone the imbibing part of the ball and had tipped over tubs of flowers on the Market Hill and had managed to break a bed and a window at the Crown. This unfortunate behaviour prompted a flurry of letters to the *East Anglian Daily Times* which naturally did not show the hunt in a good light.

The après ball meet was at Stradbroke Ivy House at twelve noon and almost all members had observed the tradition of hunting the morning after the ball but there was an interesting variety of states with some very hung over, some still tight, and some in between. After a very jolly meet we moved off and the first casualty was when Ian Cook's huge horse stepped round a large puddle, depositing Ian on his bottom in the middle of the water. Hounds were running hard when a loose horse appeared which was recognised as belonging to Mark Wayne. It was caught and some people rode back to return it to him but this proved easier said than done. After a thorough search of the countryside Mark was found asleep in a little spinney, leaning back against a tree.

The Essex and Suffolk Foxhounds invited me to bring my hounds into their country on 8th January and George Paul gave a lawn meet at Blue Gates at Wherstead. It was too foggy to hunt but George took the field for a ride round his estate, making full use of all the hunt jumps. On January 9th it started to snow with a vengeance and we had the deepest bout since 1947. I gave a hunting lecture on 28th January and about forty people turned up at the Crown Hotel. There was excellent audience participation and many good questions led to further explanations. I was most heartened to receive so many personal thank-yous the next day. During the talk I said that I was seriously considering expelling any member who did wilful damage to crops and would refund their subscription personally. We managed to hunt the next day from Brundish Crown and my threat worked miracles. In the wet conditions everyone behaved impeccably. It was hot and sunny after a frost which usually means poor scent but this day proved the exception to the rule and hounds flew. Jim brought 12½ couple of bitches and they drove on at such a pace that their cry was only half as loud as usual because of their exertions. The ditches were still full of snow in places, which made for some exciting riding. Geoff, the landlord, gave me £20 for the BFSS funds and Brian Sawyer gave three new armchairs to be raffled at the dinners in aid of the BFSS.

We did not hunt again until 5th February at Blaxhall Ship when the day started off with one grand hunt but the rest of the day was spent drawing blank as there were still no hares on Mr Kemball's estate at Wantisden. There was a very good party in the pub afterwards. I left at a quarter past four and there were still about twenty people there, with Geoffrey Ingram-Smith heartily playing his accordion. Two days' later we were at Kettleburgh Chequers and hounds found near the church and ran at a terrific pace to Earl Soham, swinging right and running parallel with the main road, crossing behind the Volunteer pub to Mount Pleasant Farm, Framlingham, and right handed again back to Kettleburgh church. This hunt had been at racing speed and almost all the field were well left behind. Later on Janet Baxter was almost drowned when her horse fell into a ditch of water, trapping her beneath it, but she was saved by Ernie Calver who managed to get her out. Rupert Montagu, who was following in my pick-up, took her to Brook Farm where Sue Scott provided her with a hot bath and clean clothes. Janet was very shaken but, fortunately, no bones were broken and the accident did not prevent a tremendous party breaking out in the Chequers afterwards. The landlady, Jackie Catling, provided a marvellous array of dishes of jugged hare for everyone, which was followed by a good singing session.

On Wednesday 11th February we held a hunt dinner at Cretingham Bell and I awarded hunt buttons to my daughter Judith, Scilla Western, Penelope Reinarz, Margaret James, Patricia Hardwick, Jim Hardwick, Richard Hickson, Tony St Quinton, Tom Walne, David Steel, Christine Novosad, Michael Buckley, and Nigel Chapman. There were twenty-one present and the landlord again generously gave ten meals for hunt funds. Colin Plumbe was present at the dinner having arrived from Scotland for his annual visit and had brought with him a grand grey mare called Countess. The next morning the meet was at the Wetheringsett Cat and Mouse and it turned out to be a most frustrating day with more hares than hounds and the usual disastrous results. I made the decision quite early to give up the unequal struggle and Jim and I separately went back to the meet with some hounds each. I set off in the pick-up truck with Rupert Montagu and we found Gordon Grover with a couple of hounds inside the Aspall apple orchards and Bill James in another wood with some hounds. Rupert rode in the back of the open pick-up holding two and half couple of hounds, and I had one and half in the front with me. Eventually, we managed to get all the hounds back. That evening there was a party in the pub which Elaine Grover had arranged as a surprise birthday party for her husband, Gordon. Colin Plumbe was on top form and sang some delightful Lakeland hunting songs.

A Gentlemen's Day to raise funds for the BFSS was held at the Hare and Hounds in Framlingham on Tuesday 17th February with seventeen men paying £15 each. The sport was anything but classical hare hunting but good fun as hounds ran and ran all day, very often changing hares. There was plenty of singing on our return at half past four with Harry Chambers, a retired farm worker, giving a rendition of *The Derbyshire Ram*. The same night a BFSS dinner was held at Tannington Hall and sixty people attended, including Jim Wickham's splendid party of twelve. An aperitif of sherry was served in the drawing room before we sat down to an excellent dinner provided by Sheila. The menu was specially selected to raise as much money as possible for the cause by using the cheapest ingredients and consisted of leek and potato soup, minced beef balls with carrots, peas and potatoes, followed by blackberry and apple pie or gooseberry fool, with cheese and coffee to finish. Sheila's expertise had produced all this for a mere £2 per head and the dinner made a profit of £360. The draw was very successful with the armchair donated by Brian Sawyer and made another £200 so, with the takings of £225 from the Gentlemen's Day, we had raised £785 for the BFSS in one day of continuous fun. In the morning, fifty-eight empty wine bottles were put out for re-cycling.

Snowdrifts were still in evidence when we met at Thorndon Black Horse on 19th February but scent was very good and hounds could hunt a line fifteen minutes after the hare had passed. When it was time to blow for home we just could not stop Royston. Jim and Robert Bothway had to go back by car and managed to pick him up. At Rendham two days later the scent was just as good and, finding at Don Mann's Rendham Grange, hounds took the line with a tremendous cry through the lovely meadows at Bruisyard Hall, running straight into Bruisyard Big Wood which is over a hundred acres. Ignoring all the deer, they came out at the far side and ran to the A1120 near the Bowling Green pub, and crossed the main road on their own as we just could not keep up. This line was eventually lost near where Badingham Old Hall once stood. The almost direct straight line that this hare had taken clearly showed he was a travelling jack. During this day Jaffa had been up to his old tricks again, making wild casts well ahead of the others. Twice he seriously distracted them and I decided definitely to put him down. We had given him so many chances but that 'jealous' streak always came out. The same night we held another BFSS dinner at Tannington Hall and sixty people enjoyed home-made tomato soup, boeuf bourguignon, apple pie and cream or a dish of meringue topped by half a peach which in the family is usually called a 'fried egg'. This made another tremendous profit, mostly thanks to Sheila's unstinting efforts in catering for one hundred and twenty people in only five days, with such low costs.

For these two fund-raising events, I quote below from my diary:

'Sunday 15th. Carried out a great deal of furniture to the garage and put up trestle tables etc.

'Tuesday 17th: Started at 5 o'clock in the morning, laying up tables for sixty etc. I worked through until 10.00am then changed for hunting and polished my boots. Sheila cooked breakfast and I sat down for five minutes to eat it. Immediately I returned from hunting, I carried on with jobs and, eventually, sat down again for five minutes in the bath. Sat down to eat each course but jumped up again to clear away and serve the next course, pouring wine etc. I was putting pressure on a certain very careful gentleman who was the only person reluctant to sign a direct debit form for the BFSS. He promised to do so if I came up to the Dennington Bell after dinner, so I

did and he finally signed it, thus making every member of the Easton Harriers a direct debit member of the BFSS. A whole crowd of members had gone up to the Bell to witness this signature and a party was soon going. I managed to slip away just after 2.00am, having sat down for a total of fifteen minutes in twenty-one hours. No one knows how much work goes on behind the scenes; this is roughly the form for all the dinners but generally not finishing quite so late, say 12.30/1.00am'.

'We are now hunting four days a week and I had to walk the country on Sunday after dinner the night before. I even missed church to walk the Pettistree draw and this took from nine o'clock until twelve thirty; meeting Sheila, Judith and Bill for a steak lunch, then walking the Kettleburgh Chequers draw well into the dark'.

'With no alcohol since 5ᵗʰ January and an extra busy time I am losing weight which must be a good thing'.

Jim hunted hounds at Kettleburgh Chequers on Monday 23ʳᵈ February, the draw running to Framlingham and Saxtead, while I was acting as Field Master. Sixty hares had recently been shot here so we had a good a day with enjoyable hound work without any distractions from fresh hares. The next day we had another Gentlemen's Day at Pettistree Greyhound but it was not quite the same as usual as one member unaccountably brought his wife to the meet. Hounds crossed the A12 twice, over and then back, near Ufford. I could not get down to the road because of an oak post and rail fence on top of a high bank and it made my stomach turn over to see the near misses. Luckily no hound was hurt partly due to the gallant efforts of a lorry driver who stopped his lorry and waved down the traffic on his side of the dual carriageway. The next draw was well away from the road and the rest of the day comparatively uneventful. The same evening another BFSS dinner was held at Tannington Hall. Another sixty people attended to enjoy a menu of leek soup, 'up market' shepherd's pie, banoffee pie or chocolate mouse, cheese and coffee. Before leaving many people congratulated Sheila on her culinary skills and appreciated just how much work she had done to make it such a special evening. One of Brian Sawyer's chairs was first prize in the raffle and Rod Thorpe gave two good prizes, one of which was an enormous box of fresh fruit weighing between three and four stone. Again this made over £200 for the funds.

As hunting was cancelled due to excessive wet on 28ᵗʰ February, I made use of the opportunity for Janet Baxter, Robert Bothway and myself to have an impromptu meeting with Geoffrey Ingram-Smith to discuss and draw up a list of all the duties

at the forthcoming Point-to-Point. As I was totally disinterested in racing I had always left these matters to Geoffrey but he was retiring and it was important that Janet, who was to be the new secretary, learnt the ropes and Robert Bothway knew a great deal about Point-to-Pointing. That evening was the last of the dinners for the BFSS. I quote from my diary: *'Drink consumed 67 bottles, 18 more than the last dinner. The Wayne family on top form and placed a photo on top of a candle, then put a silver hare on the photo, and proceeded to call for 'cheers for the hare' and then 'cheers for NO HAIR (their father); before the end of the dinner people were asking for another one like it. We had home made tomato soup, 'upmarket' shepherds pie, apple pie and blackberry mousse, cheese and coffee. I presented Chris Wells, the BFSS Secretary, with a folder of 46 direct debits to BFSS for new members which with the existing members made a total of 75 which amounted to £1,000 a year. I also handed over a cheque for £2,000 being the profits from two gents days and four dinners. A wonderful effort from Sheila, had remained calm throughout and has served over a thousand helpings for the four dinners. I don't know anyone else who would have tackled that alone whilst bringing so much credit to the E.H. WELL DONE SHEILA!'*[5]

It was the end of an era when Jim and Hilda Wickham moved out of the round house on 31st April 1987. At first I had tried not to accept Jim's resignation as kennel huntsman to the Easton. I tried various different tacks to persuade him to stay: the last being when I offered the ultimate sacrifice, of handing him the horn and promoting him to be a professional huntsman and it was when he turned this down that I had to face the fact that he was in considerable pain and would retire at the end of the season. Jim and Hilda were tailor-made for the Easton and perfectly fitted the role; they were both equally enthusiastic to deal with whatever problem came their way. Hilda had endeared herself to the local people of Easton and throughout all the hunt country. Her expertise in looking after the whelps at breeding time was insurmountable, especially with poor Lawful[78]. This bitch had no tongue as while eating raw flesh a sinew had somehow encircled the back of her tongue and stopped the circulation and, before anyone realised what had happened, it was too late. She could not lick her babies but Hilda had quickly realised the problem

---

[5] Sheila would like to add that she certainly did not do it alone. On the evenings of the dinners she had the willing assistance of Sue Scott and Dandy Corner, and Hilda Wickham organised a team of washers-up.

and cleaned them after the birth and daily attended to their nursery needs. No Master of Hounds could have wished for, or have received, more loyal support than Jim and Hilda gave to me. They had suited me and all of the Easton members, especially in their never failing good humour, even down to Jim's 'boyish pranks'. At times these pranks were 'well over the top' but Jim even accepted my rebukes cheerfully. In all the years that we were together I cannot remember a single sullen or moping day. I could go on extolling their virtues but suffice to say that it was a very lucky day for me when the Wickhams moved into the round house and I had a heavy heart when they moved out.

Farewell to the Wickhams

1987–88

David and Fiona Horsefield moved in and soon settled down and we started to break last year's puppies. Jim and I had experienced great difficulties breeding the hounds during his last few seasons. A great amount of thought was given and many evenings spent in discussion regarding which bitches should be put to which dogs but there was an insurmountable difficulty in that some of the bitches would not come into season, sometimes for two years or more. These were good, strong, young bitches, appearing to be in perfect health but just did not come into season or, if they did, it was not a normal one, perhaps lasting only two or three days. This caused us great aggravation as we could not breed to our plans but instead had to breed from whatever came into season at the correct time. I am convinced that this upset to the normal pattern of behaviour was a result of the Parvovirus. There were only 3½ couple of puppies to be broken in David's first season and they came from two litters, both dams being Rufford Forest bitches sired by our Granville[83] and Teacher[85]. It seemed that they were not affected like the Easton bitches who had been reared in kennel with the virus. I missed Peterborough Hound Show for the first time since 1960 as Sheila and I had been invited to a garden party at Buckingham Palace and I was sorry to hear that David had not had a more exciting show getting only two third prize rosettes,

both with Jasper in the restricted doghound class and the stallion hound class.

Presentations were made to Jim and Hilda at the Open Day, followed by another presentation to Vera Pulham for completing forty years as Point-to-Point secretary. Disappointing news was to arrive in that the Windermere Harriers were to be disbanded. The staff situation was David Horsefield as kennel huntsman on £105 per week: David Cook, part-time groom at the kennels, £38: and the two grooms at the Hall, Karen Wainer £70, and Karen Sills, £50, although two days into the season, I had to sack Karen Sills.

The season was late in starting due to a very late harvest because of the wet weather and there were still fields of standing corn when we started hunting in the sugar beet on 26th September. The Ride and Drive Meet on 3rd October was again at Bedfield Crown. Peter Crockford could not come to drive his Suffolk horse to deliver hounds so Bruce Smith from Hollesley Bay stepped in to fill the breech. Richard Hickson brought an Australian to see the meet which was just as much fun as ever. Both my Hackney cross driving horses were hunted, Bella ridden and driven by Michael Sawyer, while I drove Tiger to the meet for Karen Wainer to ride. Bruce Smith was called away on an emergency so I told an astounded David Horsefield that he was to drive the Suffolk horse back to the Hall. His face showed abject horror as he had never driven a horse before but I waved away his objections and the journey was successfully accomplished.

By hunting four mornings a week, we managed to fit in sixteen early mornings before the Opening Meet at Framlingham on 29th October. The late harvest and wet conditions meant the autumn drilling was well behind schedule so we had rideable country in almost every direction. There were too many hares for serious hunting but the field had a marvellous day, galloping across country wherever they wanted. A rare treat in Easton country! Two days later the Charsfield meet was sadly different as the Hennessy family were moving from Pear Tree Farm and could not offer their famous hospitality although a few of us were invited back afterwards for what was to be the very last occasion. The après hunting teas, the numerous dinners and warm-up parties en route to neighbouring hunt balls which ensured we arrived on top form; these lovely memories of Pear Tree Farm will remain in our thoughts forever. During the day we met the same tractor driver twice and each time the man had stopped and turned off the engine. The second time he had taken the opportunity to get out his flask of tea but Ernie Calver, wishing to acknowledge this kindness, rode up to offer him his flask and the driver tossed away the remainder of his tea but unfortunately, it hit Ernie's horse, which shied sideways, depositing Ernie on the road. The poor man was teased for the rest of the season for falling off while standing still.

On Tuesday, 10th November 1987, a memorial service was held in Little Glemham church for Lady Blanche Cobbold. The Easton would certainly not have survived the war without the generosity of this great lady and John Wayne, the Bishop, made reference to this fact in his address. *Horse & Hound* magazine sent a photographer to the Laxfield meet on 12th November, and amongst many others, he took a picture of Bridget holding her book which by now was completely sold out. None of the usual country around Laxfield House was available due to pheasants in wire runs all over the draw. I had come across these the day before, which proves the importance of walking the country thoroughly. I went to see Alec Comins at Wilby Hall and explained my problem and asked if I could hunt his land again although we had hunted it five days earlier. I found him and Mrs Comins with their elderly man, Jim, taking tiles off a storm-damaged roof. Alec laughed and said, 'You can hunt the farm again if you help with these tiles,' so I shinned up on the roof and handed down enough to fill their tractor-trailer. Debach Post was a disaster on 14th November as, at the last minute, five farmers had telephoned to say they were shooting. This meant that almost all the draw was unavailable and I did not know quite what to do. I drew on the only piece of country I had and with great luck, the hare ran to Dallinghoo and was lost outside Jim and Hilda's new residence. I was accused of laying a drag but it honestly was the hare and, with the usual Easton spirit, a mounted party was soon in progress and we drank Jim out of all his booze. Two men from the Holme Valley Beagles were following and they each sang a song, and Marion Saffell made a speech and declared Jim and Hilda to be honorary members of the Easton for the rest of their lives.

The Cambridgeshire Harriers invited us to meet on Cottenham Racecourse on 17th November. A fairly good day followed and the twenty who were to stay moved to Horningsea Manor to change for dinner. The demand from the Cambridgeshire members to attend this dinner was so great that Betty Gingell, Master, had to divide them and provide a second dinner a few days' later. On Thursday 10th December hounds met at Stradbroke Ivy House and the first hare ran directly to Worlingworth church. Here we noticed that a little dark bitch called Velvet was badly cut. We put her in a loose box at Worlingworth Hall but five minutes later she was with us again, having broken the glass in a window and jumped out. When we returned to the meet Harry Chambers was there on top form and we had jokes and tales galore before going home. There was a hunt dinner that night at Framlingham Crown at £8.50 per head which included half a bottle of wine. There was a tremendous atmosphere right from the start and, around midnight, I tried twice to stop but they just kept calling for more songs.

Hunting was not very good at Southolt Plough on 12th December as most of the draw had been recently ploughed and fresh plough does not hold a scent. Expert was missing at the end of the day and although I waited at the Plough until half past four he appeared the moment I left. Kaz Bryan tried to catch him but was bitten for her trouble. I returned at once in my pick-up but he had lost his nerve and I could not catch him so I went across to Jim Mutton's farm to ask if I could telephone David to bring some hounds to give him confidence. Whilst I waited for David to come, Jim pressed a drink into my hand and Peggy produced a plate of moules marinière, which made me think of the old saying, 'It's an ill wind that blows no one any good.' As soon as David arrived Expert joined the other hounds and jumped into the van with no trouble at all.

Bedfield Crown on 17th December was one of those days when everything seemed doomed right from the start. It was David Steel's birthday meet but he had influenza and could not hunt although he and I had a proper hunt breakfast in the pub. It was very foggy and it was not at all certain that we would be able to hunt. Then the boxes had been parked so badly in the lane outside the pub that an oil tanker and a pig lorry could not pass to get to Ivy Farm. Richard and Michael Nesling owned the land all round the meet and we normally spend a considerable part of the day on their farms so it was not at all helpful when Richard, who was driving the pig lorry, asked for the horsebox to be moved and was given the answer, 'Can't you go round another way?' Naturally this infuriated him and, in no time at all, both brothers were in a high state of dudgeon. As it is always the Master who takes the blame, they both vented their spleen on me. The scent was very good and hounds just flew but this was just an extra worry for me as the fog made it difficult to keep in touch with them. Rod Thorpe dispensed half-time drinks at Hartismere Grange, which gave us an opportunity to blow for missing hounds but the field made such a mess on Paul Elliott's wheat that I was furious and took hounds home immediately. David Horsefield was riding Ozzi who had run out of steam and was nowhere to be seen. Jim Wickham was out so I asked him to help me back to the pub with hounds. We both had lame horses with shoes off, but managed to get most of the hounds back. I then had the unenviable task of visiting the two Nesling brothers. I spent an hour with Michael, and then went on to see Richard, who was the more angry of the two as it was he who had received the stupid answer. In the end I left them 'reasonably'

Lynn Mace and Anne St Quinton with JAH

happy and that ended a most unfortunate day. The last entry in my diary reads: '*How I wish I could give up hounds and pass them on to someone reliable.*'

My sister, Sarah, and her husband, Michael Buckley, gave a splendid hunt breakfast before the meet at Hoxne Swan on 19th December. It was as just as well that we had such a good start to the day as there was not much country because of shooting. The Children's Meet at Helmingham Hall on Monday 21st December was rather chaotic with boxes and cars stuck on the park owing to the very wet conditions but sixty-five children had the usual fun of clattering over the drawbridge into the courtyard. There were not as many hares as usual and I was able to give the children a fairly good day, during which a fox got up from the middle of a field, from exactly the same spot as the previous year. History nearly repeated itself when, as we hacked back to the meet along a cart-way that borders the park fence, Gordon Grover spotted a fox in an oak tree which was inside the park as there was a long story about the Hamilton Harriers hunting a tree fox from Helmingham Hall in March 1877 in *All Thanks To His Grace*. As soon as we were able to re-

enter the park we rode across to the area where the fox had been seen. Robert Bothway's friend, Peter, who I believe is Canadian, climbed up the tree and poked the fox down but he only went for about fifty yards before going to ground.

The Christmas Eve meet was held at Dennington Bell, and there was a grand atmosphere and some songs before we moved off. Ian Cook had run low on port so the traditional toast to General Miller was drunk in whatever drinks we had. Tony St Quinton was riding Rose and fortunately his wife, Anne, followed on foot and was on hand when I needed her. Bantry had cut herself very badly and Anne was able to catch her for me using my whip formed into a noose. Victor Scott and Catharine Corner took her to the vet to be stitched up. The hunting had started with a good 'pipe opening' sharp run from opposite the pub to Downs Farm and back to the Chantry. There was a messy, middle part of the day with too many hares on Harvey land so we went to draw Tannington Lodge where we found at once. She ran along a valley and swung right-handed up to the Lodge, crossing Severals Lane into the osier beds right on the edge of Dennington village. They ran on strongly through various gardens before crossing the main A1120 *en route* to Framlingham Hall where she was fresh found. This hare had a love of villages and made for Dennington again, running through another garden and across the community centre playing field and then parallel to the old Roman road. It had begun to get dark when I managed to stop them at Elm Farm on the very meadow where I first sat on a saddle when trying out my first riding cob Monty in my teens. Only Robert Haag and Kaz and Mike Bryan managed to finish this run and helpfully brought on a couple of missing hounds, which made it 'all on'. Hotpot and dumplings were waiting for us on our return but I did not stay long as it was already so late.

Boxing day, as always, was at Saxtead Volunteer. We unboxed at Church Farm and, with me on Fizz and David on Max, we hacked up to the meet where a huge crowd awaited us. John Appleby, the landlord, had telephoned during breakfast to say that a car was being driven round the car park towing a hessian sack but the sack had been removed before there was a problem. There were very few regular members out as their horses had not recovered from Christmas Eve and this left me with a difficult situation as it meant that most of the seventy-six mounted followers were not knowledgeable hunters and did not have experienced people to follow. The Field Master could only look after those at the front and experienced members should, in those circumstances, have divided themselves to help with the newcomers. Sure enough, the worst happened and during the day I received a message that they had been riding four abreast round some wheat but fortunately the wheat belonged to our member Tim Last. Finding on Tim's land we ran across to Button's Hill, swinging left to Tannington Lodge where, after a circuit of the farm, she was lost in the overgrown gardens. Finding again on Fenton's Farm, hounds ran with barely a check for one and a quarter hours. I am sure that they changed hares, probably twice, but the pace was such that I was seldom close enough to be sure. They lost the line completely between the Chantry and Dennington Bell so I hacked up to the Bell for half-time thus giving our horses a chance to get their wind back. We hacked back into the draw proper, found at once, and ran hard to Bedfield Crown. There was a huge crowd there waiting for us but, as hounds were still running hard, I could only acknowledge their greeting as we passed. I finally managed to stop them in the dark at Bull's Hall and there were very few still with us as we hacked back to Saxtead. These last two days had been Yuletide sport at its best, and hounds had run all the mounted field to a standstill on both days.

On Monday 28th December the meet was at Debenham Cherry Tree and the local policeman was determined to prevent an accident like that to Jeffrey Bowden the previous year and was very concerned about how much we would be on the road. The field missed out on the only good run of the day when Ollie Knowland objected to them crossing one field. He had tried to stop me but I dare not stop as hounds were running towards the A1120 and although I went to see him afterwards he barely accepted my explanation for not stopping. Too many hares spoilt the rest of the day and the only highlight was the half-time stop at Winston Hall for mince pies, sausage rolls and hot punch. Too many hares also spoiled Stradbroke on 30th December with hounds divided for most of the day but, at the end of the day, an almost unbelievable thing happened as hounds were hunting in two groups, each with a great cry, when the two lines came together. What had happened was that the hare had run round in a circle and had crossed her own line. When hounds had reached this point where she had crossed over, some had continued on her original line while some had started hunting 'heel away' on the newer section so both packs eventually ran round to meet each other. Owing to this extraordinary but convenient phenomenon, I managed to stop them on Wingfield Green 'all on'.

At the New Year's meet at Cretingham Bell a large crowd saw over eighty mounted field move off. The hunting was again poor because of too many hares, and consisted of lots of short hunts with parts of the pack. It was very wet and cold and the half-time stop at Robbie Haag's indoor school was especially welcome as Angela provided hot punch and pies and we sheltered from the driving rain. During perhaps the best little run, I had to change on to Karen Wainer's own horse and enjoyed a good run on this quality hunter. The pub was packed to overflowing when I returned with people clamouring for songs and a great party was soon in full swing. It was rather late when I arrived home. The Hunt Ball was held again at Framlingham College on Wednesday 6th January (1988). Tickets to include dinner were £24 and £10 for after dinner. The Plumbe family deserved a medal as they had driven down from Scotland in the teeth of a gale towing a trailer for Colin's horse and Alice's pony but still appeared at the ball all bright and breezy. The marquee, although in a courtyard, was damaged by gale force winds and had to be weighed down. We had the Galvanos and the Peagreen Philharmonic Pullover Set again but this year I had arranged for a steel band to play in the ballroom during the Galvanos' break although this was not totally successful as they took so long to set up. I had not realised that steel bands had moved on from those I had heard in the past who played on barrels or part barrels. An air lock prevented the loos from working which caused a major hiccup. Even the ladies were choosing to resort to the outside and I, in my green tails, was rushing around with buckets of water to enable the loos to flush. There had been some damage in the college and the College authorities, especially the Bursar, were not very pleased with us. This was a sad ending to what could have been the greatest possible success apart from the problem with the loos. The main band, the Galvanos, was so well liked that the dance floor was packed all evening. As usual the success and wonderful atmosphere was the result of the hard work of a few stalwarts. The disco room had been decorated most artistically by a group of youngsters, Rupert Montagu, with his splendid bevy of lovely ladies to help him, ran the wine bar most successfully, my daughter Bridget worked endless hours making signs and seating plans, all of which were beautifully done, and Mary Calver, with many willing volunteers, had transformed what was basically a boy's school into a regal setting for a ball.

The meet the 'morning after' produced some woeful looking specimens but I was pleased to see that almost all had honoured the ancient custom of hunting after the ball no matter how hungover they might feel. Hunting is, after all, one of the finest cures for hangovers. Hounds met at Laxfield Oak at twelve o'clock to draw the Badingham country. It was really too wet to hunt but I went because of the tradition of hunting after the ball. A bitterly cold wind soon cleared our heads but scent was almost zero so, instead of drawing each field properly, I went from field to field across the draw and then turned and did the same in the opposite direction. This kept the field on the move with lots of ditch jumping and all were happy except my daughter Judith who managed to get knocked off her horse by an overhanging bough.

There was an outstanding day from Dennington Bell on 9th January (1988). After a few indifferent little hunts I drew a plough at Low Grange Farm, Heveningham, where the Rush family always gave us a genuine greeting. Finding there, hounds ran over David Clarke's Wood Farm, and turning on Walnut Tree Farm, she began to return home via Redhouse and the Peasenhall Manor Farm, but not to where she was found which is what I expected. Instead she ran over Sylvester's land where a convenient bridleway took us to Heveningham Long Lane, from which we began to run into Waveney country. A huge, uncrossable water-course had caused a delay so we were not on hand and I did not know if hounds killed or not although they certainly deserved to. I found hounds at Sibton Green, having had to dismount at Buttocks Lodge and be driven on in a car by Jill Graham, and they were 'all on' except for Teasel. This run was quite fast with hounds casting and putting themselves right, rather too quickly for our panting horses who could have done with a longer break, and as far as I know, they did not change hares throughout. Most of us who had finished with hounds, dismounted and stood with our horses while they fought to get their breath back. A car follower drove Ernie Calver back to the meet and he brought out my lorry and we loaded up hounds and horses at Sibton White Horse. One never knows what to expect when hare-hunting and this proved to be one of the most unusual runs I had

ever had. Hounds had run approximately five miles and were not helped by either huntsman or whipper-in. It is moments like this when, full of pride and joy, one realises that the long hours spent studying the pedigrees and the different outstanding points of hounds to be bred are worthwhile.

Christine Crisp, Master of the Waveney, was very upset that we had run into her country and said that she had received a serious complaint from a lady who lived on Sibton Green. I went the next morning to see her and she explained what had happened. She was walking along a footpath with her dog and heard hounds running in full cry. Looking back she saw them coming along the footpath behind her and immediately thought that they were hunting her dog but they ran on past her and checked where I eventually found them. Not unnaturally, she had been quite scared and was most concerned that the hounds were running around with no one to control them. She eventually accepted my apologies and explanations and assurances that they would not have hurt her dog.

The next meet should have been held at Brundish Crown on 14th January but the pub was closed and the landlord pretended he did not know about us although Ian Cook had told him what to expect. I left Rupert Montagu to redirect all boxes to the Dennington Bell. It was far too wet and I ought not to have hunted but I do so hate to lose a day. The scent was good and hounds hunted themselves while we kept to the tracks and roads. The best of the fun was on the lovely meadows at Wilby Hall. Back in the Bell afterwards I declared a 'sing, say or pay' round. We had all had such a lovely day and I took a collection from those present to buy a goose as a thank you to Alec Comins of Wilby Hall where we had spent so much of the day. The next afternoon I went to see him taking not only the goose but also a bottle of rather good claret from my cellar. I was met at the door by a furious Alec who ranted on at me, quite deservedly, for hunting in such wet conditions. He vented his anger for half an hour or so then I managed to say that I had realised that I had overstepped the mark but, as we had had such a marvellous run, the members had all contributed to send him a thank you present. When he saw the goose and the claret and realised I had planned to give it to him beforehand, he subsided a little and asked me in for a cup of tea. When I left about an hour later he had calmed down considerably. It had been a great shame to have so upset such a marvellous sportsman.

Glemham on 16th January was very foggy and three times I asked someone to drive me from the meet onto the airfield to see if the fog had cleared enough to hunt. Rather than cancel because of the excessive wet, I had decided to hunt for an hour or so on the airfield where the horses could do no harm as the hares usually stay around the runways and criss cross from one side to the other. After the third inspection, I decided to hunt but as soon as we started, down came the fog again. I called for David to stop them drawing but it was too late and hounds disappeared into the blanket of fog with me riding hard trying to keep in touch. The scent was very good and I galloped my horse almost to a standstill before eventually managing to stop 10½ couple beyond Fiddler's Hall. I was on Don Mann's farm without permission and he loomed up out of the fog but, instead of being cross with me (he was a keen pheasant shooter), he kindly helped me shut up hounds in a loose box at Fiddler's Hall. I was still 4½ couple light and hoped Robbie Haag or David Horsefield had stopped some. As I hacked back to the meet I met David who had three couple in the hound van, which meant we were now only 1½ couple light. Mike Carter, our sporting policeman, appeared to tell me that a hound had been killing the chickens of Mr and Mrs Grieves at the Old Rectory so he drove me to see them. They were upset but very kind and understanding and shared in my unhappiness, as I had not had any trouble of this sort for many seasons. Granville was the guilty hound and never came out with the Easton again. Finally, the landlord telephoned me at eleven o'clock at night to say there was a hound at the pub. David went out and collected a beautiful little bitch called Nettle. So ended a day's hunting that would have been better never to have been started.

Thursday 21st January did not start off very well as the meet was planned to be at Bedfield Crown but Michael and Richard Nesling, still smarting from their inexcusable treatment the last time we were there, said that they would rather we did not meet there mid week so I moved the meet to Worlingworth Swan little imagining that another exceptional day was before us. I drew towards Bedfield church as I intended to see as much of hounds as possible but keeping to the lanes, as it was still unbelievably wet. A few short, enjoyable, but moderate, hunts started the day until hounds found a hare on the Davy family's farm at Tannington. They ran from Wood Farm, Tannington, to Bedfield church, crossing the road at Bedfield School and had barely checked at this point. They ran on strongly over Hungers Green, leaving Monk Soham church on their left, dropping into the valley and crossed the Earl Soham to Kenton road and, at a great pace, went up over Kenton Lodge where they divided. David and Robbie Haag went with the split, eventually stopping at Blood Hall. I carried on with the main pack who ran over Crows Hall, almost to the road, then swung left handed and with barely a check, raced on to just short of Ashfield village where they swung left again, re-crossing the low road at Ashfield Lodge, running on past Ringies Arch, over Spring Hill, and across to Monk Soham Hall. Here, regretfully, I had to stop them. I jumped off my horse and made a great fuss of them saying all their names in turn. By this I hoped to lessen their disappointment at being stopped. I did not have any choice as my horse was completely blown. Luckily I was riding my quality horse Bucks Fizz who loved to gallop and was the only horse I owned who could have gone that distance at that pace. I am reasonably sure that hounds did not change hares and they had worked out every check so quickly as to give the appearance of not checking at all. This hunt had been an excellent demonstration of how a hare hunt changes character when the scent is particularly good. When hounds are driving on so fast that she does not have the time to do any classical doubles, she is soon pushed out of the area she knows well, and then she runs more like a fox. We had run through Tannington, Bedfield, Monk Soham, Kenton, Debenham, Ashfield and Monk Soham again. As we hacked back to Worlingworth Swan I ran the day through my mind again: quite good scent for the first few hunts, then exceptionally good for the great run. There was a softness in the air and I was not surprised that that night it snowed as there is frequently such an outstanding scent just before it snows.

The following Thursday our invitation by the Essex and Suffolk to Blue Gates, Wherstead, was cancelled due to deep snow and we had to cancel the next Saturday (30th) as the snow had been melted away by rain and the land was the wettest I have ever seen, but hounds met on Thursday 4th February at Thorndon Black Horse and it was to be yet another outstanding day although there were strong winds. Robert Crawford was out from the Dunston and, as usual, everyone was pleased to see him. David only brought doghounds because we thought they would be steadier in the high winds and the 12½ couple hunted beautifully, keeping tightly together and resisting the temptation of 'flightiness', which often accompanies high winds. The day was just one classical hunt after another. Hounds cast themselves so cleverly that I hardly helped them at all. Poor Jeffrey Bowden was in the wars again with a serious fall on John Edwards' farm, crushing his vertebrae. Members helped him to the road near Rishangles chapel and when the ambulance arrived, the driver said, 'Not you again, sir? Wouldn't you prefer to take up stock car racing?'

More amusement in a lighter vein happened when most of us were on one side of a high and thick 'bullfinch' and from the other side could be heard a lot of squeaking and other sounds of female distress. It was my daughter Judith and after a few minutes her plucky little mount Mickey decided that she had chickened out long enough, launched himself and, with a crashing and snapping of twigs, she appeared on our side. The day ended with a great hunt, which would have delighted any true hare hunter. This hare was hunted in two fairly large circles, which formed a figure of eight. Each time she clapped down in the same field as she was originally found, and each time she was fresh found. She clapped down for the third time on the brow of a ditch and when fresh found she was so tired that she fell over twice, which allowed hounds to catch up and get their reward. I am really far too soft-hearted to be a huntsman as tears were in my eyes to see this gallant hare falling over and I would have preferred to see her either escape or be killed as she was clapped which is the normal way. This hunt was the best of the day and to watch hounds sort out the complicated doubles in the high wind was a great credit to them and immensely pleasing to me. One and a half brace were killed, all after classic hunts. Thus we ended our day with 12½ couple 'all on' in spite of the high winds.

The Point-to-Point Races were held at Higham on 6th February with a lovely sunny day, which brought out a huge crowd and double the usual number of race cards were sold. Robbie Haag won the Members' Race riding Robert Bothway's horse, Harry Spencer was second, and Brian Sawyer third. Sadly, Karen Wainer was unseated at the open ditch and Michael Sawyer fell and broke his collar bone.

The meet on Thursday 11th February was cancelled owing to snow and wet but we managed to go from Kettleburgh Chequers on the following Saturday. Again we had high winds but this time with heavy rain and it was very cold. The country was very rideable and some average hunts were enjoyed before the Edmundson family dispensed some much needed hospitality for half-time. A great run from Church Farm, Earl Soham, concluded the day with some hounds showing untypical tiredness. One bitch curled up under a bush and David had to carry her to a car. It was later found that many hounds had yellow jaundice and David undertook a concentrated rat-poisoning exercise at the kennels. We were wet and cold but deliriously happy as we hacked back to the meet at four o'clock.

Paul and Jacky Yeldham gave a hunt breakfast for hunt funds prior to the meet at Wetheringsett Cat and Mouse on 18th February. Twenty-five people enjoyed an excellent breakfast at £2.50 each. Hunting was much better here than the previous years as the younger Mr Robinson had shot over a hundred hares on Lampitts Farm so we did not have the problem of too many hares and hounds dividing. The day ended with a great singing session with John Howson, Ted Chaplin, and Harry Chambers all there so we were entertained to new songs galore. Scent remained good and two more enjoyable days were held before a particularly good day at Occold Beaconsfield Arms on 27th February. I was delighted to see Mr Owens, the new owner of Occold Hall, at the meet and, having met him previously, I knew that he had come from great hunting country in Northamptonshire. After some good local hunting, a hare was found near the meet, which ran across Eye Park Farm and then crossed the River Dove where we could not jump it. I knew the nearest place to cross was the Blue Bridge and I was soon over it but hounds were flying and were out of sight. I galloped Demelza flat out and soon had hounds in sight again. They had crossed Ted Saunders' farm and were running straight towards the main Ipswich/Norwich road. I was scared that the hare was a travelling jack and would cross the main road but, luckily, it turned and ran parallel with the road, crossing two more side roads and then straight across Gordon Grover's farm before swinging right-handed back to Eye airfield where she was lost. There were only two horses still up with me and all three of us were highly excited and mightily relieved at the same time. Our horses were really 'done in' after what I believe to be the fastest run I have ever known with the Harriers although I am not quite sure because of the disadvantage of having to go via the bridge at the start. All the time hounds were running parallel to the main road it was at a galloping pace and every ditch was taken at that speed. I needed to keep up with them for fear that they may try to cross the main road. I went home exhilarated and was in just the right mood to go to a 'Swinging 'Twenties' party at the home of our Member of Parliament, Michael Lord, at Mellis.

It was towards the end of this season that at last I managed to find a solution to the personal problems of being Master. These had been growing steadily, year by year. I was now spending an average of forty hours a week on the Easton and at busy times such as at the main ball and other major events it would rise to 55–60 hours and I was able to do this only because I had, in Kenny Warne and Bob Pipe, two very knowledgeable and dependable men to look after my pig-fattening enterprise. The more important problem was the financial one because, as ever, I wanted to run the Easton Harriers as well as possible but this demanded far more money than the guarantee, and the disparity between the guarantee and the real costs was getting wider and wider because of inflation. Although I had always been against the idea of having a Joint Master, this seemed the only way out of the problem but the problem would be to find someone to share the costs as, even halved, it was still a considerable sum so I thought of trying to find up to five Joint Masters who would put in a few thousands each. I approached some members who I thought would make good Joint Masters but none of them were willing to dip their hands into their pockets. Each man suggested economies that I could have made myself had I felt they were acceptable. Purely

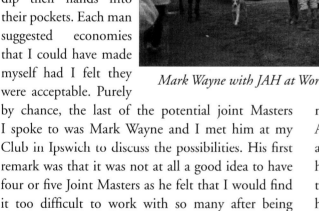

Mark Wayne with JAH at Worlingworth Swan

by chance, the last of the potential joint Masters I spoke to was Mark Wayne and I met him at my Club in Ipswich to discuss the possibilities. His first remark was that it was not at all a good idea to have four or five Joint Masters as he felt that I would find it too difficult to work with so many after being independent for so long. I explained my thinking that the more who came in to divide the shortfall, the less each would need to contribute and he asked what the shortfall was.

After digesting the shock, he said, 'I am going to make a proposal but I need a week to think about it.'

I was too excited and anxious to know what it was so he said, 'Well, if we are going to be Joint Masters, let me divide the shortfall down the middle but, don't forget, I need a week before I confirm this.' He then added something that was music to my ears. 'I want no part in the day to day running of the Hunt as I am perfectly satisfied with the way you run it now.' I was pretty sure that he would not pull out having said so much and as I was overjoyed, becoming quite emotional and close to tears. As I expected, Mark

confirmed his offer and from 1ˢᵗ May 1988 I had for the first time a Joint Master.

I was able to enjoy my hunting holiday in Leicestershire with a light heart because of this agreement with Mark and I was so euphoric that I had reverted to the happy days of song-writing and composed one regarding David Horsefield, my Kennel Huntsman, and the Easton Harriers at that time.

Terence Saffell, whom I had left in charge while I was away, cancelled the Thursday meet and David was unable to hunt hounds but I was back to hunt again at Glemham on Saturday 5ᵗʰ March, which was a modest day. The last meet of the season was at Worlingworth Swan on 12ᵗʰ March. The scent was very good but there were too many hares and hounds divided and divided again until there were only five couple hunting one hare but a lot of country was covered. At one point we were on Horham airfield and later on at Monk Soham church. At the end of the day we picked up hounds at Occold and Bedingfield; it had been a really messy sort of day and a terrible waste of good scent. At one time during the day, a man who had bought a cottage in Monk Soham, was upset because some hounds strayed into his garden. I called to see him that night en route to the End of Season ball and left him much happier. The ball was a great success with a tremendous atmosphere and, as I had a chalet so as not to have to drive home, combined with being a grass widower for the night, I had a right royal time.

1988–89

I went away on a hunting holiday after hunting finished with the Easton so we could not start to break the young hounds until early April. This year the young entry numbered eleven couple and we had them all walking off couples by mid-May. They were all bred 'in kennel' with no outside blood, the four litters having been sired by Jasper[82] (two), Expert[83] and Webster[85]. All these hounds carried the original old Easton blood. David's wife Fiona was to 'do' three horses at the kennels for him which were the everlasting Polly, Ozzi, and a new six-year-old called

B.J., and I would leave my lorry at the kennels for the whole season to bring both horses and hounds to the meet. At the Hall I had two grooms, Karen Wainer and Sam Large, to do Bucks Fizz, Max, Nicky, Demelza, Rose, and a new five-year-old, Roulette, belonging to my new Joint-Master, Mark Wayne.

The start of hunting was delayed by the very dry and hard conditions and the first day was held at Tannington on 21st September during which three brace of hares were chopped which at least gave the puppies a taste of their future quarry. A few puppies left the sugar beet and went back to the meet, one of whom was Modest who, on meeting my aged, rough-coated lurcher, started to run back to me in the beet with the old dog gamely coursing her. This first morning was short as we had only had two days of hound exercise, one round Letheringham and one round Hoo church. I had deliberately not done much exercise as I had become convinced that the harriers, when really fit, did not hunt steadily, which was not helpful to teach the young entry. Very fit hounds hunted through the sugar beet far too fast, leaving the young entry on their own to return to me. This was not ideal and the new system of reduced exercise worked well but was designed to cope with the problems of hunting in large fields of sugar beet.

The second morning was still scentless and no hares were caught but we were pleased because no puppies went back to the meet and all stayed with us until the end. The third morning it was blowing a gale and I cancelled at seven o'clock but the winds had moderated enough for us to hunt at half past two and two hours of wonderful

The Ride & Drive Meet – JAH with John Parker and David Horsfield behind

hare hunting followed. The hares ran twisting with complicated zig-zags in the beet and hounds turning tightly at each twist, thus vindicating my point about not being too fit because otherwise they would have over run. Most of the puppies were in amongst the old hounds, leaving only Modest and Calico still with me. Jumping off, I managed to retrieve one partly-eaten hare and was able to make sure that they both had a taste which I hoped would encourage them to enter. They were both a little nervous and the tremendous cry coupled with the crashing of the beet

leaves unnerved them at first. The 'morning' ended with a lovely run out of the beet round Tannington Lodge Farm and back into the beet.

Several people asked if they could come out for the early mornings but I refused as the young entry were still hesitant and would be very easily frightened and probably hide up in the beet but four mornings later I allowed six people out as all the young hounds were now going with the old ones and had done so for two consecutive mornings. On 3rd October I eventually had to cancel because of fog which just would not clear although I felt sorry for Lady Quilter and Gay Bridgford who had come a long way for a seven o'clock meet. Wednesday 5th October should have been very good but the field behaved badly and received the full extent of my wrath for riding far too close to hounds, especially the young entry. When a young hound is galloped over or kicked during its first three months or so, it usually never recovers and will go off to one side and hide up whenever the horses come near. The Ride and Drive Meet was held at Bedfield Crown on 8th October. Most people 'put to' and started from Tannington Hall with Mary Garton leading the convoy with hounds in a four-wheeled van.[6] Thirty-six horses were driven to the meet and among them were a tandem driven by Sally Waldron with a leader already saddled ready to ride, a four in hand team of black Frieslanders driven by Mike Daniels, and the famous team of greys driven by John Parker. John asked if he could follow hounds *driving* his four in hand as he had with him a group of ladies on a driving course. I helped him by following hounds via the gateways to show him the best routes and we hunted for an hour and a half with John Parker cantering his team across country. There was an abundance of stubbles and we covered a lot of country.

We carried on with threes early mornings each week and on 22nd October had a brilliant morning following the meet at Dennington Bell. This was mostly on the grass at Dennington Hall and hounds

---

[6] A van is a strong four-wheeled cart used for commercial work; the name was copied when motor vehicles appeared.

just flew. Thirty-five people were out and I failed to get home to see the beagles meet at the Hall at half past one. I met them moving off and hurried in to change and was just walking out of the drive when Mike and Kaz Bryan arrived and I was able to ride in their Range Rover, finding hounds at Severals Lane, just behind Dennington village. Unusually I hunted on a Tuesday on 25th October at the request of John Parker who wanted to bring nine of his grooms out hunting to thank them for all their help during the driving season.

The Opening Meet at Framlingham on 27th October proved to be a disaster when everything went wrong. There were only forty-two mounted, the lowest number for many years. The usual draw was almost completely drilled up with wheat so we drew Countess Wells Farm where there were still a few stubbles and enjoyed an hour or so of fun which included a fair-sized gate into some meadows. Nearly half the field jumped it. It is often said that bad luck comes in threes and so it turned out when poor Chris Bray's horse dropped dead under him on the stubbles at Countess Wells as this was the third horse to die on Opening Meet day on the same farm within my memory. There were too many hares to hunt correctly, only livened up by the fun at the beginning. When hacking to another draw we passed the place where our boxes had been left at Cransford and over half the field assumed that this was the end of the day, a mistake which should teach them to listen for 'Going Home' to be blown, as the day had not ended. There was a specially good Opening Meet Dance organised by the Supporters Club which was held in the Debenham Community Centre.

On 29th October at Charsfield Horse Shoes the ground was still rock hard and I blew for home at a quarter past two as the hounds' feet were too sore. The Hennessy hospitality was greatly missed and would have livened up the day. The same conditions prevailed at Worlingworth Swan on 3rd November and the only highlight was Graham Kerry who became a full subscriber and Bill Peart who read out an ode.

At Dennington Bell on 5th November I took only eight and a half couple as the ground was still like concrete and I left at home all the hounds that were going to Devon. When I was hunting with the Mid Devon Foxhounds at Gillingham there were two Masters out, Messrs Hickmott and Vickers. Mr Vickers and I gelled immediately and at the end of the day he invited me to bring my harriers and hunt hare on the moor. Unfortunately, Mr Vickers resigned the Mastership at the end of that season. I enquired of Mr

Hickmott if he was still willing to extend the invitation to which I had an unenthusiastic yes. I ought to have smelled a rat and not gone ahead with the idea. He was very unhelpful in the arrangements so Sheila and I went down and stayed at the Three Crowns Hotel in Chagford. It took a few days to find stabling for every member who wanted to come down. We booked the whole hotel which was nearly full, whilst some other members stayed elsewhere. I was so looking forward to this trip and hoped to hunt my harriers on the moor. I could get no direct answers from Mr Hickmott and found out too late that he appeared to be completely overawed by his huntsman, Bernard Parker, and needed his permission before replying, a state of affairs which is not to be encouraged in any hunt.

I left home on Sunday 6th November at five o'clock in the morning and picked up Tim Last and his horse. Thirty-one members elected to go and all arrived safely with their horses. A lovely party was held in the Crown that night. What a difference there is between hunts. Our hosts and the Easton were chalk and cheese. Not a single member of the Mid Devon, nor their Master, came during the evening to greet us. Such a contrast with the Easton who would have turned out had the roles been reversed.

On Monday 7th November the Easton Harriers met by invitation at Pawton Gate near Chagford in Devon. The morning started off with a little fun as my joint Master came downstairs with his spurs on upside down and paid the traditional fine by buying champagne for all present. Several members of the Mid Devon joined us at the meet, including Mr Hickmott and his huntsman, and introductions were made. Hounds behaved very strangely and would not leave me, just as they would fly to me at the slightest touch of the horn when we were visiting the Waveney or Cambridgeshire Harriers and hunting in strange country. We used to call it their 'party manners'. In Devon the worry about being in a strange place was magnified to something approaching terror. At home I could send them to draw on their own to the far side of an enormous wheat field but here in Devon they would not venture more than a hundred yards away from me. They all kept running back to me for no apparent reason other than a fear of getting lost in this strange land. Three times I got off Bucks Fizz and drew bogs on foot but they would not leave me and draw properly. Hares were very scarce as we did not find although of course I did not expect to find easily with them drawing so badly. Mr Hickmott rode up to me and nervously asked me if I would mind having a short day as 'Parker had three bullocks to skin'. What a thing to say after we had travelled 310 miles to be there.

We arrived back in Chagford and eight of us trooped into the tea shop in full hunting gear for a proper Devon cream tea. The evening was rather subdued as we were all disappointed that the Mid Devon members were not welcoming with the exception of Herbert Parr, the peculiar behaviour of the Master who was really just a messenger boy for his huntsman, and the hounds' behaviour.

I had been so looking forward to this visit, thinking it would be the climax of my Mastership, but it turned out to be such a flop. The journey to Devon and two days spent finding stables, then two weeks later the journey with the hounds and hunt horses, 31 members and their horses, all making the 310 mile journey. It was heart breaking and I have never been so upset about anything in all the years of my Mastership. The evening was brightened up by the arrival of Sue Gooderham, Jill Sillars, Sarah Edmundson, and the Quilters who were staying elsewhere, and then Herbert Parr arrived and was worth a guinea a minute. He kept insisting that the girls should wear mini-skirts for the skittles match the next night.

The next day almost all of us were out for the meet of the East Devon Foxhounds at Upton Farm, Payhembury. Mr Bartlett, the Master, made us very welcome and the hospitality was excellent. We found a fox at once in some sugar beet which they went on to catch.

The only exciting thing that happened after that was that Demelza jumped me off at a wall. Hounds had to contend with a blue haze which is a sure sign of bad scent but hunted very diligently and impressed me with their perseverance. At four o'clock I said to Mr Bartlett that I was ready to go home and he agreed and said how sad he was that he did not know we were coming down to Devon or else he would have given us a day. We had another session in the tea room and the manager was delighted to see us.

Next morning we set off very early for the meet of the North Dartmoor Beagles at the Taw Valley Inn, Sticklepath. The reason for going early was that I wanted to call at the King's Arms at South Zeal to see the landlord who had provided so much fun for us East Anglians during a folk festival. He soon had the pub open although it was before time. I introduced him to everybody. After a pleasant half an hour we moved on to the meet where the Master and Huntsman, Tim Whitley, made us most welcome. The members of the

two packs gelled together immediately and there was a good atmosphere. There were screams of laughter when I tried to pay for a round with a £50 note which my joint Master grabbed and posted into the Poppy Day Appeal box. An Easton member who was making a video film was very upset to have missed this incident and asked for a mock repeat which went well except that Mark put the second note into the box as well. This caused even louder howls of laughter mixed with astonishment at such an extravagant joke. The laughter was rekindled when the landlord calmly said 'That will go well with the £1.50 already in there.' One of our younger members who was known to be quite thrifty was all for cutting off the lid of the box. Mark refunded the second half of the joke and gave me £50 during the evening.

I followed hounds as they drew some fodder beet but the sticky red mud I found very hard going and soon accepted a lift with Mike and Kaz Bryan who were following in their Range Rover. We could see nothing as the Devon banks were so high and soon lost hounds. I suggested the Bryans might like to see a real old-fashioned pub so we adjourned to the Drewe Arms at Drewsteignton. During that evening I was told that I could not have my promised second day on the moor with my hounds. I was so upset and disappointed at the dismal failure of this trip when all the other visits to other packs had gone well, the Picardie Valois in France, and the Holcombe and Rockwood Harriers in England. This trip in my final season was to have been the grand finale with the pleasure of hunting the Easton hounds on the moor. I made the same mistake as many another and tried to drown my sorrows with the result that I needed to take myself off to bed in the middle of the party and missed some good singing.

Thursday saw us at the meet of the South Devon Foxhounds at Haytor Rocks and Friday was free for everyone to do as they pleased with the official joint dinner that evening. I went to bed at half past twelve, leaving the party in full swing which carried on until half past two. On Saturday the meet of the Mid Devon was at Postbridge near Princetown. My good friends Anne and Tony St Quinton had come down for the dinner the previous evening and we followed together on foot and managed to get a tongue lashing from an angry farmer who told us to keep to the footpath. Sunday saw us all on the road back to Suffolk.

Back at home at Henley Cross Keys on Thursday 17th November was uneventful except that a pony jumped out and the owners was very angry. Tom and Sandy Walne went to see them for me and left them reasonably happy. We enjoyed a red letter day at Stradbroke Ivy House on Saturday 19th. Hounds ran hard all day and covered a lot of country, some of which was not in our draw but fortunately none of the affected farmers minded. One well hunted hare even crossed the bridge into Ernie and Mary Calver's garden and we ended the day at dusk near Duncan Morton's Rectory Farm.

On Tuesday 22nd the Cambridgeshire Harriers met at Dennington Hall at half past twelve. This was convenient for all the visiting members but the reason was that there had been some sharp frosts in the mornings and I did not want them to come all that way then have to wait. They were again very naughty on rabbits and pheasants and I spent a considerable time guarding a pheasant release pen in Sunflower Wood. I had to stop hounds which was a great shame as they were hunting very well at the time. Theresa Rous gave us all a splendid tea. Five people put up their horses in the stables at Tannington Hall before coming in for one of Sheila's dinners. Twelve Cambridgeshire and forty-four Easton sat down to home made soup followed by salt beef, and after dinner there were some recitations, jokes, and songs, and the evening was as much fun as usual.

We were at Wetheringsett Cat and Mouse on Saturday 26th but were rather restricted for country as the foxhounds had upset so many people. There was dreadful anxiety when hounds were running hard towards the main A140 road. I turned Demelza across the wheat and she seemed to know the danger and really galloped and I was just in time to stop hounds. I dismounted and stood by her side feeling very emotional at her effort. As she galloped she seemed a hand lower than usual and I did not touch her with my whip. As I stood beside her, her heaving sides where making the saddle stand up in the air.

On Tuesday 29th we were the guests of the Dunston Harriers at Roseville, Carlton road. The day started off well with a champagne breakfast at the home of Robert Bothway and it was a good scenting day but I got fed up as hounds were continually being whipped off as so many farmers had banned the hunt. The meet at Bedfield Crown was uneventful on 3rd December providing good sport. A red letter day followed with the Special Day on Monday 5th December. This was different from the more usual Gentlemen's Days in that I had asked for twelve members to pay £250 each for four private days' hunting with dinner afterwards at Tannington Hall, each member to bring his own wines, although I provided drinks on arrival, i.e. whisky, gin, sherry, and so forth. I would bear the costs

and all moneys raised would go to hunt funds where it was desperately needed. The following volunteered immediately: Paul and Jacky Yeldham, Mike and Kaz Bryan, Bill and Margaret James, Brian and Michael Sawyer, Mick Abbot, Michael Buckley, Rod Thorpe, Chris Durrell, Idwal Humphrey, and Duncan Morton. We met at Dennington Bell where most of us sat down to a huge breakfast. Hounds ran hard all day and I was very pleased to see my second horse at half past one. We covered a lot of country between the A1120 and Laxfield village, and a brace and a half of well hunted hares were killed. We stopped for a half of bitter each at Dennington Queen and finished in the dark in the orchards at Valley Farm Brundish. A delicious dinner was provided by my long suffering wife: salmon mousse, jugged hare, fruit tart and syllabub, ending with devils on horseback.

The Essex and Suffolk Foxhounds invited us to a meet at Bluegates, Wherstead, the home of the Master George Paul. Mary Paul was in hospital but George had received good news so was in a particularly jovial mood. A large table stood in the centre of the paddock with all one could wish for upon it. The country was simply wonderful after our sticky plough, much lighter land near the Orwell River with plenty of small woods. Scent was not good but was a real 'serving' scent i.e. it lasts but the hounds have to work for it. At one time, down near the river, we saw six herons standing in a row in a field, looking like posts. We caught a brace of well hunted hares. George Paul had said that he could not give a tea as Mary was not there but did so just the same. I ended my diary entry with: '*A lovely day and a joy to be there.*' Following this day I was very pleased to receive a lovely letter from Cherry Clarke saying how impressed she was with my hounds.

Another exceptional day followed the meet at Dennington Queen on Saturday 10th December. The first run took us from Dennington village to Fiddler's Hall at Cransford during which my joint Master was knocked from his horse as he was watching hounds instead of looking where he was going. The next run was very fast and took us from Countess Wells to Laxfield Station yard. It was so fast that our horses were covered in white lather and even the hounds were puffing. We celebrated the grand day when we returned to the Queen, especially the two joint Masters, and I was not quite at my best to take my mother to the Bears Restaurant in Wickham Market. I lost all my brownie points and was not at all popular.

Dennington again produced a red letter day a week later. We drew for ages and finally found and had a very fast hunt to Laxfield. My joint Master and I were the only ones to finish this hunt and, thinking that the Field Master Terence Saffell would anticipate our intention, we went to the Low House pub for half time. To save time Mark bought 24 whiskies and was waiting for the field to appear but they did not. I suppose we had a couple each but I cannot remember what we did with the others.

Dennington Bell provided yet another grand day on 24th December. A great run started the day and hounds ran unaided for an hour and twenty minutes. Only four horses finished this run and as we rested our horses the others came up one by one until I decided to draw again. It was first class hunting all the rest of the day until we finished in the darkness. A young bitch called Wedlock was missing and Tony St Quinton and I eventually found her at Castle Farm Badingham. We heard her speaking and eventually found her staggering along like a drunken man, having hunted herself almost to a standstill.

Boxing Day attracted the usual large crowd and the collection for David Horsfield amounted to £640. Hunting was very messy with hounds constantly dividing on fresh hares. That evening I wrote four letters of resignation, one to my joint Master, one to the Chairman, one to Rupert Montagu my Secretary, and finally one to David Horsfield to terminate his employment with me on 30th April.

On 2nd January there was a huge crowd at Cretingham Bell for the New Year's Day meet. Hunting was extremely poor with seven deer and six hares in one field. I was so fed up that I went home instead of joining in the usual party afterwards. A very successful Hunt Ball was again held at Framlingham College on Wednesday 4th January with 250 sitting down to dinner and roughly the same after dinner. Tickets were £25 and £12. The members could at times bring me to tears with their lack of support and of those at the Ball only Sarah Edmundson was there the next morning to help me with Idwal Humphrey, and John Capon coming along later.

Hounds met at Stradbroke Ivy House on 5th January 1989 and an above-average day followed with two particularly good little hunts. One of our younger bachelor members was very slow in courting and Maurice Scott and I used to amuse ourselves by fixing him up with dates which produced problems such as the girl from Wickham Market who was dumped because 'it was too far out of his way'. Our latest effort was a girl who hunted and when we were in the pub afterwards, Brian Sawyer telephoned to ask me to keep everyone there. Half an hour later he arrived

from Ipswich with a ring and made an announcement saying that our bachelor had commissioned him to buy the ring, regardless of price. This was, of course, a complete fabrication and it was a cheap ring but, sadly, when he tried to put the ring on Paula's finger, it was too small. This set the scene for a party during which I sang 'Marry the girl that you love, boys!' My son-in-law, Bill Vaudrey, called in on his way back from London returning the candelabra used at the hunt ball so he was able to drive my Joint Master and myself home where we continued the fun by opening a bottle of Pure Douro Port '37 imported and bottled by R Miller & Sidgwick Ltd, Ipswich, which I had bought, with two others, from a man who did house clearances.

My sister Sarah gave a splendid hunt breakfast before the meet at Hoxne Grapes on Saturday 14th January. We enjoyed excellent beef and ham from Horham Post Office, which was well known for its quality, baked potatoes and home-made bread. There was great laughter when Dougie Ruth covered his beef with home-made marmalade mistaking it for chutney. The country was good and open and the hunting quite good but the atmosphere was spoiled by two accidents. Ian Cook's horse stumbled over a stump and Ian broke his collarbone, then David Bond had a fall and was concussed, although he might have been killed if he had not been wearing the new type of safety hat.

A Special Day took place on Monday 16th January at Dennington Bell which was one of the four private days to be held.[8] After two and a half hours of very good hunting we stopped at the Hall and stabled horses and hounds, leaving us free to go inside for lunch. Bill and Margaret James were very late coming in for lunch so, although we waited for them, we pretended otherwise and, a spy having told us when they left the stables, we all trooped out as if we had finished our lunch. Their faces were a picture and Margaret looked as if she would burst into tears. The only alcohol to be served throughout lunch was the 'John Turner', the only truly Suffolk drink which is a mixture of mild beer and gin. I had bought three gallons of mild beer and two bottles of gin and after lunch there was none left. It took some time to find after lunch and then we ran hard well into the dark and with difficulty I stopped hounds in the valley not far from Fosdyke's Bridge. As I stood blowing

---

[8] The others were on 20th January and 7th February.

and 'coping' for the missing hounds the moon was rising and shining down on us all and the sound of my 'coping' - 'Come away cup, come away cup, come away cup, co co' - was echoing down the valley. We could clearly hear the missing hounds speaking, some at Brundish Grove and some at Tannington Lodge but David Horsefield arrived bringing the last of the hounds and we were 'all on'. As it was so dark I thought it was better to go home across country but David persuaded me otherwise saying, that if we put up another hare, we would never stop them with scent as good as it was. It was pitch black as we all headed along the road from Fosdyke Bridge to the Bell and passing motorists were justly annoyed and blared their hooters at us which was not a good end to such a lovely day.

An excellent day surprised us at Crowfield Rose on 19th January. The pub was packed to overflowing and a grand atmosphere filled the whole room. I drew Paris Farm and hit off the line of a fox which I recognised because most of the hounds would not speak and those who did spoke with deeper voices. Hounds ran to a pond, cast themselves round the edge, then hit off the line and ran heel way making it easy for me to stop them. They found a hare and ran across Peter Wright's farm to the new house where the Ashbocking Nelson had once stood, crossing the road where the Pratt family ran to open their gates to allow us to gallop through their farmyard, crossing to Burghersh Place, where hounds swung right-handed and crossed the road just below Henley School. They went on Mr Self's Walnut Tree Farm where I had to gallop across the middle of a wheat field to keep hounds in sight. They eventually checked close to Henley Cross Keys. I did not let them cast themselves as we were well out of our draw. When this run started, I called to Tony St Quinton to keep close to me and this he did, apart from when I crossed the wheat. How he enjoyed himself. It took half an hour for the field to catch up and when I offered to draw again they all said they would prefer if I blew for home as their horses were spent. Once back at the Rose, we settled down to a feast of lamb chops. I had quite enough to drink but kept in sufficiently good order to dine later with Jacky and Paul Yeldham, my Joint Master being the only other guest. The main point of this dinner was to discuss the possibility of Mark and Paul as Joint Masters to take over from me.

Saturday 21st January provided yet another exceptional day when hounds met at Glemham. Firstly two small hunts took place on the airfield then they found a third hare, which ran a most unusual line. Hounds flew along with a great cry and scent was so good that every hound was speaking. They ran over to Pound Farm, then swung towards Parham North Green. Just before the green they turned towards Framlingham, then right-handed crossing Little Lonely Farm, Fiddlers Hall, to just short of Cransford. They swung left-handed almost to Herman Seggons farm then left again to Mr Larter's farm on the edge of Framlingham. During this remarkable run, hounds were not helped in any way and it was one of those occasions when I could not have done so even if I had wished, as I was never near enough to them. This had been Sheila's birthday and as a present I took her the next day to the Wentworth at Aldeburgh for a 'Bargain Break' but, as usual, I had to combine business with pleasure and I invited the Yeldhams and Mark to dine with us on Sunday night to further discuss the possible Joint Mastership.

A Committee Meeting was held on Wednesday 25th January to discuss the applications for the Mastership. There were various options to be considered, the first being Robert Bothway as Acting Master, i.e. all bills to be sent to the Honorary Secretary to be paid directly by the hunt but all other duties of administration to be carried out by the Acting Master. The second was Robert Bothway and Jeffrey Bowden as Joint Masters, with a guarantee, the third Jeffrey Bowden as sole Master, with a guarantee, and the fourth Mark Wayne and Paul Yeldham as Joint Masters, with a guarantee. After much discussion, the latter offer was considered to be the best and the committee were unanimous in their decision which would then be taken to the AGM for final approval of the members.

Occold on 26th and Knodishall on 28th January were ordinary days with a brace being caught each day but January 30th found us at the Willoughby Arms at Parham for the third Special Day. The atmosphere in this wonderful old pub was of the best; it had not been changed or decorated in over thirty years and had a nicotine and smoke patina on cupboard doors and ceiling alike. The day's hunting was above average and a brace was caught. The ladies were, as usual, asked to dine in the evening, this time at Tannington Hall and we had goose.

There was another outstanding day on 2nd February from Thorndon Black Horse. The first hare ran a very straight line to beyond the Cedars keeping uncomfortably close to the main A140 through Wetheringsett and checked behind the Manor Hotel. Hounds cast themselves and killed her on her form.

I felt it 'prudent' to rest the horses outside the hotel and was delighted when some car followers arrived and bought the drinks. I hacked back into the draw and found another hare on John Edwards' farm which gave us one of the fastest hunts I can recall with the Easton Harriers. I was riding a really good little horse called Max but could not help wishing I was on my thoroughbred Bucks Fizz. She did not run straight but took a large-scale zig-zag route to within a field of Wetheringsett Manor Hotel and I wondered if we would have a repeat performance at the hotel but she did not dwell and ran on to be caught five minutes later. During most of this hunt, although riding at maximum speed and never hesitating at ditches or crossing the four roads, I could only hear the cry and occasionally saw a tail hound. This run proved the point that we must breed for voice as well as nose.

Blaxhall Ship meet was always looked forward to as it normally had more than its share of fun but when hounds met there on 4th February it proved to be a very sad day. The first hare was found near the meet and ran to Gables Farm then swung left-handed towards the airfield. We galloped into a field which appeared to be unploughed but half of which was ploughed. Heavy rains had blended the unploughed and ploughed into one colour, just sandy light soil, and it was impossible to see the difference.

Louis Borrett

Hounds were running fast and I was the first one to hit the ploughed part. My horse plunged up to his knees in the loose, sandy soil and I was thrown up his neck but somehow managed to stay on and immediately raised my arm to signal people to stop. Sadly, Louis Borrett did not see my hand or could not stop quickly enough and his horse came down causing him serious injury. An ambulance was sent for and, because of the nature of this light land was able to drive quite close but as a result of this accident Louis was paralysed from the upper chest downwards. Louis was one of the best members, always thoughtful, generous, and cheerful.

The rest of the day was very poor. I could put no heart in what I was doing and blew for home at two o'clock. There were seven singers of local songs waiting for us as Blaxhall is renowned for its singing but I explained what had happened and that singing would not be appropriate and most of us went home quite soon.

Pettistree Greyhound was the setting for another Gentlemen's Day on 7th February but scent was absolutely non-existent. I drew right across to Dallinghoo, then Letheringham but hounds could do nothing except find their hare i.e. they could find but not hunt. Feeling flat, I decided to try to brighten things up a little so we made our way to Easton White Horse. Unfortunately it was shut but David came to the rescue and offered drinks at the kennels and after some beer and champagne, we felt quite buoyant. We found two more hares on the way back but the longest hunt was a hundred yards. Mary and Ernie Calver provided a delicious dinner at Town Farm, Wilby, for the twenty-two guests who paid £6 per head, and the two Masters elect were not charged. After dinner, Maurice Scott auctioned two day's hunting for the British Field Sports Society. These were bought by Bill James and Mike Bryan for £50 each.

Rendham White Horse proved very foggy but I waited until half past two and was then able to hunt. The new Mastership had a man on trial from the Essex and Suffolk Foxhounds and they asked me for my opinion but I thought he was not experienced enough. Too many hares ruined the day and the meet at Otley on 11th February was spoiled by the extraordinary behaviour of the Helmingham Estate keepers who had blocked almost every gateway with old machinery or barbed wire. This caused us to have to jump some ditches where the banks were riddled with rabbit holes and were very unsafe but there was one highlight in the day. Sally Dunlop, who had hunted with the Easton from childhood and was often involved in the activities, was getting married at Framsden church and I knew that Maurice Scott was driving them in his carriage so I took hounds to the church and all the field formed a guard of honour as she drove away. I think she was suitably touched by the gesture as she had tears in her eyes.

Wetheringsett Cat and Mouse provided yet another 'red letter day' on 10th February with three very good hunts all running out of our draw on to Mr Styles farm. Two more little hunts took us into the cider orchards at Aspall where we found our last hare which took us at great speed to Stoke Ash, checking just short of the A140. The Masters elect asked me to let David Horsefield hunt hounds at Easton on 18th February so I kept away and walked the country for Monday but Tony St Quinton was out on Rose and my daughter Bridget on Demelza who later told me that David had hunted them well and was quiet and steady. I was so pleased to hear this as I felt my hounds would be left in good hounds.

Brian Sawyer provided parking space for the lorries at Little Choppins for the last of the Special Days held at Coddenham Duke, now very appropriately kept by Jim and Hilda Wickham who provided breakfast of either cold beef or traditional English eggs and bacon. The scent was good enough to provide us with two good hunts which between them took us into Stonham Aspall where the Ten Bells was well-placed for half-time. Idwal Humphrey had hired a horse from Rozzie Theobald's stables which coincidentally was the same one that Louis Borrett had been riding on the day of his terrible accident, and it dropped dead but Brian Sawyer kindly provided Idwal with another horse and he joined us at the Ten Bells. An excellent dinner was held at Mr Underhill's restaurant at Stonham on the A140.

David hunted hounds again at Worlingworth on Thursday 23rd as I wanted to attend the thanksgiving service for Mary Paul. East Anglia lost one of its finest Masters with the death of Mary. She had been Joint Master of the Essex and Suffolk Foxhounds with her husband George for ten years until 1985 and would have gone on longer but for her illness. The Masters-elect had John Harrison on trial from the Vine and Craven who proved to be a good man and became first whipper-in to the Easton the following season. This would be the first time the Easton Harriers had had a professional huntsman and whipper-in since the days of the Committee-run Mastership, prior to me taking over. The Point-to-Point was held at Higham on 25th February with Jim Hardwick winning the Members' Race on Rafferty and Karen Wainer coming second riding Autumn Lady which belonged to Harry Spencer. Stephen Appleby fell at the third fence but the greatest shame of all was that Harry Spencer was far ahead when he was unseated when his horse pecked badly three fences from home. This was a terrible shame as Harry had so wanted to win the Members' Race.

A British Field Sports Society Meet was held at Laxfield Kings Head on Monday 27th February, for which everyone who rode paid £25 to the BFSS, and proved to be another exceptional day. There were two

or three nice little hunts, then hounds divided and I stood near Jill Graham's Woodlands Farm, Brundish, blowing for them until they were all on. Then I drew the nearby orchards and hounds put their noses down and, making full use of the clean, spray-free grass in the orchards, they just flew. I knew from earlier in the day that scent was first class and these wonderful hounds did not need any help as they raced through Tannington to Mr Havers at Valley Farm, Worlingworth, where they turned and ran to Horham. With only the briefest of checks, they swung back and raced across Stanway Green Farm, Worlingworth, Rectory Farm at Wilby and finally stopping at Wilby Hall. I think this hare was caught but am not sure. The horses were quite spent so I decided to hack back to Tannington Hall and left both horses and hounds there. Only Robert Bothway and Mike Bryan saw the end of this remarkable hunt and the remainder of the field stretched back for well over a mile. I went back to the meet in my pick-up to enjoy a singing session to beat all singing sessions which showed no sign of stopping until half past seven.

The Dunston Harriers met by invitation at the Kettleburgh Chequers on Wednesday, 1st March, bringing with them 12½ couple. I had sent a duplicated letter to every Dunston member telling them how to find Maurice Scott's at Brook Farm where the boxes were to be left and that there would be a taxi service to ferry everyone to the meet. In my diary I wrote: '*David the huntsman was quieter than I thought he would be but perhaps this was due to it being his first day out since he was kicked. The winds were too strong for serious hunting but they never really tried, the slightest touch on the horn brought them hurrying to David. As every check they just stood still, staring David in the face begging for help! Real Cambridgeshire "second eleven". Such a shame after how they were once which, in my opinion, the best in England.*[9] *It is terrible to think that a first-class pack should be ruined for a piece of crinkled red ribbon known as a rosette, what is their hour of glory at Peterborough compared to 250 hours of good hunting*'.

On Saturday 4th March hounds met at Brundish Crown and I was disappointed to see such a small field, only thirty or so which included four visitors from the Essex and Suffolk. I wanted to get across country to hunt near Stradbroke but every hare found ran back across Harvey land at Tannington. Scent was first class and one hare took us from Cole Street, Wilby, to

---

[9] This was during the three seasons 1968–71, between the end of my first Mastership and the beginning of the second, when I hunted with them two days a week.

Fenton's Farm, Dennington, then right-handed over Tim Last's farm at World's End. I just managed to stop them on the edge of Saxtead Green. The visitors were delighted and declared they had enjoyed a grand day. That evening the End of Season Ball was again held at Brome Grange and 146 people sat down to an excellent dinner with Brian Sawyer and Chris Durrell looking splendid in their new green tailcoats. I gave an old oil-painting of myself on Paddy, with Fred Hargreaves, my first kennel huntsman, on Embassy and hounds for auction but someone suggested that it should be a 'Dutch' auction where the auctioneer starts at a high figure and works down until he finds a bidder. I was furious as it made only £165 when, with Maurice Scott as auctioneer, I thought it might have made as much as £650. I was so angry that I knew that I would lose my temper and spoil the ball so I went to my chalet where I remained for most of the evening.

Thursday 9th March saw hounds meeting at Yaxley Cherry Tree. We drew Pip Moore's farm first but, not finding there, we crossed the Eye road and via Rapsy Tapsy Lane, reached the Grover family farm. Found at once and enjoyed a good little hunt which was enough to show me that the scent was good. When walking the country the day before I had called in, as I usually did, on my school friend Ted Saunders at Braiseworth. He was never keen on having the mounted field trooping around but after a cup of tea and something a little stronger he had said we were welcome. Nevertheless, my penultimate day of

The honour guard at the last meet

hunting hounds was spoiled and the atmosphere ruined because when I went to draw Ted's lovely low meads, which were always a highlight meandering along the river, we discovered that someone had sealed off every gateway, either by tying the gate shut or, where there was no gate, with barbed wire. There was no stock out and it had clearly been done that morning as it was all open when I had walked round the day before. I was deeply hurt but the Easton Harriers had always managed to rise above its troubles and, on this occasion, it took the form of a half-time at Gordon Grover's. Generous amounts of 'fuel' soon

put matters right and we ended the day with the best run of all and caught our hare.

My last day hunting the Easton Harriers was appropriately at Worlingworth Swan on 11th March. This was where, thirty-six years previously, a very nervous and very rustic boy had watched from the gateway at the Grange Farm to see the Easton Harriers move off and had followed, scared witless, and dismounting to lead his horse over every ditch. I carried the horn for the first time when I hunted the drag hounds from Grundisburgh Dog in November 1963 and first hunted the harriers on 27th January 1964 at Glemham Crown. Now, having carried the horn for 1,153 days, I was doing so for the last time. It was far more emotional than anyone would have realised. The meet was wonderful, with everyone full of that special Easton camaraderie. I had so many drinks offered to keep that I could have been drunk for three weeks but I kept a tight check on myself. As we prepared to move off, the area immediately around the pub suddenly became horseless as Maurice Scott had organised a mounted guard of honour which stretched up to the Grange Farm entrance, to the very spot where I had stood on my first ever day. I felt extremely moved and emotional.

Hounds found their first hare on Bull's Hall land and it was soon apparent that the scent was of the best as they raced across Bedfield Hall land and Hungers Green, Primrose Farm, Monk Soham, and the Grove, before dropping down towards the low road that runs from Earl Soham to Kenton. I thought they would cross the road but they swung right handed and ran more or less parallel to the road to just short of Kenton village where the scent was not quite as good. They managed to stick to the line and returned via Monk Soham Green Farm, where she was given best. I hacked on slowly to allow the horses a breather, returning to the intended draw towards Saxtead. Two moderate hunts followed until it was decided to hold half-time at the Saxtead Volunteer. Unbeknown to me, Bill Peart asked the landlord if he could have the tiny tumbler I had been drinking from and weeks later presented me with the same glass inscribed by John Finch with the words

'Last day, last drop.' I then did a foolish thing and drew behind the pub, knowing full well that there were usually far too many hares there. It was so, and hounds divided into three. I eventually stopped my group and then waited at Dial Farm where I blew and blew until I had them 'all on'.

No one can possibly know how I felt during these last moments with my beloved hounds. When parents have a child abducted they must feel absolutely devastated but in my case I had made the decision to stop hunting my hounds and it was more akin to parents reluctantly giving away their child and watching it go. I wanted to spend a little longer with them so I decided to hack slowly back to the kennels as it was about the same distance as back to the meet. David Horsefield was not pleased but, having taken hounds back to the kennels, I then turned round for the long hack back to Tannington. The nine miles or so were broken up with three pit stops, with Robert Taylor at Kettleburgh Rectory Farm, then with Will Edmundson at Dial Farm, and finally with David Steel's sister Libby at Red House. Old Bucks Fizz and I were both glad to see the stables and I went indoors but was soon besieged with visitors. No one could understand that I did not feel like going into the pub as I was far too emotional. They pressed me to go with them, saying that the landlady had prepared an incredible feast including a cake with huntsman and hounds on it. I would not go and they eventually left saying they would be back. The day ended round the kitchen table, eating fish and chips while drinking champagne.

I had expressed the wish to hold another tailcoat dinner but this was one too many for Sheila. I hoped to have it at my club in Ipswich but the chef left the week before so it was eventually held at Pettistree House. This was well-known for its smorgasbord menu but I planned a seven-course dinner, bringing my own wines from my cellar. Twenty-nine of us sat at a traditional horseshoe-shaped hunting table with all of us sitting round the outer edge and the serving done from the centre. Those present were Mark Wayne, Terence and Nick Saffell, Rupert Montagu, Ernie Calver, Paul Yeldham, Robert Haag, John Finch, Gordon Grover, Michael Buckley, Tim Last, Robert Bothway, Jeffrey Bowden, Patrick and Will Edmundson, Maurice Scott, Nigel Chapman, Tony St Quinton, Idwal Humphrey, Jim Hardwicke, Mike Bryan, Bill James, Brian Sawyer, John Capon, Ernie and Richard Baker, David Steel, Chris Durrell and myself. I was very pleased with the evening and the horseshoe shaped table made the perfect setting for the green coats.

It was with a psychological jolt that I realised that my mastership had really ended. My life had been so absorbed in the complexities of the mastership that it had long been the major reason for my existence. To earn a living and above all to earn enough to cover my considerable expenses with the hunt. Fattening pigs was my main business and I was lucky in that it was quite profitable at that time. I had three children to educate and this was the only expense that I would have put above the hunt if forced to make a decision. It was very convenient to me that I was registered with the taxman as a horse dealer, having earned my living solely from that during my late teens, and during that time my hunt subscription was a legitimate expense. This enabled all the expenses of the hunt to be set against my income. My accountant pointed out to the Inland Revenue that the Mastership would enable me to deal more successfully so it was agreed that the hunt guarantee should be counted as income and the expenses as outgoings since it was too complicated to separate the expenses between the hunt and dealing. The fact that there was very little dealing was conveniently overlooked so somehow or other I managed to struggle through.

I received considerable comfort from knowing that the high standards I felt so important would be maintained when Mark Wayne took over as Senior Master. Mark really loved the Easton Harriers and would go to any lengths to see that things were done well. I had always believed in the old saying that old Masters, like old hounds, should be put down. This, of course, implies that they should not meddle in the new regime and certainly not ever suggest that they would have done things differently. I believed that if I had attended any meets there would have been a strong possibility that hounds would leave their new huntsman and come to me, so strong was the bond between us. There was an even greater reason for keeping away and that was that I could not bear to look. Two summers later the Easton paraded in the Grand Ring at the Suffolk Show. When they came into the ring I was sitting in front of the Vice Presidents' tent and I got up and walked away. It must have looked terrible but I just could not help it. Later that year I was pressed by a small gang of Easton members for an explanation of this strange behaviour and I could see that they were not to be fobbed off. I needed to think of a suitable explanation and told them this story. I said to them, 'Have you ever been dumped by a girl you were very fond of? Well, it's like this. When you see her at a party with another man, it hurts and you have to look away. Then you feel compelled to look again and it hurts again so it would have been better if you had not been to the party.' And so I kept away from the hounds.

Left to right, back row:
M. Buckley, T. Last , R. Baker, N. Chapman, C. Plumb, C. Corner, W. Edmondson, E. Baker, J. Finch, W. James
Middle row:
M. Bryan, D. Steel, R. Bothway, A. St Quinton, M. Scott, J. Hardwicke, G. Grover, R. More, B. Sawyer
Front row:
I. Cook, E. Calver, R. Haag, P. Yeldham, Tony Harvey, T. Saffell, J. Bowden, C. Durrell, R. Montague

SONGS

THE BATTERED BRIGADE

The mark of a stake on the shoulder,
the brand of a wall on the knee,
are scars to the careless beholder,
and blemishes so it may be.
But every such blemish endorses
the pluck of a steed unafraid,
and the heart of a lover of horses,
goes out to the battered brigade.

Their knocks have been gathered in duty,
their scars in the front of the fray.
It isn't your cleanest legged beauty
that's there at the end of the day.
When 5ft of timber before us
has half of the pretty ones stayed,
if you mean to catch up with the chorus
come on with the battered brigade,

Turned out in the finest of fettle,
'tis sometimes the soundest that fail,
and would rather hear hooves on the metal
than follow the rattle of rail.
But out on the grass with hounds racing,
and fences as big as they're made,
the cream of the gay steeplechasing,
is left to the battered brigade

Their line is the line of the foxes,
their pace is the pace of the pack.
Though tomorrow they stand in their boxes
as stiff as the props of a stack.
But I'll lay you my cheque at the bankers
they're forward next week undismayed.
Here's good luck to the blemished front rankers,
Hats off to the battered brigade.

THE SIX FELL PACKS

Now I'll give you a toast, lads, to all the fell packs,
To Masters and Huntsmen and Whips of aw maks,
You can have your athletics and games of all sorts,
But this hunting is surely the greatest of sports,
    Tally-ho, tally-ho, tally-ho,
    Hark forrad, good hounds, tally-ho.

John Peel was t'first hunter to gain lasting fame,
At Caldbeck not long since they honoured his name.
Bill Porter, Jim Dalton are others we know,
Then rivalling Peel there came Bowman - Old Joe.
    Tally-ho, tally-ho, tally-ho,
    Hark forrad, good hounds, tally-ho.

On t'North side there's t'Eskdale, wi' Porter's son, Jack,
Harry Hardisty's proud of his laal Melbreak pack,
Geordie Bell hunted t'Cathra for many a year,
Johnnie Richardson now keeps those foxes in fear,
    Tally-ho, tally-ho, tally-ho,
    Hark forrad, good hounds, tally-ho.

And when Bowman retired, they engaged a new lad
As Ullswater Whip – and he hasn't done bad.
He's stayed 40 years and he's still going the rounds,
So here's to Joe Wear and his Ullswater hounds
    Tally-ho, tally-ho, tally-ho,
    Hark forrad, good hounds, tally-ho.

We next come to one who to hunting was born.,
He's the fourth generation to carry the horn.
Anthony Chapman's the name, as I hardly need say.,
And how those Coniston hounds love his "Hoo git away",
    Tally-ho, tally-ho, tally-ho,
    Hark forrad, good hounds, tally-ho.

So there's yan laal pack left, hunting plain open fell,
And whose foxes are apt to go straight-necked to hell,
But Walt Parkin's young pack has caught up with the rest.
And the Lunesdale can now hold its own with the best.
    Tally-ho, tally-ho, tally-ho,
    Hark forrad, good hounds, tally-ho.

So back to my toast to this greatest of sports,
Here's to hunters and hounds – and spare Reynard a
    thought.
May we follow the horn till it's our turn to die,
And if St. Peter has hounds he will hear us all cry
    Tally-ho, tally-ho, tally-ho,
    Hark forrad, good hounds, tally-ho.

D. P. Todd, Kendal. 1950's.

A FINE HUNTING DAY

'Twas a fine hunting day and as balmy as May.
And the hounds to the village will come,
Every friend will be there, and all trouble and care,
Will be left far behind us at home,
See servants and steed on their way,
And sportsmen their scarlet display;
Let's join the glad throng, and go laughing along,
And we'll all go out hunting to-day.
    Chorus:
    So we'll all go out hunting to-day,
    All nature balmy and gay;
    Let's join the. glad throng, that goes laughing along.
    And we'll all go out hunting to-day.

Farmer Hodge to his dame says "I'm sixty and lame,
Times are hard and my rent I can't pay,
But I don't care a jot, if I raise it or not,
For I must go out hunting to-day,
There's a hare in yon planting they say,
Let's find her and get her away;
I'll be first up yon hill, and be in at the kill,
For I must go out hunting to-day.
 Chorus:

See the doctor in boots, with a breakfast that suits,
Of strong home made ale and good beef,
His patient in pain says I've called once again.
To consult you in hope of relief,
To the poor he advice gives away;
To the rich he prescribes and takes pay,
But to all of them he said, you will shortly be dead.
If you don't go out hunting to-day.
 Chorus:

Then the judge sits in court and gets wind of the sport,
For the lawyers apply to adjourn,
And no witnesses come there is none left at home.
They have followed the hounds and the horn,
Says his worship, great fines they shall pay,
If they will not our summonses obey,
But 'tis very fine sport, so we'll break up the court.
And we'll all go out hunting to-day.
 Chorus:

Then the village bells chime there's a wedding at nine.
And the parson unites the fond pair;
But when he heard the sweet sound of the horn and
 the hound,
And he knew 'twas his time to be there,
Says he, "For your welfare I'll pray,
And regret I no longer can stay,
You are safely made one so quickly be gone,
For I must go out hunting to-day.
 Chorus:

None are left in the lurch, for all friends of the church,
The beadles and clerks, are all there,
They're determined to go, and shout "Tally HO"
And the bell ringers joined in the rear,
With bridegroom and bride in array,
Each one to the other did say,
Let's join the glad throng that goes laughing along,
And we'll all go out hunting to-day.
 Chorus:

Theres' only one cure for all maladies sure,
That reaches the heart to its core,
'Tis the sound of the horn on a fine hunting morn,
Whatever the heart wished for more,
It turneth the grim into gay,
Makes pain unto pleasure give way,
Turns the old into young and the weak into strong,
If they all go out hunting to-day.
 Chorus:

THE CHASE

Dedicated to Mr. Harold Floyd, Past Master of the Holme Valley Beagles.

Come out, come out, my merry, merry men,
Aye, Girls also who care,
From farm and shop, from mill and forge
Come chase the sportive hare.

The hay and corn is gathered in
The russet tints the trees
And blood runs thin, so health come win,
In autumn's cooling breeze.

September is a merry, merry month,
The month we all love well
For then we start the chase we love,
As records past will tell.

Our hills and dales with sportsmen fill,
And echoes ring all round.
Then hark away, we all feel gay,
And quickly clear the ground.

Our hares are a merry, merry lot,
We chase both brown and grey,
For hours they double, twist and turn,
At sundown, love to play

They're hardy, fleet and tricky, too,
We love their merry ways;
If one we lose, we quest around
Another one to raise.

Our hounds they are a merry, merry pack,
They fill us with delight,
For when they find a romping scent
They'll hunt from morn 'till night.

Though puss may leave them in the chase
They still stick upon the trail,
Til sportsmanship demands recall
Before her heart doth fail.

We love to rise on merry, merry morns
When breezes softly blow
When cares are light , and hearts are bright
And sun doth gently glow.

And as we roam o'er fields and woods,
And huntsman's horn doth sound
A happier lot you ne'er will find
Go search the world around.

When evening falls, a merry, merry crew,
Are found in village inn
In natures haunts we've spent the day
In man's we now begin.

With song and jest and laughter loud,
We'll pass the night away.
A happier lot you ne'er may find
Though search the world all o'er.

THE BALLAD OF THE EASTON HARRIERS

Come hear my song
I won't keep you too long,
'Tis of hounds from Easton I'll sing,
There's Sago and Tatler
And Primrose and Pratler,
Them all to the Meet I will bring.
There's Tangle the best of them all
For her help I often must call.
But the years unfold
And now she is old,
On her puppies my trust must now fall.
 Chorus:
 Let's all go a-hunting today,
 All nature is smiling and gay.
 Let's join the glad throng
 That goes laughing along,
 And we'll all go a-hunting today.

At the Opening Meet
With a jockey-type seat,
George Cooper his racehorse sat on.
When the first hare we found
Hooves began to pound
And George Cooper with the hounds was gone.
For this young man's welfare I said,
"Try behind the huntsman instead."
"Oh indeed!" said he,
"But where can he be?"
As through all my hounds he sped.
 Chorus:

I remember one day,
When fog caused a delay
And the Harriers met at Stradbroke.
We thought it great fun,
For we stayed there till one,
And then hunting was just a big joke.
We mounted our horse
With a stagger, of course,
And we had a most wonderful run.
We knew of no fear,
For we thought it was clear,
But, in fact, it was thicker at one!
 Chorus:

Said, Fred Seggons one day, "What can I say,
If the hunt on my land does come.
There'll be Clay, my Vet, I mustn't upset,
And John Moyle on my books has begun.
Capt. Marriott, my neighbour'11 be there
To fall out with him I don't dare.
I pretend to be teased,
But really I'm pleased
For without them no better I'd fare.
 Chorus:

Herbert Breeze does tell
That story so well
When the Harriers met at Southolt.
The first hare to be seen
Was killed on the green
At Wilby with never a fault.
Mr. Nesling, The Master, arrived
"Oh dear! I've no wind" he sighed.
Who can blow this horn
On this fine hunting morn,
For we've had the best run of our lives.
 Chorus:

We have often been told
About memories of old
All stories quite true, of course.
Who? In a pond one day
Had his wig float away,
'Twas the manager of Ipswich White Horse.
The poor man was quite full of shame
And never came hunting again.
We feel sorry for him,
Even though he could swim,
But misfortune has brought him to fame.
 Chorus:

He reigned over us
Without any fuss,
The Master for fourteen long years.
He'd tell us a tale
Which would never fail,
To amuse us till we were in tears.
Capt. Bernard from Ireland he came,
To take on these hounds he was game.
No-one can tell,
How he bred them so well,
But at Peterborough they quickly gained fame.
 Chorus:

"My hounds are all fed,
I'll go jumping," said Fred,
"See you all at Westerfield Show".
On that Skewbald horse
That bucks with such force,
At the open course I'll have a go.
For the water jump, Fred he was game,
But into the water he came
He said "Oh Dear!"
"I'm wet I fear,
I hope never to do that again."
 Chorus:

For his first ride,
At hunting he tried,
On the Master's old favourite mare.
Blaze jumped that first ditch
With never a hitch,
He said "'Tis fine sport I declare."
Ernie Calver with horse and cigar,
Behind hounds he's ne'er very far,
But at each thick fence
He must feel a bit tense,
But he never removes that cigar.
    Chorus:

On the Master's birthday,
We felt a bit gay,
So we went to Fram. Hare & Hounds,
Hunting songs to sing,
Till the whole house did ring
And the street was filled full of glad sounds.
The landlord's a jolly fine sport,
And the Harriers he helps to support,
He sang about wealth
And he drank to our health
For he's one of the very best sort.
    Chorus:

So cruelly the snow
In our faces did blow
When the Cambridgeshire hounds we visit.
Christine was there,
It seemed without care,
But she was soon seen to fidget,
She said "The farmers here are so kind,
Here's a hedge to spend a penny behind."
But in that snow
She did not know
That the bull would come up from behind.
    Chorus:

At Dennington one day John Graham did say
"On these Easton hounds I'll pay a call."
The hounds ran so well
And did not dwell,
Till their Master in a ditch did fall.
In good time he saw the disaster
But urged his horse on all the faster.
'Tis the season's end
You've time to mend."
And away he went, roaring with laughter.
    Chorus:

Now there's Jill Moyle,
At capping she'll toil
And collects a most fabulous sum.
And there's Marion Saffell,
Who we all know so well
For many years the same job has done.
They make a formidable pair
To cross them no-one would dare,
But which is the best
I dare not test
For we all know which one can swear.
    Chorus:

'Twas at Rendham White Horse
With a party of course,
That the Master moved off in good cheer,
From his horn cam a sound
As a jack hare he found
And the first hedge appeared to be clear,
Too late his mistake he did see
And it filled all the followers with glee.
For beyond that hedge
Noddy stopped on the edge,
And their Master in the river they see.
    Chorus:

BALLAD OF TANNINGTON HORSESHOES

I'll sing you a long ditty about Tannington Horseshoes,
where the Easton Harriers had one of their do's
'Twas the first day of February on a Saturday,
by the time we moved off, we were merry and gay.

The hunting was fair, though the scent was not good
the hounds tried hard, and did all that they should.
till the Master he said, "It must be a short day
my horse is not fit", so says Major Clay.

At half past one we returned to the meet
and into the pub the Landlord to greet.
I took my horse home and returned in the car
to buy a few drinks for my friends in the bar.

The hunting folk went, one by one away
'til only four fellas were left there that day.

In there was Stopher, and two other men,
so there were not many left in the bar then.
When I asked the Master if he'd have a drink
"Oh, yes thank you, Tony, a bitter I think".

I said "You're a damned foreigner from up Yorkshire way,
have a good Suffolk drink, a John Turner I say",
I said to the Landlord, "Gin and beer let it be"
and the Master he tasted, "Oh, 'tis good", said he.

The rounds went by 'till we'd had about eight
The master he looked, said, " 'tis getting quite late."
But Ernie said, "There's time for a song,
before we go home, It won't take very long".

At about four o'clock I said 'twould be fun
to do something now that I have never done,
to hunt again at the end of the day,
so we all said "Now Master, what do you say?"

The Master was keen, but not sure if he ought
so we all assured him 'twould be fine sport.
He gave it some thought, while he had one more drink.
By the time it was finished, like us he did think.

I said I would telephone for my fresh horse
but Stopher he said, "I will fetch one of course".
By the time it arrived, it was twenty past four
the hounds were all baying, quite eager for more.

Poor old Geoffrey climbed on to his horse
but being quite tight, fell right over of course.
He sat on the road, and giggled with glee,
while a lady in a car said "What fun this will be".

When we were all mounted, we made the first draw
in the very first field a fine Jack hare we saw,
and away we went at a cracking good pace,
those first few ditches so boldly did face.

Now during this run, the Master's horse was so slow
with the help of my whip, a little faster he'd go
So now and again I gave a small flick,
'till quite by accident, the Master I hit.

He said "You're a devil, my horse you have hit",
and made a swing at me with his whip
and being annoyed, gave chase of course
so I was quite glad of my fresh horse.

While crossing a field we heard a loud call
poor old Geoffrey from his horse did fall.
'Neath the neck of his steed, he sat on the land
so like a bellringer, with the reins in his hand.

"Debach Boy, is at home, of that I'm right glad,
'cos dear old Charlie is such a good patient lad".
He said "Oh dear, oh dear, oh dear,
I'm terribly glad that Monica's not here.

Now the Master was a-blowing of his horn
while the ethics of riding was seen to scorn.
For he laid the full length of his horses back
If Billy Smart had've seen him, no contract he'd lack.

Now midst all this revelry, a thought crossed my mind
What if my poor father us in this state find.
For being teetotal, he'd view with alarm
to see us all tight crossing over his farm.

I said to Ernie, these two are quite tight,
I'm not sure of you, though you may be alright.
So I rode in front, and to the hounds did call,
and I got them all back to Tannington Hall.

I asked Ernie with the horses to stay
whilst in the stable, the hounds put away.
But when I returned, he on the ground had sat,
with the reins of three horses all held in his lap.

We left the horses in the charge of a groom
and into the hall we retired, quite soon.
But on the way in, the swan we did meet
and being afraid out of the way we did keep.

Now the Master he laughed and he laughed at our fear
saying I'll ride that swan, just you boys watch here,
and he took a hold of the swan by the neck,
and rode him around without even a peck.

Now cups full of coffee and plates full of beef
were quickly eaten and soon brought relief,
and that was the end of a very good day
until we did hear what our wives had to say.

When the Holcombe Rode with Easton

(To be sung to the tune of 'The Mellow Rose of Texas.)

On a Wednesday in November in Nineteen Seventy Four
Some members of the Holcombe their wives and horses
    bore
Down the Motorway to Saxted, in the land of gin and
    beer,
To meet the men of Easton at the hostel – volunteer.

> *Chorus:*
> *If you're in the North of England and the best hunt wish*
>   *to see*
> *Meet the harrier pack of Holcombe who wear Royal*
>   *livery,*
> *King James had such good hunting with them in days of*
>   *yore*
> *He said they could wear Scarlet and Gold for evermore.*

On Thursday was the meeting of Green and Hunting
    Pink.
They gathered at the Queen's Head to forge this friendly
    link.
They were led away by Tony who blew a merry horn,
To hunt o'er plough and ditches and get their faces torn.
    Chorus:

Although they had good hunting they came back rather
    sad
For Alex left poor Tartan behind and felt so sad,
But spirits soon recovered - at dinner some got tight
And broke all drinking records at the Brudenell that
    night.
    Chorus:

On the afternoon of Friday they met at Tannington
And walked the Harvey acres in boot and Wellington.
After having good sport coursing, with tired and aching
    knees,
They staggered back to Sheila for cakes and ale - and teas.
    Chorus:

Those who had the strength next morning met this time
    at the Crown
and after more refreshment you could not hold them
    down.
They spent more hours out hunting and there's a funny
    thing –
Though they were tired and hungry - they still had breath
    to sing.
    Chorus:

Now in the hunting field all Newton's men ran true
But that night after dinner they met their Waterloo.
Then Alex rose to save them and much to Katie's glee
He sang them to a standstill with a song about Dundee!
    Chorus:

We left on Sunday morning with sorrow in our heart
To leave such smashing people was much the hardest part.
But we made a resolution with great alacrity
To start plans for returning such hospitality.
    Chorus:

INDEX OF PERSONAL AND PLACE NAMES

AND LIMITED SUBJECTS